SHAKESPEAREAN TRAG

Related Titles

THE ARDEN GUIDE TO RENAISSANCE DRAMA: AN INTRODUCTION WITH
PRIMARY SOURCES
Brinda Charry
978-1-4725-7224-0

THE ARDEN RESEARCH HANDBOOK OF CONTEMPORARY SHAKESPEARE
CRITICISM
Edited by Evelyn Gajowski
978-1-3500-9322-5

SHAKESFEAR AND HOW TO CURE IT: THE COMPLETE HANDBOOK FOR
TEACHING SHAKESPEARE
Ralph Alan Cohen
978-1-4742-2871-8

STUDYING SHAKESPEARE ADAPTATION: FROM RESTORATION THEATRE
TO YOUTUBE
Pamela Bickley and Jenny Stevens
978-1-3500-6864-3

SHAKESPEAREAN TRAGEDY

KIERNAN RYAN

THE ARDEN SHAKESPEARE
LONDON • NEW YORK • OXFORD • NEW DELHI • SYDNEY

THE ARDEN SHAKESPEARE
Bloomsbury Publishing Plc
50 Bedford Square, London, WC1B 3DP, UK
1385 Broadway, New York, NY 10018, USA
29 Earlsfort Terrace, Dublin 2, Ireland

BLOOMSBURY, THE ARDEN SHAKESPEARE and the Arden Shakespeare logo
are trademarks of Bloomsbury Publishing Plc

First published in Great Britain 2021

Cover design: John Stevens Design

A catalogue record for this book is available from the British Library.

Library of Congress Control Number: 2021938166

ISBN: HB: 978-1-4725-8699-5
         PB: 978-1-4725-8698-8
         ePDF: 978-1-4725-8700-8
         eBook: 978-1-4725-8701-5

Typeset by Integra Software Services Pvt. Ltd.,
Printed and bound in Great Britain

To find out more about our authors and books visit www.bloomsbury.com
and sign up for our newsletters.

For my daughters
Laura and Emerald

But the true ground of all these piteous woes

We cannot without circumstance descry.

Romeo and Juliet

Sir, in my heart there was a kind of fighting

That would not let me sleep.

Hamlet

Make not your thoughts your prisons.

Antony and Cleopatra

CONTENTS

Preface   xii

PART I

1   **The Birth of Shakespearean Tragedy:** *2 & 3 Henry VI*   3
    The Quondam King   3
    The Wild Morisco   12
    The Upstart Crow   18
    The Devil's Butcher   22

PART II

2   *Titus Andronicus*: **A Sympathy of Woe**   31
    Prototypes and Precursors   31
    A Wilderness of Tigers   35
    This Fearful Slumber   39

3   *Romeo and Juliet*: **Kissing by the Book**   45
    Strange Love Grown Bold   45
    The Prison-House of Language   46
    Empowering the Audience   50

4   *Julius Caesar*: **The Common Good**   55
    An Icy Anatomy   55
    Scorning the Base Degrees   58
    The Foremost Man of All the World   62

PART III

5   *Hamlet*: **A Kind of Fighting**   67
    The Stamp of One Defect   67
    Seeing Doubles   73
    That Within Which Passes Show   83
    Things Rank and Gross in Nature   88
    The Whips and Scorns of Time   92
    The Strong Conflux of Contending Forces   98
    A King of Infinite Space   101
    The Prophetic Soul of the Wide World   107

Contents

6   *Othello*: Thereby Hangs a Tail   113
   Expectation in Preference to Surprise   113
   Sinking Below Shakespeare   118
   True Colours   122
   The Green-Eyed Monster   125
   Who Hath Done This Deed?   129
   The Tragedy of the Handkerchief   134
   If Wives Do Fall   138
   Motiveless Malignity and the Curse of Service   143
   What You Know, You Know   153
   A Pageant to Keep Us in False Gaze   157

7   *King Lear*: Shakespeare's Leviathan   163
   A Play Fit for a King   163
   Echoes and Anticipations (i)   167
   Echoes and Anticipations (ii)   172
   A Better Where to Find   175
   The Whoreson and the Plague of Custom   180
   The Fool and the King   183
   The Art of Known and Feeling Sorrows   188
   The King and the Beggar   191
   So Distribution Should Undo Excess   197
   A Whole Dead World Galloping Over the Living Earth   203

8   *Macbeth*: The Habit of Another Nature   207
   Embracing the Butcher   207
   Supernatural Soliciting   209
   Terrestrial Tragedy   215
   The Language of Complicity   219
   Vaster Powers Without: Mirroring Macbeth   222
   So Much More the Man   230
   Dispossession and Disavowal   236
   Pity, Like a Naked New-Born Babe   241
   Blood Will Have Blood   243
   Ere Humane Statute Purged the Gentle Weal   246

PART IV

9   *Antony and Cleopatra*: Making Defect Perfection   255
   Tragedy Travestied   255
   The Nobleness of Life   259
   Past the Size of Dreaming: Utopian Realism   263
   A Lass Unparalleled   267

10 *Coriolanus*: **A World Elsewhere**   271
     Antecedents and Affinities   271
     An Inventory to Particularize Their Abundance   272
     To Unbuild the City and to Lay All Flat   278
     A Kind of Nothing   280

Works Cited   287
Index   289

PREFACE

The title of this book deliberately echoes the title of arguably the greatest and most influential modern study of its subject: A. C. Bradley's *Shakespearean Tragedy*, first published in 1904 and still in print in various editions over a century later. My study takes issue with the still widespread assumptions on which Bradley proceeds and with the general conclusions about Shakespearean tragedy at which he arrives. But it shares Bradley's belief that, notwithstanding their dazzling diversity, the four towering tragedies he deals with are informed by a distinctively *Shakespearean* vision, and that the nature of that vision is best defined through what Bradley calls the 'analytic interpretation' of each play as a whole. The subtitle of Bradley's book is *Lectures on 'Hamlet', 'Othello', 'King Lear', 'Macbeth'* and its enduring appeal owes much to its origin in the lecture hall, to the sense it gives the reader of an acute mind thinking its way through the problems the plays pose as they arise from close reading alone, and taking as much time as it needs to do so in the depth and detail the problems warrant. In his introduction to the book at the dawn of the twentieth century Bradley acknowledged that other kinds of approach, including the historical, contextualizing kind, 'are useful and even in various degrees necessary' to the study of the plays. 'But', he continued, 'an overt pursuit of them is not necessary here, nor is any one of them so indispensable to our object as that close familiarity with the plays, that native strength and justice of perception, and the habit of reading with an eager mind, which make many an unscholarly lover of Shakespeare a far better critic than many a Shakespeare scholar.' This twenty-first-century study of Shakespearean tragedy was conceived and written on the same understanding, in the hope that its readers will find its direct engagement with the plays themselves equally accessible in its own way as a result.

Not the least merit of Bradley's readings of Shakespeare's greatest tragedies is the forensic tenacity with which he disposes of common critical misconceptions for which the evidence of the text provides no support, clearing the way for the reader to confront the actual questions of interpretation posed by the play. The construction that Bradley's argument leads him to place on the play as a whole may prove unconvincing, but time and again one finds oneself indebted to him for establishing a firm basis on which to build a more cogent reading of one's own. My readings of all four of the tragedies with which Bradley deals, and of *Othello* and *Macbeth* in particular, have profited from both building on and arguing against Bradley's views of crucial interpretive issues. But they have conscripted Bradley in the service of a conception of Shakespearean tragedy and interpretations of the plays that are radically different from his. The immediate mainspring of Shakespearean tragedy for Bradley is the action that issues, with catastrophic consequences, from the conflicted character of the protagonist, envisaged as an exceptional individual rather than a social being. Bradley's chief concern is therefore to explain the psychological factors peculiar to the protagonist's character that account for the fateful course of action to which he is driven. Bradley is too astute a critic not to realize that an explanation of Shakespearean tragedy that ascribes so much to the character of the protagonist and so little to factors beyond the individual's ken or control is unsatisfactory. But whenever he attempts to bring those factors to definition, to pin down 'the ultimate power in the tragic work', the rigorous intelligence he displays in the analysis of character deserts him, forcing him to resort to such nebulous abstractions as:

> the whole system or order, of which the individual characters form an inconsiderable and feeble part; which seems to determine, far more than they, their native dispositions and their circumstances, and, through these, their action; which is so vast and complex that they can scarcely at all understand it or control its workings; and which has a nature so definite and fixed that whatever changes take place in it produce other changes inevitably and without regard to men's desires and regrets.

Whether this 'inexorable order working in the passions and actions of men, and labouring through their agony and waste towards good' deserves the name 'fate', Bradley cannot decide. But he has no doubt that Shakespearean tragedy leaves us in the end with no choice but resignation to the 'painful mystery' of its inscrutable purpose.

Illuminating and indispensable as it remains in so many respects, Bradley's study is fatally flawed by its view of Shakespearean tragedy as counselling acquiescence in intolerable human suffering, which is created by forces we cannot control under circumstances we are powerless to change. This book argues that exactly the opposite is the case: that Shakespearean tragedy reveals the fundamental source of the suffering it depicts to be the systemic injustice of the society its characters inhabit, which needs to be questioned and demands to be changed; that it's driven by a visionary commitment to the possibility of transforming an inhuman society blighted by division and subjection into a truly civilized community of equals; and that it's written in a way designed to empower its audiences and readers to change their world by changing the way they see it and the way they see themselves. As Bradley's contemporary, George Bernard Shaw, would have been happy to inform him, there's no mystery for Shakespeare about the nature of 'the whole system or order' of which his tragic protagonists form part, and 'which seems to determine, far more than they, their native dispositions and their circumstances, and, through these, their action'. The thoughts, words and deeds of Shakespeare's tragic protagonists can never be prised apart from the social circumstances that shaped them, and to write about them as if they can be is to miss the whole point of Shakespearean tragedy and rob it of its revolutionary import. Bradley would have been wiser in this regard to take as his starting point the key to Shakespearean tragedy proffered by Enobarbus in *Antony and Cleopatra*: 'I see men's judgements are / A parcel of their fortunes, and things outward / Do draw the inward quality after them / To suffer all alike.' For, once it becomes plain that character analysis will not suffice to understand

Shakespearean tragedy, because – as the Watchman in *Romeo and Juliet* perceives – 'the true ground of all these piteous woes / We cannot without circumstance descry', the protagonists' refusal to be defined completely by their circumstances, and thus the thing that makes them tragic in the Shakespearean sense, becomes equally apparent.

Shakespeare's tragic protagonists are manifestly as dissimilar in countless ways as the fictional universes that surround them and the cruel fates that await them. But they are all 'fools of Time' (Sonnet 124) inasmuch as they are all hoodwinked by history. Despite the potential they reveal to be humane, enlightened citizens of centuries to come, they are overpowered by the inescapable constraints of the barbaric times in which they have the misfortune to live rather than by some malign, metaphysical force or some fatal defect in their character. Romeo may fear that he's the victim of 'Some consequence, yet hanging in the stars'; Hamlet may wonder whether it's 'some vicious mole of nature' or 'a divinity that shapes our ends'; and Macbeth's downfall may seem to be due to the 'supernatural soliciting' of 'the secret, black, and midnight hags' who greet him on the heath. But their real tragedy, the plays make clear, is to find themselves stranded and fated to die in a hostile, alien reality, far from the transfigured future that their struggle against their plight foreshadows. Shakespeare's creation of protagonists who cannot come to terms with their world reveals the need and the capacity of all human beings – then and now – to live in a world where freedom, equality and justice prevail. The protagonists of Shakespearean tragedy are shown to be defeated and destroyed by the harrowing predicaments in which they are trapped, but their predicaments are shown to be the man-made products of an oppressive dispensation, whose continuance is neither desirable nor necessary.

When Nietzsche wrote in *The Gay Science*, 'We children of the future, how *could* we be at home in this today?', he might have been speaking for all Shakespeare's tragic heroes, who are heroic precisely because they could never have been at home in their today. Nor should that be surprising, since they sprang from the imagination of a playwright who was himself a child of the future, and who remains to this day, four centuries after his death, 'the prophetic soul / Of the wide world dreaming on things to come' (Sonnet 107). To take this view of Shakespeare and Shakespearean tragedy is to part company with the past-bound, historicist school of Shakespeare criticism that has held sway in the academy for the past forty years, and that has been responsible for subordinating absorption in the plays themselves to a peripheral engrossment in their early modern contexts. Informative though such background studies can often be, their retrospective standpoint and extraneous focus blind them to the as yet unrealized possibilities stored in the language and form of Shakespeare's plays. To do justice to the tension between historical realities and utopian ideals at the heart of Shakespearean tragedy, and to bring out the progressive implications of that tension for our time, requires as full and close a reading as possible of each play.

That is what the four main chapters that form the core of this study seek to provide. My original plan had been to confine its account of Shakespearean tragedy, as Bradley does, to the plays rightly regarded as Shakespeare's crowning achievements as a tragedian. But, on rereading his previous and subsequent tragedies in light of them, the extraordinary consistency of Shakespeare's tragic vision, from his first stab at the genre in *Titus Andronicus* to his final foray in *Coriolanus*, became too evident to ignore. The book was therefore redesigned to demonstrate this striking continuity by tracing the evolution of Shakespearean tragedy from its seeds in the two *Henry VI* plays that launched his career as a dramatist through the nine plays whose categorization as tragedies few would contest – with glances at credible contenders for inclusion such as *Richard II* and *Timon of Athens*. All the chapters have been designed to serve not only as stages in the four-part argument of the book, but also as readings in their own right of the individual plays they address. To see these plays as sharing aims, concerns, strategies and techniques that stamp them all indelibly as Shakespearean tragedies, possessed from first to last by the rebellious spirit of the 'upstart crow', is to see each of them afresh and to know why they matter more than ever today.

The argument of this study and some of its chapters draw on ideas and develop readings in previous publications of mine, especially the following: 'Shakespeare's Inhumanity', *Shakespeare Survey 66* (2013); '"The Theatre of the Invisible-Made-Visible": Shakespeare and the Politics of Perception', *Actes des congrès de la Société française Shakespeare*, 33 (2015): http://shakespeare.revues.org/3365; 'Introduction' to the Penguin Classics edition of *King Lear* (London: Penguin Books, 2015); *Shakespeare's Universality: Here's Fine Revolution* (London: Bloomsbury, 2015); 'An Introduction to Shakespearean Tragedy', '*Hamlet* and Revenge', 'Racism, Misogyny and "Motiveless Malignity" in *Othello*', 'Sovereignty and Subversion in *King Lear*' and 'Manhood and the "Milk of Human Kindness" in *Macbeth*': all published in 2016 by the British Library on its *Discovering Literature* website (https://www.bl.uk/discovering-literature); and 'The Empathetic Imagination and the Dream of Equality: Shakespeare's Poetical Justice', in *The Arden Research Handbook of Shakespeare and Social Justice*, ed. David Ruiter (London: Bloomsbury, 2020).

To free this study of footnotes, primary and secondary references have been kept to a bare minimum. Those not included within the chapters can be found in the 'Works Cited' at the end of the book.

This preface would be incomplete without an acknowledgement of how much the book owes to the unswerving friendship and sage counsel of Ewan Fernie. It was commissioned for Bloomsbury by the inestimable Margaret Bartley and its procrastinating author was patiently coaxed into completing it by the indefatigable Mark Dudgeon, ably abetted by Lara Bateman: I am indebted to all three of them for their invaluable help in the making of *Shakespearean Tragedy*. My deepest debt, as always, is to my wife, Elizabeth Drayson, for her unfailing love and support.

PART I

CHAPTER 1
THE BIRTH OF SHAKESPEAREAN TRAGEDY: *2 & 3 HENRY VI*

The Quondam King

The seeds of Shakespearean tragedy were sown right at the start of the dramatist's career in the linked pair of history plays that have a strong claim to be the first plays he wrote: *The First Part of the Contention betwixt the two Famous Houses of York and Lancaster, with the Death of the Good Duke Humphrey* and *The True Tragedy of Richard Duke of York and the Death of Good King Henry the Sixth, with the Whole Contention between the Two Houses Lancaster and York*. The plays were written and staged at the dawn of the last decade of the sixteenth century, and versions of them were published under these titles a few years later: the Quarto edition of *The First Part of the Contention* in 1594 and the Octavo edition of *The True Tragedy* in 1595. Longer versions of both plays were published in the posthumous First Folio of Shakespeare's plays in 1623, under the briefer titles that recast them retrospectively as components of a trilogy: *The Second Part of Henry the Sixth, with the Death of the Good Duke Humphrey* and *The Third Part of Henry the Sixth, with the Death of the Duke of York*. The play that precedes them in the 1623 Folio, *The First Part of Henry the Sixth*, exists in no earlier printed version and is now generally believed to have been written immediately after them, and mostly by other playwrights with whom Shakespeare collaborated, in order to capitalize on the commercial success of *The First Part of the Contention* and its sequel.

Exactly when, and in what order, the *Henry VI* plays were scripted and first performed, precisely which portions of *The First Part of Henry the Sixth* were penned by which co-authors, and the possibility of one or more collaborators having had a hand in one or both of its precursors too, will continue to be matters for debate by textual scholars. The claim that the plays subsequently relabelled *The Second Part of Henry the Sixth* and *The Third Part of Henry the Sixth* were the very first plays Shakespeare wrote will likewise remain open to dispute. But there's no disputing that with these ground-breaking history plays he announced his arrival on the theatrical scene as an ambitious young dramatist of formidable power. That Shakespeare pioneered in them a new kind of historical drama is remarkable enough. But what makes them even more remarkable is that they show him already beginning to forge a tragic vision that is unmistakably Shakespearean. In fact, we can pinpoint the moment in *The Second Part of Henry the Sixth* when that vision finds its voice for the first time.

Acts 1 and 2 give us no reason to question the court's judgement of Henry, who is repeatedly disparaged as a weak, imprudent ruler by the factious peers surrounding him.

The play opens with the king welcoming his French bride, Margaret, with a 'kind kiss' in the hope that the 'sympathy of love' will unite them (1.1.19, 23), blissfully unaware that Suffolk has already cuckolded him. Henry is as unperturbed by his wife's scandalous lack of a dowry as he is by the surrender of huge tracts of territory to France that this impolitic marriage entails. Even the Good Duke Humphrey of Gloucester, the Lord Protector upon whose loyal solicitude for king and country Henry can rely, is outraged by his pious nephew's gullibility and blindness to the priorities of a sovereign. Gloucester himself is blind to the murderous cabal closing in on him, and oblivious of York's plot to outwit him and wrest the throne from Henry, 'Whose church-like humours fits not for a crown' (1.1.244). York's disdain for the reigning monarch is dwarfed, however, by the contempt for Henry that his own wife feels.

When Margaret joins with Suffolk and the Cardinal to antagonize Gloucester in Act 2, Henry's plea that she 'whet not on these furious peers; / For blessed are the peacemakers on earth' (2.1.33–4) serves only to make the peers more furious instead of bringing them to heel. What puts a stop to their strife is not the king but the sensational arrival of the blind and lame Simon Simpcox, whose sight, he claims, has been miraculously restored at St Alban's shrine. 'Let never day nor night unhallowed pass', Henry adjures Simpcox, 'But still remember what the Lord hath done' (2.1.82–3); whereupon Gloucester exposes the hapless Simpcox as a fraud, who is neither blind nor lame, thereby underscoring the credulity of the unworldly king. The same credulity snares Henry in the trap laid for Gloucester's wife by Gloucester's enemies to bring him down. The king plays into their treacherous hands when, egged on by the Queen, he relieves the faithful Lord Protector of his staff of office, saying: 'Henry will to himself / Protector be; and God shall be my hope, / My stay, my guide and lantern to my feet' (2.3.23–5).

Gloucester's downfall is charged with pathos by the quiet dignity he displays on his dismissal; by the tears he sheds at his wife's public shaming and his speechless grief at their parting; and by the baseless charges against 'the shepherd of the flock, / That virtuous prince' (2.2.73–4), who is, the king protests in vain, 'as innocent / From meaning treason to our royal person / As is the sucking lamb or harmless dove' (3.1.69–71). The pathos is intensified by Gloucester's stirring defence of his record as a compassionate Protector, who refused to tax 'the needy commons' and whose sole judicial fault was the pity that made him 'melt at an offender's tears' of contrition (3.1.116, 125–6). And it reaches its climax in his last speech, as he's led away to what he knows is certain death, concerned only for the plight in which his sovereign has been left:

Ah, thus King Henry throws away his crutch
Before his legs be firm to bear his body.
Thus is the shepherd beaten from thy side,
And wolves are gnarling who shall gnaw thee first.

(3.1.189–92)

It's Henry's response to the sight of his guiltless uncle being taken away to die that is significant as far as the beginning, and our understanding, of Shakespearean tragedy are concerned. 'My lords,' says the king, to the lords' and his wife's disconcertment, 'what to your wisdoms seemeth best / Do, or undo, as if ourself were here.' 'What, will your highness leave the parliament?', asks the queen. 'Ay, Margaret,' Henry replies, 'my heart is drowned with grief' (3.1.195–8). He then describes the scene that has caused his grief and his own reaction to it in an extraordinary extended simile:

> And as the butcher takes away the calf
> And binds the wretch and beats it when it strains,
> Bearing it to the bloody slaughterhouse,
> Even so remorseless have they borne him hence;
> And as the dam runs lowing up and down,
> Looking the way her harmless young one went,
> And can do naught but wail her darling's loss,
> Even so myself bewails good Gloucester's case
> With sad unhelpful tears, and with dimmed eyes
> Look after him, and cannot do him good,
> So mighty are his vowed enemies.
>
> (3.1.210–20)

With that, Henry exits in tears, abandoning Gloucester to his mighty enemies. 'Free lords,' observes Margaret to Suffolk, York and the Cardinal, 'Henry my lord is cold in great affairs, / Too full of foolish pity' (3.1.224–5), before enjoining them to 'quickly rid the world' (3.1.233) of Good Duke Humphrey.

The line that rings out is Henry's 'Do, or undo, as if ourself were here.' It catches the ear not just because of the note of resigned indifference struck by 'Do, or undo,' but chiefly because of the more profound detachment implied by the phrase '*as if ourself were here*'. Henry's surrender of his sovereign authority to Gloucester's foes to deal with their prisoner – to 'Do, or undo' – as they see fit bespeaks a disengagement strikingly at odds with the tender, imaginative empathy he displays in his impotent lament for his doomed kinsman. But it chimes perfectly with his desire to withdraw *himself* from 'ourself', from the virtual royal self he appoints to remain present in his absence. So acute is Henry's anguish at seeing Gloucester borne off like a calf to be butchered and feeling helpless to save him that he recoils from his own intolerable identity. The man parts company with the monarch: the compassionate human creature splits off from the ermine-clad king, the epitome of the hierarchical regime that breeds the ruthless struggle to rule it, which will soon turn the whole nation into the 'bloody slaughterhouse' of civil war. At that moment, as the self is sundered from the social identity that normally defines it, we catch our first glimpse of the Shakespearean tragic protagonist in embryo.

What sets this new kind of protagonist apart becomes more apparent as *The Second Part of Henry VI* proceeds. But that Henry is a seminally tragic figure of a type quite different from the typical tragic hero of the Elizabethan stage is already evident at this point in the contrast between him and Gloucester. Gloucester fits the traditional *de casibus* model of the tragic figure perfectly: a famous, powerful man of high degree, who is fated to fall through misfortune or his fault, or through some combination of both. In Gloucester's case the downfall is portrayed in a manner designed to arouse our pity for a helpless, noble victim of unwarranted malevolence. The same emotion is milked from the audience in *The Third Part* by the sadistic tormenting of the defiant York, as he weeps for his murdered son: the pathos is piled on, just as it is by Henry's likening of his grief for Gloucester to a heifer that frantically seeks her slaughtered calf, 'And can do naught but wail her darling's loss'. In both cases the lachrymose impact of the character's suffering and humiliation deepens the gulf that yawns between his abject plight and his once exalted state. In both cases, too, the term 'tragedy' is used to describe the character's fate. 'Who finds the heifer dead and bleeding fresh / And sees fast by a butcher with an axe, / But will suspect 'twas he that made the slaughter?', asks Warwick, echoing Henry's imagery after the discovery of Gloucester's corpse in *The Second Part*; 'Even so suspicious', he declares, 'is this tragedy' (3.2.188–90, 194). The title of the first printed edition of *The Third Part* – *The True Tragedy of Richard Duke of York and the Death of Good King Henry the Sixth* – demotes the monarch's demise to second billing and denies his death the dignity of tragedy it confers on York. But the term 'tragedy' as applied to Gloucester and York signifies simply that their downfalls and deaths are lamentable, and lamentable because of the height from which they have fallen and what they have lost along with their lives.

The tragedies of Gloucester and York are predicated on the rank and power that they possess, and desire to possess, in a hierarchical society whose validity they accept without question. They are men who belong to their world and whose tragic fates are defined in the terms of that world. But when Henry says, 'Do, or undo, as if ourself were here', a new breed of tragic protagonist is born: a protagonist indifferent to rank and power, who does not belong to his world and does not desire to, and whose tragedy is to find himself miscast in a role he rejects in a society that makes him feel like an alien. In the eyes of his conniving, adulterous queen and the blue-blooded butchers stalking him, Henry is at best a holy fool, whose unfitness to rule is the mainspring of the civil war, and at worst a spineless usurper, who deserves to be dethroned and liquidated. Most critical accounts of the play to this day come down hard on Henry too, mistaking the other characters' views of him for the plays' view of him, because they take Shakespeare's subscription to the orthodox political ideals of his day for granted. But to trace the depiction of Henry from the standpoint of that arresting line through the rest of *The Second Part* and *The Third Part* is to acquire a quite different perspective on him and the author who depicted him.

On hearing that Gloucester is dead, Henry falls into a deathlike swoon. He is roused from it only to round on Suffolk, the 'baleful messenger' who ordered Gloucester's murder, and voice his craving to be dead indeed: 'For in the shade of death I shall find joy, / In life but double death, now Gloucester's dead' (3.2.48, 52–5). When he later beholds Gloucester's corpse, he identifies with it completely: 'That is to see how deep my grave is made', he says, 'For, seeing him, I see my life in death' (3.2.150, 152). Even after the quelling of the Cade rebellion and Henry's pardoning of the rebels, he remains unreconciled to the part historical mischance has condemned him to play against his will:

Was ever king that joyed an earthly throne
And could command no more content than I?
No sooner was I crept out of my cradle
But I was made a king at nine months old.
Was never subject longed to be a king
As I do long and wish to be a subject.

(4.9.1–6)

One need only set those last two lines against York's homicidal lust for the crown to take the measure of Henry's aversion to royalty:

I will stir up in England some black storm
Shall blow ten thousand souls to heaven or hell;
And this fell tempest shall not cease to rage
Until the golden circuit on my head,
Like to the glorious sun's transparent beams,
Do calm the fury of this mad-bred flaw.

(3.1.348–53)

If that's the cost of kingship, Henry's aversion begins to look less reprehensible than York's denunciation of him in *The Second Part* warrants: '"King" do I call thee? No, thou art not king, / Not fit to govern and rule multitudes' (5.1.93–4). For York, Henry's head 'doth not become a crown', which York's head is better qualified to wear: 'That gold must round engirt these brows of mine, / Whose smile and frown, like to Achille's spear, / Is able with the change to kill and cure' (5.1.96, 99–101). But again, if that's what it takes to be a king – if that's the kind of man a king must be – then being 'Not fit to govern and rule multitudes' begins to look less like a culpable defect and more like a commendable virtue. The entire second and third parts of *Henry VI* are nothing if not a testament to the holocaust unleashed on society when men with the same raging ambition and vaunted regal qualities as York run riot. The notion that factional feuds and civil war could have been averted, if only Henry had also possessed those qualities and an equally bellicose disposition, does not stand up to scrutiny.

More importantly, that notion misses the point of Shakespeare's characterization of Henry, which is to call kingship and all it implies increasingly into question in *The Third Part of Henry VI*. In the opening scene the fact that the right to exercise sovereignty is open to negotiation rather than innate is made farcically evident by Henry and York's bickering about who is entitled to be the other's king. 'My title's weak' (1.1.134), Henry is forced to concede, before securing York's agreement to let him reign until his death, after which the crown will pass to York and his heirs instead of through the immediate royal bloodline to Henry's son. Henry is saddened, though far from mortified, by having to disinherit his only child, merely remarking with a sigh: 'be it as it may' (1.1.194). But although it keeps civil war at bay for the moment, his capitulation to York's claim on the English throne drives a further wedge between Henry and the crown forced upon him in the cradle. When that war breaks out, his estrangement from his royal self becomes even more profound.

Henry's reaction to the sight of York's head impaled above the gates of York's own city speaks volumes. All the principal antagonists on both sides, apart from Henry, are consumed by the need to exact bloody retribution for their family. But when Margaret points to York's spiked head and asks, 'Doth not the object cheer your heart, my lord?', Henry replies, 'To see this sight it irks my very soul. / Withhold revenge, dear God' (2.2.4, 6–7). Rebuked by the bloodthirsty Clifford for that response and for disinheriting his son, Henry replies, unperturbed by the reproof:

> But, Clifford, tell me, didst thou never hear
> That things ill got had ever bad success?
> And happy always was it for that son
> Whose father for his hoarding went to hell?
> I'll leave my son my virtuous deeds behind
> And would my father had left me no more.

> (2.2.45–50)

Unfortunately for Henry his father, Henry V, left him much more than virtuous deeds along with the throne, not least the guilty legacy of the Lancastrians for their illicit seizure of the throne from Richard II. Henry inhabits, to his credit, an ethical realm that cannot come to terms with the actual realm inhabited by the rest of the characters. For them, things as they stand, however horrific, matter and make sense; they take reality as they find it and deal with it on its terms, playing the social roles in which they've been cast, and the hands they've been dealt by history, without ever wishing to be someone else or somewhere else. But for Henry things as they stand are insane and inhuman, and if he can't have the oblivion of death, then another person in a different place is exactly what he wants to be.

As he says in the soliloquy he delivers seated on a molehill, while the battle of Towton, from which he has been sidelined, rages on:

> Would I were dead, if God's good will were so.
> For what is in this world but grief and woe?
> O God! Methinks it were a happy life
> To be no better than a homely swain,
> To sit upon a hill, as I do now,
> To carve out dials quaintly, point by point,
> Thereby to see the minutes how they run:
> How many makes the hour full complete,
> How many hours bring about the day,
> How many days will finish up the year,
> How many years a mortal man may live. …
> So minutes, hours, days, weeks, months and years,

Passed over to the end they were created,
Would bring white hairs unto a quiet grave.
Ah! What a life were this, how sweet, how lovely!
Gives not the hawthorn bush a sweeter shade
To shepherds looking on their silly sheep
Than doth a rich embroidered canopy
To kings that fear their subjects' treachery?
O yes, it doth, a thousandfold it doth.

(2.5.19–29, 38–46)

The soliloquy owes nothing to Shakespeare's sources and everything to his fellow-feeling for this stranded royal misfit. That Shakespeare went out of his way to invent this scene and this speech for Henry, which runs in this vein for over fifty lines, tells us much about where his sympathies lay, and the standpoint from which the play was written. To reduce it to a pastoral fantasy, designed to buttress the monarchy by rendering the royal lot unenviable compared to that of a 'homely swain' would be mistaken. There's more to it than that, partly because the alternative life of the humble shepherd is portrayed at such length as idyllically desirable, but also because that life is imagined from a posthumous perspective, as if the speaker were looking back on its entire course from a point beyond it: 'So minutes, hours, days, weeks, months and years, / Passed over to the end they were created, / Would bring white hairs unto a quiet grave.' Henry's detachment from the calibrated constraints of time cuts deeper in this soliloquy than his disenchantment with being a monarch. It denotes a disengagement from the whole 'piteous spectacle' of these 'bloody times' (2.5.73), in which his life as a king is inescapably and culpably embroiled against his will.

Shakespeare pursues this line of thought in the scene that opens Act 3, a scene again indebted solely to the boldness of his theatrical intelligence. There Henry is confronted, recognized and taken prisoner by two gamekeepers, keen to bag the bounty on the fleeing king's head. It's perhaps the first of the trademark encounters Shakespeare will contrive, throughout his career as a tragedian, between the base-born and the royal, mingling kings and clowns in the manner Sidney scorned as unseemly in *An Apology for Poetry*. Henry reproves himself as he enters for calling England his country: 'No, Harry, Harry, 'tis no land of thine; / Thy place is filled, thy sceptre wrung from thee, / Thy balm washed off wherewith thou wast anointed' (3.1.17–18). The keepers agree: 'This is the quondam king', says the first, dismissing Henry's royalty as a thing of the past, 'let's seize upon him' (3.1.23). So much for the illusion under which Shakespeare's Richard II will later labour for a while: 'Not all the water in the rough rude sea / Can wash the balm off from an anointed king' (3.2.54–5). As far as Henry and these mercenary quondam subjects are concerned, he stopped being the sovereign as soon as someone else sat on the throne, holding the sceptre and wearing the crown. That's all it took to strip him of majesty and provoke this exchange:

2 KEEPER
Say, what art thou that talk'st of kings and queens?

KING HENRY

    More than I seem, and less than I was born to:
    A man at least, for less I should not be;
    And men may talk of kings, and why not I?

2 KEEPER

    Ay, but thou talk'st as if thou wert a king.

KING HENRY

    Why, so I am, in mind, and that's enough.

2 KEEPER

    But if thou be a king, where is thy crown?

KING HENRY

    My crown is in my heart, not on my head:
    Not decked with diamonds and Indian stones,
    Nor to be seen. My crown is called content,
    A crown it is that seldom kings enjoy.

                                 (3.1.55–65)

The First Keeper rebuts the charge that they are breaking their oaths as Henry's 'sworn true subjects': 'No, for we were subjects but while you were king'; to which Henry can only retort, 'Why, am I dead? Do I not breathe a man?', before bowing to the will of his captors with an injunction whose irony is lost on them: 'Go where you will, the King shall be commanded; / And be you kings: command, and I'll obey' (3.1.78, 80–1, 91–2).

This exchange strikes a keynote that will be struck again and again in Shakespearean tragedy, and that will resound throughout the greatest of the tragedies he will write. It's a dialogue in which the king is cut down to size, not just by nameless, insubordinate subjects, but by the king himself. Henry's description of himself as 'More than I seem, and less than I was born to' – the kind of riddling riposte at which Hamlet will excel – triggers an inversion of normal values. To be less than the king one was born to be is to be 'A man at least', a designation in which a basic human dignity resides, and which grants one the same right as a man of any rank to 'talk of kings' as one sees fit. The suspicion that this claim will be the prelude to a reassertion of majesty is soon dashed. Henry assures the keeper that he is indeed a king 'in mind', though not one who needs to wear a crown to confirm his royalty, because 'My crown is in my heart, not on my head', and that figurative crown 'is called content'. Henry is redefining royalty as the supreme state of mind, rather than the supreme position in society, that a person can attain. The First Keeper hammers home the irrefutable fact that he and his fellow keeper were Henry's subjects only while Henry happened to be king, their subjection being a construct as contingent and unstable as the sovereignty on which it hinges. But instead of haughtily demanding, as a conventionally conceived monarch might, 'Am I not still your king?', Henry asks simply, 'Do I not breathe a man?' He restates his redefinition of himself as primarily a man like the keepers, emphasizing by his choice of the word 'breathe' his innate consanguinity with his kind. From there it's but a step to the inversion of hierarchy and reversal of roles Henry envisages in lines whose sardonic tone cannot disguise their seditious import: 'the King shall be commanded; / And be you kings: command, and I'll obey'.

The contrast with the staple fantasy of omnipotent majesty that holds York and his sons in thrall could hardly be more complete. 'And, father, do but think', says Richard as he urges York to break his oath to reign only after Henry's death, 'How sweet a thing it is to wear a crown, / Within whose circuit is Elysium / And all that poets feign of bliss and joy' (1.2.28–30). Henry is obliged, of course, to maintain the charade of majesty, whenever the occasion requires it, until his murder by Richard in Act 5 releases him from his obligation. But he does so in the tacit knowledge that deep down, as Warwick shrewdly remarks of him, 'having nothing, nothing can he lose' (3.3.151–2). Hence, when Warwick frees Henry from incarceration to restore the crown to him, Henry describes his imprisonment as having been a pleasure:

> Ay, such a pleasure as encaged birds
> Conceive, when after many moody thoughts,
> At last, by notes of household harmony,
> They quite forget their loss of liberty.
>
> (4.6.12–15)

Henry wastes no time handing the reins of the realm over once again, this time jointly to Warwick and Clarence with immediate effect. Once again, he seeks to retreat behind the simulacrum of the sovereign he never sought to be, having known all along what Warwick, the once mighty 'kingmaker', realizes as he dies:

> Lo, now my glory smeared in dust and blood.
> My parks, my walks, my manors that I had
> Even now forsake me, and of all my lands
> Is nothing left me but my body's length.
> Why, what is pomp, rule, reign but earth and dust?
> And live we how we can, yet die we must.
>
> (5.2.23–8)

It's the ultimate, levelling realization that undergirds both the second and the third part of *Henry VI* and the Shakespearean tragic vision that has its roots in them. Nothing will be left to anybody – whatever their rank, gender or race, whether rich or poor, powerful or powerless – but their body's length in death's promiscuous embrace. That's why, when 'that devil's butcher, Richard' is about to 'To make a bloody supper in the Tower' (5.5.77, 85) by murdering him, Henry retains sufficient self-conscious detachment to ask his killer, 'What scene of death hath Roscius now to act?' (5.6.10). The question casts the future Richard III, and Henry himself perhaps, as the legendary Roman actor synonymous with tragedy. It invites the audience to read the king's assassination through the lens of that genre, framing it in theatrical terms that subtly underline the play's status as a staged 'tragic history' (5.6.28). In so doing, it also theatricalizes the historical figures being portrayed, retrospectively revealing them as people who happened to be cast in those aristocratic roles, just like the actors now playing them.

'And men may talk of kings, and why not I?': it's tempting to hear in Henry's rhetorical question the audacious voice of the aspiring dramatist who created him and a host of kings to come. Right from the start of his career Shakespeare rarely forgets the vulnerable, human creature beneath the carapace of royalty, or the mortality that makes a mockery of eminence and privilege. A playwright bridled by a more tractable mind would have probed no deeper than the nobility's denigration of Henry as a 'faint-hearted and degenerate King, / In whose cold blood no spark of honour abides' (*3HVI* 1.1.183–4). But Henry's utter unfitness for the royal office that repels him is precisely what fascinates Shakespeare. So much so, that he goes out of his way to invent scenes and speeches designed to make Henry's disaffection sympathetic, unsettling the assumptions on which monarchy rests and the allure of sovereignty relies. To treat Henry as a fully drawn tragic protagonist, or the final part of the trilogy as a cohesive tragedy, would be to go too far. But as Henry's visceral aversion to playing the king begins to make sense amid the senseless slaughter, and wishing he were dead begins to seem a perfectly sane response to the insanity that surrounds him, there's every reason to believe that what we're witnessing is the birth of Shakespearean tragedy.

The Wild Morisco

It requires no stretch of the imagination to discern in the Henry of *The Second Part* and *The Third Part* the progenitor of Richard II, Hamlet, King Lear and Timon of Athens, who all find themselves, like Henry, so alienated from the identity that once defined them and the society that shaped them that their only refuge lies in the oblivion of death, to which their minds repeatedly turn. The less immediately apparent affinities between Henry and characters such as Romeo and Juliet, Othello, Macbeth, Antony and Cleopatra and Coriolanus become apparent too, when one considers that every one of them is doomed, like Henry, by having been cast in the wrong role in the wrong place in the wrong time. Every one of them – just like Richard II, Hamlet, King Lear and Timon – becomes a stranger in a world where they had once felt at home, and a stranger to the person they used to be or thought they were. And in the process every one of them reveals the potential they possess to be another kind of person in another kind of world, which they will never live to see. The respects in which Henry VI can be seen as the prototype of Shakespeare's greatest tragic protagonists will become clearer in the course of this book. But that's by no means the only debt Shakespearean tragedy owes to the brace of plays with which the actor from Stratford transformed himself into a trailblazing dramatist. For in *The Second Part of Henry VI* Shakespeare also dramatized the political rationale of Shakespearean tragedy, establishing the premises that would continue to underpin the perspective from which his tragedies were written.

It's no coincidence that the scene that marks the start of Henry's tragic self-division in the line 'Do, or undo, as if ourself were here' is the same scene that heralds the outbreak of a violent popular rebellion under the leadership of Jack Cade. It's no coincidence, because the appeal of a man in revolt against his own sovereignty, and the appeal of a plebeian revolt against the injustice of the regime over which that sovereign presides, were inseparable in Shakespeare's rebellious imagination: the same imagination that will later confront Hamlet with the Gravedigger and King Lear with Poor Tom, and that will begin the last tragedy Shakespeare wrote, almost two decades later, with another plebeian uprising in *Coriolanus*. The playwright who gave Henry VI the lines 'Go where you will, the King shall be commanded; / And be you kings: command, and I'll obey' – the dramatist who has the dying kingmaker Warwick say, 'what is pomp, rule, reign but earth and dust?' – is also a playwright audacious enough to stage at length scenes of popular rebellion, whose anarchic energy and fierce utopian spirit are unparalleled in early modern drama.

These scenes are ushered in by the beheading of Suffolk by a man he reviles as an 'Obscure and lousy swain', 'a jaded groom' and 'base slave' (4.1.50, 52, 67). But the 'base slave' denounces the arrogant aristocrat in his turn as a 'kennel, puddle, sink, whose filth and dirt / Troubles the silver spring where England drinks' (4.1.70–2). 'It is impossible that I should die', declares Suffolk, shortly before his headless corpse is lugged back onstage, 'By such a lowly vassal as thyself' (4.1.110–11). As the duke's body and head are lugged back off again, the scene shifts to this exchange between two of the rebels – commoners of the same stamp as those scorned by Suffolk as 'these paltry, servile, abject drudges' (4.1.105):

GEORGE

I tell thee, Jack Cade the clothier means to dress the commonwealth, and turn it, and set a new nap upon it.

NICK

So he had need, for 'tis threadbare. Well, I say it was never merry world in England since gentlemen came up.

GEORGE

O miserable age! Virtue is not regarded in handicraftsmen.

NICK

The nobility think scorn to go in leathern aprons.

GEORGE

Nay, more, the King's Council are no good workmen.

NICK

True; and yet it is said, 'Labour in thy vocation'; which is as much to say as, 'Let the magistrates be labouring men'; and therefore should we be magistrates.

(4.2.4–16)

The commonwealth needs completely reforming, George and Nick contend, in order to restore the 'merry world', where wealth was literally held in common, before the advent of class society, when 'gentlemen came up' and looked down, as Suffolk does, on those who actually work for a living, as the likes of Suffolk do not. To put things right, the existing order of things must be turned upside down, which means that society should be ruled not by the parasitical nobility but by those who are qualified to run it by the fact that they labour. The sort of people George and Nick have in mind as legitimate rulers ('magistrates') are people who belong to the same class as the followers of 'Jack Cade the clothier', who are about to join them onstage: 'Dick the butcher', 'Smith the weaver', and the first rebel they see approaching, 'Best's son, the tanner of Wingham', who 'shall have the skins of our enemies to make dog's leather of' (4.2.19–23, 26). The hides of the nobles will be good enough, that is, to make only the cheapest kind of leather gloves. The barbed quip is a reminder that the man who wrote it was the son of a glover, born into the same artisan class as Cade's rebels.

'For our enemies shall fall before us,' proclaims Cade, 'inspired with the spirit of putting down kings and princes' (4.2.31–2). He then launches into a ludicrous genealogical claim to the throne, which Dick the butcher and Smith the Weaver debunk in asides, and which itself debunks York's serious genealogical claim by parodying it. Cade's credibility as a revolutionary leader is tainted from the outset by the fact that he's a tool of York, an *agent provocateur* suborned 'To make commotion' (3.1.357) in York's interests. So when Cade 'vows reformation', promising that 'All the realm shall be in common', and immediately undercuts the promise of communal ownership by saying, 'And when I am king, as king I will be' (4.2.59–60, 63–5), the entire rebellion might seem irredeemably discredited by its leader's self-serving cynicism. But to draw that conclusion would be to ignore the complexity of Shakespeare's depiction of Cade and the political sophistication of his view of the revolt. Cade, as York himself points out, is York's 'substitute' (3.1.370). Thus, when he absurdly knights himself, declares 'I am rightful heir unto the crown' (4.2.122), publicly proclaims Henry a usurper, 'And vows to crown himself in Westminster' (4.4.30), Cade is burlesquing the pretensions of his aristocratic alter ego as well as flaunting his own selfish motives. When he brags, 'my mouth shall be the parliament of England' (4.7.12–13), has Lord Saye and Sir James Crowmer summarily beheaded, and their heads stuck on poles and made to kiss, he is also mimicking England's tyrannical nobility, to whose savage cruelty the entire trilogy attests.

Cade's grotesque mirroring of their tyranny does not detract from his critique of the systemic injustice over which the nobility presides, or from the power of the age-old demand for social justice that is Cade's rallying cry. Insofar as he is the mercenary pawn of York, masquerading as 'Sir John Mortimer', Cade is a caricature of the despotic mentality and fatuous pretensions of the patrician class he serves. But insofar as he is *at the same time* plain Jack Cade the clothier, he is also the fearless champion and convincing spokesman of the oppressed class he belongs to. When Cade indicts Lord Saye for appointing judges 'to call poor men before them, about matters they were not able to answer' because they were illiterate, and for imprisoning and hanging them in effect 'because they could not read' (4.7.38–40), the justice of the indictment is undeniable, and may have seemed especially just to the son of an illiterate provincial glover, who signed his name with an 'X'. When Cade upbraids Saye for riding on the sumptuous footcloth adorning his horse's back, because 'thou ought'st not to let thy horse wear a cloak when honester men than thou go in their hose and doublets' (4.7.45–7), the rank injustice of a regime in which the horses of the wealthy are treated better than human beings who must graft for their living is laid bare in a single, stinging sentence. It's inconceivable that Dick the Butcher's line, 'The first thing we do, let's kill all the lawyers' (4.2.71), didn't meet with the same jocular roar of approval from its first audiences that greet it to this day; or that the mass of the play's earliest spectators didn't thrill to Cade's revolutionary summons:

> And you that love the commons, follow me.
> Now show yourselves; 'tis for liberty.
> We will not leave one lord, one gentleman:
> Spare none but such as go in clouted shoon,
> For they are thrifty honest men, and such
> As would, but that they dare not, take our parts.
>
> (4.2.171–6)

'They are all in order and march towards us', observes Dick of the enemy, to which Jack replies with the Delphic dictum, 'But then are we in order when we are most out of order' (4.2.177–9), turning the rulers' view of what constitutes 'order' on its head. We will be 'in order' at last, in other words, on the day when the existing order has been overthrown and 'all things shall be in common' (4.7.16) instead of hogged by the high-born elite to the detriment of the labouring masses they despise.

The Jack Cade who voices these ideals is far from being the object of mockery he is when he's impersonating a ridiculous pretender to the throne in flat contradiction of those ideals. After Sir Humphrey Stafford and his brother have been slain in battle by the men they had addressed as 'Rebellious hinds, the filth and scum of Kent' (4.2.113–14), Cade commends Dick, 'the butcher of Ashford', for his gallantry: 'They fell before thee like sheep and oxen, and thou behaved'st thyself as if thou hadst been in thine own slaughterhouse' (4.3.1–5). The scene concludes with the rebels marching on to London, with Cade resolving to drag the corpses of the Staffords behind his horse, and Dick the valiant butcher saying that if they 'mean to thrive and do good', when they reach the capital they must 'break open the gaols and let out the prisoners' (4.3.14–15). At no point in this short scene are the audience being invited to regard what either character says and does as risible or monstrous. On the contrary: they are being invited to relish the spectacle of Jack Cade, the capering 'wild Morisco' (3.1.364), and his band of rebellious tradesmen being unleashed to run riot and give the likes of Lord Saye and the Stafford brothers a taste of their own cruel medicine. Why would the plebeian majority of playgoers in Shakespeare's day have been appalled rather than enthralled to see aristocrats get their comeuppance at the hands of commoners like themselves in a popular crusade for social justice?

The fundamental validity of that crusade is not impugned by the fact that its rambunctious mouthpiece is also – though only initially and intermittently – York's hireling and mordant caricature. Nor is its credibility scuppered by its ultimate defeat, when all but Cade surrender to the king and Cade is cut down on the run and beheaded by a country squire. Cade doesn't foment rebellion by arousing baseless grievances and spurious aspirations in the lower orders; the grievances and aspirations are real, long-standing and justified, otherwise they couldn't be aroused and mobilized so effectively. That's why Shakespeare is careful to begin his dramatization of the revolt before Cade enters with the exchange in which we overhear his foot soldiers, Nick and George, reasoning things out for themselves. He takes equal care to draw a distinction between Cade and his followers from the start by having them puncture his grandiose genealogical claims in asides to the audience. They plainly don't swallow the twaddle Cade's peddling about being the true-born heir to the throne. But they play along with it in the same carnivalesque spirit in which the clothier delivers it, and they are happy to hail Cade anyway as king of the commonwealth to come. They remain as oblivious as Cade is, however, to the satirical point Shakespeare makes by foregrounding that unconscious contradiction in terms. The point being that a realm whose wealth is held in common wouldn't be a realm at all, because it wouldn't by definition have a king. The creation of a true commonwealth presupposes the abolition of the monarchy and the entire social hierarchy on which monarchy is predicated.

The serious joke here is certainly on Cade and his crew, but it's not at the expense of the egalitarian ideal they are unwittingly at odds with. It's a joke that could be cracked only by a dramatist who perceived the contradiction, because he understood, quite remarkably for a man of his time, that the problem lay not with the concept of a collectively owned and ruled society, but with the hierarchical mentality fettering the imagination of those most committed to creating it. Shakespeare broached this still crucial political issue in what may well be his first play, and in the last play he wrote single-handed he came back to it again. In Act 2 of *The Tempest* Gonzalo's flight of fantasy to the Land of Cockaygne is grounded in mid-sentence by Sebastian's and Antonio's sarcastic heckling. 'Had I plantation of this isle,' opines Gonzalo, 'And were the king on't ... / I'th' commonwealth I would by contraries / Execute all things' (2.1.144, 146, 148–9). He proceeds to outline the key features of his utopian commonwealth, in which masters and servants, riches and poverty, private property, the exploitation of the earth's resources, and labour itself would no longer exist, and there would be 'No sovereignty – '; at which point Sebastian interjects, 'Yet he would be king on't' and Antonio underscores Gonzalo's gaffe: 'The latter end of his commonwealth forgets the beginning' (2.1.157–9). But the flaw in the honest old councillor's reasoning doesn't invalidate his utopian dream, only the premise on which it's based and the means by which it's to be achieved. The chief target of Antonio's and Sebastian's derision is not the idyllic dispensation Gonzalo envisages or its feasibility. It's the vanity betrayed by his fantasy of benign omnipotence, which blinds him to the contradiction between his wish to be king of his utopian colony and his knowledge that the precondition of a just and civilized society is 'No sovereignty'. Gonzalo is mocked because 'The latter end of his commonwealth forgets the beginning', not because the notion of a society free from tyranny and toil, where poverty is unknown because wealth is shared, and an undefiled nature produces 'All things in common' (2.1.160), is innately preposterous.

Like the exposure of Gonzalo's gaffe in *The Tempest*, the mockery of Cade's communist kingdom entails the knowledge that sovereignty cannot solve the problems of social and economic inequality that spring from its very existence. Shakespeare, needless to say, did not express that knowledge in those terms; he articulated his profound grasp of this fundamental political problem as he dramatized these scenes in the language dictated by his characters. The fact that Shakespeare was wrestling with a matter of such moment at the dawn of his theatrical career, and that he was still wrestling with it as that career drew to a close, shows how enduring its hold was on his mind. But what his first engagement with it tells us about his view of Jack Cade is that there's more to it than mockery. Cade doesn't just survive being the butt of his rebels' ragging and the patricians' contempt, he *thrives* on it and he remains defiant to the death.

Nothing illustrates the complexity of Cade's characterization more clearly than his denunciation of his followers for their craven capitulation to Buckingham and Old Clifford, when they are offered a free pardon from the king:

> Will you needs be hanged with your pardons about your necks? Hath my sword therefore broke through London gates, that you should leave me at the White Hart in Southwark? I thought ye would never have given o'er these arms till you had recovered your ancient freedom; but you are all recreants and dastards and delight to live in slavery to the nobility. Let them break your backs with burdens, take your houses over your heads, ravish your wives and daughters before your faces.
>
> (4.8.21–30)

That is not the speech of a character we're supposed to discount as a hypocritical buffoon. By this point in Act 4, Cade's role as York's cat's paw has been forgotten. After a final display of spinelessness by his brothers-in-arms, he washes his hands of them in disgust. 'Was ever feather so lightly blown to and fro as this multitude?' (4.8.55–6), he asks the audience in a rhetorical aside, which assumes they will agree and take his part:

> My sword make way for me, here is no staying. In despite of devils and hell, have through the midst of you! And heavens and honour be witness that no want of resolution in me, but only my followers' base and ignominious treasons, make me betake me to my heels.
>
> (4.8.62–4)

When King Henry enters five lines later, it's not to crow in public over the crushing of the rebels and the defeat of Cade, but to confess to the audience, 'Was never subject longed to be a king / As I do long and wish to be a subject' (4.9.5–6), which undercuts the Crown's triumph immediately before Buckingham and Old Clifford arrive to proclaim it.

It's no accident that the king's private disclosure to the audience follows hard on the heels of the rebel leader's appeal to them. Both characters are granted a downstage intimacy with the audience which the other characters are denied. That privilege reflects the dramatist's empathy with their points of view at such moments, an empathy the spectators are confidentially induced to share. For the disenchanted monarch and the rootless demagogue are both internal exiles, united by their discontentment with the world as they find it. That's the source of Shakespeare's attraction to these secret allies, which explains, amongst other things, why he dramatizes Cade's death scene as he does.

The scene begins with the famished renegade in hiding with a price on his head, standing alone onstage and explaining to the audience, in the same demotic prose as before, how he's been forced to climb into a private garden to stave off starvation with a 'sallet' (4.10.8) of raw herbs and vegetables, the staple resort of the destitute. When the squire, Alexander Iden, confronts him, Cade again enlists the audience in an explanatory aside – 'Here's the lord of the soil come to seize me for a stray for entering his fee-simple without leave' (4.10.24–5) – before drawing his sword. 'Look on me well', he tells Iden, 'I have eat no meat these five days, yet come thou and thy five men, an if I do not leave you all as dead as a doornail, I pray God I may never eat grass more' (4.10.37–40). The 'wild Morisco' is still alive and kicking, his bravado unbowed despite his emaciation, and still keen to put a comical spin on the fix he's in: 'Steel, if thou turn the edge or cut not out the burly-boned clown in chines of beef ere thou sleep in thy sheath, I beseech God on my knees thou mayst be turned to hobnails' (4.10.55–8). Though he's no physical match for his well-fed, upper-class opponent, Cade runs him through with an insolent quip that turns the squire into his boorish social inferior and into the joints of beef his ravenous belly craves. As he lies dying at Iden's feet, the last words Shakespeare gives Cade are:

> O, I am slain! Famine and no other hath slain me. Let ten thousand devils come against me, and give me but the ten meals I have lost, and I'd defy them all. Wither, garden, and be henceforth a burying place to all that do dwell in this house, because the unconquered soul of Cade is fled. ... For I, that never feared any, am vanquished by famine, not by valour.

> (4.10.59–64, 73–4)

Any doubts one might harbour about Shakespeare's sympathy with Cade should be dispelled by his granting the play's most charismatic character a death scene and a dying speech worthy of a hero. That sympathy is tempered by Cade's having also served as the parodic epitome of callous autocracy and by his blindness to the contradiction between his demand that everything be held in common and his bombastic fantasies of regal omnipotence. But it cleaves without qualification to the Cade who denounces his followers' 'base and ignominious' surrender to their oppressors, disdains to surrender himself, and dies fighting, 'vanquished by famine, not by valour'.

The Upstart Crow

It's 'the unconquered soul of Cade' that resonates above all with his creator's ungovernable spirit as a dramatist. That spirit never leaves him, and Shakespearean tragedy is possessed by it. It's the spirit of the 'upstart crow', whose dazzling debut in the plays first published as *The First Part of the Contention* and *The True Tragedy* provoked the older playwright Robert Greene to take him to task for his effrontery in presuming to vie with Greene and his peers. In *Greene's Groatsworth of Wit*, published posthumously in 1592, well before both the plays were published, but shortly after they had been performed, Greene addresses three of his fellow playwrights from the groatless gloom of his deathbed:

> Base minded men all three of you, if by my miserie you be not warned: for unto none of you (like me) sought those burres to cleave: those Puppets (I meane) that spake from our mouths, those Anticks garnisht in our colours. Is it not strange, that I, to whome they all have beene beholding, is it not like that you, to whome they all have been beholding, shall (were yee in that case as I am now) bee both at once of them forsaken? Yes trust them not: for there is an upstart Crow, beautified with our feathers, that with his *Tygers hart wrapt in a Players hyde*, supposes he is as well able to bombast out a blanke verse as the best of you: and being an absolute *Johannes fac totum*, is in his owne conceite the onely Shake-scene in a country.

Much scholarly ink has been spilled over this passage since its citation in the 1778 edition of Shakespeare's works. But what it reveals about the dramatic debutant, as viewed through the jaundiced eyes of a resentful rival, has not been fully appreciated. Greene's warning, it's generally agreed, is directed at three of his fellow 'University Wits': Christopher Marlowe, Thomas Nashe and George Peele, all of whom are '*Gentlemen*', like him, '*that spend their wits in making plaies*'. Necessity has obliged them all, as Greene's disparaging phrase implies, to turn minds fitted by rank and education for better things to penning plays for the commercial theatre. But they would be 'Base minded' indeed, says Greene, if they failed to heed his warning not to place any trust in those ungrateful, parasitic 'Puppets', the actors who play the parts and speak the lines that they and Greene have written for them. These 'Anticks garnisht in our colours' – these grotesque buffoons decked out in our verbal livery – are 'beholding' to us, Greene fumes, for their living. But when he fell into his present sick and destitute state, he says, the players who had once clung to him like 'burres' forsook him, as they are sure to forsake his fellow playwrights, should they find themselves in Greene's plight.

'Yes trust them not', cautions Greene, at which point his rancorous tirade against the players for their ingratitude switches tack to single out one of them as untrustworthy, but not for the same reason. The actor who has really got Greene's goat is William Shakespeare, first disguised as 'an upstart Crow, beautified with our feathers', but swiftly unmasked, through a tweaked quotation from his latest play and the 'Shake-scene' pun on his name. In his capacity as an actor, Shakespeare is stigmatized as a drab, vulgar bird, transfigured by the splendid plumage for which, like his fellow actors, he is entirely indebted to the playwrights. But the real sting in the phrase is delivered *de haut en bas* by the barbed word 'upstart', an insult aimed at someone seen as having risen suddenly and impertinently to undeserved prominence, to the aggravation of their avowed superiors. Although the patronage of the Crown and great noblemen could draw them into the orbit of the most privileged spheres, Elizabethan actors were commonly viewed, not least by enemies of the stage, as perched on the bottom rung of the social ladder alongside vagabonds and itinerant pedlars. As a university-educated gentleman playwright, Greene would have found it especially galling that a mere player, who was neither a gentleman nor university-educated, fancied himself a match for the University Wits as a playwright too; in fact, more than a match for them, because, as a Jack of all theatrical trades (*'an absolute Johannes fac totum'*), he could write and speak his own blank verse, leaving him 'beholding' to none of them, and thus 'in his owne conceite the onely Shake-scene in a country'.

Greene's aggrieved gibe is as illuminating in its way about what drove Shakespeare as the dramatist's successful application four years later, in 1596, for the coat of arms with its motto '*Non sans droict*' ('Not without right') that entitled him to be called a gentleman. Whether the charge of arrogant egotism levelled at him by Greene was warranted or not, it's impossible to say. That Greene was not alone in regarding the grammar-school lad as a cocky upstart for turning his hand to penning as well as performing plays is a plausible surmise. Nor does it seem unreasonable to assume that Shakespeare was aware of being perceived as such by the likes of Greene. But at least three things may be inferred with certainty from Greene's fit of pique. The first is that the success of the upstart crow's first stabs at play-making had been spectacular enough to provoke it. The second is that Shakespeare clinched that success with the play we know now as *The Third Part of Henry VI*, because Greene deliberately misquotes a striking phrase from it, and in a way that leaves no doubt about its having become so widely known that he can play on it satirically without needing to explain the allusion. And the third, which obviously follows from the second, is that Shakespeare's success, to Greene's chagrin, stems first and foremost from his superb command of dramatic verse, to which the thrilling eloquence of the travestied phrase attests.

The travesty backfires on Greene, however, by turning into a backhanded compliment. The original version of the line Greene has twisted reads: 'O, tiger's heart wrapped in a woman's hide' (1.4.137). Having decried Shakespeare as a common crow dressed in the feathers of his betters, Greene exploits the further derogatory animal comparison and the same idea of deceitful disguise in the original line, changing 'woman's hide' to 'Players hyde' to turn the line against its author. In a society whose sumptuary laws strove to enforce the distinctions between its ranks by prescribing the kind and colour of clothes its citizens were permitted to wear, Greene's resort to masquerading metaphors to traduce Shakespeare and his fellow 'Anticks' may have had the desired effect on like-minded readers. But, although his aim was to vilify Shakespeare by likening him to a savage beast lurking within the skin of a common player, Greene couldn't prevent the line from having the opposite effect of hailing Shakespeare as an actor and author with the heart of a tiger. Nor could he avoid creating the impression of Shakespeare as a unique, indomitable, seismic new force in the nation's theatre by invoking his capacity 'to bombast out a blanke verse', by granting that he is 'an absolute *Johannes fac totum*', and above all by dubbing him 'the onely Shake-scene in a country'. Instead of smearing Shakespeare unequivocally as a braggart and a parvenu by imputing such boasts to him, Greene winds up paying the scene-shaking tyro an unintended compliment.

It's worth pausing over the electrifying line Greene seized upon to sabotage, because it encapsulated for him Shakespeare's essential quality as a player and a playwright. The line occurs in the searing diatribe York directs at his captor, Queen Margaret, the 'She-wolf of France' (1.4.111), who has just offered him a napkin soaked in the blood of his youngest son, Rutland:

> O, tiger's heart wrapped in a woman's hide,
> How couldst thou drain the lifeblood of the child
> To bid the father wipe his eyes withal,
> And yet be seen to bear a woman's face? ...
> That face of his the hungry cannibals
> Would not have touched, would not have stained with blood;
> But you are more inhuman, more inexorable,
> O, ten times more than tigers of Hyrcania.

(1.4.137–40, 152–5)

The 'ruthless queen' remains unmoved by the 'hapless father's tears' (1.4.156). Pausing only to reproach Northumberland for weeping too in sympathy, Margaret joins Clifford in stabbing York to death. And she closes the scene as he dies with the command: 'Off with his head and set it on York gates, / So York may overlook the town of York' (1.4.179–80).

In choosing the line he did to epitomize and lampoon Shakespeare, Greene took a line charged with the violent passions of the scene from which it was torn. In doing so, he identified Shakespeare implicitly with a ferocious, implacable, foreign female: a vengeful French she-wolf exulting in the humiliation, torture and slaughtering of a grief-stricken English nobleman. Greene fastened instinctively on the genuine ferocity at the tiger's heart of Shakespeare's drama right from the beginning. Unaware that what he ridiculed as a duplicitous defect was the source of one of that drama's greatest strengths, Greene recognized in the stage's rising star a subversive affinity with characters 'more inhuman, more inexorable, / O, ten times more than tigers of Hyrcania'. We cannot fully understand Shakespearean tragedy if we fail to understand that affinity, the upstart's appetite for scenarios that put the high and mighty on the rack. The fact that Shakespeare kicked off his career with a brace of plays in which predatory patricians relentlessly betray and murder each other speaks for itself. Add to that the mounting death toll of rulers and aristocrats in subsequent history plays, both English and Roman, as well as in the tragedies, and Cade's words to Dick the butcher of Ashford might be addressed no less aptly to their author: 'They fell before thee like sheep and oxen, and thou behaved'st thyself as if thou hadst been in thine own slaughterhouse.'

To put the point another way: it's not difficult to discern in the wild Morisco an avatar of the upstart crow himself, who was likewise 'inspired with the spirit of putting down kings and princes' in the second and third parts of *Henry VI*, and who would continue to be inspired with it in the mature tragedies that grew out of them. Jack Cade leaps into riotous life in the same play that sees the birth-pangs of the Shakespearean tragic protagonist, because the perspective he embodies is integral to Shakespeare's tragic vision. The bewildered beings who wake to find themselves imprisoned in minds and lives they never chose are indivisible in Shakespearean tragedy from the utopian critique of the unjust society that imprisoned them to begin with. Cade's 'We will not leave one lord, one gentleman' and 'All the realm shall be in common' spring from the same source as the king's 'Do I not breathe a man?' and 'in the shade of death I shall find joy'. That source is the egalitarian frame of mind in which Shakespeare constructs these plays, fashions the characters and writes their lines. It's a frame of mind profoundly at odds with the rigidly hierarchical regimes in which the plays are set. For Shakespeare never forgets that 'pomp, rule, reign' are nothing 'but earth and dust' in the end, and that the entrenched disparities they sanction throughout society are as baseless as the insubstantial pageants that replicate them in the theatre. Shakespeare is under no illusion about how deeply entrenched those disparities are, and how hard it is for any mind inured to them to think of the world without them. There's nothing naïve or sentimental about the utopian viewpoint from which the plays are conceived and crafted. On the contrary, it's grounded in a realistic grasp of what is socially and historically feasible. The conflict incarnate in Cade between the demand for a true commonwealth of equals and thraldom to the divisive dispensation that obstructs its creation is rooted in the broader conflict between the *already* imaginable and the *as yet* unachievable that drives Shakespearean tragedy. No account of Cade would do justice to his character if it didn't also glimpse in him, alongside the carnivalesque plebeian clown, the makings of a proletarian tragic protagonist defeated, like his royal antagonist, by history and his own insuperable contradictions.

The Devil's Butcher

To appreciate the full extent of Shakespearean tragedy's debt to the second and third parts of *Henry VI*, it's vital to recognize the covert kinship not only of Henry and Cade, but of 'that valiant crookback prodigy' (*3HVI* 1.4.75) with both of them. Just as Cade bursts into *The Second Part* to steal the fourth act from the king who longs to be a subject, so Richard of Gloucester springs suddenly into demonic life in the middle of *The Third Part* to steal the limelight there and at the close of the play. Nor is it fortuitous that his first stunning soliloquy is delivered in the scene that follows Henry's encounter with the contemptuous keepers, or that his second follows immediately upon his assassination of the monarch he will eventually succeed on the English throne in *Richard III*. For they have more in common as characters than meets the eye, especially when one views them from the vantage point of the tragedies to come. Richard turns out on closer inspection to be a fusion of core qualities of Henry and Cade, incorporating as he does the vulnerable, tragic disposition of the one and the domineering, parodic prowess of the other.

Richard shares with Henry and Cade, through soliloquies and asides, the same direct downstage connection with the audience that's designed to elicit from them, at key moments, a degree of identification and empathy not granted to any other characters in these plays. But nothing Henry and Cade have confided could prepare us for the kind of rapport 'the foul misshapen stigmatic' (2.2.136) secures when we are left alone with him in the second scene of Act 3. The soliloquy begins conventionally enough with Richard explaining his predicament: the seeming impossibility of removing the human obstacles that stand between him and the throne he craves. But then the speech turns inward to reflect on the flaws in his own personality – 'My eye's too quick, my heart o'erweens too much' (3.2.144) – and to ponder the only alternative life seems to offer him. As it does, it becomes the first soliloquy in Shakespeare in which we witness a character thinking self-consciously and unpredictably out loud, as he strives to articulate why he is the way he is, how he sees himself, and what he's capable of being and doing to achieve his end.

> Well, say there is no kingdom then for Richard:
> What other pleasure can the world afford?
> I'll make my heaven in a lady's lap,
> And deck my body in gay ornaments
> And witch sweet ladies with my words and looks.
> O miserable thought, and more unlikely
> Than to accomplish twenty golden crowns!
> Why, love forswore me in my mother's womb,
> And, for I should not deal in her soft laws,
> She did corrupt frail Nature with some bribe
> To shrink mine arm up like a withered shrub;
> To make an envious mountain on my back,
> Where sits deformity to mock my body;
> To shape my legs of an unequal size;
> To disproportion me in every part,
> Like to a chaos or an unlicked bear whelp,
> That carries no impression like the dam.
> And am I then a man to be beloved?
> O monstrous fault to harbour such a thought!
> Then, since this world affords no joy to me
> But to command, to check, to o'erbear such
> As are of better person than myself,
> I'll make my heaven to dream upon the crown
> And whiles I live t'account this world but hell,
> Until my misshaped trunk that bears this head
> Be round impaled with a glorious crown.

(3.2.153–71)

The cruelty of nature has conspired with the constraints of society to leave Richard no option, as he sees it, but to seize supreme political power to find fulfilment: 'What other pleasure can the world afford?' In this respect, the contrast with Henry, 'the easy-melting King' (2.1.170), who longs to be a subject, who would rather be a shepherd or dead than be a monarch, could hardly be stronger. But what unites them is their sense of having been given no alternative, of being coerced by factors beyond their control, despite their capacity to imagine or wish themselves otherwise. Like Henry, moreover, but to a far greater degree, Richard is able to withdraw mentally to a point from which he can consider the person he is obliged to inhabit as if it were a self apart. Richard is not only talking to the audience about himself, but also talking to himself about the self that life and the world have assigned him. So when he says, 'this world affords no joy to me / But to command, to check, to o'erbear such / As are of better person than myself', he opens a space between the 'me' to whom the world affords no other joy and the Richard resolved 'to command, to check, to o'erbear' all those to whom the world has made him feel inferior. He opens the space, that is, in which tragedy as Shakespeare has begun to see it becomes possible.

That space, which Henry shares to a less developed degree with Richard, becomes clearer as the soliloquy proceeds, as does the main distinction to be drawn between them, and what 'that devil's butcher, Richard' (5.5.77) has in common with Jack Cade.

> And I, like one lost in a thorny wood,
> That rents the thorns and is rent with the thorns,
> Seeking a way and straying from the way,
> Not knowing how to find the open air,
> But toiling desperately to find it out,
> Torment myself to catch the English crown:
> And from that torment I will free myself,
> Or hew my way out with a bloody axe.
> Why, I can smile, and murder whiles I smile,
> And cry 'Content!' to that which grieves my heart,
> And wet my cheeks with artificial tears,
> And frame my face to all occasions.
> I'll drown more sailors than the mermaid shall,
> I'll slay more gazers than the basilisk,
> I'll play the orator as well as Nestor,
> Deceive more slyly than Ulysses could,
> And, like a Sinon, take another Troy.
> I can add colours to the chameleon,
> Change shapes with Proteus for advantages.
> And set the murderous Machiavel to school.
> Can I do this, and cannot get a crown?
> Tut, were it farther off, I'll pluck it down.   *Exit.*

(3.2.174–95)

Although Richard never evolves into a fully fledged tragic protagonist, the divided selves that find expression in the soliloquies of Shakespeare's greatest tragedies descend directly from the character that found its voice in this speech. Again, Richard objectifies himself, speaking about himself as though he were someone else, or rather a series of other selves. In a rapid succession of similes he likens himself to 'one lost in a thorny wood', a mermaid, a basilisk, Nestor, Ulysses, Sinon, the chameleon and Proteus. The dizzying multiplicity of alternative identities he conjures up creates an exhilarating sense of boundless, transformative potential at the command of an ulterior, indeterminate self. All that boundless potential is doomed to be wasted, however, in lying and murdering his way to 'a glorious crown', because wielding power over everyone else is the ultimate prize his hierarchical world, which is indeed 'but hell', can offer him. The nascent tragedy of Richard's plight lies in the tension between all that he might be and what he's reduced to becoming by assumptions and expectations he can't escape.

It's easy to overlook the essential similarity between Richard and Henry as proto-tragic characters, because it's overshadowed by the glaring difference between the ways they react to the same basic bind. The regal role Henry recoils from in dismay is coveted by Richard as the one thing he must have at all costs. Henry shirks decisions and delegates responsibility, relapsing under pressure into lassitude to avoid shouldering the burden of sovereignty; Richard is unflinching and resourceful in his energetic pursuit of absolute power. Henry's crown is the invisible crown of inner contentment that he wears in his heart, not on his head; Richard cannot rest until his head is 'impaled with a glorious crown', the glittering symbol of supreme authority. In that respect he's no different from his own father or his brother Edward, who are equally single-minded in their quest to be king. Unlike them, however, Richard resolves on reflection to turn himself into the kind of person he needs to become to reach that goal, because he feels that's the only choice his noble birth and disfigured body have left him. Unlike his sire and his sibling too, Richard embraces the villainous task that faces him with a theatrical gusto designed to disarm and seduce the audience in whom he's confiding. He takes delight in his own histrionic virtuosity and rhetorical verve, exults in his capacity to plot, dissimulate and slay without conscience, and defies us not to suspend moral judgement and simply admire his mutation into a monster as a brilliant, amoral performance.

The future King Richard III might appear to have nothing in common with a base-born rebel, whose battle-cry is 'All the realm shall be in common'. But, despite the social chasm that divides the king from the clothier, 'this scolding crookback' (5.5.30) shares a great deal with the bricklayer's son who 'vows to crown himself in Westminster' (*2HVI* 4.4.30). Both are egotistical underdogs, accustomed to being cursed and derided, and thus bound to appeal to an upstart crow scoffed at for thinking himself the only Shake-scene in the country. Both solicit the audience's applause for their flamboyant caricatures of the power-crazed, rapacious patrician class. Both are licensed by Shakespeare to wreak havoc on the nobility whose barbarism they epitomize and burlesque with such brio. 'I am the besom that must sweep the court clean of such filth as thou art' (*2HVI* 4.7.27–9), says Cade to Lord Saye, casting himself in the role of scourge of the aristocracy that Richard, the 'devil's butcher' (5.5.77), takes over from him in *The Third Part* and in *Richard III*. In contrast to Cade, Richard doesn't see himself as a scourge, and his motives are selfish rather than subversive. Yet insofar as he exacts retribution from the ruling class he mirrors and mocks by paying them back in their own cruel currency, he is as much a demonized scourge as his plebeian counterpart.

Richard has the same warrant from Shakespeare as Cade to create carnage, unfettered by conscience, fear or contrition, among those whose vicious power-struggles are responsible for the bloodbath of the civil war. Shakespeare does nothing to disguise the pitiless savagery in which both characters are capable of indulging. But it would be disingenuous to deny that it's a pitiless savagery which the playwright with the tiger's heart takes vicarious pleasure in staging for his audience's entertainment. As scapegoats as well as scourges, Richard and Cade incur within their plays all the caustic abuse and righteous condemnation their villainy attracts, even though the worst atrocities they commit are no worse than those committed or countenanced by their aristocratic antagonists. As scapegoats they are doomed, sooner or later, to bear the guilt and pay with their lives for the barbarism of the society that produced them. They must be demonized and killed off *as if* they were exceptional abominations from which their society had to be saved, when what their society in fact beholds in them are personifications of its own ethos. As such, however, they acquire immunity from unequivocal denunciation by the audience for their odious deeds, which the brutalized society that fostered them has brought upon itself. The amoral allure with which Shakespeare invests these outrageous characters and their confidential alliance with the audience reinforce that immunity. The audience in turn finds itself licensed to enjoy watching Cade and Richard terrorize the regimes whose inhumanity they distil in their exactions of poetic justice.

There's nothing about the way Cade and Richard are characterized that invites the audience to adopt the moralistic attitude to them that criticism has so often adopted. Onstage or in the theatre of the mind their magnetism renders the pious urge to censure their conduct irrelevant. Even when Richard butchers Henry in the Tower at the end, stabbing him mid-sentence to cut off his abusive tirade, then stabbing his corpse again, it's not the pitiful fate of the hapless king but the thrilling audacity of the assassination and Richard's final soliloquy that capture our attention:

Down, down to hell, and say I sent thee hither!
I that have neither pity, love nor fear.
Indeed, 'tis true that Henry told me of,
For I have often heard my mother say
I came into this world with my legs forward.
Had I not reason, think ye, to make haste,
And seek their ruin that usurped our right?
The midwife wondered and the women cried,
'O, Jesus bless us, he is born with teeth!'
And so I was, which plainly signified
That I should snarl, and bite and play the dog.
Then, since the heavens have shaped my body so,
Let hell make crook'd my mind to answer it.
I have no brother; I am like no brother.

And this word 'love', which greybeards call divine,
Be resident in men like one another
And not in me: I am myself alone.

(5.6.67–83)

After a rapid review of those he must dispose of next to clear his path to the throne, Richard drags the king's carcase unceremoniously offstage. 'I'll throw thy body in another room' (5.6.92) he informs the corpse, as he exits with a line and a cavalier callousness that Hamlet will reprise as he drags what he'd hoped would be the corpse of a king out of his mother's chamber, saying 'I'll lug the guts into the neighbour room' (3.4.210).

All Shakespeare's imaginative empathy in this seductive soliloquy is reserved for a regicide who boasts that he feels 'neither pity, love nor fear' and expects us to admire him for it. He proceeds, on the unspoken understanding established in his first soliloquy, to assume that he can count on our condoning both the brutal murder of a monarch, which we alone have witnessed, and the future murders he is planning of his royal kith and kin. Note the sly shift of tone and deft sleight of diction that pull us into Richard's conversation with himself, and thus into tacit dialogue with him, before we know it. From his exclamatory consignment of the sovereign's soul to hell Richard switches without blinking into reflective mode, pausing to consider what he has become and why. His tone relaxes, as he concedes that Henry was right, after all, about his alarming physical precocity at birth. The language then slips seamlessly into the informal vein of anecdotal reminiscence. The phrase 'For I have often heard my mother say' imputes to the audience a foregone familiarity with the speaker, which he presumes upon and deepens in his appeal to them for corroboration, couched in a joke about his breech-birth being deliberate ('Had I not reason, *think ye*, to make haste … ?'). The jocular note is sustained through the reported response of the midwife and the women to the infant Richard's premature dentition. The colloquial register of their exclamation forges a further demotic bond with the spectators whose idiom it echoes.

The humorous tone prevails over the sinister thrust of the lines as Richard portrays himself as dentally doomed to 'snarl, and bite and play the dog'. The verb 'play' keeps the touch of innocuous levity alive for a moment, before the soliloquy reverts to the steely tone in which it commenced. But, by treating Richard's aggressive, canine character as a role, the word paves the way for his resumption in the next six lines of the rationale he developed in his first soliloquy and will restate in the enthralling soliloquy with which *Richard III* begins. As in the first soliloquy, Richard is at pains to explain that he has become a villain – indeed, is still in the process of becoming one – *as a consequence* of his congenital deformity, but not because his congenital deformity made him innately villainous: 'Then, since the heavens have shaped my body so, / Let hell make crook'd my mind to answer it'. He doesn't say that hell *has made* his mind as crooked as the heavens have made his body; he employs a subjunctive locution ('*Let* hell make … ') to express his wish that it *would* make it equally crooked. So, when he declares in the following, chilling line, 'I have no brother; I am like no brother', that emphatic, indicative statement still harbours the subjunctive wish that spawned it. The same is true of Richard's declaration 'I am myself alone', which is prefaced by his wish that 'love', which for him is merely a 'word', would confine itself to men who resemble each other, and avoid him as one set apart from the rest of his kind. 'I have no brother; I am like no brother' and 'I am myself alone' are proleptic assertions, in which Richard defines himself as already being what he is willing himself to be by the act of uttering them. They betray the pressure under which he is asserting his absolute autonomy and the price of severing himself irrevocably from his fellow human beings and the possibility of love. At this moment we catch, once again, a glimpse of the tragic protagonist Richard might have become in *Richard III*, and of his unexpected affinity in that regard with the reluctant sovereign he has just stabbed to death.

We also catch a glimpse in these lines of some of Shakespeare's fully evolved tragic protagonists, who are driven to a similar point of defiant isolation under extreme pressure and at an unbearable cost to themselves. Richard's egocentric credo will resurface over a decade later in Macbeth's 'for mine own good, / All causes shall give way' (3.4.133–4). It will still be echoing in Shakespeare's final tragedy, in Coriolanus's resolution to 'stand / As if a man were author of himself / And knew no other kin' (5.3.35–7) and his repeated insistence on having achieved everything 'alone'. To cast one's mind forward to that aspect of these characters is to appreciate how much they owe to the Richard of *The Third Part of Henry VI*. No less indebted to this charismatic villain in his solitary, destructive stance against the world are Aaron, Iago and Edmund, all of whom cast a spell on the audience which charms and disarms them, just as Richard does. All of them revel like Richard in causing mayhem in societies whose ethos they both violate and embody. All of them bear witness, like Richard and Jack Cade, to Shakespeare's penchant for dramatizing the agony and grief such characters relish inflicting on a world from which they feel excluded.

Understanding what's distinctive about Shakespearean tragedy demands an honest recognition of the streak of punitive cruelty that runs through it from beginning to end, and the gratification it secretly affords both author and audience. The nightmare of mutual butchery that grips *Titus Andronicus* is otherwise inexplicable. What else could account for Shakespeare ditching his chief source's benign resolution in *King Lear* in order to kill off every member of the play's two noble families bar one, after first torturing the fathers, Lear and Gloucester, beyond endurance? This powerful animus is already at work in the second and third parts of *Henry VI*, where it finds its most forceful expression in the theatrically sanctioned violence of Jack Cade and Richard. That Shakespeare should choose as the themes of his first crack at serious drama the slaughterhouse of civil war, aristocratic treachery, popular rebellion, dethronement and regicide is as telling as the fact that he began to forge his own brand of tragedy in political plays explicitly concerned with the struggle for sovereignty, the possibility of revolution, and the dream of a land whose wealth is held in common. The deep structure of all the tragedies Shakespeare would go on to write after *Henry VI* is already discernible in these amazing plays. They are the crucible in which the vital elements of Shakespeare's tragic vision were forged, as we shall see when we turn to the play with the most compelling claim to be the first tragedy that he wrote.

PART II

CHAPTER 2
TITUS ANDRONICUS: A SYMPATHY OF WOE

Prototypes and Precursors

Most critical studies of Shakespeare's tragedies commence with the play first published in a quarto edition in 1594 as *The Most Lamentable Roman Tragedy of Titus Andronicus*. As it's the first play by Shakespeare unequivocally conceived and billed as a stand-alone tragedy, it seems a reasonable place to begin any account of his ventures in that genre. But, given that Shakespeare had begun to forge his own tragic vision in the second and third parts of *Henry VI*, *Titus Andronicus* should really be regarded as the first flowering of that vision rather than its root. We view *Titus* quite differently, if we view it as a tragedy which evolved out of the two plays that launched Shakespeare's dramatic career, instead of as his first attempt to write another kind of play altogether.

It's rare these days to find a critic echoing the once routine disparagement of *Titus* as the crude Senecan sensationalism of a prentice hand pandering to his audience's basest appetites. Although the play was a huge hit in its day, as the three quarto editions it went through in Shakespeare's lifetime attest, the critical consensus from Samuel Johnson in the eighteenth century to T. S. Eliot in the twentieth was dismissive, if not contemptuous. But from the second half of the twentieth century onwards, as cultural tastes and critical values changed, the way *Titus* was perceived changed too. The play that, in Johnson's opinion, 'could scarcely be conceived tolerable to any audience', because of 'The barbarity of the spectacles and the general massacre which are here exhibited', struck a chord, and continues to resonate, with audiences accustomed to seeing barbarous spectacles and massacres beamed daily into their homes in news footage and for their fictional entertainment. The tragedy trashed by Eliot as 'one of the stupidest and most uninspired plays ever written' revealed under sharper scrutiny, moreover, formidable intelligence and sophistication. Nevertheless, the critical and theatrical rehabilitation of *Titus* hasn't stopped it continuing to be seen, like *Timon of Athens*, as an essentially anomalous part of Shakespeare's tragic repertoire. Its salient affinities with later tragedies, especially *King Lear*, have of course been noted. And the play slots readily into a subgroup of Roman tragedies, although the fact that it draws on no known main source for its plot and *dramatis personae* also sets it apart from *Julius Caesar*, *Antony and Cleopatra* and *Coriolanus*. The observed points of resemblance between *Titus* and Shakespeare's other tragedies have been overshadowed, however, by what's commonly felt to mark it out as an eccentric manifestation of its author's genius: the extreme nature of the unremitting horrors to which it treats the audience, and the brazen black humour with which it treats those horrors.

The gruesome pageant of dismemberment, rape, mutilation, decapitation and cannibalism staged by Shakespeare's earliest tragedy is certainly without parallel in the tragedies that follow it. Nor could a credible case be made for any other tragedy finding the same incongruous grim comedy in its atrocities with the same frequency and panache. But the difference between *Titus* and the tragedies that came after it turns out to be one of degree rather than kind in these respects, when it's reappraised in the light of the second and third parts of *Henry VI*, whose basic stance and tone *Titus* takes over for its own darker ends.

After all, there's no shortage of atrocities in *2* and *3 Henry VI*, which are full of the deeds and discourse of the killing field that the war-torn English nation has become. Think of the ghoulishly graphic description of the murdered Gloucester's corpse in *The Second Part*:

> But see, his face is black and full of blood,
> His eyeballs further out than when he lived,
> Staring full ghastly like a strangled man;
> His hair upreared, his nostrils stretched with struggling;
>
> (3.2.168–71)

Think of the guilt-stricken Cardinal in his death throes, *'raving and staring as if he were mad'* at the imaginary sight of that corpse: 'Comb down his hair; look, look, it stands upright / Like lime twigs set to catch my winged soul' (3.3.0. s.d., 15–16). Think of the 'barbarous and bloody spectacle' (4.1.146) of Suffolk's body and severed head being hauled on and offstage by his plebeian executioners, before his head comes to rest two scenes later, bizarrely cradled in the grieving queen's arms before the eyes of the cuckolded king. Think of the severed heads of Lord Saye and Sir James Crowmer stuck on poles, carried through the streets of London by the advancing rebels, and obscenely made to kiss each other 'at every corner' at Jack Cade's amused behest (4.7.123). Or think of Cade's own severed head, presented to the king by his killer, who is rewarded on the spot with a knighthood and a thousand marks (5.1.64–82).

The severed-head count does drop in *The Third Part of Henry VI*, but before the first act is over Rutland, an 'innocent child' (1.3.8), has been butchered by Clifford in revenge, and his father, York, has been stabbed to death by Clifford and Margaret, after being taunted with a napkin soaked in his dead boy's blood. York's head is impaled on the gates of the city whose name he bears, but it's soon replaced by the head of 'Clifford, that cruel child-killer' (2.2.98), whose lifeless body is addressed in mock earnestness by York's surviving sons. With the mutilation inflicted on Titus in mind, and the filial blood he tricks Tamora into consuming, it's worth noting, too, the terms in which Richard expresses his wish that Clifford were still alive:

> If this right hand would buy two hours' life,
> That I in all despite might rail at him,
> This hand should chop it off, and with the issuing blood

Stifle the villain whose unstaunched thirst
York and young Rutland could not satisfy.

(2.6.80–4)

The same self-maiming motif recurs in Warwick's refusal to kneel to Edward after the latter has imprisoned Henry: 'I had rather chop this hand off at a blow / And with the other fling it at thy face' (5.1.50–1). Four scenes later, York's three sons stab Henry's young son before his mother's eyes in savage reprisal for the slaying of York and Rutland; 'Bloody cannibals', cries Margaret, 'You have no children, butchers; if you had, / The thought of them would have stirred up remorse' (5.5.61, 63). In the following scene Richard enjoys 'a bloody supper in the Tower' (5.6.85). He cracks a crass gag as he stabs Henry to death: 'Will the aspiring blood of Lancaster / Sink in the ground? I thought it would have mounted' (5.6.61–2). Then he stabs the king's corpse again for good measure, dispatching Henry *con brio* to hell – 'and say I sent thee hither' (5.6.67) – before dragging his royal remains breezily offstage.

Titus Andronicus takes its trademark mingling of unspeakable cruelty and tasteless comedy straight from Shakespeare's previous two plays. But it redeploys much more of them than that. Titus inherits Henry's envy of the dead, 'Secure from worldly chances and mishaps', from treason and from envy, in 'silence and eternal sleep', as well as his aversion to assuming sovereignty and wielding power: 'Give me a staff of honour for mine age, / But not a sceptre to control the world' (*TA* 1.1.155–8, 201–2). Like Henry, Titus becomes utterly disillusioned with the society he was born to serve and defend. The Goth queen, Tamora, on whom Titus wreaks revenge for the rape and mutilation of his daughter, Lavinia, and for the framing and beheading of two of his sons, is clearly a reincarnation of the ferocious Queen Margaret, on whom York's sons likewise took revenge by butchering her offspring. Like Margaret, Tamora is a foreign queen from a vanquished nation with her own grounds for revenge, who is passed from her conqueror to a ruler whom she cuckolds. And just as Margaret was reviled by York as a 'tiger's heart wrapped in a woman's hide' (*3HVI* 1.4.137), so the queen of the Goths and empress of Rome is reviled by Titus's son, Lucius, as 'that ravenous tiger, Tamora' (5.3.194). But nowhere in the cast of *Titus* is the play's debt to its immediate precursor more transparent than in the rebirth of 'that devil's butcher, Richard' (*3HVI* 5.5.77) as 'the incarnate devil' (5.1.40) Aaron, the 'barbarous Moor' (5.3.4) and 'Chief architect and plotter of these woes' (5.3.121). Like his crookbacked progenitor, the charismatic Aaron enjoys the amoral immunity conferred by his privileged intimacy with the audience. His delight in his own villainous ingenuity plainly derives from Richard too, but Aaron takes gleeful malevolence to another level, and he reveals a capacity for compassion that Richard would find incomprehensible.

If we fast-forward to the later tragedies, *Titus Andronicus* looks less like a generic anomaly and more like the emergence of a pattern of dramatic thought that binds all the tragedies together. Titus has long been recognized as a prototype of Lear, because of the catastrophic consequences of his obstinate inhumanity and political folly in the opening scene; the unhinged state of estrangement in which he grasps and decries the iniquitous dispensation he epitomized; and the poignant parallels between Lear's relationship with Cordelia and Titus's relationship with Lavinia, 'The cordial of mine age to glad my heart' (1.1.170) as Titus calls her. Titus's revulsion from the Rome that once lionized him is mirrored in Timon's raging against the Athens whose adulation vanished overnight with his wealth. Titus's vengeful one-man revolt against the imperial might of Rome engenders the full-scale rebellion led by the banished Lucius, whose invading army of Goths marches right into the urban heart of the empire in the final act. The same scenario, in which a hitherto loyal warrior turns in anger against his society, will be replicated a decade later in Alcibiades' march on Athens in *Timon*, and reworked yet again in Shakespeare's last tragedy, *Coriolanus*. Lucius is explicitly conceived as another Coriolanus in *Titus*: the Goths, Saturninus is informed, are marching on Rome

> ... under conduct
> Of Lucius, son to old Andronicus,
> Who threats in course of this revenge to do
> As much as ever Coriolanus did.

(4.4.64–7)

The ambiguous referent of the relative pronoun 'who' fuses 'old Andronicus' with his son as an avatar of Coriolanus too. In Lucius's description of himself in the final scene of *Titus* the prefiguration of Coriolanus as Shakespeare will portray him fifteen years later is uncannily prescient; indeed, these lines could be transferred from *Titus* to *Coriolanus* and spliced almost verbatim into its hero's speech as they stand:

> Lastly myself, unkindly banished,
> The gates shut on me, and turned weeping out
> To beg relief among Rome's enemies,
> Who drowned their enmity in my true tears
> And oped their arms to embrace me as a friend.
> I am the turned-forth, be it known to you,
> That have preserved her welfare in my blood,
> And from my bosom took the enemy's point,
> Sheathing the steel in my adventurous body.
> Alas, you know I am no vaunter, I;
> My scars can witness, dumb although they are,
> That my report is just and full of truth.

(5.3.103–14)

It's not just that the seeds of the final tragedy are being so plainly sown in the first, but that *Coriolanus* attests, along with *Lear* and *Timon*, to Shakespeare's deep-rooted, enduring attraction to figures who revolt heroically against their society and are even prepared to ally themselves with its enemies, or who are driven by pain and anger to reject everything it stands for.

In Titus we can also discern a harbinger of Hamlet. The determination to revenge is indivisible for both from a profound disillusionment with their world; Titus, too, feigns lunacy to throw his enemies off the scent: 'I am not mad,' he says to Tamora, transparently disguised as Revenge, 'I know thee well enough' (5.2.21); and Titus, too, defers the execution of his revenge until prompted from without towards the end, when Revenge personified turns up to 'Knock at his study, where they say he keeps / To ruminate strange plots of dire revenge' (5.2.5–6). The genealogical line that runs back from the ravenous tigress Tamora to the tiger-hearted Margaret also runs forward through those 'Tigers, not daughters', Goneril and Regan (*KL* 4.2.41), to the equally exotic and erotic enemy of Rome, Cleopatra, and Coriolanus's devouring mother, Volumnia. Aaron, the devilish theatrical progeny of Richard and subversive black stepchild of Jack Cade, prefigures not only Iago and Edmund, but also the noble Moor whom Iago maliciously destroys. The kinship of Aaron and Othello as characters is more than skin-deep. Both are aliens within European societies, who are abused for being black and loathed for the threat their relationships with white women pose to the fabric of those societies. As we shall see, however, both also unlock for us the possibility of ways of life founded on values which are the reverse of those that blight their worlds.

A Wilderness of Tigers

I've been attempting so far in this chapter to bring into focus some of the ways in which *Titus Andronicus* draws on Shakespeare's first two *Henry VI* plays and leaves its imprint on the sequence of tragedies it inaugurates. What I want to do now is pull back to consider the perspective from which the play is dramatized, because it can tell us much about the fundamental frame of mind in which the subsequent tragedies were written. I'll then try to define the specifically tragic quality of *Titus Andronicus* in a way that illuminates the evolving vision of Shakespearean tragedy as well as *Titus* itself.

I argued in the previous chapter that Robert Greene unwittingly captured the nascent spirit of Shakespearean tragedy when he derided the author of the final part of *Henry VI* as 'an upstart Crow' and as having a '*Tygers hart wrapt in a Players hyde*'. In choosing that line from the play to twist into that gibe, Greene inadvertently acknowledged Shakespeare's seditious kinship with characters like the vicious foreign female to whom the original insult was addressed: characters 'more inhuman, more inexorable, / O, ten times more than tigers of Hyrcania' (*3HVI* 1.4.154–5); characters whose inhumanity Shakespeare turns with relish against the inhuman dispensation they caricature. His elective affinity with such characters found confirmation in his next play's likening of Aaron as well as Tamora to a 'ravenous tiger' (5.3.5,194) in a Rome revealed as nothing 'but a wilderness of tigers' (3.1.54).

In the *Henry VI* plays Shakespeare had drawn on the chronicles of Hall and Holinshed to show his nation crippled by the atavistic greed and belligerence of its aristocracy. In *Titus Andronicus* he renewed his assault on the patriciate, this time transposed to ancient Rome instead of England a century earlier. That double displacement of focus, both temporal and geographical, combined with his imaginative independence of any major source, gave Shakespeare the latitude to lash out with even more ferocity in *Titus*. He could count on few of his audience being blind to the oblique bearing of his Roman tragedy on the England they inhabited, an England that looked to classical Rome as a model for its own embryonic empire. 'If wee present a forreigne History,' wrote Shakespeare's fellow playwright, Thomas Heywood, in *An Apology for Actors* (1612), 'the subject is so intended, that in the lives of *Romans*, *Grecians*, or others, either the vertues of our Countrymen are extolled, or their vices reproved.' Shakespeare could expect many of his audience to share Sidney's view of the aim of tragedy in *An Apology for Poetry* (1595), published the year after the First Quarto of *Titus*: 'the high and excellent tragedy,' wrote Sidney, pointedly employing the present tense, 'openeth the greatest wounds, and showeth forth the ulcers that are covered with tissue; that maketh kings fear to be tyrants, and tyrants manifest their tyrannical humours; that with stirring the affects of admiration and commiseration teacheth the uncertainty of this world, and upon how weak foundations gilden roofs are builded'.

Titus Andronicus fits Sidney's formula for tragedy perfectly. It lays bare the physical and figurative wounds that tyranny inflicts on society and the fragility of the ephemeral foundations on which the power and wealth of the mighty rest. In *Henry VI*, the farcical frequency with which the English crown changes heads in a whirlwind of abdication, usurpation, restoration and assassination had made the arbitrariness and instability of its possession as palpable as the tenuousness of the genealogical arguments advanced to secure it. In the same spirit, *Titus* reveals at the outset the absurdly irrational chain of events that lead to the psychopath Saturninus being elected emperor rather than his more suitable brother, Bassianus, or the original choice of the people, Titus himself. The politically implausible Rome Shakespeare invents for this tragedy is an eclectic confusion of republic, elective monarchy and hereditary monarchy, making the acquisition of sovereignty arise from a process as prudent as tossing a coin. Titus's blind insistence that the right of primogeniture determine who rules Rome, despite the will of the people and the superiority of the rival candidate, compounds the consequences of his deafness to Tamora's plea that he spare her son, Alarbus, instead of having him carved up and burned to appease the shades of Titus's sons. The rigid compliance of this austere epitome of *romanitas* with the dictates of tradition sparks a reign of terror and a spate of reprisals that put the barbarism of ancient Rome, the supposed apotheosis of western civilization in Shakespeare's day, beyond doubt.

Shakespeare takes pains to anchor the demented universe of *Titus Andronicus* in a recognizable ancient Rome through references to classical myths, real historical figures, actual places, institutions and customs, and authors such as Virgil, Seneca, Horace, Cicero and Ovid. He takes equal pains, however, to plant in the play subliminal reminders of its resonance with the Elizabethan present. When one Goth recalls reading a verse from Horace in Lily's Latin grammar, the standard textbook in English schools from 1540 onwards, and another reports having 'strayed / To gaze upon a ruinous monastery' (5.1.21), which he could have encountered only in post-Reformation England, the play's location and time frame slip surreptitiously into the place and time of its first audiences. But the tragedy's most blatant resort to anachronism occurs in Act IV, when the Clown, with his pathetic brace of pigeons, steps into the action straight out of Shakespeare's world. Through the incongruous, colloquial prose in which he talks at cross-purposes with the protagonist, this ostensibly unwitting wise fool debunks the portentous predicament into which he's stumbled by translating its exalted concerns into his own mundane terms. The humorous effect of his artful naivety and irreverent ignorance is to secure the audience's sympathy with this thinly disguised compatriot stranded centuries away from his home in Elizabethan England. But by his very presence in Shakespeare's ancient Roman dystopia, and by the nature of the fate he suffers, he also intimates that the nightmare into which he's wandered is not as alien to the audience as it might seem.

The wretched innocent's reward for delivering a threatening letter from Titus to Saturninus is summary execution. For Shakespeare's Elizabethan audience the dispatching of the harmless, amiable Clown to instant death would have been a chilling reminder of the vulnerability of ordinary English citizens to the capricious malice of absolute power. The monstrous injustice of his hanging serves to remind us, too, of the staggering scale on which the condemned subjects of Elizabeth and James were routinely gibbeted throughout their reigns. To remember the forgotten plebeian victims of seven decades of systematic judicial slaughter is also to be reminded that the beheadings and mutilations meted out in revenge or for sadistic gratification in *Titus* would have been less likely to appal early modern audiences inured to similar, legally sanctioned atrocities unthinkable in societies that think themselves civilized today. Elizabethans didn't have to go to the theatre to see impaled heads on public display, hands chopped off for theft, human beings branded, disembowelled and decapitated, or hanged, drawn and quartered on the authority of the crown. Viewed in this light, *Titus Andronicus* looks less like a wildly unrealistic travesty of a Roman revenge tragedy and more like something closer to home: a terrifying reflection of the reality of early modern England in the guise of ancient Rome.

In *Titus* Shakespeare dramatizes the essence of that insane reality by multiplying and magnifying the atrocities it fosters, and by pushing its depraved logic to its bestial conclusion in cannibalism. He dramatizes it from a perspective which enables us to see the mechanism that perpetuates the madness, the play's complicity in its perpetuation, and the potential for deliverance at the heart of inhumanity itself. The Rome promoted as an imperial prototype of Elizabethan England is exposed from a standpoint far beyond it as a decadent society in the throes of self-destruction. It's a society which has arrived at the point that Albany in *King Lear* fears will come: the point when 'Humanity must perforce prey upon itself, / Like monsters of the deep' (4.2.50–1). Like that mighty British tragedy it foreshadows in so many ways, *Titus* has a post-apocalyptic air about it, an air of being written in the aftermath of the catastrophe it portrays with such gusto. It dramatizes nothing less than the demise of ancient Rome and everything it stood for. That's why the time frame of *Titus* is a fictional fusion of every epoch in the history of Rome, from the earliest days of the republic to the last days of imperial decadence in which it's ostensibly set. The different forms of Roman government, like the equally eclectic names and cultural referents of the characters, coexist anachronistically in *Titus*, because Shakespeare has collapsed the entire history of Rome into the era of its decline and fall.

Nothing in *Titus* reflects more plainly Shakespeare's view of the Rome his nation sought to emulate than the play's sardonic tone. That tone can be heard in Titus's outburst of laughter instead of grief or fury at the sight of his mutilated daughter kissing his sons' severed heads; it lards his speech with facetious puns on Lavinia's and his own handless plight; and it informs the cannibalistic sequence over which Titus, as homicidal cook and avenging host, presides with grim jocularity. But it's Aaron, the *spiritus rector* of the tragedy, who most consistently embodies and articulates the attitude that governs it. The 'inhuman dog' (5.3.14) who casually kills the nurse of his own child with a vicious quip ('"Wheak, wheak" – so cries a pig prepare`d to the spit' (4.2.148)), and who confesses to his captors that, after tricking Titus into having his hand chopped off, he 'almost broke [his] heart with extreme laughter' (5.1.113), remains unrepentant to the end. Superbly indifferent to his impending death and wishing that he were indeed 'a devil, / To live and burn in everlasting fire' (5.1.147–8), Aaron brags of the vile deeds he has committed and has only one regret:

> Tut, I have done a thousand dreadful things
> As willingly as one would kill a fly,
> And nothing grieves me heartily indeed
> But that I cannot do ten thousand more.

(5.1.141–4)

Shakespeare's delight in Aaron's liberty to wreak havoc on his behalf, in contempt of conventional morality and regardless of the consequences, is undeniable. His attachment to his 'irreligious Moor' (5.3.120) is unswerving enough to bring him back onstage, after the formal political denouement of the final act, to deliver the penultimate speech of the whole play: a speech in which he refuses once more to repent before being buried 'breast-deep in earth' (5.3.178) and starved to death. Productions, adaptations and audiences from the seventeenth century onwards have shared Shakespeare's predilection for his Moorish villain, treating him time and again as the true chief protagonist, if not the real hero, of the play.

Why Shakespeare should set such store by Aaron, and invest so much imaginative energy in him, becomes clear if his kinship with his fellow scapegoats and scourges, Jack Cade and Richard of Gloucester, is borne in mind. Like them, he is authorized to kill and solicit killing – not with impunity, because he is the scapegoat of the Rome his villainy reflects, but with the tacit approval of author and audiences, because Rome has brought the agony and horror the tragedy depicts upon itself. Like the Richard of *Richard III*, Aaron is an avatar of the dramatist inasmuch as he is, like Shakespeare, the 'Chief architect and plotter of these woes' (5.3.121). As such, he could indeed be seen as the true protagonist of the dark revenge comedy that underlies the tragedy of *Titus Andronicus*. At the core of that tragedy is Titus's quest for revenge against Saturninus,

Tamora and her sons for the appalling crimes committed against his daughter, his sons and himself; a quest in which Titus shows no awareness of having triggered those crimes by his immolation of Tamora's son. But from the vantage point vested in Aaron, the deeper purpose of the play is to pass sentence on the dehumanized world it arraigns by having Titus tortured beyond despair before being wiped out, along with Lavinia, Tamora, her sons and Saturninus, in an obscene massacre of his own devising.

This Fearful Slumber

If imputing such a vindictive cast of mind to the man who would shortly write *A Midsummer Night's Dream* seems unwarranted, it seems less so if one glances back to the *Henry VI* plays and forward to the deliberate cruelty with which the royalty and nobility of *King Lear* are treated; to the intransigent misanthropy of Timon, whom nothing but his own extinction and the extermination of mankind will satisfy; or to Hamlet and Macbeth in their equally misanthropic, nihilistic moods. It's surely telling that, given a free rein in *Titus Andronicus*, unfettered by chronicles, Shakespeare invents an infernal plot in which the stomach-turning savagery of the battlefield, the torture-chamber and the scaffold invades the private, domestic realm of those responsible for such institutionalized savagery and destroys them. There's a touch of the Draconian terrorist about Aaron, the effect of whose scheming is to force Rome's all-conquering military commander to feel what it's like to be one of his own victims. In the process, however, the Moor also becomes the paradoxical exemplar of the principle on which any genuinely civilized society must be founded.

When Titus turns a deaf ear to Tamora's plea for her son's life, the terms in which she frames her plea establish that principle at the start of the play. 'Victorious Titus', she begs him on her knees, 'rue the tears I shed, / And if thy sons were ever dear to thee, / O, think my son to be as dear to me' (1.1.108–11). Her sons were, after all, she reminds him, only fighting like his sons 'in their country's cause': 'O, if to fight for king and commonweal / Were piety in thine, it is in these' (1.1.117–18). Tamora appeals to Titus as a parent like herself, who loves his sons as she loves hers, to judge and treat her children exactly as he would his own. She asks him, in other words, to identify emotionally with her on the basis of what they and their sons have in common, when differences of gender, rank and race are set aside. But Titus refuses to set them aside and acknowledge the human respect in which Tamora and he are the same. In sanctioning the sacrifice of Alarbus, he shows the patriarchal virtue of *pietas* he reveres to be a 'cruel, irreligious piety' (1.1.133) indeed. Moments later, he underscores how incapable he is of the empathy Tamara solicits by slaying his son Mutius for defying his demand that Lavinia be surrendered to the vile Saturninus against her will – an act so outrageously unjust that even his eldest son Lucius is compelled to rebuke him.

The ensuing carnival of horrors is caused by Titus's inability to empathize with the Goth queen as a mother, whose son's life he sacrifices, just as he sacrifices the life of Mutius and his daughter's choice of husband, to the soulless code of conduct that enslaves him. Hence, when Lavinia begs Tamora to be 'something pitiful' for her 'father's sake' as she is about to be raped and mutilated, Tamora replies, 'Even for his sake am I pitiless' (2.2.156–62), replicating Titus's refusal to show her child pity when she begged him to. Then, when his sons Quintus and Martius are falsely accused of murdering Bassianus, Titus is forced to his knees in tears before Saturninus to intercede in vain on their behalf (2.2.288–305), just as the tearful Tamora had knelt in vain to him. To his desperate public plea, 'Be pitiful to my condemned sons' (3.1.8), the tribunes, who have sentenced them to death, are as deaf as Titus had been to Tamora. They pass him by without a word, leaving him prostrate in the dust, weeping uncontrollably and seeking in the stones the compassion denied him by the tribunes. It's at this point that the scales fall from Titus's eyes, as he realizes that the Rome to which he has devoted his life, in whose name he has conquered nations and lost so many sons, is not the pinnacle of civilization but 'a wilderness of tigers'. But his awakening, like Lear after him, to the inhumanity of his society does not spare him, any more than it spares Lear, far worse torments for having been the incarnation of that inhumanity.

The fearful symmetry of his children's suffering with the suffering inflicted at his command on Alarbus is underlined by Shakespeare. As Alarbus is led off to be sacrificed, Lucius says, 'Let's hew his limbs till they be clean consumed' (1.1.132), repeating the same callous phrase, 'hew his limbs', that he'd used earlier in the scene (1.1.100). Afterwards he reports to his father that 'Alarbus' limbs are lopped / And entrails feed the sacrificing fire' (1.1.146). Thus, when Lavinia's uncle, Marcus, encounters his horribly disfigured niece, the wording of his first question to her is anything but accidental: 'Speak, gentle niece, what stern ungentle hands / Hath lopped and hewed and made thy body bare / Of her two branches [?]' (2.3.16–18). Titus, Marcus and Lucius remain oblivious of the monstrous poetic justice not only of Lavinia's mutilation, but also of Aaron hewing off Titus's hand and the heads of Quintus and Martius being lopped off too. Neither Tamora nor Aaron draws attention to it either. But Shakespeare ensures that the point is made graphically by the play. Titus must be paid back in kind, and with interest, for authorizing the original abomination. Nor is the play done with making Titus pay through Aaron's machinations until he has been made to feel the empathy with another human being that he felt for neither Tamara nor her son.

The first sign of Titus's emotional transformation is his response to the sight of Lavinia's violated body. 'This was thy daughter', says the distraught Marcus, to which Titus replies in the present tense: 'Why, Marcus, so she is' (3.1.63–4). What makes Titus's simple, declarative sentence so moving is its recognition of his daughter as a human being rather than his patriarchal property, and his complete acceptance of her as she is now, not as the physical ruin of the daughter she used to be. 'Give me a sword', says Titus, seized by a new-found need to empathize, 'I'll chop off my hands too' (3.1.73). Because he can now identify with Lavinia, he needs to feel the same as her physically and emotionally. Not content with that, he expands the circle of empathy to embrace Marcus and Lucius. His shift from the first-person singular into the first-person plural emphasizes the shared nature of their compassion, the fusion of his feelings with Lavinia's and theirs. Shall we sit around some fountain, he asks Lavinia, and weep into it with you?

And in the fountain shall we gaze so long
Till the fresh taste be taken from that clearness
And made a brine pit with our bitter tears?
Or shall we cut away our hands like thine?
Or shall we bite our tongues and in dumb shows
Pass the remainder of our hateful days?

(3.1.128–33)

'O, what a sympathy of woe is this' (3.1.149), sighs Titus. The line encapsulates the tragic irony at the heart of the play: the fact that only through suffering and witnessing intolerable pain and grief does Titus acquire the capacity to sympathize, whose repression was the source of all his woe.

This sequence in Act 3 marks the point at which *Titus Andronicus* begins to become the first truly Shakespearean tragedy. It enshrines at the play's core the ability to identify with one's fellow human beings, an ability founded on the recognition of what we have in common rather than what divides us. That's why the word 'pity' and its variants and synonyms reverberate throughout the play, right down to its closing couplet: 'Her life was beastly and devoid of pity, / And being dead, let birds on her take pity' (5.3.198–9). Lucius refuses here to show Tamora pity even in death, but the identical rhyme insists that pity has the last word, because compassion, and the primal kinship of humanity it presupposes, are what the tragedy pits against the brutality of the society it portrays. Shakespeare dramatizes them not as abstract ideals, but as thoughts and feelings forged in response to the experience of brutality. That's why the potential of human beings to create a compassionate society acquires a credibility in this horrific tragedy that it wouldn't otherwise possess. The murderous reality of Rome prevails in *Titus*, but the play's revelation of that potential is what makes its tragic vision Shakespearean.

The revelation is engineered by Aaron, the 'swart Cimmerian' (2.2.72) and 'breeder of these dire events' (5.3.177). Shakespeare appoints the play's most vilified figure not only as his proxy and the scourge of Rome, but also as the spokesman for the visionary ideals to which the tragedy is committed. There's an extraordinary glimpse of just how visionary they are, and how closely identified with Aaron they are, in the banquet scene, which appears only in the First Folio. As Titus, Lavinia, young Lucius and Marcus sit at table traumatized by grief, Marcus casually kills a fly with his knife, provoking this startling response from Titus:

Out on thee, murderer. Thou kill'st my heart.
Mine eyes are cloyed with view of tyranny;
A deed of death done on the innocent
Becomes not Titus' brother. Get thee gone;
I see thou art not for my company.
MARCUS
Alas, my lord, I have but killed a fly.

TITUS

'But'?

How if that fly had a father and a mother?

How would he hang his slender gilded wings

And buzz lamenting doings in the air.

Poor harmless fly,

That with his pretty buzzing melody

Came here to make us merry, and thou hast killed him.

MARCUS

Pardon me, sir, it was a black ill-favoured fly,

Like to the empress' Moor. Therefore I killed him.

TITUS

Oh, Oh, Oh!

Then pardon me for reprehending thee,

For thou hast done a charitable deed.

Give me thy knife; I will insult on him,

Flattering myself as if it were the Moor

Come hither purposely to poison me.

[*Takes knife and strikes*]

There's for thyself, and that's for Tamora.

Ah, sirrah!

Yet I think we are not brought so low

But that between us we can kill a fly

That comes in likeness of a coal-black Moor.

(3.2.54–79)

Titus's reproachful echoing of that single syllable 'But' speaks volumes. It extends the empathy he feels for his daughter to a tiny, universally detested creature, which is a byword for worthless insignificance, as in Aaron's boast of having done 'a thousand dreadful things / As willingly as one would kill a fly'. Titus humanizes the fly by personifying it as the innocent victim of murderous tyranny, whose death would grieve its parents' hearts. He projects Lavinia's and his own plight, in other words, into the fate of the fly. In performance the ludicrous incongruity of Titus's reaction to the insect's demise is likely to elicit laughter from the audience. But the laughter should be uneasy, because Titus suddenly speaks here as if the taking of *any* creature's innocent life were an act of murder that should not be tolerated, a view which is anything but risible. This is the Titus who once slew his son Mutius without a second thought for defying him. Moments later, however, thanks to Marcus's quick thinking, the 'Poor harmless fly' has changed into 'a black ill-favoured fly, / Like to the empress' Moor' in Titus's eyes. Titus reverts immediately to the revenger's posture, stabbing manically at the 'likeness' of his 'coal-black' adversary. But the farcical abruptness of his *volte-face* detracts not a whit from the significance of the episode. On the contrary, it throws into relief the conflict *Titus* stages between a culture devoted to killing and an empathetic imagination incapable of taking even the killing of a fly lightly.

'"But?" / How if that fly had a father and a mother?' That Shakespeare used the licence of Titus's momentary madness to give such a thought expression at all is a sign of his capacity to disengage himself completely from the mindset of his day. How else can one explain the theatrically privileged position Aaron occupies in *Titus*, the eloquent praise of blackness and contempt for all religion (5.1.71–85) placed in his mouth, and the fierce, protective love for his newborn son that Shakespeare gives him? *Titus* was staged and first published at a time when the number of free and enslaved Africans in England had increased to the point where the government deemed it necessary to act. In 1596 a royal warrant ordered the deportation of 'blackmoores brought into this realme, of which kinde of people there are allready here to manie'. In defiance of the fear and loathing with which black people were routinely regarded by his fellow citizens, Shakespeare chose to make 'the incarnate devil' his charismatic anti-hero and the secret agent of his aims. For the Romans and all the Goths bar Tamora, who dotes on her 'raven-coloured love' (2.2.83), Aaron is a stereotypical villain, whose 'body's hue' is 'Spotted, detested and abominable' (2.2.73–4). For Shakespeare, however, he is not just the bane of the Roman barbarians, but a standing rebuke to their racism and a vessel for the humanity they lack.

The nurse calls the bastard that Tamora has borne Aaron 'A joyless, dismal, black and sorrowful issue' and 'as loathsome as a toad / Amongst the fair-faced breeders of our clime' (4.2.68–70). 'Zounds, ye whore, is black so base a hue?', retorts his father, outraged at hearing that Tamora wants him to kill his baby. 'Sweet blowze,' says Aaron, gazing fondly upon the child, 'you are a beauteous blossom, sure' (4.2.74). Nothing, he swears, will part him from or harm his 'flesh and blood', his 'first-born son and heir' (4.2.86, 94): 'This before all the world do I prefer, / This maugre all the world will I keep safe' (4.2.111–12). He sneers at the Caucasian complexion of Chiron and Demetrius, because it can redden or be cosmetically disguised, and is thus inferior to the constant, authentic colour of his skin and his child's: 'Ye white-limed walls, ye sanguine, shallow-hearted boys, / Coal-black is better than another hue / In that it scorns to bear another hue' (4.2.100–2). When Chiron and Demetrius rebuke him for the shame brought on them by the dusky sibling they are itching to kill, Aaron counters with the same irrefutable appeal to consanguinity that Shylock will later employ: 'He is your brother, lords, sensibly fed / Of that self blood that first gave life to you' (4.2.124–5). The only thing stopping him growing up to be a mighty ruler, Aaron tells the infant, is that he happened to be born black: 'Did not thy hue bewray whose brat thou art, / Had nature lent thee but thy mother's look, / Villain, thou mightst have been an emperor' (5.1.28–30).

The 'hellish dog' (4.2.79), whose torturers cannot quell the 'venomous malice' of his 'swelling heart' (5.3.13), prizes his baby above all else as 'this treasure in mine arms' (4.2.175), the sole repository of genuine value in the heartless world his father replicates and strives to destroy. The subliminal link between Titus's solicitude for the 'poor harmless fly', simply because it is a guiltless living being, and Aaron's devotion to his baby son is not hard to discern. Both bear witness to the moral power and egalitarian import of innocent infancy for Shakespeare, who will return to this theme with a vengeance in *Macbeth*. The audacity of anchoring the moral standpoint of *Titus Andronicus* in Aaron can scarcely be overstated. Aaron's cry, 'Away with slavish weeds and servile thoughts!' (1.1.517), might be Shakespeare's own watchword in this tragedy. Through the Moor he can vent his anarchic rage at the insanity of his world tricked out as ancient Rome, but in the name of everything that Aaron personifies as the proud black father of the 'beauteous blossom' he cradles in his arms.

The 'extreme laughter' that almost broke Aaron's heart after chopping off Titus's hand is the horrified laughter of Shakespeare at the nightmare of early modern reality his tragedy depicts. The Shakespeare who dreamt up *Titus* would have known what Nietzsche meant when he wrote in *Beyond Good and Evil*: 'even if nothing else of today has any future, our laughter may yet have a future'. *Titus Andronicus* is the laughter of the liberated future at the present that imprisons it and that still imprisons it, which is why the tragedy speaks to us today with such immediacy. 'When will this fearful slumber have an end?' (3.1.253), asks Titus in bewilderment, as the rising tide of horror leaves him no choice but to laugh. It's a question we might well ask ourselves, as the carnage continues unabated in our time, although we already know the answer: not until we wake up in the future from which we hear Shakespeare laughing in *The Most Lamentable Roman Tragedy of Titus Andronicus*.

CHAPTER 3
ROMEO AND JULIET: KISSING BY THE BOOK

Strange Love Grown Bold

The idea that Shakespearean tragedy is conceived and scripted from the vantage point of a possible future foreshadowed by the present becomes clearer, when we turn from *Titus Andronicus* to the first of Shakespeare's three great tragedies of love, written just a few years after *Titus* in 1595. Romeo and Juliet have become a global byword for lovers driven apart and to their deaths, because they belong to feuding factions that refuse to countenance their love. During the last four centuries the tragedy has spawned countless adaptations and offshoots on stage and screen, as well as operas, symphonies, paintings, novels and poetry. But it could never have continued to resonate around the world if its vision had been trapped in the ethos of the time when Shakespeare wrote it. That *Romeo and Juliet* can't be fully understood without some knowledge of the early modern era in which it's rooted goes without saying. But no production or critical account can do justice to the tragedy if it's blind to the ways in which it was far ahead of Shakespeare's time and is still ahead of ours.

The love that Romeo and Juliet discover may be fleeting and doomed, but its trailblazing quality is repeatedly underscored in the language they use to describe it. This 'Prodigious birth of love' (1.5.139), this 'strange love grown bold' (3.2.15), propels them beyond the horizon of Shakespeare's world and remains an inspiring ideal to this day. Romeo's infatuation with Rosaline before he meets Juliet is justly mocked by Mercutio as the stale Petrarchan scenario of pining swain tortured by unrequited love for a cold, sadistic mistress. But Mercutio's cure for Romeo's love-sickness is merely its inverted mirror image, the male subjugation of the female in an aggressive act of physical self-gratification: 'If love be rough with you, be rough with love; / Prick love for pricking, and you beat love down' (1.4.27–8). Both scenarios lock both parties into an unequal relationship that submits one of them to the will of the other. Until his masked encounter with Juliet at the Capulet ball breaks the Petrarchan spell, Romeo is the prisoner of a degrading charade of domination and subjection, from which he feels alienated: 'I have lost myself. I am not here. / This is not Romeo, he's some otherwhere' (1.1.195–6).

That other, absent Romeo, the lost 'myself' of whom he speaks in the third person, is the potential, transfigured self that becomes, however briefly, a startling reality in his relationship with Juliet. For the relationship that they forge is founded on reciprocity rather than subservience. As the Chorus is at pains to stress: 'Now Romeo is beloved and loves again' (i.e. 'loves her in return'); they are equally attracted to each other: 'Alike bewitched with the charm of looks'; and, unlike Rosaline, Juliet is 'as much in love' with Romeo as he is with her (2 Chorus 5–6, 11). When Friar Laurence reproves him 'For doting, not for loving' (2.3.78), for having simply transferred his infatuation from Rosaline to Juliet, Romeo explains precisely what makes his relationship with Juliet different: 'one hath wounded me / That's by me wounded'; 'As mine [i.e. my heart] on hers, so hers is set on mine'; 'Her I love now / Doth grace for grace and love for love allow; / The other did not so' (2.3.46–7, 55, 81–3). Romeo's syntax and diction reflect the perfect balance of attraction and power between them. Above all, their love is mutually enriching and limitless. In Juliet's wonderful words to Romeo: 'My bounty is as boundless as the sea, / My love as deep; the more I give to thee, / The more I have, for both are infinite' (2.2.133–5). It's a kind of love that can't be quantified or priced. When Romeo asks Juliet to 'Unfold the imagined happiness that both / Receive in either by this dear encounter', she demurs, saying: 'They are but beggars that can count their worth, / But my true love is grown to such excess, / I cannot sum up sum of half my wealth' (2.6.28–9, 32–4). A decade later, that thought will be voiced again in Cordelia's refusal to calculate her love for Lear and put it into words, and its phrasing echoed when Cleopatra asks Antony, 'If it be love, tell me how much', and Antony replies, 'There's beggary in the love that can be reckoned' (*AC* 1.1.14–15).

The fate of Romeo and Juliet's 'true-love passion' (2.2.104) does more than dramatize the calamitous consequences of the blood-feud that divides their families. It's long been recognized that the play vindicates the individual's basic human right to love whomever they choose, unconstrained by irrational prohibitions or mindless prejudice. But *Romeo and Juliet* goes further than that. It envisions, and invents the language to evoke, a form of love free of the drive to dominate and exploit. Four hundred years on, the play is as committed as ever to showing that mutual love between equals is not just desirable but possible by bringing it alive in the theatre and the mind's eye of the reader. What makes the fate of Romeo and Juliet *tragic* for Shakespeare is not their vulnerability to chance adversities. Nor is it the inscrutable enmity of some malign metaphysical force or the fatal flaw inherent in young love, whatever Friar Laurence may say or Romeo believe. It's the fact that they live at a time when a boundless love like theirs can't be sustained and can't survive, because it belongs to a future men and women are still striving to create. The tragedy of Romeo and Juliet lies in their being born before their time, trapped in alien identities in a hostile society, far from their home in the world they prefigure through their resistance to their plight.

The Prison-House of Language

The part played by language in defining the terms of the tragedy and determining the fate of the protagonists is as crucial in *Romeo and Juliet* as it is in *Titus Andronicus*. Like *Titus*, *Romeo and Juliet* draws attention throughout to words, books, reading and writing, and thus to its own scripted nature. In *Titus* the rape of Lavinia is explicitly modelled on 'the tragic tale of Philomel' (4.1.47) in Ovid's *Metamorphoses*, a copy of which Lavinia seizes on to show that her violation was 'Patterned by that the poet here describes' (4.1.57). So too is the vengeance Titus wreaks upon the rapists, because, as he tells them before he cuts their throats: 'worse than Philomel you used my daughter, / And worse than Progne I will be revenged' (5.2.194–5). Lavinia's death at her father's hand is dictated by the story of Virginius, who slew his daughter 'with his own right hand, / Because she was enforced, stained and deflowered' (5.3.37–8): for Titus the tale provides 'A reason mighty, strong, and effectual; / A pattern, precedent, and lively warrant / For me, most wretched, to perform the like' (5.3.42–4). The play is acutely aware, and makes us aware, of the complicity of canonical literary works in the atrocities the characters commit. The classical narratives enshrined in the set texts of early modern culture authorize the violence perpetrated by furnishing it with precedents.

Shakespeare highlights not only the unconscious, prescriptive hold such narratives have over the protagonists of *Titus*, but also the public and private means by which they are transmitted and their grip on the mind perpetuated. That's why the books among which Lavinia finds the copy of *Metamorphoses* are not random tomes she stumbles across, but the school textbooks dropped by Lucius's young son. That's why we hear the distraught Titus saying to Lavinia, 'I'll to thy closet and go read with thee / Sad stories chanced in the times of old' (3.2.83–4), and Lucius saying to his son, as they stand beside the corpse of Titus: 'Many a story hath he told to thee, / And bid thee bear his pretty tales in mind / And talk of them when he was dead and gone' (5.3.163–5). But the coercive power of written language in *Titus* is not confined to narratives read or retold in school or in the home. The success of Aaron's 'complot' (2.2.265) to pin Bassianus's murder on Quintus and Martius depends on the 'fatal-plotted scroll' (2.2.47) he forges. When Tamora and her sons, disguised as Revenge, Rape and Murder, interrupt Titus as he sits in his study drafting 'strange plots of dire revenge', he tells them: 'what I mean to do / See here in bloody lines I have set down, / And what is written shall be executed' (5.2.6, 13–15). It shall indeed in this tragedy, where what is executed is also written in the flesh, turning the body of the victim into a text to be read and deciphered. 'I can interpret all her martyred signs', Titus assures Marcus, gazing intently at Lavinia, to whom he says:

Thou shalt not sigh, nor hold thy stumps to heaven,
Nor wink, nor nod, nor kneel, nor make a sign,
But I of these will wrest an alphabet
And by still practice learn to know thy meaning.

(3.2.42–5)

Language itself, whether written, spoken or speechless, and its interpretation are implicated in the scenes of suffering penned in *Titus* for the entertainment of the audience.

So potent do words and names become in *Romeo and Juliet* that they seem to acquire their own identities and independent will to kill. 'Hath Romeo slain himself?', Juliet asks the Nurse. 'Say thou but "Ay", / And that bare vowel "I" shall poison more / Than the death-darting eye of cockatrice. / I am not I if there be such an "Ay"' (3.2.45–8). When she hears of the sentence passed on Romeo for killing Tybalt, she cries: 'Some word there was, worser than Tybalt's death, / That murdered me. ... / That "banished", that one word "banished" / Hath slain ten thousand Tybalts' (3.2.108–9, 113–14). Likewise, when Romeo is told of the anguish he has inflicted on Juliet by slaying her cousin, he replies:

> As if that name,
> Shot from the deadly level of a gun
> Did murder her, as that name's cursed hand
> Murdered her kinsman. O, tell me, Friar, tell me,
> In what vile part of this anatomy
> Doth my name lodge?
>
> (3.3.101–6)

The lovers realize that language can be as lethal in effect as poison or a bullet. But the very act of recoiling from that realization expresses their resistance to the power such words have over them. It drives a wedge between them and the intolerable selves the language of their world is foisting on them.

Throughout the tragedy their incarceration in the prison-house of language is underlined. Words are the chains that bind Romeo and Juliet to the sexual norms and social imperatives of Verona. Their doomed struggle to liberate their love is dramatized as a struggle to free themselves from the way Verona has taught them to speak and the destinies to which their names have bound them. It's no coincidence that they meet and fall in love while Romeo is masked and before they learn each other's name. For a moment the patriarchal obligations inscribed in their surnames are suspended. They are released not only from the strict proscriptions of the family feud, but also from the codes of courtship that would normally forbid such a frank encounter between any man and woman of their rank. But at the uttering of the patronymics 'Montague' and 'Capulet' the festive licence of the moment is revoked, and the tragic battle between the lovers and their world begins. The linguistic dimension of the tragedy is made explicit in the celebrated balcony scene, when Juliet meditates on the issue at the heart of their dilemma:

> O Romeo, Romeo, wherefore art thou Romeo?
> Deny thy father and refuse they name,
> Or if thou wilt not, be but sworn my love,
> And I'll no longer be a Capulet …
>   … O be some other name!
> What's in a name? that which we call a rose
> By any other word would smell as sweet;
> So Romeo would, were he not Romeo called,
> Retain that dear perfection which he owes
> Without that title. Romeo, doff thy name,
> And for thy name, which is no part of thee,
> Take all myself.
>
> (2.2.33–6, 42–9)

And Romeo replies:

> By a name
> I know not how to tell thee who I am.
> My name, dear saint, is hateful to myself,
> Because it is an enemy to thee.
> Had I it written, I would tear the word.

(2.2.53–7)

The exchange goes right to the heart of Shakespearean tragedy, because it captures the conflict between the manifest potential of these two individuals to live the fulfilling life together that they have the right to live and the crippling constraints encapsulated in the names they never chose.

'The tradition of all the dead generations', Marx observed in *The Eighteenth Brumaire*, 'weighs like a nightmare on the minds of the living.' *Romeo and Juliet* makes clear the extent to which that tradition is felt as the weight of words, the discursive gravity that pins people to destinies against which their unrealized selves revolt. In *Titus Andronicus* and *Romeo and Juliet* Shakespeare makes the same point as Marx by giving physical and symbolic prominence to the tomb that houses the dead generations of the Andronici in the first act of *Titus*, and to the Capulet crypt in which Romeo and Juliet meet their deaths. And in *Romeo and Juliet* as in *Titus* Shakespeare uses the book to foreground the role of internalized discourse in preserving the oppressive legacy of the dead. Thus, when Romeo punctuates the second love-sonnet he shares with Juliet at their first meeting with a kiss, Juliet sabotages the poem by turning the fourth line back against him in playful mockery of his textbook courtship:

ROMEO
> Thus from my lips by thine my sin is purged.

JULIET
> Then have my lips the sin that they have took.

ROMEO
> Sin from my lips? O trespass sweetly urged!
> Give me my sin again.   [*Kisses her.*]

JULIET   You kiss by th' book.

(1.5.106–9)

Juliet's teasing quip registers the gap already divorcing authentic feelings from the trite poetic parlance that distorts and displaces them. The correspondence between Romeo's initial bondage to the mentality epitomized by that parlance and Juliet's reduction to a nubile commodity at her father's disposal is made evident by the protracted metaphor her mother employs to persuade her to accept Paris's suit. The metaphor reifies the prospective couple, turning the suitor into a 'precious book of love', for which the beauty of his betrothed furnishes the 'cover': 'That book in many eyes doth share the glory / That in gold clasps locks in the golden story' (1.3.92–3). Marriage to Paris would lock Juliet, like Romeo before they meet, into a set book, which forbids them to write their own story, create their own roles and speak lines of their own devising.

'Love goes toward love', remarks Romeo, 'as schoolboys from their books' (2.2.156). The mutual union of equals emerging between them demands that they toss aside the obsolete texts of the school of love in which they've been educated and learn a new language. That their time and place and culture render it impossible for that mutual union to take root and blossom makes the injustice of their plight unbearably poignant. The tragic sense of being turned into a character in a script beyond one's control informs Juliet's reflection as she braces herself to drink the fateful potion: 'My dismal scene I needs must act alone' (4.3.19). It also informs Romeo's unexpected compassion for his dead rival, Paris, in whom he recognizes a fellow victim of the same unswerving narrative: 'O, give me thy hand, / One writ with me in sour misfortune's book' (5.3.81–2). The final chapter of that book is penned by Capulet, when he insists on Juliet marrying the husband he has chosen. The drug plot concocted by Friar Laurence is a desperate attempt to rewrite Romeo and Juliet's truly 'precious book of love' and give it the ending it deserved, instead of a denouement in the Capulets' ancestral sepulchre, 'that nest / Of death, contagion and unnatural sleep' (5.3.151–2).

Empowering the Audience

Romeo and Juliet dramatizes the potential its hero and heroine possess to live and love on terms radically different from those that ultimately destroy them. But it's equally intent on enlarging *our* capacity as the audience to take the command of our lives and relationships that its protagonists cannot take of theirs. The function of foregrounding language, narratives and books in this tragedy, as in *Titus Andronicus*, is explanatory, insofar as it makes the discursive determinants of the tragedy immediately intelligible. It does that by giving the unseen, unconscious pressures on the lovers' hearts and minds concrete, visible form. The Capulet crypt, like the tomb of the Andronici and the actual copy of *Metamorphoses* in *Titus*, makes the intangible forces it signifies materialize as a physical object on the stage. The recurrent references to words, names and books achieve a similar effect by means of virtual or figurative visualization. When Romeo says, 'My name, dear saint, is hateful to myself, / Because it is an enemy to thee. / Had I it written, I would tear the word', or when Paris is transmuted into a book and Juliet into its ornate binding, the alienating assumptions absorbed and transmitted through names, words and narratives become palpable in the theatre of the mind.

But the function of this rhetorical strategy isn't confined to explanation. By enabling us to grasp the discursive machinery of the tragedy in objectified, imaginable forms, it also reveals the extraneous source and artificial nature of that machinery. It invites *us* to see what the protagonists trapped inside their play cannot: that their fate is the product of forces that are neither natural nor supernatural nor inevitable, but man-made and therefore mutable, as their struggle to unspeak the murdering words they utter implies.

The tragedy is written in such a way as to make us envisage the alien cultural restraints that rob the lovers of agency, of their innate right to act freely in their own legitimate interests. By making us theatrically and poetically conscious of the lovers' unconscious thraldom to their time, place and preconceptions, it seeks to make us aware of our own forms of unconscious thraldom, and in so doing activate in us the agency that Romeo and Juliet are denied.

To be the unknowing prey of involuntary thoughts and emotions, of predetermined reactions and intents, and to act in unwitting compliance with them is the opposite of self-possession. It is to be dispossessed of oneself, as Romeo senses he has been by his infatuation with Rosaline: 'I have lost myself. I am not here. / This is not Romeo, he's some otherwhere'; and as Othello intimates after murdering Desdemona, when Lodovico asks, 'Where is this rash and most unfortunate man?', and Othello replies, 'That's he that was Othello: here I am' (5.2.280–1). It's a state akin to trance, the somnambulant state that Titus calls 'this fearful slumber' (3.1.253), which he fears will never end, and that Romeo calls 'Still-waking sleep that is not what it is' (1.1.79). It's the dream-state induced by Queen Mab (1.4.53–94), in which everyone's desires and destinies are prescribed by their social identities, despite its being 'Begot of nothing but vain fantasy, / Which is as thin of substance as the air' (1.4.98–9). Seeing this simulacrum of existence as a waking dream or nightmare does at least hold out the possibility, if not the promise, of eventual awakening. The metaphor harbours, at least for us, the prospect of deliverance from the spurious forms of selfhood Shakespeare's tragic protagonists strive in vain to shed: 'I am not I, if there be such an "Ay"'.

There can be no deliverance for Romeo and Juliet, because what they show to be *humanly* possible is not *historically* possible *for them*. From this point of view the lovers' lives look more like a living death than a waking sleep. Just as the tomb of the Andronici casts its shadow forward over the five acts of *Titus Andronicus*, so the Capulet crypt, symbol of the patriarchal family, casts its shadow back over the entire tragedy of Romeo and Juliet. Both of them have been a 'Poor living corse, closed in a dead man's tomb!' (5.2.29) from the start. Their self-inflicted deaths turn that virtual entombment into a harrowing reality. Without diminishing the power or credibility of their utopian love, they are repeatedly conceived, long before they actually die, as animated corpses, as the walking dead: 'in that vow', says Romeo of Rosaline's sworn refusal to be wooed, 'Do I live dead that live to tell it now' (1.1.221–2); 'Alas, poor Romeo', quips Mercutio to Benvolio after their friend has fallen for Juliet, 'he is already dead' (2.4.13); 'Thy Juliet is alive', Friar Laurence assures Romeo, 'For whose dear sake thou wast but lately dead' (3.3.134–5); 'Methinks I see thee now', says Juliet to Romeo, 'thou art so low, / As one dead in the bottom of a tomb' (3.5.55–6); having assumed, after drinking the Friar's potion, the 'borrowed likeness of shrunk death' (4.1.104), Juliet is interred as if she were really dead; 'I dreamt my lady came and found me dead', muses Romeo as the fifth act begins, 'Strange dream that gives a dead man leave to think' (5.1.6–7); and as he stands over the slain body of Paris at the Capulet tomb, he says, 'Death, lie thou there, by a dead man interred' (5.3.87).

The tone may be flippant or sardonic, baleful or grim, but the cumulative import of such lines is clear. Romeo and Juliet's love is indeed 'death-marked', as the Prologue to Act 1 puts it, but not only in the sense that it's inexorably doomed. Shakespeare thinks of his lovers proleptically as 'already dead' in the more profound sense that they could never be authentically alive in the society in which they've been marooned. So complete and uncompromising does their estrangement from this living death become that, as the tragedy proceeds, actual death becomes increasingly for them a state to be desired rather than feared. As early as Act 3 we hear Juliet telling the Nurse, 'I'll to my wedding bed / And death, not Romeo, take my maidenhead' (3.2.137) and Romeo crying, 'Come, death, and welcome!' (3.5.24). 'I long to die,' says Juliet to the Friar, 'If what thou speak'st speak not of remedy'; 'Or bid me go into a new-made grave, / And hide me with a dead man in his shroud' (4.1.66–7, 84–5). 'O, here / Will I set up my everlasting rest', declares Romeo, as he prepares to kiss Juliet for the last time before taking his life, 'And shake the yoke of inauspicious stars / From this world-wearied flesh' (5.3.109–12).

The entire *Liebestod* in which the tragedy culminates is erotically charged to the point where the catastrophe can be construed as an apotheosis, a moment of sublime consummation. 'Well, Juliet,' says Romeo, having decided to end his life, 'I will lie with thee tonight' (5.1.34). Juliet's 'beauty makes / This vault a feasting presence full of light' (5.3.85–6), transforming the tomb into a bridal chamber. 'Death, that hath sucked the honey of [her] breath' (5.3.92) is imagined as a rival lover by Romeo. As he gazes at his wife, he fancies 'That unsubstantial death is amorous, / And that the lean abhorred monster keeps / Thee here in dark to be his paramour' (5.3.103–5). Romeo's final act before drinking the vial of poison is to embrace his beloved Juliet and 'seal with a righteous kiss / A dateless bargain to engrossing death' (5.3.114–15). Juliet's final act is to kiss her husband's poisoned lips to 'die with a restorative' (5.3.166), and her last words are 'Thy lips are warm!' (5.3.167). It's as if they have both been brought to life by dying. But the familiarity of that romantic paradox, the purely rhetorical consolation the play allows the lovers and the audience, shouldn't blind us to the craving for oblivion at its heart.

Weltschmerz and a longing to die are far from peculiar to the protagonists of *Romeo and Juliet*. Both Henry VI and Titus, as we've seen, envy the dead for being free to enjoy what Romeo calls an 'everlasting rest' from the miseries of life as they know it. 'Nor I nor any man that but man is', Richard II comes to realize, 'With nothing shall be pleased till he be eased / With being nothing' (5.5.39–41). Hamlet is seized from the outset by a disillusionment so complete that 'all the uses of this world' seem 'weary, stale, flat and unprofitable', and he wishes 'that the Everlasting had not fixed / His canon 'gainst self-slaughter' (1.2.131–4). The hunger for extinction finds its most extreme expression in Timon, who prepares his grave, inscribes his epitaph on the gravestone, and declares on the brink of dying: 'My long sickness / Of health and living now begins to mend / And nothing brings me all things' (5.2.71–3). And dying will be erotically transfigured once again in the closing moments of *Antony and Cleopatra*: 'The stroke of death is as a lover's pinch / Which hurts and is desired' (5.2.294–5). Hostility to the world as it is, and the yearning to be released from a reality that cannot be borne, run deep in Shakespearean tragedy. The eagerness with which death is embraced by its protagonists is the measure of the undesirability of life in a world they are impatient to leave, like the speaker of Sonnet 66: 'Tired with all this, for restful death I cry'. It's a frame of mind that leads Shakespeare to adopt a posthumous perspective in these plays ('Poor living corse, closed in a dead man's tomb!'), because it allows him to view their concerns from a point beyond the immediate scope of his protagonists. That viewpoint is inextricable, however, from the fundamental utopianism of Shakespearean tragedy, which finds such enthralling expression in *Romeo and Juliet*: 'My bounty is as boundless as the sea, / My love as deep; the more I give to thee, / The more I have, for both are infinite'.

CHAPTER 4
JULIUS CAESAR: THE COMMON GOOD

An Icy Anatomy

With *Julius Caesar*, the tragedy he wrote to open the new Globe theatre in 1599, Shakespeare returned to the Roman world whose civilized façade he had torn down with such gusto in *Titus Andronicus*. This time, however, his imagination was not unleashed to run riot as it had been in *Titus*, but tied more tightly to the historical narrative furnished by Plutarch. For Dr Johnson, Shakespeare's fidelity to the basic facts of his source was responsible in part for the forbidding *froideur* he detected in the tone of the tragedy: 'I have never been strongly agitated in perusing it, and think it somewhat cold and unaffecting, compared with some other of Shakespeare's plays; his adherence to the real story, and to Roman manners, seems to have impeded the natural vigour of his genius.' Absorbed, as so much of it is, in argument, rumination and oratory, *Julius Caesar* undoubtedly strikes a sustained note of decorous restraint quite foreign to the lurid extravagance of *Titus Andronicus*. But the gory assassination round which the play revolves, the frenzied mob's dismembering of an innocent poet, the mass bloodletting of civil war and the suicides that end it, plainly spring from the same barbaric Rome as the horrors spawned in *Titus*. The tone of the treatment may have changed, but Shakespeare's judgement of the empire Elizabethan England sought to emulate has not.

To turn from *Titus Andronicus* to *Julius Caesar* is to turn from a grotesque caricature to an icy anatomy of the patrician class under whose sway Rome became a slaughterhouse, camouflaged as the shining citadel of western civilization. It's also to return with Shakespeare to re-examine in Roman terms the subject of the second and third parts of *Henry VI* and *Richard III*: a society ripped apart by aristocratic factions vying for supreme power after the assassination of the aristocrat who possessed it. Four years before *Julius Caesar* Shakespeare had also dramatized the forced deposition and cold-blooded murder of Richard II, which secured the English throne for the Lancastrian clan. And after *Julius Caesar* the killing of the king was at the forefront of his mind again in *Hamlet* and *Macbeth*. If that doesn't amount to an obsession on Shakespeare's part, it does evince a fascination with regicide persisting through a sequence of plays, in which *Julius Caesar*, the tragedy about the most notorious assassination in the ancient world, clearly has a paradigmatic place. The murder of Caesar was already in his thoughts as he was writing the *Henry VI* plays: Suffolk cites the fact that 'Brutus' bastard hand / Stabb'd Julius Caesar' as a consoling precedent for his own impending death at the hands of 'pirates' (*2HVI* 4.1.138–40); while his mistress, Queen Margaret, cries, 'They that stabb'd Caesar shed no blood at all' (*3HVI* 5.5.52) compared with the killers of her young son,

Edward. The subject of his previous tragedy is still reverberating in *Hamlet*: in Horatio's evocation of the fearful portents observed 'In the high and palmy state of Rome / A little ere the mightiest Julius fell' (1.1.112–13); in Polonius's recollection of playing the part of Caesar at university and being killed in the Capitol by Brutus (3.2.94–100); and in Hamlet's wry reflection in the graveyard that 'Imperious Caesar, dead and turned to clay, / Might stop a hole to keep the wind away' (5.1.202–3).

Hamlet's couplet echoes lines with the same levelling thrust in *Julius Caesar* itself. 'How many times shall Caesar bleed in sport', wonders Brutus in the immediate aftermath of the murder, 'That now on Pompey's basis lies along, / No worthier than the dust?' (3.1.114–16). 'O mighty Caesar!', exclaims Antony moments later, 'Dost thou lie so low? / Are all thy conquests, glories, triumphs, spoils, / Shrunk to this little measure?' (3.1.148–50). Left alone with Caesar's corpse, he begs its forgiveness: 'O pardon me, thou bleeding piece of earth, / That I am meek and gentle with these butchers' (3.1.254–5). The colossus who once bestrode the narrow world, 'the noblest man / That ever lived in the tide of times' (3.1.256–7), is now nothing more, even in the grieving eyes of Antony, than a 'bleeding piece of earth': a carcass as worthless as the dust it lies in at the foot of the statue of Pompey the Great, Caesar's assassinated rival for supremacy in the Roman state. Shakespeare's urge to puncture the pretensions of the powerful and lay the mighty low remains as strong in *Julius Caesar* as it was when he had the once omnipotent kingmaker Warwick ask, as he lies dying alone onstage, 'Why what is pomp, rule, reign but earth and dust?' (*3HVI* 5.2.27).

That anti-authoritarian attitude is announced at the start of the play. It begins with the tribunes, Flavius and Murellus, rebuking the commoners crowding the stage as 'idle creatures' for treating 'a labouring day' as 'a holiday' and not wearing clothes that bear 'the sign' of their 'profession' (1.1.1–5). The plebeians have seized on Caesar's triumphant return as a cue to take liberties and break ranks, creating a festive mood of licensed transgression. The tribunes fasten at once on the absence of the insignia that tether each man's identity to his trade, and thus to his prescribed place in the social order. The commoners' unauthorized abandonment of their work and working clothes flouts that order, which the tribunes seek to restore by demanding that the revellers declare their occupations. The Carpenter respectfully complies, accepting without demur Murellus's reproof for sporting his 'best apparel' instead of his 'leather apron' (1.1.7–8). But Murellus and Flavius get more than they bargained for from the leader of this unruly crew. The Cobbler's insolent quibbling and bawdy innuendo maintain the spirit of misrule, driving the bamboozled tribunes to distraction, until he decides he's pushed his luck far enough. The tribunes soon clamp down on the plebeians' brief outbreak of illicit jollity. Exuding contempt for the class whose interests they profess to defend – 'You blocks, you stones, you worse than senseless things!' (1.1.36) – Murellus upbraids them for the alacrity with which they've switched their adulation from the dead Pompey to Caesar, oblivious to what that says about the transience of mundane glory. The plebeians troop off 'tongue-tied' at the tribunes' behest to do penance with 'all the poor men of [their] sort' for their alleged 'ingratitude' to Pompey (1.1.56, 58, 63). The scene ends with the spokesmen for the people heading off to 'drive away the vulgar from the streets' and strip all the trophies from the images of Caesar, 'Who else would soar above the view of men, / And keep us all in servile fearfulness' (1.1.71–2, 75–6).

The opening scene encapsulates the conflict round which the tragedy revolves: the conflict between the oppressive reality of a rigidly hierarchical state, prone by its nature to breed tyrants, and the utopian drive, rooted in the latent power of the bridled multitude, to subvert the foundations on which the state rests. That conflict is staged in the first scene as a confrontation between an anonymous crowd of common tradesmen on the loose, led by a smart-mouthed cobbler, and two officers of the Roman state, whose supposed function is to serve the 'vulgar' they are driving from the streets, but whose actual function is to bring them to heel to preserve the status quo.

The class antagonism between the tribunes and the tradesmen is amplified by the audible idiomatic difference between them. The tribunes speak blank verse, the tradesmen the same colloquial prose spoken by the Capulet and Montague servants in the opening scene of *Romeo and Juliet*; by the hapless Clown hanged in *Titus*; and above all by Jack Cade and his fellow rebels in *2 Henry VI*, who are all tradesmen and commoners like the carpenter and the cobbler. The cobbler's speech is the living, demotic speech of early modern Londoners. As he speaks it, the remote world of ancient Rome is conflated with the Elizabethan present of the play's original audiences, making its issues implicitly theirs too. The other flagrant anachronisms that notoriously pepper the play – the allusions to kings, crowns, the commons, pulpits, striking clocks and books – are likewise designed to keep it anchored in both times. The Elizabethan audience is discreetly induced to see *Julius Caesar* as a mirror of their world, but also to look back on their world in Roman guise as the strange world of another age. Translating the present into the distant past defamiliarizes it, enabling the audience to view this version of their own times, in which they have a vested interest, with an objectivity that city comedies set in contemporary London could never afford them.

When the crafty Elizabethan cobbler runs punning rings round the Roman authorities bent on quelling the holiday high jinks, there's no doubt with whom most members of the first Globe audiences, themselves taking time off to watch the play in London's Liberties, would have identified. What the opening scene of the tragedy would have shown them was their onstage counterparts being browbeaten into 'servile fearfulness' by the eloquence of the tribunes. In *Richard III* Shakespeare had invited audiences of London citizens to watch the charade of reluctant piety Richard performs before their eyes to dupe the citizens of London onstage and bend them to his will. Before that, in *2 Henry VI*, he had shown the rebel forces swallowing Old Clifford's jingoistic hogwash and abandoning Cade, to Cade's disgust: 'Was ever feather so lightly blown to and fro as this multitude?' (4.8.55–6). And in the electrifying oration scene of Act 3 of *Julius Caesar* he invites the theatre audience again to see their onstage alter egos, a crowd of ordinary Roman citizens, being rhetorically manipulated into adopting views of Caesar and Brutus diametrically opposed to those they initially held. So keen have most critics been to believe Shakespeare shared the patricians' contempt for the lower classes, that they haven't considered the possibility of his being more interested in exposing the methods used to secure their subjection than in despising them for their gullibility.

Nor have they considered the enormous untapped power the plebeians possess without being aware that they possess it. Note how anxious all the patrician protagonists are at every stage to win the people over to their cause by force of argument or brazen deceit. Think of the offstage pantomime Caesar reportedly performs in the second scene, thrice refusing the proffered crown to seduce 'the tag-rag people', who 'clap him and hiss him', in Caska's jaundiced account, 'as they use to do the players in the theatre' (1.2.257–9). Think of Brutus insisting that the conspirators assassinate Caesar in a way which 'shall make / Our purpose necessary and not envious, / Which so appearing to the common eyes, / We shall be called purgers, not murderers' (2.1.176–9); or Brutus again, immediately after the assassination, saying to Antony, 'Only be patient till we have appeased / The multitude' (3.1.179–80). The first thought of both Brutus and Antony after Caesar's murder is to head for the marketplace. 'There shall I try / In my oration', says Antony, 'how the people take / The cruel issue of these bloody men (3.1.292–4). The next scene begins with Brutus and Cassius leading the plebeians into the marketplace, where, Brutus assures them, 'public reasons shall be rendered / Of Caesar's death' (3.2.7–8). There 'the rabblement' with their 'chopped hands' and 'stinking breath' (1.2.243–5), 'the common herd' (1.2.263) that Cassius reviles as 'trash', 'rubbish', 'offal' and 'base matter' (1.3.108–10) for fawning on Caesar, are magically transformed in the speeches of Brutus and Antony into 'Friends, Romans, countrymen' (3.2.74). The patricians are politically impotent without the approval and support of the multitude, whom they despise but are forced to placate and deceive.

Why? Because the republican constitution of ancient Rome claims to be democratically designed to serve the interests of all its citizens, to meet the needs of patricians and plebeians alike, whereas its real purpose is to serve the interests of the patricians at the expense of the plebeians, without the plebeians realizing that they're being gulled. *Julius Caesar* is an uncompromising critique of a ruling class, and thus of a whole society, in the grip of a political lie that dooms that society to destruction. The tragedy displays the verbal and theatrical means by which the people are cynically duped by their political masters. There are few things of its kind more chilling in Shakespeare than Antony's words, spoken *solus* to the audience, after the plebeians he's whipped into a homicidal frenzy storm off to wreak havoc and he lets the mask of grief for Caesar drop: 'Now let it work. Mischief, thou art afoot: / Take thou what course thou wilt' (3.2.251–2). Shakespeare is equally intent, however, on showing us how Rome's fraudulent republican ideology is used by the members of its aristocratic elite to beguile not only each other but also themselves. For it's in Brutus's tormented self-delusion that the key to the true tragedy of *Julius Caesar* lies hidden.

Scorning the Base Degrees

On the face of it, the tragedy consists in Brutus finding himself compelled to conspire in the assassination of his dearest friend, who might otherwise become a tyrant, for the greater good of the Roman republic. A man of exemplary probity, forced to weigh the life of a man he loves against his duty to society as a whole, and choosing the latter at the cost of his own life: that's how Brutus has been portrayed more often than not, and more often than not for political reasons one can readily understand. That view of him is not without warrant in the text. Brutus certainly seeks to see himself, and be seen by others, in such terms. 'Though now we must appear bloody and cruel', he says to Antony, indicating their blood-smeared hands and 'the bleeding business they have done', it was 'pity to the general wrong of Rome' that 'Hath done this deed on Caesar' (3.1.165–72). If any friend of Caesar's 'demand why Brutus rose against Caesar', Brutus tells the plebeians assembled in the marketplace, 'this is my answer: not that I loved Caesar less, but that I loved Rome more. Had you rather Caesar were living, and die all slaves, than that Caesar were dead, to live all freemen?' (3.2.20–4). Brutus could hardly have a more impressive character witness than Antony, who delivers this eulogy over his enemy's corpse:

This was the noblest Roman of them all:
All the conspirators save only he
Did that they did in envy of great Caesar.
He only, in a general honest thought
And common good to all, made one of them.

(5.5.68–72)

But Brutus's euphemistic phrase 'this bloody business', like his delegation of responsibility to the conspirators' hands and the abstraction 'pity', betrays the insecurity of his stance. So does the riddling syntax of 'not that I loved Caesar less, but that I loved Rome more', which demands a rapid double take of auditor or reader. And a eulogy for Brutus from the man who delivered such a blatantly duplicitous speech to the plebeians over Caesar's corpse, and who is then shown signing death warrants, including one for his sister's son, without turning a hair, should be taken in context *cum grano salis* rather than at face value.

This, after all, is a play in which Shakespeare goes out of his way to prompt us not to take things at face value, to make us aware of the need to interpret, and the risk of misinterpreting, what we see and hear. No less an authority than Cicero is given a cameo role expressly to warn that 'men may construe things after their fashion / Clean from the purpose of the things themselves' (1.3.34–5); the significance of prophecies and portents is repeatedly contested, with contradictory constructions being placed on Calphurnia's dream; and towards the end of the play Titinius says to the dead Cassius before taking his own life too: 'Alas, thou hast misconstrued everything' (5.3.84). Failure to take Shakespeare's hermeneutic hint to heart means accepting Brutus's and Antony's version of Brutus, as Swinburne did when he hailed him as the 'very noblest figure of a typical and ideal republican in all the literature of the world'. Long before Swinburne, however, the first great close reader of Shakespeare put his finger on the problem the tragedy poses, when he confessed himself nonplussed by the soliloquy in which Brutus rationalizes his decision to kill Caesar:

It must be by his death: and for my part
I know no personal cause to spurn at him
But for the general. He would be crowned:
How that might change his nature, there's the question.
It is the bright day that brings forth the adder,
And that craves wary walking. Crown him that,
And then I grant we put a sting in him
That at his will he may do danger with.
Th' abuse of greatness is when it disjoins
Remorse from power; and to speak truth of Caesar
I have not known when his affections swayed
More than his reason. But 'tis a common proof
That lowliness is young ambition's ladder
Whereto the climber upward turns his face;
But when he once attains the upmost round
He then unto the ladder turns his back,
Looks in the clouds, scorning the base degrees
By which he did ascend. So Caesar may.
Then, lest he may, prevent. And since the quarrel
Will bear no colour for the thing he is,
Fashion it thus: that what he is, augmented,
Would run to these and these extremities.
And therefore think him as a serpent's egg
Which hatched, would as his kind grow mischievous,
And kill him in the shell.

(2.1.10–34)

'This speech is singular', comments Coleridge; 'at least, I do not at present see into Shakespeare's motive, his *rationale*, or in what point of view he meant Brutus's character to appear.' 'Surely', he continues,

> nothing can seem more discordant with our historical preconceptions of Brutus, or more lowering to the intellect of the Stoico-Platonic tyrannicide, than the tenets here attributed to him – to him, the stern Roman republican; namely, – that he would have no objection to a king, or to Caesar, a monarch in Rome, would Caesar but be as good a monarch as he now seems disposed to be! How, too, could Brutus say that he found no personal cause – none in Caesar's past conduct as a man? Had he not passed the Rubicon? Had he not entered Rome as a conqueror? Had he not placed his Gauls in the Senate? – Shakespeare, it may be said, has not brought these things forward – True; – and this is just the ground of my perplexity.

Coleridge's perplexity is a testament to his critical acuity and perfectly understandable, given his laudatory 'preconceptions' of Brutus. But the speech ceases to be perplexing, once one realizes that 'Shakespeare's motive, his *rationale*' is to demolish such preconceptions by exposing the speciousness of Brutus's argument and disclosing the real reason, which Brutus is shown striving to disguise. Nothing makes it clearer that the demolition is deliberate than the fact that, as Coleridge observes, Shakespeare could easily have given Brutus strong and credible grounds for seeing Caesar as a budding tyrant, but chose to withhold them.

He withheld them not to exculpate Caesar and paint him as an innocent victim, but to focus our attention on a man in the process of deluding himself that the murder he's resolved to commit is being committed for sound, high-minded, altruistic reasons ('for the general', i.e. the common good) and not for selfish, personal motives that are indefensible. Brutus's speech begins by stating its conclusion – 'It must be by his death' – which the rest of the soliloquy proceeds to rationalize unconvincingly. The indefinite pronoun 'It' (to what does 'It' refer?) is characteristic of the evasiveness that marks the speech throughout under the pressure of disavowal. Because, by his own admission, there's no case for killing Caesar as things stand, Brutus is forced to fabricate subjunctive scenarios to supply one: 'So Caesar may. / Then, lest he may, prevent', he argues, masking the murder such spurious reasoning entails with that euphemistic 'prevent'; 'And since the quarrel / Will bear no colour for the thing he is, / Fashion it thus', which means twisting it to support the conclusion he has already reached. So baseless is the case for assassination that Brutus is forced to enlist extended metaphors and similes to furnish the plausible corroboration his conscience requires. He twice resorts to depicting Caesar as a snake: first as a poisonous adder and again, at the end of the soliloquy, as an embryonic serpent, which must be destroyed before it hatches. But it's the equally tenuous analogy with a man climbing a ladder that gives Brutus's true motive for murdering Caesar away. What really galls Brutus is the idea of one of his aristocratic peers, a man of the same birth and breeding, climbing above him to the topmost rung of the social hierarchy and thus degrading him, reducing him to one of 'the base degrees', the inferior ranks, to be scorned.

Brutus is possessed by the same pathologically competitive, hierarchical mentality as the rest of 'the breed of noble bloods' (1.2.150) to which he belongs. Like Cassius and the other conspirators, like Antony and Octavius, and like Caesar himself above all, he's driven by emulation, by envious rivalry, but he's obliged by the republican ideology he espouses to disguise it as disinterested concern for 'the general good' (1.2.85). The charge Caesar levels at Cassius – 'Such men as he be never at heart's ease / While they behold a greater than themselves' (1.2.207–8) – could be levelled at all of them, including Caesar. In his eulogy for Brutus, Antony pointedly absolves him of acting out of the 'envy' that motivated his fellow conspirators. But in doing so he foregrounds the fact that Brutus is as vulnerable to the charge as Antony is, because he needs to be defended against it. When Cassius first sounds Brutus out in the second scene of the play, Shakespeare leaves us in no doubt that Brutus is ripe for conscription to the conspiracy, because his own secret thoughts, what he calls 'Conceptions only proper to myself' (1.2.41), are already turning in that direction. That Brutus's and Cassius's views of Caesar are essentially identical is established by having Cassius offer himself as a mirror in which Brutus may behold the

Brutus who is privately thinking exactly what Cassius is thinking. Brutus could never have been so swiftly coaxed by his friend into leading the conspiracy against Caesar unless he were predisposed to do so by the same egotistical dread of subordination.

That is the fear Cassius plays on, the same fear that makes Brutus reach later for 'ambition's ladder' to forge his justification of murder: 'I had as lief not be as live to be / In awe of such a thing as I myself', says Cassius, 'I was born free as Caesar, so were you' (1.2.95–7). But 'this man / Is now become a god, and Cassius is / A wretched creature, and must bend his body / If Caesar carelessly but nod on him' (1.2.115–18). Yet, as far as their physical constitution is concerned, says Cassius, changing tack, Caesar is manifestly inferior to him, which makes it astonishing that 'A man of such feeble temper' should 'bear the palm alone' (1.2.131). Then he presses his argument home by appealing to Brutus's personal pride, asking him to measure Caesar's claims to precedence against his own:

> 'Brutus' and 'Caesar': what should be in that 'Caesar'?
> Why should that name be sounded more than yours?
> Write them together: yours is as fair a name:
> Sound them, it doth become the mouth as well.
> Weigh them, it is as heavy: conjure with 'em,
> 'Brutus' will start a spirit as soon as 'Caesar'.
>
> (1.2.141–6)

At no point does Cassius seek to sway Brutus by advancing the *political* argument that their overriding priority must be to preserve the republic and the supposedly democratic rights of all its citizens. That's the last thing on their minds in this decisive exchange. What they both find unbearable is the prospect of being 'underlings' to 'one man', 'but one man', 'but one only man' (1.2.140, 152, 154, 156), whom they must look up to, not the oppressive consequences for society as a whole, or the notion of a monarch as such, as Brutus's subsequent soliloquy makes plain.

The Foremost Man of All the World

Brutus may think of himself, and would doubtless wish to be remembered, as having acted 'in a general honest thought / And common good to all', as Antony puts it. But the assassination neither preserves nor restores the republic, even if one believed that was its purpose. On the contrary, it plunges the republic into 'Domestic fury and fierce civil strife' (3.1.263), which destroys it by paving the way for 'another Caesar' (5.1.53) – Octavius Caesar – to become its emperor. The conspirators bring about the very catastrophe they profess to be killing to avert. But that's hardly surprising, since they patently have no plan of action beyond the assassination, the be-all and end-all of which is cutting Caesar down to size for good by killing him. 'Let's be sacrificers but not butchers, Caius', Brutus counsels Cassius before the deed. 'Let's carve him as a dish fit for the gods, / Not hew him as a carcass fit for hounds' (2.1.165, 172–3). Otherwise, he explains, the assassination will appear 'envious … to the common eyes' and they'll be called 'murderers' instead of 'purgers' (2.1.176–9). But butchers hewing a carcass is exactly how they appear as they bathe their arms 'in Caesar's blood / Up to the elbows' (3.1.106–7) at Brutus's behest – as Shakespeare emphasizes by having Antony call them 'these butchers' (3.1.255) in the hearing of the audience alone. Brutus exhorts them all to walk into the marketplace, crying 'Peace, Freedom and Liberty' as they wave their blood-stained swords over their heads (3.1.108–10). To the glaring incongruity of that cry with the sight they will present to the citizens of Rome Brutus is oblivious. He shares Cassius's fantasy of their being forever called 'The men who gave their country liberty' (3.1.118). But by killing Caesar, the play makes plain, they have given their country neither peace nor liberty, and what the audience sees are not the heroic 'purgers' of tyranny but the envious 'murderers' Brutus feared they would be called.

If there's anything tragic about Brutus, it's not that he's ultimately destroyed by an agonizing choice between sacrificing his dear friend Caesar to save the people of Rome from a potential tyrant and sacrificing the republic and the freedom of its citizens to his love for his friend. To view the tragedy in those terms is to buy the version of Brutus that Brutus sells himself and wants Antony to buy when he says that he 'did love Caesar when [he] struck him' (3.1.182). It's to miss the deeper, far-sighted tragedy to which *Julius Caesar* points through its unflinching judgement of Brutus. That tragedy is the betrayal of the principles enshrined in the phrases 'the general good' and 'common good to all' by a Rome in thrall to the urge to subjugate that drives its ruling class. The patriciate pays lip service to those principles but in practice rides roughshod over them to the detriment of the entire society. What's tragic about *Julius Caesar* is that a truly free and just society, organized and governed in the common interests of all its members, is *already conceivable* but *not yet realizable*. Nor can such a society become a reality so long as rulers and ruled collude in pretending that it already exists, while remaining the divided slaves of subjection.

That understanding is nowhere stated in such abstract terms by any character. It's dramatized through the stark contradiction between the republican cant and the actual ethos of ancient Rome. When Caesar's assassins cry 'Liberty! Freedom! Tyranny is dead!' and 'Liberty, freedom and enfranchisement!' (3.1.78, 81), nothing could matter more than the things they are crying out for, but nothing could be more tragic than the fact that for Shakespeare they are empty words mouthed by 'hollow men' (4.2.23) – the phrase that captured for T. S. Eliot the essence of the play and of the modern world. Likewise, when Brutus tells the plebeians that all of them may rest assured of 'a place in the commonwealth' (3.2.43) now that Caesar is dead, and the plebeians' response is 'Let him be Caesar', 'Caesar's better parts / Shall be crowned in Brutus' (3.2.51–2), the hopelessness of a society whose populace have been so effectively brainwashed stands revealed. '*Julius Caesar* has great relevance to our time', W. H. Auden told his New York audience when he lectured on the play there in 1947, 'because it is about a society that is doomed'. The parallels with society at the end of the Second World War did not escape him. That sense of doom is intensified by the apocalyptic imagery that pervades the play: the slave whose hand 'did flame and burn / Like twenty torches joined' and yet 'remained unscorched' (1.3.16–18); 'Men, all in fire' walking 'up and down the streets' as 'a hundred ghastly women' look on in terror (1.3.23–5); graves that 'have yawned and yielded up their dead', while 'ghosts did shriek and squeal about the streets' (2.2.18, 24); 'pure blood' running from Caesar's statue, 'like a fountain with an hundred spouts' (2.2.76–8); 'The sun of Rome is set. Our day is gone' (5.3.63).

As Caesar observes of Calphurnia's ominous nightmare, 'these predictions / Are to the world in general as to Caesar' (2.2.28–9). So they are, because Caesar is the master spirit of a world whose ruthless, narcissistic individualism he epitomizes and both his killers and his successors share. That's why the tragedy is entitled *Julius Caesar*, despite Brutus stealing the spotlight and the lion's share of the lines. 'Caesar doth bear me hard,' muses Cassius, 'but he loves Brutus. / If I were Brutus now, and he were Cassius, / He should not humour me' (1.2.312–14). The confusion of the three characters with each other, compounded by the indefinite referent of the second and third 'he', is symptomatic of the recognition that they are essentially the same. The blurring of identities when Antony says, 'But were I Brutus, / And Brutus Antony, there were an Antony' (3.2.219–20) carries the same implication. When the ghost of Caesar appears to Brutus, and Brutus demands, 'Speak to me what thou art', the apparition replies, 'Thy evil spirit, Brutus' (4.3.279–80). In the evil spirit of Caesar Brutus beholds the mirror image of himself, just as he had beheld it in Cassius at the start of the play. In the final act both Antony and Brutus address Octavius as 'Caesar' (5.1.24, 55), whose imperious spirit is reincarnated in his heir. Both Cassius and Brutus die with the word 'Caesar' on their lips. Before he dies, Brutus realizes that in the end it will have been neither he nor Cassius who has taken their lives. As he stands over Cassius's body, he says, 'O Julius Caesar, thou art mighty yet. / Thy spirit walks abroad and turns our swords / In our own proper entrails' (5.3.94–6).

Caesar has indeed killed them, inasmuch as they have been destroyed by the psychotic male fantasy Caesar personifies to this day: the fantasy of being one of whom, as Caesar boasts, 'There is no fellow in the firmament' (3.1.62); 'but one / That unassailable holds on his rank' (3.1.68–9); in short, 'the foremost man of all the world' (4.3.22). The chill Johnson felt when he read *Julius Caesar* was a fitting response to the tragedy's clinical indictment of a society in its death throes: a society that privileges the gratification of the powerful few over the needs and rights of the powerless multitude, while masquerading as a society that has the best interests of all its citizens at heart. *Julius Caesar* offers us not only a mordant dramatic metaphor for Shakespeare's world, but also a parable foretelling the fate of the self-obsessed, self-deluding class society most of us still inhabit. It can do that because it's imagined and written from the standpoint of 'the general good', the 'common good' of humanity, which is to say from the standpoint of a time to come 'In states unborn' (3.1.113), where 'Peace, Freedom and Liberty' are no longer empty words.

PART III

CHAPTER 5
HAMLET: A KIND OF FIGHTING

The Stamp of One Defect

For centuries critics have tied themselves in knots trying to solve the baffling problem they believe *Hamlet* poses. On the face of it, the nature of the problem and the reason for the bafflement are clear. In Act 1 Hamlet is charged by the ghost of his father to 'Revenge his foul and most unnatural murder' (1.5.25) by his brother Claudius, who has robbed him of his wife and his throne as well as his life. Hamlet assures the apparition that 'with wings as swift / As meditation, or the thoughts of love', he will 'sweep to [his] revenge' (1.5.29–31). His response to the plea with which the dead king's spirit exits, 'Adieu, adieu, adieu, remember me', is 'thy commandment all alone shall live / Within the book and volume of my brain' (1.5.91, 102–3). Hamlet then spends most of the play spectacularly failing to keep his word, despite the ghost's reappearance in Act 3 to remind him: 'Do not forget! This visitation / Is but to whet thy almost blunted purpose' (3.4.110–11). After his departure for England in Act 4, the ghost and the obligation to avenge his father have been all but forgotten. On his return to Denmark in Act 5, after restating the compelling grounds he has for exacting retribution, Hamlet shows no sign of planning to take his uncle's life. When he does at last kill Claudius in the dying moments of Act 5, he does so suddenly, without forethought, stabbing and poisoning the king for conniving to poison him and for inadvertently poisoning his mother. 'Here, thou incestuous, murderous, damned Dane!', cries Hamlet, 'Drink off this potion' (F: 5.2.279–80). It remains unclear whether the word 'murderous', which appears only in the Folio version of the play, refers to Claudius's part in the killing of Hamlet and Gertrude or implicitly includes his murder of old Hamlet. The other characters onstage at this moment, apart from Horatio, can only assume Hamlet to have the deaths of himself and his mother in mind. At no point in any version of the play, not even at this climactic moment, does Hamlet confront Claudius with his crime of regicide or make his own knowledge of it public.

It's purely by chance, therefore, and not by design, that Hamlet finally takes the revenge he swore to take for his father's murder, which might otherwise have remained unavenged. Furthermore, the retribution he happens to exact is exacted too late to avert all the deaths that need not have occurred, if only he had killed Claudius sooner. As a direct or indirect consequence of his procrastination, Hamlet unwittingly slays Polonius instead of Claudius; Ophelia goes mad after her father's murder and drowns; Rosencrantz and Guildenstern are dispatched by Hamlet to their deaths; and in the fatal duel that concludes the tragedy Gertrude drinks from the lethal goblet intended for her son, who is mortally wounded by Laertes in revenge for the deaths of his father and his sister. It's not difficult to see why most commentators on the play have drawn the conclusion that the main cause of the whole tragic train of events is Hamlet's compulsion to avoid or postpone performing the deed he had solemnly promised to perform – a compulsion that no one finds more inexplicable than Hamlet himself. On this understanding, there's no dispute about where the blame for the tragedy lies, which is squarely on the prince's shoulders. It's the reason *why* Hamlet prevaricates and delays that's proved the source of endless speculation.

Most stabs at cracking the conundrum with which the tragedy ostensibly presents us have been variations on the views of some of its earliest, most influential critics. For the eponymous hero of Goethe's *Wilhelm Meister*, what we see in *Hamlet* is 'An oak tree planted in a precious pot, which should only have delicate flowers. The roots spread out, the vessel is shattered'; in short, 'the effects of a great action laid upon a soul unfit for the performance of it'. The flaw that renders Hamlet unfit for the performance of that great action is, according to Coleridge, who happily confesses to being hobbled by the same disposition, a propensity to sacrifice action to reflection:

> Hamlet's character is the prevalence of the abstracting and generalizing habit over the practical. He does not want courage, skill, will, or opportunity; but every incident sets him thinking; and it is curious, and at the same time strictly natural, that Hamlet, who all the play seems reason itself, should be impelled, at last, by mere accident to effect his object. I have a smack of Hamlet myself, if I may say so.

August Schlegel concurred with this take on the play, famously dubbing *Hamlet* 'a tragedy of thought', which 'is intended to show that a calculating consideration, which exhausts all the relations and possible consequences of a deed, must cripple the power of acting'. Over a century later, a cut-price version of much the same conclusion was still being peddled in Laurence Olivier's voice-over at the start of his 1948 screen adaptation of *Hamlet*: 'This is the tragedy of a man who could not make up his mind.' That basic view of the protagonist, in more or less sophisticated guises, has maintained its tenacious hold on popular and academic conceptions of the play ever since.

Latter-day critics of this persuasion have naturally sought to put their own diagnostic spin on the cast of mind that seems to hamstring 'the overmeditative Hamlet', as Coleridge called him. The most common diagnosis is that the prince is suffering from some pathological disorder, of which his compulsive flight from action into thought is a symptom. In *Shakespearean Tragedy*, A. C. Bradley disposes superbly of several specious critical theories, only to propose his own equally unsatisfactory explanation in their stead. The cause of Hamlet's irresolution, Bradley maintains, 'was not directly or indirectly an habitual excess of reflectiveness. The direct cause was a state of mind quite abnormal and induced by special circumstances – a state of profound melancholy.' Hamlet himself cannot account for the dejected state of lassitude into which he is prone to relapse: 'I have of late', he tells Rosencrantz and Guildenstern, 'but wherefore I know not, lost all my mirth' (2.2.261–2). But Bradley has 'no doubt that many readers of the play would understand it better if they read an account of melancholia in a work on mental diseases'. Ernest Jones, on the other hand, the influence of whose study *Hamlet and Oedipus* has proved as enduring in various ways as Bradley's, was equally convinced that the heart of the play's mystery could best be plucked out by subjecting its protagonist to Freudian analysis. For Jones, the unconscious source of Hamlet's suicidal melancholy and reluctance to avenge his father turns out to be his repressed sexual desire for his mother, because by killing his mother's lover, her new husband Claudius, he would be killing the mirror image of his secret Oedipal self.

It would be otiose to review all the permutations there have been of this line of thought about the play. The point is that, whatever incidental insights such accounts produce, they all rest on the same misconception of Hamlet's plight and what makes it tragic in the Shakespearean sense. They proceed on the assumption that the problem lies with Hamlet rather than with the world and the situation in which he finds himself. The terms of that world and Hamlet's predicament are taken as read, as the *données* of the dramatic narrative: the prince has a legitimate obligation to avenge his royal father's murder by the man who stole his crown and his wife, because the fact that his father's killer is the king leaves him no option but to take the law into his own hands to achieve through revenge what Bacon termed 'a kind of wild justice'. The *tragedy* is thus taken to be Hamlet's unfortunate possession of an emotional, intellectual or psychological flaw, however virtuous its origin, however understandable its cause, which prevents him from meeting that obligation at the first opportunity. The presumption is that if Hamlet's character hadn't been marred, for whatever reason the critic infers, by 'some vicious mole of nature' and 'the stamp of one defect' (1.4.24, 31), the tragic catastrophe would not have transpired and the only corpse left at the end of the play would have been Claudius's. Hence the fixation on working out what's wrong with Hamlet, which time and again reduces the play to a case study in failure and a travesty of the tragedy Shakespeare actually wrote.

In their defence, critics bent on identifying the one defect whose stamp Hamlet allegedly carries might reasonably reply that they are taking their cue from Hamlet. After all, Hamlet repeatedly expresses his bewilderment at not having discharged his filial duty to his father's shade, and he interrogates himself in his own attempts to diagnose the cause of his dereliction. In the soliloquy that begins 'O, what a rogue and peasant slave am I!' he rebukes himself for his laxity after watching an actor really weep, convulsed with simulated sorrow for an imaginary character, who means nothing to him.

> Is it not monstrous that this player here,
> But in a fiction, in a dream of passion,
> Could force his soul so to his own conceit
> That from her working all the visage waned
> – Tears in his eyes, distraction in his aspect,
> A broken voice, and his whole function suiting
> With forms to his conceit – and all for nothing –

(2.2.486–92)

The actor's performance, 'But in a fiction, in a dream of passion', makes Hamlet feel ashamed, because 'the motive and the cue for passion' (F: 2.2.555) that Hamlet has are, unlike the actor's, real and compelling. Yet all that he, 'A dull and muddy-mettled rascal', can do, he declares, is mope about 'Like John-a-dreams, unpregnant of my cause, / And can say nothing. No, not for a king / Upon whose property and most dear life / A damned defeat was made. Am I a coward?' (2.2.502–6).

A whole act later, when the ghost's reappearance interrupts his verbal assault on his mother, Hamlet remains at a loss to explain why, 'lapsed in time and passion', he still 'lets go by / Th'important acting' of his father's 'dread command', obliging the forgotten wraith to return to chide his 'tardy son' (3.4.103–5). Deep into Act 4, en route to the coast to take ship for England, the prince finds himself shamed by comparison yet again for dragging his heels. This time what mortifies him is the sight of Fortinbras's army marching without a qualm to their doom, merely 'to gain a little patch of ground / That hath in it no profit but the name' (4.4.17–18). The sight prompts Hamlet to give vent once more to his perplexity at his inertia in his last great soliloquy. 'How all occasions do inform against me', he thinks, 'And spur my dull revenge' (4.4.31–2):

> How stand I then
> That have a father killed, a mother stained,
> Excitements of my reason and my blood,
> And let all sleep; while to my shame I see
> The imminent death of twenty thousand men
> That for a fantasy and trick of fame
> Go to their graves like beds …
>
> (4.4.55–61)

Hamlet is persuaded by none of the possible reasons he cites for having 'let all sleep', because he cites them without pausing to give any of them credence before confessing himself utterly mystified:

> Now whether it be
> Bestial oblivion or some craven scruple
> Of thinking too precisely on th'event
> (A thought which quartered hath but one part wisdom
> And ever three parts coward) I do not know
> Why yet I live to say this thing's to do,
> Sith I have cause and will and strength and means
> To do't.
>
> (4.4.38–45)

The charge of 'Bestial oblivion', of succumbing to a state of mindless torpidity, can be dismissed out of hand as the last thing Hamlet could be accused of, not least because the opposite charge of 'thinking too precisely on th'event' seems so plausible at first glance and precludes it. But the notion that Hamlet's capacity to act is paralysed by an innate predisposition to think himself out of acting doesn't square with his obvious ability to act decisively when he wants to. There's no sign of pensive dithering, no ducking the need for immediate action, when he plunges after his father's ghost on first sight of it, heedless of the consequences and with no concern for himself: 'Why, what should be the fear? / I do not set my life at a pin's fee' (1.4.64–5); or when he sets *The Mousetrap* to 'catch the conscience of the King' (2.2.540); or when he runs his sword through Polonius in the belief that he has run it through Claudius: 'Thou wretched, rash, intruding fool, farewell: / I took thee for thy better' (3.4.29–30); or when he foils Claudius's plot to have him beheaded on his arrival in England, consigning the treacherous Rosencrantz and Guildenstern to the fate meant for him; or when he escapes the ship transporting him by boarding the pirate ship attacking it and negotiating his release with his captors; or when he kills Claudius without hesitation in the heat of a duel he agreed at once to fight, despite his sense of foreboding: 'Thou wouldst not think how ill all's here about my heart' (5.2.190–1). Such conduct makes nonsense of portrayals of the prince as constitutionally unfit for the performance of a great action, his power to act crippled by the prevalence of the abstracting and generalizing habit over the practical, and the consequent inability to make up his mind.

On this evidence, too, Hamlet's fears that his procrastination might be provoked by cowardice are equally unfounded. The answer to the blunt question he asks himself and the audience in his second soliloquy, 'Am I a coward?' (2.2.506), is clearly 'No'. The worry that he might be does crop up once more in the passage quoted from his last soliloquy: '(A thought which quartered hath but one part wisdom / And ever three parts coward)'. But it's only glanced at in parenthesis within a sentence whose point is Hamlet's frank admission that he doesn't know, and it never takes root in his mind. As Bradley proves in a single paragraph, nothing could be further from the truth than the sentimental characterization of Hamlet that he quotes from *Wilhelm Meister*: 'a lovely, pure and most moral nature, *without the strength of nerve which forms a hero*, sinks beneath a burden which it cannot bear and must not cast away' (Bradley's emphasis). On the contrary, 'the Hamlet of the play', Bradley insists, 'is a heroic, terrible figure', who 'would have been formidable to Othello or Macbeth', and to buy the effete, romanticized view of him is not only 'grossly unjust to Hamlet', but it also 'turns tragedy into mere pathos'.

The ascription of 'a lovely, pure and most moral nature' to Hamlet in Goethe's novel fits neatly with the theory that overthinking is his Achilles heel. But there's no textual corroboration for the surmise that Hamlet is consciously or unconsciously deterred not just from taking revenge on Claudius, but from taking another human life at all, by the Christian objections of his conscience, or by any other kind of moral scruple, whether craven or commendable. Hamlet is never troubled in the least by such objections, as he shows by his keenness to kill Claudius in a state of mortal sin rather than in the shriven state of redemptive grace his father was denied:

Up sword, and know thou a more horrid hent
When he is drunk, asleep or in his rage,

> Or in th'incestuous pleasure of his bed,
> At game a-swearing, or about some act
> That has no relish of salvation in't.
> Then trip him that his heels may kick at heaven
> And that his soul may be as damned and black
> As hell whereto it goes.

(3.3.88–95)

'This speech,' wrote Dr Johnson, 'in which Hamlet, represented as a virtuous character, is not content with taking blood for blood, but contrives damnation for the man that he would punish, is too horrible to be read or uttered.' But the speech makes it clear that Hamlet is neither conceived nor represented by Shakespeare as 'a virtuous character' in the conventional moral sense Johnson assumes he must be. Lest that fact escape us, Shakespeare drives it home a few moments later, when Hamlet displays not a trace of guilt or remorse for having mistakenly killed Polonius, whose corpse he just leaves lying there until he's finished berating his mother; after which he drags it away to dump it elsewhere, adopting the same sardonic air with which the humpbacked killer of Henry VI hauled the latter's corpse offstage:

> I'll lug the guts into the neighbour room
> Mother, goodnight indeed. This councillor
> Is now most still, most secret and most grave,
> Who was in life a foolish prating knave.
> Come, sir, to draw toward an end with you.

(3.4.210–14)

Hamlet is equally unperturbed by his decision to have Rosencrantz and Guildenstern 'put to sudden death' in his place, with the express stipulation 'Not shriving time allowed' (5.2.46–7). Indeed, he makes a point of stressing how impervious to compunction their deserved fate leaves him, when he forestalls the reproof he expects from Horatio: 'Why, man, they did make love to this employment, / They are not near my conscience. Their defeat / Doth by their own insinuation grow' (F: 5.2.57–9). Moreover, when Horatio, appalled by the outrageousness of Claudius's plot against Hamlet's life, exclaims moments later, 'Why, what a king is this!' (5.2.61), Hamlet's reply invokes his conscience once again, but only to emphasize the absolute consistency of killing Claudius with its dictates:

> Does it not, think'st thee, stand me now upon?
> He that hath killed my king and whored my mother,
> Popped in between th' election and my hopes,
> Thrown out his angle for my proper life
> And with such cozenage. Is't not perfect conscience
> To quit him with this arm?

(F: 5.2.63–7)

'If he hesitates to kill his uncle', as Hippolyte Taine observed a century and a half ago, 'it is not from horror of blood or from our modern scruples'.

So far is Hamlet from being hampered by pangs of conscience on any count, before or after the fact, that, as Taine also observed, he shows no sign of remorse for his part in precipitating Ophelia's breakdown and subsequent death. Not a word of grief at her passing leaves his lips, despite his public declaration at her graveside: 'I loved Ophelia – forty thousand brothers / Could not with all their quantity of love / Make up my sum' (5.1.258–60). Nor does he seize the opportunity offered by his apology to Laertes before the duel to express remorse, let alone beg forgiveness, for the manslaughter of Laertes' father or the ensuing derangement and demise of his sister. On the contrary, he denies responsibility for what he euphemistically refers to as 'What I have done / That might your nature, honour and exception / Roughly awake' (5.2.208–10), mentioning neither Polonius nor Ophelia by name; he lays the blame instead upon 'His madness', casting himself as its victim too: 'Hamlet is of the faction that is wronged – / His madness is poor Hamlet's enemy' (5.2.216–17); and he invites Laertes, by means of an evasive metaphor, to regard the deaths of his father and his sister as merely an unfortunate accident: 'Let my disclaiming from a purposed evil / Free me so far in your most generous thoughts / That I have shot my arrow o'er the house / And hurt my brother' (5.2.218–21). Idealized visions of Hamlet as wittingly or unwittingly baulked by the claims of a higher moral code upon his conscience couldn't be wider of the mark. It would be nearer the mark to see him as overriding whatever moral constraints might impede him and dispensing with conscience altogether, except when adducing it serves his purpose.

Seeing Doubles

In sum, none of the motives for procrastination mooted by Hamlet himself, or canvassed by commentators on the play, pass muster. However plausible some of the reasons advanced might sound, attention to the text invariably proves fatal to them. It proves fatal to them, because they rest on the uncontested premise that the tragedy springs from Hamlet's failure to appease his father's shade more promptly, at the cost of five more lives, including his own, which would otherwise have been spared. But what if we adopt a diametrically opposed point of view? What if Hamlet's tormented resistance to performing the role of revenging prince is seen not as his fatal flaw, but as the heroic virtue that sets him at odds with his world for reasons he can't comprehend but the play makes plain to us? In that case, the problem posed by *Hamlet* and its solution become quite different, and so does our understanding of what makes the play tragic.

For a start, the futility of attempts to explain Hamlet's stalling as a diagnosable defect that causes the tragedy becomes immediately apparent, because Shakespeare is at pains to make it apparent. Why else take such care to have Hamlet consider in soliloquy, in tacit downstage dialogue with the audience, the explanations most likely to strike him and them, and find none of them satisfactory? Why else but to prevent Hamlet and the play being explained away, as critics and productions have sought to explain them away for centuries? To lay the blame on Hamlet, for whatever reason one chooses, is to take for granted the world he inhabits and the task it demands of him, and to find the tragedy in his inability to act as an early modern man of his rank in such a situation would be expected to act. Whereas to find the explanatory exits to that view of the tragedy blocked is to be forced to call into question the world and the task that confront Hamlet, and to rethink both the character of Hamlet and the nature of his tragedy.

That Shakespeare deliberately makes the source of Hamlet's temporizing and fits of lassitude as puzzling to the audience as they are to Hamlet is not in dispute. What's at issue is the construction *the play* leads us to place on them – the sense that *we* are left to make of the puzzle the protagonist can't solve – once the solutions that make his personality the culprit are discounted. For the play does guide us towards its own quite different conception of Hamlet's tragic predicament. It does so, however, not by giving us overt directions, but by the indirect art of implication that Shakespeare preferred and perfected. The critical task the play sets us, like the task Polonius sets Reynaldo, is 'By indirections' to 'find directions out' (2.1.63): to make explicit the tragic vision implicit in the play.

Consider, for example, the way Hamlet's incompatibility with the part he's expected to play is thrown into relief by juxtaposing him with Fortinbras and Laertes. The son of old Hamlet is placed between two conventional sons who are also determined to avenge their fathers, but who have no problem whatsoever about doing so. In the case of Laertes, the parallel is so obvious that even Hamlet can't avoid pointing it out after his last attempt to rouse himself to vengeance: 'But I am very sorry, good Horatio, / That to Laertes I forgot myself, / For by the image of my cause I see / The portraiture of his' (F: 5.2.75–8). Yet the difference between their attitudes to the cause they have in common could not be starker. As soon as he hears of his father's death, Laertes slips secretly back into Denmark from France, leads a rebellious insurrection right into the heart of the palace and, with his rioting followers crying 'Laertes shall be king!' (4.5.106, 108), breaks down the doors to the royal quarters to demand answers from Claudius, whom he suspects of complicity in Polonius's murder:

How came he dead? I'll not be juggled with.
To hell allegiance, vows to the blackest devil,
Conscience and grace to the profoundest pit.
I dare damnation. To this point I stand –
That both the worlds I give to negligence.
Let come what comes, only I'll be revenged
Most throughly for my father.

(4.5.129–35)

On the strength of mere suspicion, Laertes confronts the chief candidate for his father's killer face to face at the first chance he gets. We're left in no doubt that, sweeping every moral qualm and religious consequence aside, he would have slain Claudius on the spot, had his suspicion been confirmed, without a second thought. He thinks and acts exactly as Hamlet does not, both immediately after the ghost confirms what his 'prophetic soul' (1.5.40) suspects and when catching Claudius alone at prayer gives him the perfect opportunity. Hamlet can and does deliver speeches in the same revenger's vein as the lines Laertes addresses to Claudius; but he delivers them only in soliloquy, never to Claudius's face, and he does not act on them. Whereas the moment Laertes learns that Hamlet is to blame for his having 'a noble father lost, / A sister driven into desperate terms' (4.7.26–7), he declares 'But my revenge will come' (4.7.30) and conspires at once with Claudius to set a lethal trap for the prince in the ensuing duel.

In the case of Fortinbras, the parallel with Hamlet is made more precise by the fact that he, too, is the son of a lately deceased king of the same name, whose brother has succeeded him, and is resolved to avenge his father by hook or by crook, which he ultimately succeeds in doing, despite his uncle's efforts to thwart him. When Hamlet chances upon the army led by 'The nephew to old Norway' heading for Poland, merely 'to gain a little patch of ground / That hath in it no profit but the name' (4.4.13, 17–18), the comparison his soliloquy draws to his detriment also draws an oblique distinction between the prince of Denmark and the 'delicate and tender prince' (4.4.47) of Norway as revengers. So does Hamlet's prophecy in his last speech that 'th' election lights / On Fortinbras; he has my dying voice' (5.2.339–40). It seals the success of Fortinbras's campaign to avenge his father's defeat by Hamlet's father on the day that Hamlet was born. In exacting his own revenge by finally killing Claudius, Hamlet foregrounds his affinity with his fellow revengers, both of whom gain their revenge at the end, and gain it by Hamlet's death. The fact that all three find themselves in the same basic predicament also makes it clear that the causes of that predicament are systemic and not specific to Hamlet. But the respects in which their situations are alike serve only to emphasize the respects in which Hamlet's reaction to his situation differs from theirs. Laertes and Fortinbras are set alongside Hamlet by Shakespeare to embody the norm to which he strives in vain to conform: to give us the measure of how drastically out of sync Hamlet is with 'the drossy age' and all those who have 'only got the tune of the time' (5.2.169–70), which he perceives is 'out of joint' (2.1.186). The juxtaposition defines and endorses Hamlet's abnormality, his inability to think and act in tune with the time like the textbook avengers Fortinbras and Laertes.

For Hamlet to find avenging his father unproblematic, to regard it purely as a matter of when and how instead of whether, would mean his being not just the same kind of man as Fortinbras and Laertes, but the same kind of man as his father's murderer, in step with the world as it stands. Hamlet, of course, says nothing to suggest that he knows or thinks that. But once again the point is made apparent in ways that are more effective for being implicit. The play repeatedly draws parallels between Hamlet and Claudius, conflating the prince who seeks revenge with the king on whom he seeks to be revenged. The conflation invites the inference that complying with the revenge code and killing the king would make Hamlet a mere clone of Claudius, who makes his subscription to that code clear to Laertes: 'No place indeed should murder sanctuarize. / Revenge should have no bounds' (4.7.125–6). Hamlet's involuntary refusal to comply with the code bespeaks a refusal to be Claudius's counterpart in the revenge scenario and a revolt against the entire ethos the revenge scenario sanctions.

One of the most striking subliminal equations of Hamlet and Claudius is woven into the prince's first encounter with the players, just two scenes after his encounter with his father's ghost. Immediately before it we've had our first taste of Hamlet's antic disposition in his cryptic replies to Polonius's attempts to converse with him, and we've heard him tipping Rosencrantz and Guildenstern the wink, in equally cryptic terms, that his antic disposition is an act: 'I am but mad north-north-west. When the wind is southerly I know a hawk from a handsaw' (2.2.315–16). So it's already evident that, instead of sweeping to his revenge with wings as swift as meditation or the thoughts of love, Hamlet is playing for time by employing strategies of evasion and diversion. The unexpected advent of 'the tragedians of the city' (2.2.292) couldn't be more timely, since it provides him with further pretexts for postponement, culminating in *The Mousetrap*. The player scenes allow Hamlet to keep the actual killing of Claudius at bay by acting it out imaginatively in fictional guise through surrogate versions of himself, and thus gaining vicarious satisfaction from his virtual performance of the deed by proxy.

After welcoming the troupe warmly back to Denmark, Hamlet asks the leading actor to deliver part of a speech from a play: ''twas Aeneas talk to Dido, and thereabout of it especially when he speaks of Priam's slaughter' (2.2.384–5). Hamlet cues the actor by delivering the first dozen lines himself, which describe how, '*roasted in wrath and fire, / And thus o'ersized with coagulate gore, / With eyes like carbuncles, the hellish Pyrrhus / Old grandsire Priam seeks*' (2.2.399–402). Then the actor continues:

> Anon he finds him,
> Striking too short at Greeks. His antique sword,
> Rebellious to his arm, lies where it falls,
> Repugnant to command. Unequal matched,
> Pyrrhus at Priam drives, in rage strikes wide,
> But with the whiff and wind of his fell sword
> Th'unnerved father falls. Then senseless Ilium
> Seeming to feel this blow, with flaming top
> Stoops to his base and with a hideous crash
> Takes prisoner Pyrrhus' ear: For lo, his sword
> Which was declining on the milky head
> Of reverend Priam seemed i' th' air to stick.
> So as a painted tyrant Pyrrhus stood
> And, like a neutral to his will and matter,
> Did nothing.
> But as we often see against some storm
> A silence in the heavens, the rack stand still,
> The bold winds speechless and the orb below
> As hush as death, anon the dreadful thunder
> Doth rend the region, so after Pyrrhus' pause

A roused vengeance sets him new a-work
And never did the Cyclops' hammers fall
On Mars's armour, forged for proof eterne,
With less remorse than Pyrrhus' bleeding sword
Now falls on Priam.

(2.2.406–30)

Why this part of this speech comes to Hamlet's mind at this juncture isn't hard to see. On one level it's chosen to evoke afresh the brutal murder of old Hamlet by his brother and whet his son's blunted appetite for revenge. That Priam stands for Hamlet *père* in this reading and Pyrrhus for Claudius is clear from the characterization of 'hellish Pyrrhus' as 'a painted tyrant' bringing his sword down on 'the milky head / Of reverend Priam', the vulnerable 'unnerved father' and the king whose slaughter is a national catastrophe. That this is the primary connotation of the speech for Hamlet is corroborated by his urging the actor to hurry on to the part that describes Queen Hecuba's heart-rending cries of grief at the sight of her husband being butchered; the effect of which must be to bring back to the boil Hamlet's outrage at the glaring lack of grief shown by his mother following his father's death.

But on another level the speech can be construed as a projection of what Hamlet the avenging prince desires to do to his father's assassin. In this reading it serves likewise to revive his thirst for revenge, but this time by conjuring up a killing fit for him to emulate, because it resembles so closely the deferred dispatching of Claudius he anticipates. 'The rugged Pyrrhus' morphs from this perspective into an avatar of Hamlet the revenger, 'total gules, horridly tricked / With blood', stalking his royal prey 'roasted in wrath and fire'. The lines in which he's described with his sword poised above Priam's head, but inexplicably frozen and, '*like a neutral to his will and matter*', unable to deliver the death blow, mirror the prince's plight and even prefigure his suspension of Claudius's death-sentence when he has him at his mercy at prayer. The lines that follow them also presage Hamlet's no less 'remorseless' dispatching of the king with a 'bleeding sword', when, after his more protracted 'pause', '*A roused vengeance sets him new a-work*'. Once Pyrrhus is perceived as an avatar of Hamlet too, the passage about the Trojan queen becomes a vindictive envisaging of her Danish counterpart, blinded by tears ('With bisson rheum') and stripped of her royalty ('a clout upon that head / Where late the diadem stood'), watching in horror as old Hamlet's avenger makes 'malicious sport / In mincing with his sword her husband's limbs' (2.2.444–5, 451–2).

Hamlet offers no explanation for his choice of this speech by Aeneas, from a play which 'pleased not the million, 'twas caviar to the general' (2.2.374–5). But the twin motives the speech prompts one to infer are psychologically and emotionally consistent with his situation and state of mind at this point. The speech feeds Hamlet's need to rouse his vengeance from its slumber by reimagining the reason for it, and by giving him the imaginary experience, and the imaginary gratification, of eventually exacting the delayed revenge. In the process, however, it also identifies the play's protagonist with his antagonist by fusing them in the person of Pyrrhus. That fusion points to the true rationale for recoiling from revenge that Hamlet can neither grasp nor articulate, but that we are placed in a position to apprehend.

Nor is that the only moment when the play offers us a vantage point from which the same insight can be gleaned. The Hamlet who feels honour-bound to secure justice for his father's restless shade is tacitly identified with his treacherous uncle again in *The Murder of Gonzago* in Act 3. This time Hamlet makes his purpose in having this dramatic piece enacted clear from the outset, both in soliloquy (2.2.523–40) and to Horatio, whom he enlists to observe the king's reactions (3.2.71–6). The dumb show and the play proper are transparent depictions of old Hamlet's poisoning, and Gertrude's swift seduction, by his brother, whose 'occulted guilt' they are designed to 'unkennel' (3.2.76–7). In that aim they succeed spectacularly as far as Hamlet is concerned, although they also furnish another fictive device for postponing and displacing retribution. The Player King's speech cautioning the Player Queen to beware of swearing never to remarry glances at that very problem, and in terms which leave no doubt that the likelihood of Hamlet's reneging on his oath is being addressed too:

> *I do believe you think what now you speak.*
> *But what we do determine oft we break.*
> *Purpose is but the slave to memory,*
> *Of violent birth but poor validity,*
> *Which now like fruit unripe sticks on the tree*
> *But fall unshaken when they mellow be.*
> *Most necessary 'tis that we forget*
> *To pay ourselves what to ourselves is debt.*
> *What to ourselves in passion we propose,*
> *The passion ending doth the purpose lose.*
> *The violence of either grief or joy*
> *Their own enactures with themselves destroy.*

(3.2.180–91)

Hamlet had earlier asked the actor who delivered Aeneas's speech, and who presumably takes the part of the Player King, to 'study a speech of some dozen lines, or sixteen lines', which Hamlet 'would set down and insert' (2.2.477–8) in *The Murder of Gonzago*. Exactly which lines of the abortive performance that ensues were penned by the prince it's impossible to ascertain, but that passage is the obvious prime candidate, along with these gnomic lines from later in the same speech: '*Our wills and fates do so contrary run / That our devices still are overthrown. / Our thoughts are ours, their ends none of our own*' (3.2.205–7). Even though they can't be ascribed with certainty to Hamlet, their bearing on his own dilemma is as plain as their bearing on his mother's inconstancy.

In the context of its court performance, the Player King's speech has the uncanny effect of a thinly veiled Old Hamlet at once reproving and reassuring his widow and his son from beyond the grave. The reproof of Gertrude, as she sits watching the play, is retrospective and meant to gall her for the alacrity with which she forgot her dead husband and swapped her widow's weeds for a bridal gown; the reproof of Hamlet, on the other hand, is of urgent relevance to the impasse at which he finds himself, and meant to goad him into action by reminding him of his failure to remember what he once swore with such passion he would never forget. At the same time, the reprehension of both widow and son is cushioned by the broader perspective in which the Player King places their forgetting of the bonds between them and him. He presents it in the first person plural as a delinquency of which people in general are habitually guilty; indeed, as a human failing so widespread and inevitable that we may as well resign ourselves to its ubiquity, and even regard it pragmatically as something we have to do to get by: '*Most necessary 'tis that we forget / To pay ourselves what to ourselves is debt.*' If 'Our thoughts are ours, their ends none of our own', because things rarely turn out as we intend ('our devices still are overthrown'), such an attitude to even our most binding promises is inescapable.

Whether we think of Hamlet as having drafted this passage or not, its conflicted expression of censure and exculpation fits Hamlet's frame of mind. The Player King's speech rebukes the faithless widow and the faltering son and simultaneously rationalizes their defaulting on their debt to him as a frailty that flesh is heir to. The Player Queen rejects her spouse's pre-emptive pardon out of hand, reaffirming her pledge of posthumous fidelity with a vehemence calculated to throw Gertrude's posthumous infidelity into relief by comparison. That the cloaked rebuke of Gertrude has hit its intended target is confirmed by her response to Hamlet's barbed enquiry, 'Madam, how like you this play?': 'The lady doth protest too much, methinks', says Gertrude, to which Hamlet replies, 'O, but she'll keep her word', leaving the insinuation 'unlike you, mother' audible though unspoken (3.2.223–5). The dual focus of the Player King's coded speech to his queen has narrowed by this point to focus on the impact of their exchange on Gertrude; but not before giving veiled expression to the struggle in Hamlet between self-recrimination and the unvoiced disavowal of his obligation to avenge. In its conclusion that '*Our thoughts are ours, their ends none of our own*', we even have a foretaste of the dispassionate view of his life and death as beyond his control that he voices in the play's last scene.

At this moment in the play, however, it's Hamlet's sense of shame for shirking his sacred duty to his father that prevails and dictates his behaviour. As the Player King is left asleep by the Player Queen, and the scene shifts to his murder, Hamlet turns his mind to nettling Claudius. He informs him that the play is called *The Mousetrap*, that it's 'the image of a murder done in Vienna', and that 'Gonzago is the Duke's name, his wife Baptista' (3.2.232–3): information supplied too late for Claudius and Gertrude to distance the hitherto nameless characters onstage from their offstage equivalents. 'You shall see anon 'tis a knavish piece of work, but what of that?', adds Hamlet with feigned insouciance, as the mousetrap is about to be sprung; 'Your majesty and we that have free souls – it touches us not. Let the galled jade wince, our withers are unwrung' (3.2.233–6). At that moment, as Hamlet sardonically declares his fellowship with the king as a guiltless soul, '*Enter* Lucianus', whom Hamlet identifies at once: 'This is one Lucianus, nephew to the king' (3.2.237). It's a remarkable moment because, given the context and the whole point of staging the poisoning scene before the poisoner himself, one would expect Lucianus to be introduced as *brother* to the king. In no suggested source for *The Murder of Gonzago* is there any precedent for the Lucianus figure being the nephew of his victim. Moreover, having just identified the character played by the Player King as the 'duke' Gonzago, Hamlet calls Lucianus 'nephew to the *king*' instead of 'nephew to the duke'. There is no doubt that Shakespeare's decision to make Lucianus the same relation to Gonzago as Hamlet is to Claudius was deliberate. Thus, when Hamlet calls out to the actor playing Lucianus, 'Begin, murderer: leave thy damnable faces and begin. Come, "the croaking raven doth bellow for revenge"' (3.2.245–7), he's addressing both a projection of Claudius and a projection of himself in the hackneyed role of ranting revenger evoked by his parodic quotation. The sight of the Player King's kinsman creeping up as he sleeps to poison him replicates Claudius's murder of old Hamlet to steal his throne and wife; but Hamlet's identification of the regicide as the king's nephew, whose motive for murder is revenge, transforms the scene into a simultaneous dramatization of Hamlet avenging his father by murdering Claudius in exactly the same way as Claudius murdered his brother.

The murder scene of *The Mousetrap* is meant by Hamlet to be read by the king as both a provocative depiction of his fratricide and his nephew's threat of retribution. Hamlet certainly gives him no choice but to read it as the former: ''A poisons him i'th' garden for his estate', says Hamlet as Lucianus pours poison in the Player King's ears; 'You shall see anon how the murderer gets the love of Gonzago's wife' (3.2.254, 256–7). Whereupon Claudius rises, calls for lights and exits with Gertrude and attendants, leaving a jubilant Hamlet to exult over the success of his theatrical ploy. That Claudius also reads it as Hamlet's promise of impending reprisal may be inferred from his speech to Rosencrantz and Guildenstern shortly afterwards, which begins: 'I like him not, nor stands it safe with us / To let his madness range', and which ends: 'The terms of our estate may not endure / Hazard so near us as doth hourly grow / Out of his brows' (3.3.1–2, 5–7). Once again, as with Pyrrhus in Aeneas's speech to Dido, the dual deployment of the same fictional character – in this case Lucianus – to stand for both Claudius and Hamlet harbours a deeper import.

The play's implicit twinning of Hamlet with Claudius doesn't stop there. Still reeling from the shock of *The Mousetrap* and left alone onstage, the king resorts to soliloquizing on the bind in which he finds himself:

> O, my offence is rank: it smells to heaven;
> It hath the primal eldest curse upon't –
> A brother's murder. Pray can I not:
> Though inclination be as sharp as will,
> My stronger guilt defeats my strong intent
> And like a man to double business bound
> I stand in pause where I shall first begin
> And both neglect.

(3.3.36–43)

Although his quandary is different from Hamlet's, the echo of the latter's deadlock in these opening lines is unmissable. The last three could have been spoken in soliloquy by Hamlet as they stand, because they describe the same feeling of being immobilized by conflicting imperatives. Claudius cannot both 'be pardoned and retain th' offence' (3.3.56) any more than Hamlet can both exact revenge and refrain from exacting it. As Claudius kneels nevertheless to pray for forgiveness, saying 'Bow, stubborn knees, and hearts with strings of steel / Be soft as sinews of the new-born babe' (3.3.70–1), Hamlet materializes on cue, as if to clinch their resemblance in this regard. In a matching soliloquy, of which the praying king is oblivious, he proceeds to perform his version of the basic dilemma they share. No sooner does he have his father's murderer at his mercy and his sword unsheathed than his reluctance to revenge produces a pretext he finds cogent enough to sheathe his sword and withdraw, leaving his dilemma unresolved:

> Up sword, and know thou a more horrid hent
> When he is drunk, asleep or in his rage,
> Or in th'incestuous pleasure of his bed,
> At game a-swearing, or about some act
> That has no relish of salvation in't.
> Then trip him that his heels may kick at heaven
> And that his soul may be as damned and black
> As hell whereto it goes. My mother stays;
> This physic but prolongs they sickly days
>
> (3.3.87–96)

Ironically, as Hamlet exits on that line, Claudius rises from prayer and exits likewise with a couplet, which reveals his prayers to have been in vain and leaves his dilemma as unresolved as his unwitting alter ego's: 'My words fly up, my thoughts remain below. / Words without thoughts never to heaven go' (3.3.97–8).

The two characters merge unmistakably again in Act 4 for a moment through a kind of discursive contagion, when Claudius tests Laertes's mettle and motivation for avenging his father. He begins by closely echoing the argument of the Player King cautioning the Player Queen not to protest her love for him too much – an argument which itself carries echoes of the prince's reflections and locutions. The speech then segues seamlessly into lines that might have sprung as easily from Hamlet's lips as Claudius's:

> That we would do
> We should do when we would, for this 'would' changes
> And hath abatements and delays as many
> As there are tongues, are hands, are accidents,
> And then this 'should' is like a spendthrift's sigh
> That hurts by easing.
>
> (4.7.116–21)

When Claudius, hearing that Laertes would gladly cut Hamlet's throat in a church, replies 'No place indeed should murder sanctuarize. / Revenge should have no bounds', the emotional arc of his thinking mimics Hamlet's habitual resort to reproach to ignite resolution. To hear the murderer of Hamlet's father mouthing the revenger's staple platitudes to manipulate Laertes is also to be reminded that Hamlet, as the man who slew Polonius, stands in the same relation to Laertes as Claudius does to Hamlet. By killing Hamlet in the duel, Laertes avenges his father's murder at the same time as Hamlet avenges his by killing Claudius; and both killings incidentally complete by proxy the revenge of Fortinbras on the throne of Denmark.

These discursive echoes and structural symmetries stitch into the fabric of the play a recognition that the Hamlet sworn to revenge is the mirror image not only of his fellow avengers, Laertes and Fortinbras, but also of the king on whom he is doomed to wreak revenge. The tragedy makes no essential distinction between the character guilty of the deed that demands to be avenged and the character whose duty is to exact revenge. On the contrary, unlike the latter, it dissolves the distinction, because the object of its indictment is the iniquity of the kind of society of which revenge is a symptom. The inference we're prompted to draw from the play's recurrent equating of Hamlet with Claudius is clear. To kill Claudius, as Hamlet eventually does, is not just to duplicate the original crime of homicide he feels bound to avenge; it's to be complicit in the culture that fosters such crimes by forging the conditions that give rise to them. Complying with the revenge code means acting not merely as if revenge makes sense and matters, but as if the social order that generates the reasons for revenge makes sense and matters. That's why Shakespeare casts as the hero of his revenge tragedy a protagonist who finds acting as if that were the case impossible, for reasons that elude him, until circumstances force his hand.

Even then, the thought that he is finally avenging his father's murder and thus keeping his promise to the ghost is anything but uppermost in Hamlet's mind. He is prompted to stab and poison the king only by Laertes's dying revelation that 'the King, the King's to blame' (5.2.305) for the fatal poisoning of both Hamlet and his mother. After wounding Claudius with the envenomed point of his rapier, Hamlet forces the same lethal draft quaffed by Gertrude down his throat, crying, 'Here, thou incestuous, murderous, damned Dane! / Drink off this potion. Is thy union here? / Follow my mother' (F: 5.2.279). In the Second Quarto's version of this speech, whose first line reads simply, 'Here, thou incestuous, damned Dane!' (5.2.309), Hamlet says nothing that might refer to his having avenged his father's murder. In fact, the whole speech in Q2 suggests that foremost in Hamlet's mind at that moment is requiting Claudius for marrying his mother and for her poisoning. But even in the Folio version, as was noted at the beginning of this chapter, there's no basis for taking 'murderous' as a reference to Claudius's murder of old Hamlet rather than to his responsibility for the murder of Hamlet and the death of Gertrude. Neither in this speech nor in anything Hamlet says before he dies is there any mention of his father, the ghost of his father or the vow he made to the ghost. Nothing would have been simpler for Shakespeare than to give the dying prince the consolation of having at last kept his oath to his father's spirit to remember him and 'Revenge his foul and most unnatural murder' (1.5.25). But Shakespeare does not do so, and it would strike a false note if he did, because long before the end of the play the revenge has clearly ceased to matter to Hamlet and to Shakespeare. It has ceased to matter to them because it's *beside the point* of the play, for which much more than revenge is at stake.

That Within Which Passes Show

If one looks back through the tragedy from the final scene, it's obvious that Hamlet's heart was never in the role of revenger from the outset, any more than Shakespeare's heart was in writing a conventional revenge tragedy. In *Hamlet* Shakespeare sabotages revenge tragedy by creating a tragic protagonist who bridles at playing the stock part in which, it soon transpires, he's been miscast. As a Renaissance prince, steeped in the values of his class and culture, Hamlet is naturally appalled to find himself failing to perform the prescribed royal role of righteous avenging son, and at a loss to explain why. He strives repeatedly to stick to the stage-revenger's script, contriving impromptu performances of Aeneas's speech to Dido and *The Murder of Gonzago*, which incite him for a time to emulation when his resolution flags. Giddy with the triumph of his *Mousetrap*, and itching to berate his mother, he whips himself into a fit of melodramatic wrath by declaiming:

'Tis now the very witching time of night
When churchyards yawn and hell itself breaks out
Contagion to this world. Now could I drink hot blood
And do such business as the bitter day
Would quake to look on.

(3.2.378–82)

But the parodic ring of the lines succeeds only in betraying the fact that the part Hamlet's playing here, and the language he's speaking, are creaking theatrical clichés of which he's acutely aware. We know that he's acutely aware of them, because a few minutes earlier we've heard him saying to the actor playing the counterpart of Claudius/Hamlet about to murder the counterpart of old Hamlet/Claudius: 'Begin, murderer: leave thy damnable faces and begin. Come, "the croaking raven doth bellow for revenge". The scolding of the actor for his stereotyped mugging in the role and the sarcastically garbled quotation from *The True Tragedy of Richard III* (1591) – 'The screeching raven sits croaking for revenge, / Whole herds of beasts come bellowing for revenge' – betray Hamlet's ironic attitude to the part he's struggling to play in earnest himself. So when we hear him declaiming shortly afterwards in the same trite, bombastic vein, it's hard to imagine any accomplished actor delivering those lines without showing by his tone that Hamlet can hear himself doing precisely that.

His scorn for that overblown vein is such that even Laertes doesn't escape Hamlet's derision when he leaps into Ophelia's grave and spouts the hackneyed hyperbole beloved of sworn avengers of fathers and sisters on the Elizabethan stage:

Now pile your dust upon the quick and dead
Till of this flat a mountain you have made
T' o'ertop old Pelion or the skyish head
Of blue Olympus.

(5.1.240–3)

Hamlet is having none of this physical and verbal posturing, this overwrought public pantomime of grief, notwithstanding the genuine bereavement that prompted it:

'Swounds, show me what thou'lt do.
Woul't weep, woul't fight, woul't fast, woul't tear thyself,
Woul't drink up eisel, eat a crocodile?
I'll do't. Dost come here to whine,
To outface me with leaping in her grave?
Be buried quick with her, and so will I.
And if thou prate of mountains let them throw
Millions of acres on us till our ground,
Singeing his pate against the burning zone,
Make Ossa like a wart. Nay, an thou'lt mouth,
I'll rant as well as thou.

(5.1.263–73)

It's in keeping with Shakespeare's characterization of Hamlet that his difference from Laertes as an exemplary revenger should be expressed not only through stalling, but also through this caustic stylistic critique of Laertes's second-hand gestures and shopworn rhetoric. A deep-seated distrust of the theatricality of everything that's said and done in the rotten state of Denmark lies at the heart of what troubles him from the very beginning.

Every attempt to force his revenge tragedy back on track when it's derailed is doomed to fail, because even before the play is under way, even before the ghost's revelation and demand for revenge, Hamlet has 'that within which passes show' (1.2.85): a grief-stricken sense of disillusionment so consuming that life seems pointless and he wishes he were dead. It 'passes show' inasmuch as it defies expression in the language and demeanour of a world from which Hamlet feels cut off. Hence the first two sentences he speaks in the play take the evasive form of an acerbic, quibbling aside and a punning riposte, which show that he has *already* put on the 'antic disposition' (1.5.170) that he warns Horatio and Marcellus he might assume after his encounter with the ghost. 'But now, my cousin Hamlet, and my son –' (1.2.64), says Claudius, turning from matters of state and court affairs to deal with his nephew's dejected mood. 'A little more than kin, and less than kind' (1.2.65), retorts Hamlet, bristling at Claudius's callous displacement of his father in presuming to address him as his son. The first thing we hear from Hamlet, who is visually set apart from the entire court by his mourning suit before he speaks, is an insolent interjection uttered out of the king's hearing for our benefit alone. It immediately establishes a confidential relationship between the prince and the audience, drawing both into an alliance against king and court, even before the basis of the alliance is apparent. That it should be delivered and heard as an aside (which most editors mark it as) is confirmed by Claudius's completion of his interrupted sentence in his next line: 'How is it that the clouds still hang on you?' 'Not so much, my lord, I am too much in the "son"' is Hamlet's barbed reply (1.2.66–7). The pun rejects his uncle's appropriation of the term and reasserts the paternity of the king whose death, unlike Claudius and Gertrude, he has not ceased to mourn.

The recently widowed queen gets equally short shrift from Hamlet, when she attempts to persuade him with a platitude to snap out of his downcast state and get over his father's demise, as she obviously has: 'Thou knowst 'tis common all that lives must die, / Passing through nature to eternity' (1.2.72–3). 'Ay, madam, it is common' (1.2.74), replies her son, fastening on her word and turning it against her, just as he turned the king's use of the word 'son' against him. The echoing of 'common' makes the glib banality of the sentiment audible and upbraids the royal speaker for making herself common by resorting to a commonplace. Undeterred by the slight, Gertrude takes it as a cue to press home her argument, unaware of the tirade her question is about to trigger:

HAMLET
    Ay, madam, it is common.
QUEEN   If it be
    Why seems it so particular with thee?
HAMLET
    'Seems', madam – nay it is, I know not 'seems'.
    'Tis not alone my inky cloak, cold mother,
    Nor customary suits of solemn black,
    Nor windy suspiration of forced breath,
    No, nor the fruitful river in the eye,
    Nor the dejected haviour of the visage,
    Together with all forms, moods, shapes of grief,
    That can denote me truly. These indeed 'seem',
    For they are actions that a man might play,
    But I have that within which passes show,
    These but the trappings and the suits of woe.

                                        (1.2.74–86)

Again, Hamlet pounces on a single word to protest at its connotations. Again, he interrupts the speech of his interlocutor, refusing to treat language that he perceives to be loaded as innocuous. For to do that would mean not just taking what's being said by the speaker at face value, but participating in the parlance that underpins the status quo, which he can no longer countenance. From the first act to the last, Hamlet's hypersensitivity to the language his world speaks rarely leaves him. On the threshold of the catastrophe in the final scene he still finds time to burlesque at length the fatuous diction of the foppish courtier Osric (5.2.67–173), because he understands the power of language to keep people in tune with the time, to inure them to 'the drossy age' (5.2.169), through the mindless parroting of its habits of speech. Osric is only a particularly ludicrous instance of a general syndrome, which Hamlet's verbal heckling of everyone he encounters in his 'antic disposition' seeks to subvert.

In his attitude to language, Hamlet aligns himself with the protagonists of *Romeo and Juliet*, who become as acutely aware as he is from the start that being in conflict with one's world means being in conflict with the presiding discourse of that world. But, as his riposte to his mother's unguarded query reveals, Hamlet is equally suspicious of conventional body language and the symbolic significance of raiment as reliable gauges of character, emotion and intent. Sighing, weeping, looking sad and dressing in mourning clothes, 'Together with all forms, moods, shapes of grief', cannot tell you, Hamlet says in effect, what someone thus attired and exhibiting such behaviour is truly feeling and thinking. They are 'but the trappings and the suits of woe', which can be donned and doffed at will like a costume. Insofar as Hamlet is making a general observation about people's ability to put on a convincing public display of sorrow they don't feel, he's glancing at the charade of mourning he's just witnessed at court; his checklist of the staple signs of grief, including the 'windy suspiration of forced breath' and 'fruitful river in the eye', makes the satirical slant and butt of these lines plain. But insofar as they also pertain to Hamlet, their purpose is to distinguish his heartfelt emotions from such transparent histrionics.

There's more to this speech, though, than a contrast between sincerity and hypocrisy. Hamlet himself is wearing an 'inky cloak', a 'customary suit of solemn black', to signal publicly that he remains, unlike the court, in mourning for his father. The queen has just admonished him for continuing to exhibit 'the dejected haviour of the visage' that he cites as one of the easily faked signs of sadness: 'Do not for ever with thy vailed lids / Seek for thy noble father in the dust' (1.2.70–1). Although neither the 'windy suspiration of forced breath' nor 'the fruitful river in the eye' is meant to be self-mocking, the sentence that contains them presumes him to be capable of producing both, 'Together with all forms, moods, shapes of grief'. What Hamlet's saying in the final sentence of the speech is that, even though his 'shapes of grief' are sincere expressions of true grief, they still can't 'denote' him 'truly': they can't hope to reflect faithfully how he feels and what he's thinking. 'These indeed "seem"', he says, 'For they are actions that a man might play, / But I have that within which passes show'. There's something suspect, in other words, about 'customary' actions and appearances of any kind, even when the inward thoughts and emotions they denote are genuine, because they can be convincingly simulated – as the player turning pale and shedding real tears for Hecuba, 'But in a fiction, in a dream of passion' will shortly demonstrate. That's why Hamlet sets such store by his possessing '*that within* which passes show', something beyond mere grief that defies dissimulation.

We don't have to wait long for Hamlet to make the full significance of 'that within' clearer in his first soliloquy. It follows hard upon Claudius's forceful reiteration of

Gertrude's appeal to Hamlet to curtail his 'obsequious sorrow', because 'to persever / In obstinate condolement is a course / Of impious stubbornness, 'tis unmanly grief' and 'a fault to nature, / To reason most absurd, whose common theme / Is death of fathers' (1.2.92–4, 102–4). He begs Hamlet to 'think of us / As of a father' instead (1.2.107–8), evidently unfazed by Hamlet's objection to being addressed as his 'son'. Then, after Hamlet's feigned consent to his mother's wishes, Claudius invites him to 'be as ourself in Denmark' (1.2.122), which is the last thing Hamlet wants to be, but exactly what conformity with convention demands that he become: the same kind of self-serving, disingenuous cynic as the man squatting on his dead father's throne. As soon as the stage has cleared, leaving Hamlet to open his heart in confidence to us, we are left in no doubt about how far he is from the 'gentle and unforced accord' (1.2.123) expected of him:

> O that this too too solid flesh would melt,
> Thaw, and resolve itself into a dew,
> Or that the Everlasting had not fixed
> His canon 'gainst self-slaughter. O God, O God!
> How weary, stale, flat and unprofitable
> Seem to me all the uses of this world!
> Fie on't! O fie, fie, 'tis an unweeded garden
> That grows to seed: things rank and gross in nature
> Possess it merely. That it should come to this!
>
> (F: 1.2.127–35)

Here, in the first nine lines of the soliloquy, we gain our first glimpse of 'that within which passes show': the other Hamlet, for whom the thought of compliance with 'all the uses of this world' is unbearable, because they strike him now as 'weary, stale, flat and unprofitable'. So much so, that he craves the annihilation of his physical being, imagining it dissolving by a process of slow deliquescence as easy and natural as melting snow or condensing dew; and then, turning his mind to a more realistic means of terminating his existence, laments that suicide is forbidden by divine law.

The importance of Hamlet's divulging this in soliloquy at this point and soliciting our sympathy by making us privy to his private anguish, is impossible to overstate. Before the ghost has laid its injunction to revenge upon him – before whether, when and how to take revenge has become an issue – Hamlet has had enough of living as the person he's supposed to be in the world as he finds it, which is tiresome, predictable, disgusting and pointless. Before the action of the play begins, he is terminally disenchanted not only with everything the people around him habitually think, feel and do ('all the *uses* of this world'), but with everything that being Hamlet, Prince of Denmark entails thinking, feeling and doing. A space has already opened within him, which frees him to stand back from the self he can no longer unthinkingly inhabit but cannot escape, except by dying. We repeatedly catch Hamlet the man uncoupling himself from Hamlet the Prince, holding him at arm's length, observing his behaviour and overhearing his speech. For *that* Hamlet belongs to a society, he now perceives, most of whose members are not so much living as going through the motions of living: performing the customary 'actions that a man might play', and saying the things they are accustomed to say, in mindless compliance with 'the uses of this world'.

Things Rank and Gross in Nature

It's as if Hamlet the distraught son has snapped out of the trance in which Hamlet the royal prince and most of the cast of his tragedy are doomed to remain trapped. That awakening has changed everything irrevocably. He can now see people, including himself, as they really are and his world for what it really is, 'an unweeded garden' possessed by 'things rank and gross in nature'. As a result, he can never be at home in himself or his world again. The trauma that has torn through the fabric of normality, revealing the fact that it's a fabrication, is triggered by his mother's response to his father's sudden death. Hamlet makes this crystal clear in the rest of the soliloquy. His mother gave every appearance, he recalls, of returning her husband's adoration: 'Why, she should hang on him / As if increase of appetite had grown / By what it fed on' (1.2.143–5). At his funeral too, he remembers, 'she followed my poor father's body, / Like Niobe, all tears' (1.2.148–9). Yet, 'Within a month, / Ere yet the salt of most unrighteous tears / Had left the flushing in her galled eyes, / She married' (1.2.153–6). Moreover, the man she married with 'most wicked speed', and incestuously according to Judaeo-Christian law, was the brother of her husband, who 'was to this / Hyperion to a satyr', and 'no more like my father / Than I to Hercules' (1.2.156, 139–40, 152–3). Hamlet is not alone in regarding the 'dexterity' with which his mother has posted 'to incestuous sheets' (1.2.156–7) as indecent; Claudius's first thought in his first speech is to excuse the unseemly haste of the marriage to the court as romantically motivated and readily endorsed by his councillors' 'better wisdoms, which have freely gone / With this affair along' (1.2.15–16). What's shattered Hamlet, however, is not the shameless alacrity with which 'the funeral baked meats / Did coldly furnish forth the marriage tables' (1.2.179–80). Nor is it the taint of incest or his uncle's unworthiness of his mother in comparison with his father. It's that all these things have combined to expose his mother's ostentatious adoration of his father while he lived, and the floods of tears she shed over his corpse, as counterfeit. Whatever Gertrude seemed to feel about her husband, in the wake of her wedding to Claudius both her love and her grief for Hamlet's father are revealed to have been perfunctory, disposable emotions, as her plea to Hamlet to grieve no more for such a 'common' loss confirms.

By the time we first meet Hamlet, his justified disillusionment with his mother and his parents' marriage has expanded into a general disillusionment with the ways of his world that proves equally justified. His encounter with his father's ghost and his subjection to its 'dread command' do not precipitate the existential crisis that grips Hamlet, because he's been gripped by it from the outset; they intensify it beyond measure, bringing it to a head and forcing it into the open, but they don't create it. Lest we fall like Bradley into the trap of misconstruing Hamlet's frame of mind as an unfortunate mental affliction rather than a state of enlightenment, the play provides corroboration throughout for the objective validity of his view of Denmark and its denizens. Hence the care Shakespeare takes to have the apparition that 'bodes some strange eruption to our state' (1.1.68) first witnessed by Horatio, Barnardo and Marcellus, so that its ominous import for the fate of the kingdom is established before its personal claim on Hamlet is revealed. Before the Prince of Denmark has even appeared, we're aware that the nation has been thrown into turmoil by the need to arm itself against an impending invasion by young Fortinbras, and that 'heaven and earth together' have 'demonstrated / Unto our climatures and countrymen' portents as fearful as those seen in Rome 'A little ere the mightiest Julius fell' (1.1.123–4, 113). We're given independent corroboration of the fact that 'Something is rotten in the state of Denmark' (1.4.90), as Marcellus later concludes, in advance of Hamlet's discovery of its source.

After the second scene's exchange between Claudius, Hamlet and Gertrude has exposed the heartless cant and brazen expedience that rules the court, Shakespeare inserts before Hamlet's meeting with the ghost the scene in which we watch Ophelia being browbeaten, first by Laertes and then by Polonius, into rejecting Hamlet's advances as mere ploys to seduce her. The scene mirrors the previous one, because it shows Ophelia being pressed to comply with her father's and brother's will, just as Claudius and Gertrude had pressed Hamlet to comply with theirs. Both scenes display the same manipulative attitude that governs the most intimate relationships at Elsinore, and that does not afflict Hamlet alone. The oft-quoted 'few precepts' (1.3.56) Polonius drills into Laertes are commonplaces consistent with the commonplace mind of the speaker, who can think only in clichés. Their veneer of commendable prudence cloaks the naked self-interest they really serve, summed up in the specious doctrine: 'This above all, to thine own self be true / And it must follow as the night the day / Thou canst not then be false to any man' (1.3.77–9). The mindset that foists such invidious precepts upon Laertes is the same as that of Gertrude and Claudius urging Hamlet to cease mourning because the mortality of fathers is nature's 'common theme'. Anyone who thinks Polonius's advice worth committing to memory would do well to reflect that two scenes later Shakespeare shows us the same sagacious patriarch enlisting Reynaldo not just to spy on Laertes in Paris but to stain his character amongst his fellow Danes with whatever 'forgeries' (2.1.20) are necessary to find out what he's up to. The following scene finds Polonius conniving with the king to eavesdrop on Hamlet, using the hapless Ophelia as a decoy. When Hamlet is walking in the lobby, he tells Claudius, 'I'll loose my daughter to him' (2.2.159), and his use of that stockbreeding metaphor, which likens Ophelia to a cow being loosed to a bull, betrays his true view of her. The king's loyal councillor is indeed a 'wretched, rash, intruding fool', who finds to his eternal cost that 'to be too busy is some danger' (3.4.29, 31), and who merits every ounce of the contempt for his corpse Hamlet voices as he drags it offstage. He's more than just 'a foolish prating knave' (3.4.213); behind the façade of verbose old buffoon lurks a malign pawn of absolute power, who epitomizes everything Hamlet loathes about the vulpine mentality of the governing class.

It's a mentality whose assumptions and values Rosencrantz and Guildenstern share, and at whose service they are only too eager to place themselves. They are, we learn,

Hamlet's closest friends, 'of so young days brought up with him' and, by his own mother's account, 'two men there is not living / To whom he more adheres' (2.2.11, 19–20). They have been hastily summoned by the king and queen to spy and inform on Hamlet, much as Reynaldo has been instructed by Polonius to spy and inform on Laertes. Their task, Claudius tells them, will be 'to gather / So much as from occasion you may glean, / Whether aught to us unknown afflicts him thus' (2.2.15–17). Without the least sign of reluctance or distaste, Rosencrantz and Guildenstern submit completely to the royal will: 'we both obey', says Guildenstern, 'And here give up ourselves in the full bent / To lay ourselves freely at your feet / To be commanded' (2.2.29–32). The king thanks them by name in turn, and when the queen echoes his thanks but pointedly reverses their names (often reaping a laugh in performance), it highlights the abject conformity that makes such time-serving ciphers interchangeable. Shortly afterwards, we watch Hamlet light up with pleasure at the sight of them, greeting them as 'My excellent good friends' (2.2.219), and beginning to share his feelings with them, only to realize that they have been suborned to rat on him.

Act 3 opens with the venal duo reporting back to Claudius and Gertrude, which keeps their servile duplicity in view. That leaves them ripe for Hamlet's confounding of their every utterance in the next scene, and his mordant proof with a recorder of how far out of their depth they are. 'Will you play upon this pipe?', he asks Guildenstern, 'It is as easy as lying'. 'I have not the skill', says Guildenstern, to which Hamlet replies:

> Why, look you now how unworthy a thing you make of me: you would play upon me! You would seem to know my stops, you would pluck out the heart of my mystery, you would sound me from my lowest note to my compass. And there is much music, excellent voice, in this little organ. Yet cannot you make it speak. 'Sblood! Do you think I am easier to be played on than a pipe? Call me what instrument you will, though you fret me, you cannot play upon me.
>
> (3.2.342–3, 349, 354–63)

Moments later, not in the least abashed, the two-faced toadies are back in cahoots with the king, at one in their zeal to protect him by spiriting Hamlet away to England. 'Most holy and religious fear it is / To keep those many many bodies safe / That live and feed upon your majesty' (3.3.8–10), fawns Guildenstern, projecting their parasitic relationship to the crown into the polity as a whole. Thus, when Hamlet refers to Rosencrantz and Guildenstern on the verge of his departure as 'my two schoolfellows – / Whom I will trust as I will adders fanged' (3.4.200–1), his view of them, like his view of Polonius, has been borne out by the audience's independent observation of them. Their fate has indeed been sealed 'by their own insinuation' (5.2.58) of themselves into the role of Claudius's accomplices – witting or not – in his plot to have Hamlet beheaded upon his arrival in England. Having been 'thus benetted round with villains' (5.2.29), Hamlet has every reason to regard the apt retribution he contrived for his perfidious friends with no more regret than he felt for killing Polonius.

The fear Hamlet voices in soliloquy at the end of Act 2, that the spirit he has seen may be a lying devil in his father's guise, is dispelled for us before it's dispelled for Hamlet by Claudius's confession of guilt in an aside fifty lines later:

> How smart a lash that speech doth give my conscience!
> The harlot's cheek beautied with plastering art
> Is not more ugly to the thing that helps it
> Than is my deed to my most painted word.
> O heavy burden!
>
> (3.1.49–53)

Claudius is damned again out of his own mouth, overheard by the audience alone, in the soliloquy that reveals him so loath to give up the fruits of his 'foul murder' (3.3.52) that he cannot repent and beg forgiveness. All the subsequent scenes in which he's seen conspiring to have Hamlet murdered too, first with the tacit complicity of Rosencrantz and Guildenstern and then explicitly with Laertes, serve only to deepen Shakespeare's characterization of the king as irredeemably vile.

As for the queen Claudius has killed his brother to possess, one act after urging her son to cease mourning his father, because 'all that lives must die', Gertrude reveals the shabbiness of that gambit herself. In a private exchange with Claudius, she shows that she knows not just what's troubling Hamlet but the part she's played in unhinging him: 'I doubt it is no other but the main – / His father's death and our o'er-hasty marriage' (F: 2.2.55–6). We're given a further glimpse of her guilty conscience in her irritation at the Player Queen's protestation of eternal fidelity to the Player King. That Gertrude is innocent of collusion in her husband's murder is evident from her unruffled reaction to the murder scene in *The Mousetrap* and her baffled shock at the accusation Hamlet levels at her in the closet scene: 'A bloody deed – almost as bad, good mother, / As kill a king and marry with his brother' (3.4.26–7). The First Quarto gives her an emphatic denial to boot: 'But, as I have a soul, I swear by heaven / I never knew of this most horrid murder' (11.85–6). But Gertrude doesn't deny everything else Hamlet charges her with, namely making a mockery of her marriage vows to Hamlet's father by rushing headlong into wedlock with 'A cutpurse of the empire and the rule, / That from a shelf the precious diadem stole / And put it in his pocket' (3.4.97–9). On the contrary, her response to his brutal castigation of her conduct is:

> O Hamlet, speak no more.
> Thou turn'st my very eyes into my soul
> And there I see such black and grieved spots
> As there will leave their tinct. ...
>   ... O speak to me no more!
> These words like daggers enter in my ears.
> No more, sweet Hamlet.
>
> (3.4.86–9, 92–4)

Lest the authority of that confession be thought compromised by being wrenched from her under duress, Shakespeare gives Gertrude this aside as the demented Ophelia enters: 'To my sick soul, as sin's true nature is, / Each toy seems prologue to some great amiss, / So full of artless jealousy is guilt / It spills itself in fearing to be spilt' (4.5.17–20). So much lurid psychoanalytic speculation has been spun round Hamlet's relationship with his mother to make him the source of his problem that it's easy to forget the fact that Gertrude acknowledges the validity of Hamlet's recriminations and makes no attempt to defend or excuse her behaviour. Given the complacent ease with which she has so swiftly swapped one brother for another, whom Hamlet now knows to have poisoned his way into her bed, her son might be forgiven for finding her shallowness shameful and her physical intimacy with 'A murderer and a villain' (3.4.94) repugnant.

The Whips and Scorns of Time

Shakespeare lets the audience see and hear for themselves the objective proof that Hamlet's disabused revulsion from life in Denmark is warranted, and not the result of his morbidly warped perception of the reality everyone else accepts and he should come to terms with. The vision of his world that he voices in his first soliloquy, before his father's ghost demands revenge, becomes increasingly understandable as the tragedy unfolds and we learn what the place and the people he must contend with are like. By the time we reach the scene where Polonius gets his first dose of the prince's antic disposition, we know why Hamlet's come to the conclusion that 'to be honest as this world goes is to be one man picked out of ten thousand' (2.2.175–6). The fact that Polonius attests in asides to the method in Hamlet's madness ensures that we take note of his pronouncements in this mood. They include the wish that he was dead, which he expressed so movingly in his first soliloquy, and which has not left him. 'My lord, I will take my leave of you', says Polonius, preparing to depart. 'You cannot take from me anything that I will not more willingly part withal', the prince replies, 'except my life, except my life' (2.2.210–12). For Hamlet, given what he now knows, 'Denmark's a prison' and so, for that matter, is the whole world, 'in which there are many confines, wards and dungeons – Denmark being one o'th' worst' (F: 2.2.242–5).

He continues in the same vein to Rosencrantz and Guildenstern until his global disenchantment mutates into misanthropy:

I have of late, but wherefore I know not, lost all my mirth, forgone all custom of exercise; and, indeed, it goes so heavily with my disposition that this goodly frame, the earth, seems to me a sterile promontory. This most excellent canopy the air, look you, this brave o'erhanging firmament, this majestical roof fretted with golden fire – why it appears no other thing to me but a foul and pestilent congregation of vapours. What a piece of work is a man! How noble in reason! How infinite in faculty! In form and moving how express and admirable! In action, how like an angel! In apprehension, how like a god! The beauty of the world, the paragon of animals – and yet to me what is this quintessence of dust? Man delights not me – no, nor woman neither, though by your smiling you seem to say so.

(F: 2.2.294–309)

We know from Hamlet's first soliloquy and the ghost's revelation that his claim here to find his dejection inexplicable is not the diagnostic key to some mental disease that Bradley mistakes it for, but a wise withholding of the reasons from friends he perceives he cannot trust. Guildenstern himself reports later that Hamlet 'with a crafty madness keeps aloof / When we would bring him on to some confession / Of his true state' (3.1.8–10). But the rest of the speech rings true, because it chimes with speeches that sound the same note throughout the play. Hamlet's heavy disposition isn't a vicious mole in his nature, his unfortunate tragic flaw; it's the commensurate emotional response of an exceptionally sane man to an insoluble dilemma in an intolerable reality. It's the response not of a man who is innately morose, but of a dismayed idealist who, as this speech makes clear, has been driven to think the worst of his kind and the world he inhabits by matters not of his making. It's because Hamlet knows that human beings have the physical and mental potential to be 'The beauty of the world, the paragon of animals' that he's plunged into misanthropic gloom by seeing them speak and act as if they were merely the 'quintessence of dust'.

To have been driven to that point of total alienation before the tragedy begins is to have travelled too far beyond the orbit of his world for anything his world demands of him, let alone the exaction of revenge, to draw him back into it. 'The time is out of joint', he laments at the close of Act 1, as he completes his solemn oath to the ghost; 'O cursed spite / That ever I was born to set it right!' (1.5.186–7). It should be noted that he doesn't lament being charged to avenge the murder of his father by killing his murderer. In fact, he doesn't define his cursed plight in terms of having to take revenge at all. He defines it as the task of setting right the *time* in which he's living, of fixing the way things now are in the world in general. That's what it would take, the couplet implies, to do true justice to the situation that confronts him. It's a task impossible to accomplish simply by killing his father's killer, which would be pointless, because it would leave the world Hamlet now abhors just as it is, and thus the fundamental problem unsolved; a task so desperately impossible that Hamlet wishes that he'd never been born rather than be faced with it. If he thought carrying out the revenge equal to the task of setting the time right, cursing his fate to the point of wishing he'd never been born wouldn't make sense, because killing Claudius would be enough for justice to be done, and Hamlet would be the same kind of man as Laertes and Fortinbras, content to take the world as it is. But, as that wish intimates, mere revenge could never satisfy Hamlet, even if he cared enough to exact it – not because he has ethical qualms about killing, or is too depressed or pensive to act, but because his deepest desire is *not to have to exist at all* in a world to which he no longer belongs.

For his most compelling expression of that desire we need only turn to Hamlet's third soliloquy, which picks up the thread of his first:

Shakespearean Tragedy

To be, or not to be – that is the question;
Whether 'tis nobler in the mind to suffer
The slings and arrows of outrageous fortune
Or to take arms against a sea of troubles
And by opposing end them; to die: to sleep –
No more, and by a sleep to say we end
The heartache and the thousand natural shocks
That flesh is heir to: 'tis a consummation
Devoutly to be wished – to die: to sleep –
To sleep, perchance to dream – ay, there's the rub,
For in that sleep of death what dreams may come
When we have shuffled off this mortal coil
Must give us pause: there's the respect
That makes calamity of so long life.
For who would bear the whips and scorns of time,
Th' oppressor's wrong, the proud man's contumely,
The pangs of despised love, the law's delay,
The insolence of office and the spurns
That patient merit of th'unworthy takes,
When he himself might his quietus make
With a bare bodkin? Who would fardels bear
To grunt and sweat under a weary life
But that the dread of something after death
(The undiscovered country from whose bourn
No traveller returns) puzzles the will
And makes us rather bear those ills we have
Than fly to others that we know not of?
Thus conscience does make cowards of us all
And thus the native hew of resolution
Is sicklied o'er with the pale cast of thought,
And enterprises of great pitch and moment
With this regard their currents turn awry
And lose the name of action.

(3.1.55–87)

Although the line of thought he pursues in this speech is obviously prompted by his own predicament, it's striking that at no point does Hamlet use the first-person singular. The entire meditation is conceived and framed impersonally, using the first-person plural and the third-person singular. Hamlet is wrestling with fundamental questions of intense importance to him, but in terms which treat them as questions that concern all of us as human beings, regardless of rank, gender or race.

Addressed in confidence to the audience, the soliloquy assumes our agreement with its postulates and conclusions, which betray not a trace of Christian thought or doctrine.

(Compare the first soliloquy's wish 'that the Everlasting had not fixed / His canon 'gainst self-slaughter'.) The entire eschatology on which the ghost's credentials as a revenant from Purgatory rest has receded. The world view this soliloquy presumes we share is that of the humanist agnostic, for whom nothing can be known beyond death, from which no one comes back alive. That fact alone reveals the gulf dividing Hamlet in this state from the prevailing mindset of Elsinore and Elizabethan England – the mindset he will reassume when he reassumes the role of revenger and cannot kill Claudius at prayer. But that gulf is evinced no less vividly by the examples Hamlet chooses to illustrate the 'whips and scorns of time' that no one in their right mind would bear, if they could take their own lives with posthumous impunity. These include 'Th' oppressor's wrong, the proud man's contumely' and 'The insolence of office', none of which would rank high on the list of things a prince one step from the throne is likely to suffer from. Most telling of all is his instance of those who 'fardels bear' and 'grunt and sweat under a weary life'. This empathy with the physical misery of the labouring class, reversing the normal hierarchical priorities, puts the levelling spirit of Hamlet's soliloquy beyond doubt. It points to the profound link forged in this tragedy between that levelling spirit and the absolute liberation from oneself and one's world that Hamlet craves and hopes death will deliver.

The craving is so strong that only the dread of not ceasing 'To be' after death, but having to suffer unknown torments, deters him, the soliloquy implies, from taking his own life. 'Thus conscience does make cowards of us all', Hamlet concludes, meaning that introspective reflection on the possibility of further, posthumous suffering makes not just him but everyone cowards by making us afraid to die by our own hands. The word 'conscience' carries no moral connotations, religious or secular, in this context, as is clear from the expanded restatement of the conclusion in the next two lines, where it's paraphrased as 'the pale cast of thought'. Moreover, the whole six-line sentence that completes the passage quoted is couched like the rest of the soliloquy in general terms, which preclude restricting its application to Hamlet. Insofar as 'conscience' can be said to have made a coward of Hamlet in particular, the context again makes it clear that his cowardice consists in his fear of the consequences of suicide, not in his fear of suicide itself on moral grounds, and not in his fear of taking revenge, which is not uppermost in his mind here. That it is, nevertheless, stealing back into Hamlet's subconscious in these closing lines is undeniable. As the focus on suicide widens to embrace all 'enterprises of great pitch and moment' that 'With this regard their currents turn awry / And lose the name of action' (3.1.85–7), the self-recriminating impulse of Hamlet the sworn revenger strives to turn his generalization to its own account.

That it fails to do so and regain control of him is evident from his ensuing exchange with Ophelia. The animosity with which Hamlet treats her has understandably been censured as unjustified. But the torrent of bitter misogyny and misogamy he subjects her to springs from the same utter disenchantment as his previous misanthropic assertions. That doesn't absolve Hamlet of undue cruelty to Ophelia, but it does place it in a broader perspective, which explains why he says what he says to her in this mood at this point. Our response to the exchange is qualified, too, by our awareness that Claudius and Polonius are eavesdropping on it, and that Ophelia is being exploited, with her knowledge, to enable them to do so. There is also strong textual evidence to suggest that Hamlet suspects this, and that everything he says to Ophelia is intended for the ears of the eavesdroppers too. His sudden question, 'Where's your father?', lets them know that Polonius's concealed presence is suspected by Hamlet, while the answer it elicits from Ophelia, 'At home, my lord', lets us know, and must arouse Hamlet's suspicion, that it's a barefaced lie she is forced to tell (3.1.129–30). When Hamlet declares on the verge of exiting, 'Those that are married already – all but one – shall live' (3.1.147), it's hard to believe that his pointed parenthesis, 'all but one', isn't inserted for the benefit of the king he thinks may be listening too.

Even if one assumes Hamlet to be ignorant of the fact that he's being overheard and Ophelia knows it, the fact that *we* know it is enough to underscore the point he's making with his diatribe against her and her sex. The point being that, as her lie demonstrates, Ophelia is inescapably complicit with Polonius and Claudius and everything they stand for, which Hamlet rightly reviles. Innocent though she is of any desire to harm him, her impotence as a woman, a daughter and a subject makes her objectively guilty, whether she likes it or not. Once one realizes that Hamlet is assailing her in *that* capacity, as a woman unconsciously but irredeemably tainted by her incarceration in the prison-house of Denmark, his rant makes perfect sense. Hamlet is seeing Ophelia now as he sees his former self: as a stranger observed from outside. Thus, when she says she has 'remembrances' from him that she wishes to return, and Hamlet replies, 'No, not I. I never gave you aught' (3.1.92, 95), he's right, because he's no longer the person who gave her them – the lovelorn prince who once sent hackneyed verses '*To the celestial and my soul's idol, the most beautified Ophelia*' (2.2.108–9). Likewise, when Hamlet abruptly declares, 'I did love you once', only to contradict himself almost immediately by saying, 'I loved you not', he means that the man he was then 'loved' her only in the prescribed, conventional sense, and thus didn't love her at all.

The unsparing harshness of his harangue makes it easy to overlook the fact that Hamlet doesn't spare himself in this encounter. His response to Ophelia's saying that he made her believe he loved her is: 'You should not have believed me. For virtue cannot so inoculate our old stock but we shall relish of it' (3.1.116–17). In other words, however honest Hamlet's intentions were when he said that to her, the habit of lying to women about loving them has been ingrained in men for so long as to be second nature to them, and he is no exception. 'I was the more deceived', says Ophelia, provoking this angry rejoinder from Hamlet:

> Get thee to a nunnery! Why wouldst thou be a breeder of sinners? I am myself indifferent honest but yet I could accuse me of such things that it were better my mother had not borne me. I am very proud, revengeful, ambitious, with more offences at my beck than I have thoughts to put them, imagination to give them shape, or time to act them in. What should such fellows as I do crawling between earth and heaven? We are arrant knaves – believe none of us. Go thy ways to a nunnery.

> (3.1.119–29)

Hamlet castigates himself as no less culpable than Ophelia and all 'such fellows' (all the other men like him) simply by virtue of existing in the world as it is. For the man that he has been, and cannot break free from, he has nothing but the same contempt that vents itself in his misogynistic railing against Ophelia and women in general. The only thing that could save him from being an arrant knave like other men would be never having been born. For men and women alike to be part of society as it stands is to be contaminated and controlled by what Hamlet calls its 'uses': by the degrading habits of thought, speech and conduct to which its members become inured, and which they perpetuate through marriage and the children they rear. The next best thing to never having been born is thus to withdraw from society and sexual reproduction altogether. That's why Hamlet repeatedly exhorts Ophelia to confine herself in a convent, why he excoriates her sex for their cosmetic facades and seductive posturing, and why he calls for an end to the matrimonial state the latter are employed to induce: 'Go to, I'll no more on't. It hath made me mad. I say we will have no more marriage' (3.1.145–6).

After Hamlet exits, Ophelia bewails what she takes to be the mental breakdown of the prince who was 'Th' expectation and rose of the fair state, / The glass of fashion and the mould of form, / Th' observed of all observers' (3.1.151–3). She is forgivably unaware that the enviable epitome of the ideal young Danish aristocrat is the last thing Hamlet could be, or would want to be, any longer. She thinks him bereft of his 'most sovereign reason / Like sweet bells jangled out of time' (3.1.165–6), but he's never been more fully possessed of his senses than now, when he's 'out of time', out of sync with the sensibility of his society. As G. K. Chesterton observes: 'the whole point of Hamlet is that he is really saner than anybody else in the play; though I admit that being sane is not identical with being sensible. Being outside the world, he sees all round it; where everybody else sees his own side of the world, his own worldly ambition, or hatred or love.' Hamlet's sanity inevitably seems insane to anyone still locked inside the world that he's looking into from outside and that he can see round, because he's seen through it. Seeing all round it, as Chesterton intimates, means seeing it from a common human standpoint rather than the standpoint of one's own interest and advantage within that world. Hamlet's world keeps trying to pull him back inside it, and back into step with the time, by pulling him into the role of revenger his society has scripted for him. But its attempts to reclaim him are in vain. Not even his murdered father's ghost, nor his own subsequent endeavours to work himself back up into a fit of homicidal rage, can bring Hamlet back from the state of estrangement he has arrived at before the tragedy begins.

That state, for which the sole cure is to cease existing, stays with him till the end, by which point he can contemplate the prospect of his death with equanimity, content for it to deliver him from the world when it will:

We defy augury. There's a special providence in the fall of a sparrow. If it be now, 'tis not to come. If it be not to come, it will be now. If it be not now, yet it will come. The readiness is all. Since no man has aught of what he leaves, what is't to leave betimes?

(F: 5.2.197–202)

The tone is different from the tone of his first soliloquy in Act 1, and so is his attitude to death, the aftermath of which he no longer dreads. But, as the last sentence quoted attests, Hamlet's profound detachment from his world has not changed. Nothing belongs to any of us, once we no longer belong to the world; we own nothing of it, and know nothing of it, when we're dead, so it doesn't matter whether we die sooner rather than later, because we won't care. Note, too, that the whole speech, like 'To be, or not to be', is couched in impersonal terms as a statement of the case that holds true not only for Hamlet but for all human beings: 'Being outside the world, he sees all round it.'

The Strong Conflux of Contending Forces

To regard *Hamlet* as the tragedy of a man who, for one reason or another, or for reasons that remain obscure, fails to do what he has sworn to do until it's too late, causing his own death and the deaths of others as a result, is to miss the whole point of the play and Shakespearean tragedy. Viewing *Hamlet* in those terms robs it of its revolutionary vision by reducing it to a politically anodyne morality play or psychological case study, in which the catastrophe is brought about by the fatal flaw that prevents the protagonist from acting as convention, then and now, expects him to act.

The study and performance of *Hamlet* have suffered for centuries from what Swinburne denounced as 'the indomitable and ineradicable fallacy of criticism which would find the keynote of Hamlet's character in the quality of irresolution', despite the fact that 'the signal characteristic of Hamlet's inner nature is by no means irresolution or hesitation or any form of weakness, but rather the strong conflux of contending forces'. The nature of the forces contending for Hamlet's heart and mind should be clearer by this point. On one hand, the claims of the part his society demands that he play, which includes the role of royal, avenging son, but entails everything a man of his rank in such circumstances is supposed to think and feel and do; on the other, the claims of the disabused human being awoken within him by the realization that the entire order of things to which he had hitherto subscribed is a despicable charade in which he can no longer collude. Whenever the role of prince repossesses him, Hamlet berates himself for being 'a rogue and peasant slave', 'A dull and muddy-mettled rascal', and fires himself up again to take the bloodcurdling revenge convention requires him to take. But the role never possesses him for long, because it's impossible for him to return to being the unconflicted prince he was before his traumatic awakening. At the end of the play, a poisoned rapier delivers him from this intolerable impasse into eternal silence and he is ready to die. But until then the impasse leaves him stranded in limbo, killing time instead of killing Claudius or himself.

What else, after all, can Hamlet do, having no adequate course of action open to him? To kill Claudius in revenge would be to act on and endorse the terms of a society whose ethos he rejects. It would mean submitting to 'That monster Custom, who all sense doth eat / Of habits devil' (3.4.159–60). Whatever satisfaction Hamlet might derive from killing Claudius at last in the heat of the moment, the fact remains that, as George

Bernard Shaw perceived, 'this is no solution of his problem: it cuts the Gordian knot instead of untying it'. The only thing that could untie the Gordian knot for Hamlet would be the transformation of his society into one fit for what human beings could be, instead of one fit for the scoundrels, pawns and parasites it forces most of them to become. The tragedy is designed to show that nothing less than that would do to set the time right. Shrewd unsocial socialist that he was, Shaw had no more trouble understanding this than he had understanding Hamlet, 'the philosopher who went, at the bidding of his father's ghost, in search of a revenge he did not feel and a throne which he did not want'. Shaw's Hamlet

> finds somehow that a crown for which his uncle committed fratricide does not interest him as much as the players, and that revenge is not worth the mess the king's blood would make on the floor. He asks himself whether he is a coward, pigeon-livered and lacking gall to make oppression bitter. All this is quite natural. Men who are superior to vulgar cupidities and ambitions, and to vulgar rancours, always do seem weak and cowardly to men who act on them. Sometimes they seem so to themselves. There is no contradiction or inconsistency in Hamlet to anyone who understands this.

Shaw recasts Hamlet, needless to say, in his own Shavian image, distorting and simplifying Shakespeare's protagonist more than somewhat in the process. But he gets to the heart of Hamlet in portraying him as deaf to the siren call of sovereignty, devoid of a genuine desire for revenge, and morally superior to those who are driven by cupidity, ambition and rancour, and who think there's something wrong with Hamlet because he's not like them. Hamlet himself, as Shaw acknowledges, thinks so too at times, but it's only at those moments when he's in the grip of 'That monster Custom' again. There's nothing contradictory or inconsistent in Hamlet's behaviour on this understanding of him, Shaw concludes in his keenness to refute those who find Hamlet unfathomable. But it would be truer to say that on this understanding of Hamlet the reason why he behaves in an inconsistent or contradictory manner becomes perfectly clear. It has nothing to do with being indecisive, and everything to do with not wanting to be where he is or who he's supposed to be, but having to keep pretending, not least to himself, that he does.

The tension between these contending forces is evident from the moment Hamlet is told of his father's ghost. Within minutes of wishing that his 'too solid flesh would melt, / Thaw and resolve itself into a dew', freeing 'that within which passes show' from the unreality of seeming, he suddenly becomes the archetypal avenger closing the scene *solus* with a couplet that would pass muster in any revenge tragedy of the day:

> I doubt some foul play. Would the night were come.
> Till then sit still my soul – foul deeds will rise
> Though all the earth o'erwhelm them to men's eyes. *Exit.*

(1.2.254–6)

Hamlet stays in character as outraged, sworn revenger throughout his exchange with the apparition. But the plea with which it vanishes, 'Adieu, adieu, adieu, remember me' (1.5.83), anticipates – indeed almost prompts – the marked shift in attitude Hamlet displays as soon as he's left alone. It elicits from him a long, passionate protestation that he will remember for as long as 'memory holds a seat / In this distracted globe', that everything else will be wiped from his memory and the ghost's 'commandment all alone shall live / Within the book and volume' of his brain (1.5.96, 102–3). The resort to such hyperbole is itself enough to cast doubt on the depth of Hamlet's commitment to the task of remembering. But by the time he's finished reminding himself of the reason for remembering and revenging, and literally written it down in a notebook to ensure he doesn't forget, his emotional disengagement from the task is virtually complete:

> Yes, by heaven,
> O most pernicious woman,
> O villain, villain, smiling damned villain,
> My tables! Meet it is I set it down
> That one may smile and smile and be a villain –
> At least I am sure it may be so in Denmark.
> So, uncle, there you are. Now to my word.
> It is 'Adieu, adieu, remember me.'
> I have sworn't.

> (1.5.104–12)

The fustian apostrophes he enlists to rouse himself ('O most pernicious woman, / O villain, villain, smiling damned villain') ring hollow. Hamlet's heart isn't in the words he's mouthing, as his need to set them down in writing, and thus detach them from himself, suggests. When he adds, 'So, uncle, there you are', transmuting his father's murderer into a maxim in his commonplace book, he places himself at a further remove from his uncle in the flesh. The prospect of killing him, which Hamlet never mentions in this speech, has already receded, its urgency having vanished with the ghost. But it had begun to recede with the ghost's parting injunction, which assumes that the issue is not whether Hamlet will remember to sweep to his revenge, but whether he will remember his father at all. Hamlet's response, containing not a word about revenge, confirms that caring enough about his father and his fate to keep him in mind is the issue for him too.

The conclusion of the scene provides further corroboration of Hamlet's emotional retreat from what he's just pledged with such fervour to do. When Hamlet exhorts Horatio and Marcellus to swear not to breathe a word of what they've seen, the ghost returns as an eerie, discarnate voice to enforce their oaths three times from three different points beneath the stage. Having the three men move twice to swear thrice gives Hamlet the opportunity to milk humour from their bizarre situation by addressing the unseen spirit beneath them in strikingly incongruous language: 'Ha, ha, boy, sayst thou so? Art thou there, truepenny? / Come on, you hear this fellow in the cellarage? / ... *Hic et ubique*? Then we'll shift our ground. ... / ... Well said, old mole, canst work i' th' earth so fast? / A worthy pioneer!' (1.5.150–1, 156, 161–2). The shift in register from formal to colloquial, the change in tone from earnest intensity to jocular familiarity, and the knowing theatrical nod to the actor under the stage ('this fellow in the cellarage') combine to place Hamlet at an ironic distance from the ghost of his murdered father and its claims on him. It's here, too, that Hamlet hits upon the expedient of putting on 'an antic disposition', into which he can subsequently retreat at will to keep memory at bay with the cryptic quibbling of his feigned derangement.

He ends the scene by bewailing not the dreadful fact that his father has been murdered and must be avenged, but the 'cursed spite' of having been born to set the time right. Yet again, in this crucial definition of his plight, what one might think would be foremost in Hamlet's mind has already been eclipsed. It remains eclipsed the next time we hear of him, which is in Ophelia's report of his accosting her in the stereotypical guise of the distraught, dishevelled lover whom he was plainly impersonating (2.1.72–97). When Hamlet does turn his mind back to avenging his father's death, he can do so likewise only by proxy, at a coded theatrical remove from reality, first through the player's speech about Pyrrhus killing Priam, and then by staging *The Mousetrap*. As Dr Johnson drily remarks, 'The apparition left the regions of the dead to little purpose'. Its return in Act 3 to jog Hamlet's memory proves fruitless and, after Hamlet's final soliloquy in Act 4, neither his father nor revenge crosses his mind again, apart from the single occasion in Act 5 quoted earlier, when he refers to old Hamlet tellingly not as 'my father' but impersonally as 'my king'. Indeed, with the exception of that allusion, as John Middleton Murry observes, 'The fifth act rises utterly free of the Ghost and his influence' and, as the duel begins, 'there is no thought in Hamlet's mind now of revenge upon the king'.

A King of Infinite Space

Critics who regard complying with convention and accommodating oneself to the status quo as normal and reasonable, and who assume that Shakespeare shared their views, have inevitably found Hamlet's aversion to doing so a source of endless puzzlement and made this tragedy seem to be 'the most problematic play ever written by Shakespeare or any other playwright', as Harry Levin famously dubbed it. But for those who, like Shaw, approach the play from a diametrically opposed standpoint, the tragic conflict the play dramatizes could not be plainer. It's the conflict, to put it simply, between the man Hamlet could be and the prince he must be: between the radically different human being struggling for life within him and the socially conditioned self in which history has trapped him. What's tragic is not that some fatal defect in his character prevents him from avenging his father as readily as Laertes or Fortinbras would in his place; it's being forced to live and die on the terms of such a society at all, repelled by everything it stands for and demands of him, yet having to think, speak and act as if he still felt part of it, and castigate himself for failing to.

Shakespeare's favourite contemporary philosopher would certainly have understood the nature of the war within Hamlet the dramatist was staging. 'There is no man (if he listen to himselfe)', wrote Montaigne in 'Of Repenting', 'that doth not discover in himselfe a peculiar forme of his, a swaying forme, which wrestleth against the institution, and against the tempest of passions, which are contrary unto him'. It would be hard to better that as a description of what Hamlet, who listens constantly to himself, undergoes: the discovery within himself of a strange, compelling form of being, violently at odds with what institutionalized usage – what Hamlet calls 'damned custom' (3.4.35) – is forcing him to feel. Reflecting on the play while in exile over two centuries later, Montaigne's countryman, Victor Hugo, homed in on this uncanny sense of self-estrangement as the key to understanding the character:

> Hamlet is not upon the spot where his life is. He has ever the appearance of a man who talks to you from the other side of a stream. He calls to you at the same time as he questions you. He is at a distance from the catastrophe in which he takes part, from the passer-by whom he interrogates, from the thought that he carries, from the action that he performs. He seems not to touch even what he grinds. It is isolation in its highest degree. … It is as if your own self was absent and had left you there.

Hugo captures perfectly Hamlet's dislocation, the impression he gives of being there and elsewhere at the same time, and thus severed not only from the events in which he is involved and the characters with whom he is speaking, but also from his own deeds and even from his own thoughts, as this remark to Horatio attests: 'Ere I could make a prologue to my brains / They had begun the play' (5.2.30–1).

The last sentence of that quotation from Hugo describes the uncoupling of man and prince in terms that recall Romeo's bewildered couplet: 'I have lost myself. I am not here. / This is not Romeo, he's some otherwhere' (1.1.195–6). With a change of name those lines could be spoken at some point by any of Shakespeare's great tragic protagonists, and by no one more aptly than Hamlet, whose dejected fits of lassitude afflict Romeo too. The sensation Hugo and Romeo describe is also a sensation with which Shakespeare as a seasoned player as well as a playwright would have been long familiar, and from which he drew profound philosophical and political insights that found imaginative expression in his plays. That Hamlet feels such an affinity with the players, greets them with such informal warmth, holds their art in such high esteem, and insists that they be treated with respect, is not fortuitous. When he's with them he is with his own kind, which is his creator's kind. For they know exactly what it feels like to lose themselves – to lose who they would otherwise be – while acting and talking as if they were someone else in another place and time.

More recent commentators on the play than Hugo, apart from Swinburne and Shaw, can be cited in broad support of this view of its protagonist. Murry puts the bind in which Hamlet finds himself like this: 'He desires to remember himself and forget himself at the same moment.' Jan Kott sums it up thus: 'The situation has been imposed on him. Hamlet accepts it, but at the same time revolts against it. He accepts the part, but is beyond and above it.' For John Bayley 'Hamlet is a man dispossessed of himself, or rather one who has no chance to become himself.' In truth, however, one need look no further than the shrewdest observer of Hamlet within the play. After welcoming Rosencrantz and Guildenstern to Denmark, Claudius explains the mystery he needs their help to solve:

> Something have you heard
> Of Hamlet's transformation – so call it
> Sith nor th' exterior nor the inward man
> Resembles that it was. What it should be
> More than his father's death, that thus hath put him
> So much from the understanding of himself
> I cannot dream of.

(2.2.4–10)

Claudius perceives that Hamlet has been so outwardly and inwardly transformed as to be not just unrecognizable but no longer capable of *understanding* the Hamlet he no longer resembles. Nothing but Hamlet's death, he soon realizes, 'shall expel / This something settled matter in his heart / Whereon his brains still beating puts him thus / From fashion of himself' (3.1.171–4).

Being put so much from the fashion and understanding of himself is a harrowing experience for Hamlet. But it's a liberating experience too, which opens up the possibility of profoundly different, more desirable ways of living. That possibility is expressed primarily *as* Hamlet's perplexed rebellion against the obligation to take revenge, and thus against the entire dispensation on which the revenge code rests. By confounding the expectations built into the conventions of Elizabethan revenge tragedy, *Hamlet* calls into question the beliefs and values that conventional revenge tragedy endorses. It does so from a standpoint anchored in beliefs and values which are the antithesis of those against which Hamlet rails, and from whose clutches he yearns to be freed. As the play develops, the alternative principles to which Shakespeare's tragic vision is committed become increasingly explicit, finding their most powerful expression in the graveyard scene that opens the final act.

They are foreshadowed long before that, as we've seen, in Hamlet's most celebrated soliloquy, whose levelling standpoint disturbed Dr Johnson's sense of decorum: 'It may be remarked, that Hamlet, in his enumeration of miseries, forgets, whether properly or not, that he is a prince, and mentions many evils to which inferior stations only are exposed.' Johnson is shrewd enough to concede that Hamlet's obliviousness of rank might be 'proper', by which he means apt or justifiable, in some sense. But he's too struck by the prince's ostensible solecism to perceive its actual consistency with Hamlet's characterization and the democratic drift of the soliloquy. Murry, on the other hand, sees at once what the lines in question connote: 'Hamlet, for one moment, has escaped his local particularity and become pure human.' What Murry fails to see is that his acute comment applies not only to the entire speech, whose class-transcending perspective becomes conspicuous in these lines, but also to other moments and other speeches throughout the play. 'To be, or not to be' is delivered from the start not by Hamlet in his capacity as Prince of Denmark, but by the human being released within him by his revolt against his fate as a prince. Below the threshold of his socially conditioned identity and consciousness Hamlet harbours everything that makes him one with the rest of humanity as opposed to what divides him from them. This is 'that within which passes show', the realm of boundless, unrealized potential he shares with his kind, the 'infinite space' of which he could count himself a king, were it not for the 'bad dreams' that plague him as the Prince of Denmark (F: 2.2.253–4). For the duration of the soliloquy Hamlet dwells in that realm, speaking from a universal human perspective that erases his rank and empowers him to empathize with the downtrodden and oppressed, as if he were one of them. As we watch Hamlet deliver the soliloquy onstage, we *see* the sixteenth-century prince trapped in his class-bound destiny, but we *hear* the egalitarian voice of the virtual community he forges with the audience as he speaks. The tension between what we see and what we hear encapsulates the conflict between historical reality and transformative possibility at the heart of Shakespearean tragedy.

If we look back from there to the beginning of the play, there are signs of Hamlet's possessing a far from princely cast of mind from the outset, well before the ghost's revelation turns his quandary into a crisis. Take his response to Horatio's saying that he had seen Hamlet's father once in the flesh, and that he was 'a goodly king': ''A was a man', replies Hamlet, 'take him for all in all' (1.2.185–6). What matters to Hamlet is what kind of man, not what kind of king, his father was; his royalty is irrelevant to determining the respect he deserves, which Hamlet judges by criteria applicable to anyone of the male gender, regardless of their class. His reply's deliberate revision of the terms of Horatio's praise, which one might expect him to echo, suggests that for Hamlet being a good man is superior to being 'a goodly king', and that he can think of no higher accolade. A similar inversion of values is discernible in Hamlet's self-deprecating references to himself as 'poor' in his exchanges with Horatio and Marcellus: 'for my own poor part / I will go pray'; 'As you are friends, scholars and soldiers, / Give me one poor request'; 'so poor a man as Hamlet is' (1.5.130–1, 140–1, 182). Such locutions might be dismissed as routine politeness, but they bear the stamp of this unprincely prince, whose antic disposition, it soon appears, is to exalt the humble and stand hierarchy on its head: 'I hold ambition of so airy and light a quality', says Rosencrantz, 'that it is but a shadow's shadow'; to which Hamlet replies, 'Then are our beggars bodies, and our monarchs and outstretched heroes the beggars' shadows' (F: 2.2.259–62). Which end of the social hierarchy he identifies with may be inferred from his ironic response to his mendacious friend a few lines later: 'Beggar that I am, I am even poor in thanks' (F: 2.2.270).

Hamlet's instinctive alliance with the 'common players' (F: 2.2.346), who ranked alongside vagrants in Elizabethan England, and his informed esteem for their craft reflect the same reversal of established attitudes. 'Do you hear', he instructs Polonius, 'let them be well used, for they are the abstracts and brief chronicles of the time: after your death you were better have a bad epitaph than their ill report while you live'. 'My lord, I will use them according to their desert', answers Polonius, who plainly holds the players in lower regard, prompting Hamlet to retort: 'God's bodkin, man, much better!

Use every man after his desert and who shall scape whipping? Use them after your own honour and dignity' (2.2.461–9). The levelling thrust of the riposte is delivered with the spontaneous passion of a man speaking his mind, and speaking it man to man, not prince to lord: none of us is in a position to pass judgement on the worth of anyone else and everybody, without exception, deserves to be treated with the same honour and dignity that we would expect to be treated with. Hamlet the man can never sever himself completely, of course, from Hamlet the prince while the latter remains powerful enough to lay claim to him. Thus, within moments of rebuking Polonius, Prince Hamlet is rebuking himself for being 'a rogue and peasant slave' instead of a royal revenger. When Rosencrantz presses him later for the location of Polonius's corpse, he puts the presumptuous cat's paw in his place with an imperious reminder of the social gulf that divides them: 'Besides, to be demanded of a sponge! What replication should be made by the son of a king?' (4.2.11–12).

At no point is his reassertion of his royalty more emphatic than when he declares, as he confronts Laertes over Ophelia's corpse, 'This is I, / Hamlet the Dane' (5.1.246–7). But such reversions to the posture thought proper to a prince become increasingly infrequent after 'To be, or not to be', as Hamlet's sense of our common humanity deepens and his keenness to subvert sovereignty itself intensifies. Just before *The Mousetrap* Hamlet says to Horatio:

> Nay, do not think I flatter,
> For what advancement may I hope from thee
> That no revenue hast but thy good spirits
> To feed and clothe thee? Why should the poor be flattered?
> No, let the candied tongue lick absurd pomp
> And crook the pregnant hinges of the knee
> Where thrift may follow fawning.
>
> (3.2.52–8)

Hamlet's satirical assurance commends the involuntary integrity of the poor, for whom the basic human need to feed and clothe oneself takes priority, and contrasts it with the disgusting spectacle of the rich and powerful, whose 'pomp' is dismissed as 'absurd', being fawned on for advancement and financial gain. The prince's ironic envy of the freedom of the poor from the corruption of court life is superbly enshrined in that trenchant rhetorical question, 'Why should the poor be flattered?'.

His growing contempt for kingship, captured in the image of 'the candied tongue' licking 'absurd pomp', is soon audible again in the flippant rhyme with which Hamlet celebrates the success of *The Mousetrap*: 'For if the King like not the comedy / Why then he likes it not, perdie' (3.2.285–6). His sneering caricature of Claudius as 'a king of shreds and patches' (3.4.99) turns the social order upside down by figuratively stripping the sovereign of his robes and dressing him in rags. The second scene of Act 4 concludes with this exchange:

ROSENCRANTZ

   My lord, you must tell us where the body is, and go with us to the King.

HAMLET

   The body is with the King, but the King is not with the body. The king is a thing.

ROSENCRANTZ

   A thing, my lord?

HAMLET

   Of nothing. Bring me to him.   *Exeunt*

(4.2.23–8)

It should come as no surprise that four lines after we've heard Hamlet say that 'The King is a thing … Of nothing' Shakespeare has the king in question voice his fear of the danger Hamlet poses, because 'He's loved of the distracted multitude' (4.3.4) and thus capable of mobilizing them. The king's derogatory view of his subjects doesn't detract from the aptness of the play's alignment of the prince with the nameless mass of the populace, whose plight he understands and who have taken him to their heart.

If Claudius required confirmation of the strength of Hamlet's contempt for him, and of his sympathy with popular, egalitarian attitudes, he hasn't long to wait before Hamlet provides it in person:

KING

   Now, Hamlet, where's Polonius?

HAMLET

   At supper.

KING

   At supper! Where?

HAMLET

   Not where he eats but where 'a is eaten. A certain convocation of politic worms
   are e'en at him. Your worm is your only emperor for diet. We fat all creatures to
   fat us, and we fat ourselves for maggots. Your fat king and your lean beggar is
   but variable service, two dishes but to one table. That's the end.

KING

   Alas, alas.

HAMLET

   A man may fish with the worm that hath eat of a King and eat of the fish that
   hath fed of that worm.

KING

   What dost thou mean by this?

HAMLET

   Nothing but to show you how a king may go a progress through the guts of a
   beggar.

(4.3.16–30)

It's a magnificent moment, surpassed only by Hamlet's dialogue with the Gravedigger and his ensuing reflections, for which it paves the way. Hamlet's scorn is not confined to Claudius: it reaches beyond the king confronting him to assail monarchy itself and the presumption of innate social inequality upon which monarchy rests. (In the dialogue, and in virtually all the speech-prefixes and stage directions, of all three texts of *Hamlet* Claudius is referred to only as 'King', never as Claudius; his status as sovereign was clearly foremost in Shakespeare's mind throughout.) From the posthumous perspective of Death the Leveller, there's no distinction to be drawn between starving beggar and gluttonous king, since the corpses of both wind up as food for maggots. The grave makes nonsense of the artificial differences of rank, power and wealth by which societies set such store. Hence the only creature that merits the title of emperor is the worm that devours our remains in the grave, because its power, unlike that of mortal rulers, is truly supreme and absolute. The universal, classless standpoint from which Hamlet is speaking is apparent in his choice of the first-person plural to describe what applies to all human beings without exception: 'We fat all creatures to fat us, and we fat ourselves for maggots.' Viewed from that standpoint, a monarch accustomed to having his majesty confirmed by the public adulation that greets every royal journey ('progress') needs reminding of the ignominious fate nature might have in store for him – such as passing through the bowels of a beggar. That such a vitriolic insult should be delivered directly to a king by the son of a king, and with such palpable relish, says much for the nerve of the man who penned it for performance by a company soon to be known as the King's Men.

The Prophetic Soul of the Wide World

Hamlet has much more to say in the same vein in the graveyard scene, which makes the spirit in which the whole tragedy has been written unmistakable. But not before the Gravedigger has threatened to upstage him in the wily double-act with a Second Man, his fellow 'Clown', that opens the scene. 'If this had not been a gentlewoman', says the anonymous stooge to the nameless sexton digging Ophelia's grave, 'she should have been buried out of Christian burial.' His astute interlocutor pounces on his cue:

GRAVEDIGGER

Why, there thou sayst. And the more pity that great folk should have countenance in this world to drown or hang themselves more than their even-Christian. Come, my spade. There is no ancient gentlemen but gardeners, ditchers and grave-makers. They hold up Adam's profession.

2 MAN

Was he a gentleman?

GRAVEDIGGER

He was the first that ever bore arms.

2 MAN

Why, he had none.

GRAVEDIGGER

What, art a heathen? How dost thou understand the Scripture? The Scripture says Adam digged. Could he dig without arms?

(F: 5.1.23–37)

The Gravedigger's ironic gibe at 'great folk', who enjoy the privilege of killing themselves with impunity that their equals before Christ are denied, sets the broad theme and the tone of what follows. But the terms of the riddling repartee he initiates are dictated by the tool of his trade, as he literally labours with it onstage: 'Come, my spade'. Those who make their living by digging the earth like him are in fact, he maintains, the noblest gentlemen of the most ancient stock, because they can trace their lineage back to Adam. 'The Scripture says Adam digged', the Gravedigger explains, so he must have been the first gentleman, since he was 'the first that ever bore arms' and he couldn't have dug without them. The Gravedigger's punchline hinges on his sly pun on 'arms', meaning both a coat of arms and the sword that only gentlemen were allowed to carry, as well as the arms Adam used to dig with, just like the Gravedigger as he speaks these lines. His quibble does more, however, than clinch his claim that 'There is no ancient gentlemen but gardeners, ditchers and grave-makers'. It turns the established value-system on its head by implying that the arms used by those who work the earth for a living are indeed their escutcheon: the physical symbol of their social superiority, precisely by virtue of their manual labour, to the noblest lords in the land.

The allusion to Adam digging also echoes the text on which John Ball famously preached on Blackheath during the Peasants' Revolt of 1381: 'When Adam delved and Eve span, / Who was then a gentleman?' Like the Gravedigger, the question attacks the very notion of a gentleman, but in this case by reminding us that there was once no such thing, because there was once no such thing as a society that divided human beings into higher and lower ranks; and that there's nothing natural or immutable, therefore, about the hierarchical distinctions and attendant inequalities enforced by such a society. Like the Gravedigger, too, the question invokes Scripture to exalt the humble, who toil with their hands as our first ancestors did in Eden. In the words of Ball's sermon: 'We be all come from one father and one mother, Adam and Eve: whereby can they say or shew that they be greater lords than we, saving by that they cause us to win and labour for that they dispend?' The spirit of Shakespeare's Jack Cade and his followers in *2 Henry VI* is alive and kicking in the Gravedigger. The latter's inclusion of gardeners among the elite descendants of Adam recalls Cade's riposte to Sir Humphrey Stafford's attempt to put him in his place. 'Villain, thy father was a plasterer', sneers Stafford, 'And thou thyself a shearman', to which Cade retorts, 'And Adam was a gardener' (4.2.123–5). It's the Gardener, too, in *Richard II* who tells his man in the hearing of the Queen: 'Go thou, and, like an executioner, / Cut off the heads of too fast-growing sprays / That look too lofty in our commonwealth. / All must be even in our government' (3.4.32–6).

There's also more than an echo in the Gravedigger's reverse reasoning of the exchange (quoted in Chapter 1) between Cade's rebels Nick and George on the very site where Ball had preached seventy years before. 'Well, I say it was never merry world in England since gentlemen came up', remarks Nick, indignant that 'The nobility think scorn to go in leathern aprons.' 'Nay, more,' says George, 'the King's Council are no good workmen.' 'True', replies George, 'and yet it is said, "Labour in thy vocation"; which is as much to say as, "Let the magistrates be labouring men"; and therefore should we be magistrates' (*2HVI* 4.2.7–8, 11–16). Scholars keen to quash any idea that Shakespeare himself espoused such views are quick to cite the fact that in 1596 Shakespeare was granted the coat of arms his father had earlier failed to secure. Its half-defiant, half-defensive motto, '*Non sanz droict*' ('Not without right'), certainly suggests how much the right to be called a gentleman meant to the self-made dramatist. But nor does it leave much doubt about his view of the notion that gentlemen are born, not made, and that gentility can't be acquired. Given the relish with which the Gravedigger's case is made, and the roots of that case in the Cade scenes of his seminal play, Shakespeare may well have thought that he had as much right to the name of gentleman as those born with it, *because* he was a glover's son and a common player, not in spite of it.

Be that as it may, one would have to be deaf not to hear in the speech of the Gravedigger 'the great heroic song of human democracy' that Chesterton heard in it, and that we hear sung by Hamlet too from the moment he enters with Horatio. As he watches one skull after another being turfed up by the Gravedigger, Hamlet imagines the lords, ladies, courtiers, politicians, lawyers and buyers of land they might once have belonged to. He does so not to lament the fate that awaits humanity in general, but to foreground the fate that awaits those whom the Gravedigger calls 'great folk': the fate that strips them of everything they preened themselves on while alive. From the Gravedigger's rough treatment of one of the skulls Hamlet draws a further conclusion: 'And now my Lady Worm's – chapless and knocked about the mazzard with a sexton's spade. Here's fine revolution if we had the trick to see't' (F: 5.1.87–9). He reinforces it with a similar image of plebeian violence being inflicted on an upper-crust cranium: 'Why, might not that be the skull of a lawyer? Where be his quiddities now – his quillets? His cases? His tenures and his tricks? Why does he suffer this rude knave now to knock him about the sconce with a dirty shovel and will not tell him of his action of battery?' (5.1.96–101). Editors routinely insist that the word 'revolution' refers here to the wheel of fortune or the whirligig of time, and that to take the term in its modern political sense would be anachronistic. It would indeed, but it would also be consistent with Shakespeare's profoundly anachronistic imagination. Given the dramatic context in which Hamlet uses the word, it would be perverse not to see its modern political meaning already emerging here, especially when it can also be seen surfacing in Henry IV's wish 'that one might read the book of fate, / And see the revolution of the times / Make mountains level' (*2HIV* 3.1.44–6). As George Steiner observes in *After Babel*: 'Shakespeare at times seems to "hear" inside a word or phrase the history of its future echoes.'

After conceding victory to the Gravedigger in their battle of wits, Hamlet concludes his reflections on the vanity of grandeur by returning to the theme of his last exchange with Claudius about a king ending up in a beggar's guts. Holding up the putrid skull of Yorick, the king's jester, he asks Horatio, 'Dost thou think Alexander look'd o' this fashion i'th' earth?'. 'E'en so', replies Horatio. 'And smelt so? Puh!', exclaims Hamlet, flinching from the stench. 'E'en so', his friend assures him, prompting Hamlet to dilate upon that incontrovertible fact:

HAMLET

> To what base uses we may return, Horatio! Why may not imagination trace the noble dust of Alexander till he find it stopping a bung-hole?

HORATIO

> 'Twere to consider too curiously to consider so.

HAMLET

> No, faith, not a jot. But to follow him thither with modesty enough and likelihood to lead it: as thus, Alexander died, Alexander was buried, Alexander returneth into dust, the dust is earth, of earth we make loam, and why of that loam whereto he was converted might they not stop a beer-barrel?
>
> Imperial Caesar, dead and turned to clay,
> Might stop a hole to keep the wind away.
> O, that that earth which kept the world in awe
> Should patch a wall t'expel the winter's flaw!
>
> *Enter* KING, QUEEN, LAERTES, *a* Priest, *and a coffin, with Lords attendant and a* Gentleman
>
> But soft, but soft – aside – here comes the King.

(5.1.195–214)

So much for history's most glorious exemplars of the governing elite into which Hamlet himself was born. The faculty he enlists to 'trace the noble dust of Alexander till he find it stopping a bung-hole', to view the way the world wags from below instead of from above, is 'imagination': the faculty Shakespeare harnessed to create *Hamlet* itself. Hamlet's imagining of Alexander the Great reduced to dust and 'Imperial Caesar' reduced to 'earth' echoes the reduction of Caesar to both in the tragedy he penned immediately before *Hamlet*. 'How many times', wonders Brutus, 'shall Caesar bleed in sport / That now on Pompey's basis lies along, / No worthier than the dust?' (3.1.114–16). 'O pardon me, thou bleeding piece of earth', begs Antony, addressing Caesar's corpse, the sight of which had first moved him to exclaim: 'O mighty Caesar! Dost thou lie so low? / Are all thy conquests, glories, triumphs, spoils, / Shrunk to this little measure?' (3.1.148–50, 254). Shakespeare's disdain for those who glory in their sovereignty over their fellow mortals remains as undisguised in the first of his greatest tragedies as it was at the dawn of his tragic vision in *2 Henry VI*. It's not only expressed in such undisguised terms, however, as Hamlet's last line in the exchange quoted above illustrates. 'But soft, but soft – aside – here comes the King' discreetly underscores the prince's internal exile from the entire regime incarnate in Claudius. It brackets the dialogue that precedes it as an extemporal digression from the business of the plot proper, whose resumption is announced by 'Here comes the King'. Hamlet's use of the term 'aside' to signal that he and Horatio should now stand and speak apart highlights the play's framing of a virtual time and space that power cannot police.

For those whose past-bound perspective on history, and of Shakespeare's place in it, baulks at regarding his dramatic vision as fundamentally egalitarian, let alone revolutionary, this audacious sequence in the graveyard poses a serious problem. It's not by chance that the prince gazing at the skull in his hand, as he stands beside the grave in which a common gravedigger toils, has become for millions the iconic image that captures the essence of Shakespeare's drama. In this scene Hamlet's tragic plight as the son of a king, stranded in that society at that moment in history, is placed in a perspective that reaches back, through the Gravedigger's riddles, to our common human origin in Adam before class society and forward to 'doomsday' (F: 5.1.59), when everybody, irrespective of rank, gender, wealth or power, will have equal rights at last in the perfect democracy of death. Shakespeare wasn't alone in observing that death lays its icy hand on commoners and kings, revealing the cultural fictions that divide the living to be shadows, not substantial things. But he was unique among the playwrights of his day not only in never forgetting that fact, but also in understanding its political implications and embodying them in a revolutionary poetic drama beyond anything his fellow dramatists were capable of conceiving.

That dramatic vision is embodied and enacted as much as it's voiced. The urge not just to invert but to collapse and dissolve hierarchy is overtly articulated in the speeches of the Gravedigger and Hamlet. But no less powerful, indeed arguably more powerful, than the tenor of those lines is the boldness of having this disaffected, royal intellectual and this amiably insolent, anonymous labourer converse informally on an equal footing, as the latter toils at his trade onstage. The normally insuperable social barrier between them is abolished by the circumstances under which Shakespeare contrives their encounter. It's an encounter that may be without precedence in theatrical history, though not without parallels in Shakespeare's plays. That Shakespeare felt compelled to stage such an exchange at such a crucial point in the tragedy, allowing the wise plebeian fool – the only character who shares Hamlet's antic language of licensed equivocation – to quibble the prince into submission, leaves the standpoint from which the play was written in no doubt.

Shakespeare wrote *Hamlet* from the same utopian perspective as his previous tragedies, but in a spirit of dissidence more blatantly defiant than ever before. *Hamlet* is a tale of its time told in the language of its time, *but not from the perspective of its time*, which it judges from the vantage point of a future humanity is still struggling to create. Shakespeare's imaginative commitment to the potential of all human beings to live according to principles of freedom, equality and justice is what drives this tragedy's fierce dissatisfaction with the reality it reflects. The play's vision can justifiably be called revolutionary insofar as the fulfilment of that potential demands the transformation of society as it was in Shakespeare's time and as it is today. *Hamlet* epitomizes the refusal of Shakespearean tragedy to make complete sense in the terms of its time, because the assumptions and values that govern it are ahead of its time and ours.

Shakespeare, as Ralph Waldo Emerson observed, is 'as unlike his contemporaries as he is unlike us'. Emerson owed his observation to Coleridge, who was the first to grasp this anachronistic aspect of Shakespeare's dramatic art, and who saw the same turning towards the future as a defining characteristic of Hamlet as distinct from Polonius, that tireless purveyor of maxims. 'A maxim is a conclusion upon observation of matters of fact, and is merely retrospective: an Idea, or, if you like, a Principle, carries knowledge within itself, and is prospective. Polonius is a man of maxims.' Which is why, Coleridge explains, 'Hamlet, as the man of ideas, despises him. A man of maxims only is like a Cyclops with one eye, and that eye placed in the back of his head.' Those who take a retrospective, historical view of *Hamlet* and its hero, remaining blind to the prospective disposition of both, are one-eyed Cyclopses like Polonius: cursed with incorrigible hindsight and thus incapable of fathoming the prince's 'prophetic soul' (1.5.40). But when one realizes, as Hazlitt did, that 'This play has a prophetic truth, which is above that of history', then what Dowden called 'the mystery, the baffling vital obscurity of the play' is soon dispelled.

One can only regret Bradley's decision not to pursue this approach to *Hamlet* himself, after pausing to concede the powerful appeal it clearly held for him:

> How significant is the fact (if it be fact) that it was only when the slowly rising sun of Romance began to flush the sky that the wonder, beauty and pathos of this most marvellous of Shakespeare's creations began to be visible! We do not know that they were perceived even in his own day, and perhaps those are not wholly wrong who declare that this creation, so far from being a characteristic product of the time, was a vision of
>
> the prophetic soul
> Of the wide world dreaming on things to come.
>
> [Sonnet 107]

If Bradley had followed in the footsteps of Coleridge and Hazlitt, instead of diagnosing Hamlet as a suitable case for treatment, he would have applauded Wilson Knight's discerning in the prince 'a creature of another world', whom the other characters, like most critics, inevitably strive in vain to understand. But he would have known, unlike Knight, that the other world to which the king of infinite space belongs has yet to be created. For he would have felt the tidal pull of futurity in every scene of the play. As it turned out, it took another radical dramatist rather than a critic to grasp immediately both the visionary anachronism and the militant political spirit of *Hamlet*. In 'Shakespeare: Eine Differenz' Heiner Müller, the author of *Hamletmachine*, his savage homage to the tragedy, called *Hamlet* 'an attempt to describe an experience that has no reality at the time of its description. An endgame in the red dawn of an unknown day.' If any lines in the play could be said to distil the essence of its protagonist and the mood in which Shakespeare wrote it, they would not be the best known and most quoted. They would be those simple, moving words Hamlet speaks to Horatio at the beginning of the final scene: 'Sir, in my heart there was a kind of fighting / That would not let me sleep' (5.2.4–5). Here's fine revolution, if we have the trick to see it.

CHAPTER 6
OTHELLO: THEREBY HANGS A TAIL

Expectation in Preference to Surprise

Anyone who doubts that Shakespeare's greatest tragedies were written from a visionary standpoint far ahead of his time need only think of *Othello*. The play has become so well known that it's easy to forget the audacity of Shakespeare's decision to transmute Cinthio's cautionary tale of a doomed mixed-race marriage into a heartbreaking tragedy. Centuries before the issues the tragedy compels its audiences to confront became as urgent and ubiquitous as they are today, Shakespeare forged in *Othello* a critique of racial and sexual injustice which is more powerful now, in the twenty-first century, than it could ever have been at the dawn of the seventeenth.

The tragic chain of events commences with the elopement of Othello and Desdemona. The fact that they are forced to elope makes the illicit nature of their relationship in the eyes of Venice immediately clear. But in their eyes and in Shakespeare's eyes there's nothing illicit about their love, to which they regard themselves, and the play regards them, as fully entitled. Undeterred by the paternal wrath and widespread disapproval they are bound to incur, Othello and Desdemona act as if a black man from Africa and an upper-class white woman from Venice have every right to fall in love, marry and be left to live in peace as husband and wife. They act, in other words, as if they were already free citizens of a truly civilized future, instead of prisoners of a time when racial prejudice and sexual inequality are so pervasive that even their heroic hearts are tainted by them.

This view of Desdemona and Othello owes nothing to Cinthio's story and everything to Shakespeare's decision to make their scandalous defiance of convention the starting point of his tragedy. Cinthio's story is one of a series that revolves around the infidelity of husbands and wives. Its professed aim is to illustrate the dire consequences of a gullible husband being duped by a villain into believing his virtuous wife unfaithful. The interracial aspect of the marriage is far from the forefront of Cinthio's mind. His nameless Moor and his 'Disdemona' have no need to elope. At the point where their tale begins they have been enjoying an untroubled life of connubial bliss, having overcome her family's objections: 'So propitious was their mutual love that, although the Lady's relatives did all they could to make her take another husband, they were united in marriage and lived together in such concord and tranquillity while they remained in Venice, that never a word passed between them that was not loving.' The sole explicit reference to the colour of the Moor's skin occurs well into the narrative, when the unnamed Ensign, whom Shakespeare christens Iago, tells the Moor 'The woman has come to dislike your blackness' to explain her adultery with the Corporal, the counterpart of Cassio. The notion that racial difference might be a factor in the breakdown of her marriage is implicitly adduced by Disdemona later on: 'I fear greatly that I shall be a warning to young girls not to marry against their parents' wishes; and Italian ladies will learn by my example not to tie themselves to a man whom Nature, Heaven, and manner of life separate from us.' But neither of these admonitions furnishes the moral Cinthio draws from his tale once it is told. The blame for the ensuing deaths of Disdemona and the Moor is divided at the end between the Ensign's malevolence, the folly of Disdemona's father in giving her a name that means 'unfortunate', and the Moor's equally foolish credulity. For Cinthio, the blackness of Othello is a matter of incidental significance, insofar as it matters at all; whereas for Shakespeare it's so crucial that he opens the play with Iago and Roderigo breaking news of the elopement to Desdemona's outraged father, Brabantio, in the middle of the night, forcing him to imagine her copulating like an animal in the heat of interracial lust: 'Even now, now, very now, an old black ram / Is tupping your white ewe', cries Iago, 'your daughter and the Moor are now making the beast with two backs' (1.1.87–8, 114–15).

Shakespeare begins *Othello* in coarse comedic rather than high tragic style by pandering to the stereotyped views of Moors and Venetian women that he could count on most of his audience sharing. In a scene that might serve as the farcical climax of a Jacobean city comedy, a venerable citizen of Venice is roused from sleep in the middle of the night to be told by two men out to torment him that his beautiful white daughter has run off with a blackamoor, who is ravishing her as they speak. At this stage the audience's only image of the runaway lovers is the one peddled by Iago and Roderigo to a Brabantio ready to buy it. Their hot-blooded, priapic barbarian is the stock caricature of a Moor, as firmly ensconced in the popular imagination as the stock caricature of Venetian women as licentious. '[Y]our fair daughter', Roderigo informs her father, has been 'Transported with no worse nor better guard / But with a knave of common hire, a gondolier, / To the gross clasps of a lascivious Moor' (1.1.120, 122–4), thereby demeaning herself socially as well as racially and sexually. 'Your daughter', Roderigo assures Brabantio, 'hath made a gross revolt, / Tying her duty, beauty, wit and fortunes / In an extravagant and wheeling stranger / Of here and everywhere' (1.1.131–5). 'This accident is not unlike my dream', replies Brabantio, 'Belief of it oppresses me already' (1.1.140–1). He gives Roderigo's view of the eloping couple immediate credence, because it confirms his worst fears and the bigotry that fosters them. Nor does the audience have any reason yet to disbelieve the version of events and portrayal of the lovers purveyed by Iago and Roderigo in the first scene. Malicious though their intentions plainly are, there's nothing to warrant our thinking that they've traduced the true characters of the couple, or that the Moor and his bride's father don't deserve the aggravation Iago's so keen to cause them.

Thus far, we've been offered no alternative view of the newly-wed lovers, who have yet to appear and whose names we have yet to learn. The names of the three men speaking about them are rapidly established, but Othello and Desdemona are not referred to by their names, which Shakespeare withholds throughout the scene. Desdemona's name is first mentioned by Othello in scene 2, and it's not until scene 3 that we hear the play's eponymous protagonist addressed as 'Othello' rather than referred to merely as 'the Moor'.

By delaying their appearance onstage and the use of their names, Shakespeare keeps the elopers at an initial remove from us as anonymous, faceless clichés. But this comedic scenario of the delinquent daughter absconding with 'a lascivious Moor' turns out to be a trap set for the audience's assumptions. The trap is sprung when they at last see and hear Othello and Desdemona for themselves. It's impossible to square the lecherous 'old black ram' reviled in scene one with the eloquent, commanding figure who strides onto the stage in scene two, superbly unfazed by Iago's news of Brabantio's fury at his elopement: 'My services, which I have done the signiory,' he assures Iago, 'Shall out-tongue his complaints' (1.2.18–19). Far from being an alien vagrant, 'an extravagant and wheeling stranger / Of here and everywhere', the Moor (at this point still unnamed) has modestly refrained from boasting of his noble birth: 'I fetch my life and being / From men of royal siege' (1.2.21–2). Above all, sating his lust for a Venetian magnifico's daughter was patently not what impelled him to elope with her: 'For know, Iago, / But that I love the gentle Desdemona / I would not my unhoused free condition / Put into circumscription and confine / For the sea's worth' (1.2.24–8). Dismissing Iago's advice that he make himself scarce, Othello insists on openly confronting his father-in-law, confident that 'My parts, my title and my perfect soul / Shall manifest me rightly' (1.2.31–2).

'But that I love the gentle Desdemona': with that line, in which her name is first heard on her husband's lips, a quite different picture begins to emerge of the daughter who 'hath made a gross revolt' by running off with a Moor. Even before she enters in the next scene, the account of their courtship by the man the Duke of Venice greets respectfully as 'Valiant Othello' (1.3.49) has undermined the first impressions of Desdemona we've received from Iago, Roderigo and Brabantio. Far from being driven to elope with Othello by a wanton 'treason of the blood' (1.1.167), by the 'drugs' he has given her (1.2.74) or by the 'spells' he has cast on her (1.3.62), Desdemona fell in love with him, we learn, through such conversation 'As soul to soul affordeth' (1.3.114), in which 'she was half the wooer' (1.3.176) and was loved by him in return. Until they met and fell in love, Desdemona had been as firmly 'opposite to marriage' (1.2.67) as Othello. When she does finally enter and speak, we're left in no doubt by Shakespeare that Othello's bride is a woman of formidable courage, intelligence, passion and resolve.

To her father's request that she declare before the assembled company to whom she most owes obedience, Desdemona replies:

> I am hitherto your daughter. But here's my husband:
> And so much duty as my mother showed
> To you, preferring you before her father,
> So much I challenge that I may profess
> Due to the Moor my lord.

$$(1.3.185-9)$$

On hearing that, Brabantio concedes defeat, but Desdemona has not finished speaking her mind. When she pleads with the Senate to let her sail with her husband to Cyprus, she does so in a fearless speech of startling frankness:

That I did love the Moor to live with him
My downright violence and scorn of fortunes
May trumpet to the world. My heart's subdued
Even to the very quality of my lord:
I saw Othello's visage in his mind,
And to his honours and his valiant parts
Did I my soul and fortunes consecrate,
So that, dear lords, if I be left behind,
A moth of peace, and he go to the war,
The rites for which I love him are bereft me,
And I a heavy interim shall support
By his dear absence.

(1.3.249–60)

The nerve required for a woman in Desdemona's position to make such a declaration in such terms in that society at that time, in the presence of her father and the men who rule her world, can hardly be overstated. All too often, however, as Bradley observes, critics have failed 'to realize how extraordinary and splendid a thing it was in a gentle Venetian girl to love Othello', how 'exceptional' she is 'in the active assertion of her own soul and will', and what a 'strange freedom and energy of spirit' she displays in loving a man branded in Venice as inferior by the colour of his skin. The 'downright violence' with which Desdemona flouts a fundamental taboo of her culture, and her 'scorn' for whatever misfortune she may incur as a result, are qualities, contends Bradley, that we expect to find 'only in a hero'. By embodying them in Desdemona and inviting us to admire the stand she takes as heroic, Shakespeare is redefining heroism as an attribute equally apparent in the actions of women.

Othello's response to Desdemona's plea to accompany him is to second it, with an assurance that his reason for doing so is not what the Senators might think:

Let her have her voice.
Vouch with me, heaven, I therefore beg it not
To please the palate of my appetite,
Nor to comply with heat, the young affects
In me defunct, and proper satisfaction,
But to be free and bounteous to her mind.

(1.3.261–6)

It's not uncommon for recent critics to read these lines as evidence of Othello's having a psychosexual hang-up about female sexuality, a fear of the physical desire fuelling Desdemona's reluctance to be denied 'The rites for which I love him'. There's no doubt that, as the drama develops, Othello's attitude to women is exposed to increasingly intense scrutiny. But it's important not to overlook the main purpose of giving Othello these lines at this moment, whatever they might also reveal about him when reread in

116

the light of later events. Othello rightly assumes that his motive for begging the Senate to grant his bride's wish will be seen by them as the satisfaction of his 'proper', authorized lust for her body as her husband. He is keen to stress, therefore, that his actual reason is his wish 'to be free and bounteous to her mind'. He's not saying, as some critics and editors have inferred, that he doesn't *want* to please the palate of his sexual appetite for his wife. Nor does he mean by 'the young affects in me defunct' that his desire for sex is dead; he just means that he's no longer as urgently driven by that desire as his younger self would have been, and thus can more easily defer its satisfaction. As soon as the couple are joyfully reunited in Cyprus, Othello makes his desire to consummate their marriage plain as they retire for the night: 'Come, my dear love, / The purchase made, the fruits are to ensue: / That profit's yet to come 'tween me and you' (2.3.8–10). What Othello's saying in effect, in his plea to the Senate, is that his wife's right to know her own mind, speak it and be heard matters *more* to him than his right to gratify his physical desire for her. To hear any man on the early modern stage being so 'free and bounteous' as to give his wife's liberty of mind priority over his prerogatives as her husband, and to take pride and pleasure in doing so, is remarkable. But for such an enlightened attitude to be so warmly espoused by a man vilified in the opening scene as 'an old black ram' and 'a lascivious Moor' is even more remarkable, and a further index of Shakespeare's estrangement from the ethos of his age.

Only a dramatist unswayed by the racial and sexual prejudices of that age could appear to reinforce them in the first scene in order to subvert them by the third. Having been led to expect a racy low comedy revolving round racial and sexual caricatures, the audience is confronted with something radically different and unforeseen: a marriage between a strong, spirited, young white woman and a dignified, cultivated, older black man; a brazenly transgressive marriage, which we are invited to admire as a freely chosen love match, founded undoubtedly on sexual attraction, but above all on mutual regard for each other's mind and personality. Othello's wish 'to be free and bounteous to her mind' chimes with Desdemona's line, 'I saw Othello's visage in his mind'. Her line likewise puts what she calls 'the very quality', or inner essence, of the beloved's character before their external physical attributes and the sexual rites of love she is so impatient to enjoy. (That the ideal love for Shakespeare is defined primarily by the lovers' mental affinity finds corroboration in the opening of Sonnet 116: 'Let me not to the marriage of true minds / Admit impediments'.) When we meet and hear Othello and Desdemona themselves, what we learn doesn't just demolish the travesty of their relationship broadcast by Iago and Roderigo. It portrays their relationship as admirable *because* it violates the racial and sexual codes that still govern most societies to this day.

Brabantio is acutely aware that there's more at stake in this disruptive union than an affront to his honour as Desdemona's father, and Shakespeare makes sure he spells it out for the Senate and for us:

Mine's not an idle cause, the duke himself
Or any of my brothers of the state,
Cannot but feel this wrong as 'twere their own.

For if such actions may have passage free
Bond-slaves and pagans shall our statesmen be.

(1.2.95–9)

If we turn a blind eye to this outrage, Brabantio protests, then we're turning our world upside down: we're treating those whom we despise as our inferiors as our equals, which means there's nothing to stop the subhuman underclass or the heathen outcasts of society taking our places as statesmen and having power over us. From his point of view Brabantio is absolutely right. His fellow senators know that, and the sole reason for their turning a blind eye is that Othello's military prowess makes him indispensable and his marriage to Desdemona a *fait accompli*, which they are obliged to countenance. One need only imagine their reaction to Desdemona's eloping with any other black foreigner, on whose services the Venetian state did not depend, to appreciate the exceptional nature of their acquiescence in this case. As Brabantio strives in vain to remind them, their toleration of this marriage strikes at the foundations of the society over which they preside, because it tacitly sanctions the assumption of equality and independence on which a white woman and a Moor have had the gall to act. That the play solicits the audience's approval of their acting on that assumption establishes its author's standpoint as the exact opposite of Brabantio's.

Shakespeare's misdirection of the audience in the opening scene in order to reverse their viewpoint and sympathies by scene three illustrates two allied features of his art first singled out for praise by Coleridge, although their joint function in *Othello* escaped him: Shakespeare's 'management of first scenes' and his exploitation of 'expectation in preference to surprise', which Coleridge deemed the prime characteristic of the dramatist's genius. *Othello* begins by undermining the expectations it arouses, because the audience must be won round at the outset to the cause of the newly-wed couple so that their fate will be seen *as* a tragedy, rather than as the price they had to pay for the liberties they took. Before the play probes the complex reasons for that tragedy, it brings the possibility of the love Othello and Desdemona discover dramatically alive and makes their right to enjoy it matter to us. To see and hear a white woman and a black man speak of each other and to each other as free individuals, drawn together as much by mutual respect as by mutual desire, is to make such a relationship feasible by making it imaginable in a world, and at a time, when for most people it would have been literally unthinkable. Fragile and fleeting though it proves to be in the racially prejudiced patriarchy of Venice, the fact that such an ideal form of love could be envisaged by Shakespeare, and its possibility made the premise of the tragedy, should be the starting point of any critical account that seeks to do justice to *Othello*.

Sinking Below Shakespeare

In *Romeo and Juliet* Shakespeare had already imagined true love as a mutually rewarding emotional bond between equals. He had put what love like that might feel like into Juliet's thrilling lines: 'My bounty is as boundless as the sea, / My love as deep; the more I give to thee, / The more I have, for both are infinite' (2.2.133–5). And in *Antony and Cleopatra*, the last of his three great tragedies of love, he would imagine another defiant 'mutual pair' (1.1.38) for whom 'There's beggary in the love that can be reckoned' (1.1.15). But in *Othello*, taking its cue perhaps from that sentence in Cinthio cited above, his imagination took a further leap beyond his time by embodying this idea of mutual love between equals in a vividly dramatized mixed-race marriage. That it could take such a leap is what sets Shakespeare's imagination apart from even the most gifted playwrights of his day. In his opening remarks on *Othello* Bradley writes: 'There is in most of the later heroes something colossal, something which reminds us of Michael Angelo's figures. They are not merely exceptional men, they are huge men; as it were, survivors of the heroic age living in a later and smaller world. … Othello is the first of these men.' Bradley captures admirably here the qualities that make Othello stand out as a hero of exceptional character and colossal stature, constrained to live at the wrong time in a world too small for him. But he gets the anachronistic aspect of Othello's plight the wrong way round, when he depicts him as a throwback to 'the heroic age' stranded in a 'later' era to which he doesn't belong. For Othello, like Hamlet before him, is a man of the future tragically marooned in an *earlier* era. His heroism consists not in his resemblance to the mighty protagonists of ancient epics, but in his loving and marrying Desdemona, whose own heroism, as Bradley observes, consists in her loving and marrying Othello. The sheer existence of their extraordinary union at such a time, and the egalitarian principles on which it is tacitly based, make Othello and Desdemona harbingers of the racially and sexually emancipated society whose advent we still await. That they are so swiftly and cruelly destroyed does nothing to lessen the subversive power of their marriage. On the contrary, it only confirms the seriousness of the threat their marriage poses – as Brabantio perceives – to the systemic inhumanity the tragedy reveals.

Nothing corroborates the amazing modernity of Shakespeare's positive portrayal of Othello and Desdemona's marriage more clearly than the critical resistance it subsequently provoked. In *A Short View of Tragedy* (1693) Thomas Rymer launched his vitriolic attack on the play for what he saw as its violation of tragic decorum and its flagrant improbability, writing it off as 'a Bloody Farce, without salt or savour'. Repugnant though his most benighted objections now sound, they retain the virtue of throwing Shakespeare's actual aims in *Othello* into sharp relief. The very title of the play makes Rymer's hackles rise, because Shakespeare 'bestows a name upon his Moor, and styles him the Moor of Venice: a Note of pre-eminence which neither History nor Heraldry can allow him'. But to allow his Moor that normally forbidden note of pre-eminence is precisely why Shakespeare gives him a name, delaying its revelation to distinguish Othello from the derogatory stereotype that initially obscures him. Shakespeare's individualizing and elevation of his black protagonist, not least through the woman he imagines him marrying, are an intolerable affront to Rymer's sense of propriety and plausibility. Just because it was the custom of Venice 'to employ Strangers in their Wars', he asks, shall a Poet thence fancy that they will set a Negro to be their General; or trust a Moor to defend them against the Turk? With us a Black-amoor might rise to be a Trumpeter; but Shakespear would not have him less than a Lieutenant-General. With us a Moor might marry some little drab, or Small-coal Wench: Shakespear, would provide him the Daughter and Heir of some great Lord, or Privy-Councillor …

Rymer finds it inconceivable that a 'Negro' could rise to the rank of general, let alone wed a woman of Desdemona's birth and status, though he might win the heart of a common prostitute ('some little drab'). He's likewise appalled by Shakespeare's thinking that a woman of Desdemona's breeding would be so distraught at the loss of a Moor's love as to cry, 'O God, Iago, / What shall I do to win my lord again?' (4.2.150–1). 'No woman bred out of a Pig-stye', comments Rymer, 'cou'd talk so meanly'. Desdemona's sexual desire for Othello renders her too vulgar, in Rymer's view, for the spectator to find her fate moving. Because it breaks the iron laws of racial, social and sexual propriety, *Othello* forfeits its credibility as a tragedy for Rymer, degenerating into exactly the kind of coarse farce its first scene leads us to expect. But the venomous intensity of Rymer's assault on the play is a testament to Shakespeare's success in making the transgressive love of Othello and Desdemona so credible, appealing and heroic *despite* the manifest unlikelihood of such a marriage in his day.

Rymer's reaction to the tragedy might be dismissed as risibly antediluvian, if the bigoted stance on race, gender and class it buttresses wasn't still so widely shared. The same goes, unfortunately, for Coleridge's revulsion, over a century later, at the thought of Desdemona in the arms of an African:

No doubt Desdemona saw Othello's visage in his mind; yet, as we are constituted, and most surely as an English audience was disposed at the beginning of the seventeenth century, it would be something monstrous to conceive this beautiful Venetian girl falling in love with a veritable negro. It would argue a disproportionateness, a want of balance, in Desdemona, which Shakespeare does not appear in the least to have contemplated.

Writing a century after Coleridge, Bradley's comment on this quotation skewers the gross misunderstanding of the play in which Coleridge's prejudice mires him:

Could any argument be more self-defeating? It actually *did* appear to Brabantio 'something monstrous to conceive' his daughter falling in love with Othello – so monstrous that he could account for her love only by drugs and foul charms. And the suggestion that such love would argue 'disproportionateness' is precisely the suggestion that Iago *did* make in Desdemona's case: 'Foh! One may smell in such a will most rank, / Foul *disproportion*, thoughts unnatural' [3.3.236–7].

In short, concludes Bradley, to adopt Coleridge's view of Desdemona's marriage to Othello is to 'regard her love, in effect, as Brabantio regarded it, and not as Shakespeare conceived it'. In a footnote he also takes Coleridge's contemporary, Charles Lamb, to task for failing to make the same vital distinction between Brabantio's and the dramatist's perception of Desdemona in *Tales from Shakespeare*: 'I cannot believe that even Lamb is true to Shakespeare in implying that Desdemona is to some degree to be condemned. What is there in the play to show that Shakespeare regarded her marriage differently from Imogen's?'

Earlier in the same footnote, however, Bradley's notorious aside on the question of Othello's colour betrays his thraldom to the same visceral bigotry that Coleridge and Lamb share with Brabantio and Iago:

> I will not discuss the further question whether, granted that to Shakespeare Othello was a black, he should be represented as a black in our theatres now. I dare say not. We do not like the real Shakespeare. We like to have his language pruned and his conceptions flattened into something that suits our mouths and minds. And even if we were prepared to make an effort, still, as Lamb observes, to imagine is one thing and to see is another. Perhaps if we saw Othello coal-black with the bodily eye, the aversion of our blood, an aversion which comes as near to being merely physical as anything human can, would overpower our imagination and sink us below not Shakespeare only but the audiences of the seventeenth and eighteenth centuries.

Unlike Coleridge and Lamb, Bradley to his credit is at least aware that 'the aversion of the blood' he'd be constrained to feel for a 'coal-black' Othello would not be what Shakespeare himself felt, but a regression to an atavistic attitude of which Bradley himself would be ashamed. And on the next page Bradley does proceed to clinch the case for viewing Desdemona's love for Othello as heroic, even if her heroism depends on Bradley's seeing the colour of Othello's skin in his mind's eye alone. But the fact remains that at the dawn of the twentieth century we find the greatest Shakespearean critic of his day still struggling to come to terms with the standpoint of 'the real Shakespeare' in *Othello*, with the 'failure to rise to Shakespeare's meaning' in his portrayal of interracial love, three hundred years after the tragedy was first performed.

It took the rest of the twentieth century for academic criticism and editions of the play to purge themselves of the flagrant and latent racial prejudice that had tainted them from Rymer onwards. It was not until the end of the last century, too, that it became inconceivable for white actors to go on playing the part of Othello with their skin bronzed or in blackface, as they had since the time of Shakespeare. This aspect of the tragedy's critical and performance history right up to the present has been amply documented elsewhere. What's been overlooked in accounts of that history of prejudice is the most important thing it tells us: that the tragedy is conceived and crafted by Shakespeare from an imaginative standpoint on race and interracial marriage four centuries ahead of his time. In this regard as in others, *Othello* testifies like *Hamlet* to the truth of Emerson's observation that Shakespeare 'is as unlike his contemporaries as he is unlike us'.

Shakespearean Tragedy

The idea of a revenge tragedy whose royal hero feels so severed from his world and himself that life, let alone revenge, becomes pointless, and the idea of a marital tragedy whose black hero and white heroine fall victim to a hostile world in which their love has no place, sprang naturally from the same creative mind. The rebellious disposition of that mind was hard-wired into Shakespearean tragedy from the start. *Titus Andronicus* affords clear proof that the elective affinity with aliens and the alienated that made Shakespeare choose a black man married to a white woman as the hero of his next tragedy after *Hamlet* had also made him choose a black man who impregnates a white queen as the charismatic anti-hero of the first tragedy he ever wrote. The taboo against such interracial liaisons appealed early on to the English stage's upstart crow, because its irrational inhumanity fired his instinctive empathy with its victims. How else could one explain those extraordinary lines he wrote for the 'hellish dog' (4.2.79) Aaron to speak not just in defence, but in praise of the fruit of his adultery with Tamora? Not content with making the otherwise heartless monster reviled by Rome as 'a barbarous Moor' (2.2.78) the play's most magnetic personality, Shakespeare makes him the spokesman for the concept of common humanity racial prejudice defiles. 'Zounds, ye whore, is black so base a hue?', he retorts, when the Nurse calls his newborn baby 'A joyless, dismal, black and sorrowful issue / ... as loathsome as a toad', unlike 'the fair-faced breeders of our clime' (4.2.68–70). For Aaron, the child is 'a beauteous blossom', his 'flesh and blood', whose 'Coal-black' colour 'scorns to bear another hue', unlike 'the fair-faced breeders' who conceal their 'white-limed' skin with cosmetics (4.2.100–2). Moreover, as he reminds the appalled Chiron and Demetrius, 'He is your brother, lords, sensibly fed / Of that self blood that first gave life to you' (4.2.124–5) in the same womb; the same mother's blood runs in his veins as in theirs, dissolving the superficial physical difference between them and what Aaron vows 'maugre all the world' to 'keep safe': the helpless, innocent human creature he calls 'this treasure in mine arms' (4.2.112, 175).

For Shakespeare, there was nothing incongruous about placing such sentiments in the mouth of a villainous Moor (whom he chose to dignify, as he did Othello, with a name). On the contrary, who better to voice them than the tragedy's 'Chief architect and plotter' (5.3.121), the remorseless scourge of a ruthless Rome, the implacable outsider who mocks and defies his foes to the end? As the villain of the piece, Aaron could hardly be more different in obvious respects from his noble fellow Moor, Othello, being cut from the same cloth as Richard III and Othello's nemesis, Iago. But as the proud black father of a beautiful black baby born of a white mother, a mixed-race child of whom he declares, as he cradles him in his arms, 'This before all the world do I prefer' (4.2.111), he embodies the same ideal that the tragedy of *Othello* seeks to vindicate.

True Colours

Othello vindicates the utopian ideal that informs it by arraigning the forces that conspire to destroy the couple whose love threatens to make that ideal a reality. Shakespeare makes it clear from the start that it's not just Iago the newly-weds are up against, but a deep-rooted power-structure, and a concomitant view of the world, which Iago epitomizes in its most virulent form. It's not only Iago whose speech is infected with the vile racial abuse of 'the Moor' he vents in the first scene to goad Brabantio: 'you'll have your daughter covered with a Barbary horse; you'll have your nephews neigh to you, you'll have coursers for cousins and jennets for germans!' (1.1.109–12). Roderigo calls Othello 'the thicklips' (1.1.65), turning into a racist sneer the feature employed by Aaron as an affectionate epithet for his son: 'Come on, you thick-lipped slave, I'll bear you hence' (*TA* 4.2.177). On learning that Roderigo is one of the men whose 'terrible summons' (1.1.81) has shattered his sleep, Brabantio reminds him that he's been banned from hanging around Brabantio's house in the hope of wooing Desdemona: 'In honest plainness thou hast heard me say / My daughter is not for thee' (1.1.96–7). But moments later, having been convinced by Roderigo of Desdemona's 'gross revolt' (1.1.132) in marrying 'the Moor' (1.1.162), Brabantio exclaims, 'O, would you had had her!' (1.1.173). The man hitherto forbidden to court his daughter suddenly becomes 'good Roderigo' (1.1.181), because he at least has the virtue of being white.

It's Brabantio the Venetian senator, not the ensign Iago, who's the most vocal and persistent in his hostility to Othello on racial grounds, and to Othello's face:

> Damned as thou art, thou hast enchanted her,
> For I'll refer me to all things of sense,
> If she in chains of magic were not bound,
> Whether a maid so tender, fair and happy,
> So opposite to marriage that she shunned
> The wealthy, curled darlings of our nation,
> Would ever have, t'incur a general mock,
> Run from her guardage to the sooty bosom
> Of such a thing as thou?
>
> (1.2.63–71)

For Brabantio, it's incomprehensible that Desdemona would choose of her own free will to reject the most eligible bachelors of her own colour and class in favour of marriage to 'such a thing' as a Moor, making herself the butt of public ridicule. The only explanation, as he says in his appeal to the Senate, is that

> She is abused, stolen from me and corrupted
> By spells and medicines bought of mountebanks,
> For nature so preposterously to err
> Being not deficient, blind, or lame of sense,
> Sans witchcraft could not.
>
> (1.3.61–5)

No white woman in her right mind, in other words, who could see Othello's 'sooty' skin with her own eyes, would be capable of doing something so unnatural, unless she'd been bewitched. Brabantio harps obsessively on this idea:

>   ... and she, in spite of nature,
> Of years, of country, credit, everything,
> To fall in love with what she feared to look on?
> It is a judgement maimed and most imperfect
> That will confess perfection so could err
> Against all rules of nature, and must be driven
> To find out practices of cunning hell
> Why this should be.

>   (1.3.97–104)

Through Brabantio, Shakespeare gives full rein to the racist mindset at its most blinkered and toxic. His immediate dramatic purpose in doing so is plain. The cumulative pressure of the charges Brabantio levels at Othello makes Othello's patient, eloquent rebuttal of them, followed by Desdemona's dignified assertion of her autonomy, all the more impressive. Brabantio's bigoted reasoning and hysterical allegations are no match for the ethical integrity and rhetorical intelligence of Othello, who adroitly refutes the allegations on Brabantio's own terms. Promising to reveal 'what drugs, what charms, / What conjuration and what mighty magic' (1.3.92–3) he did indeed employ to win Desdemona, he explains that telling her the enthralling story of his life was the only kind of witchcraft that he used. In response to his daughter's testimony Brabantio can say nothing but 'Come hither, Moor: / I here do give thee that with all my heart / Which, but thou hast already, with all my heart / I would keep from thee' (1.3.193–7).

But Brabantio's tirades also establish that the racist mentality is not confined to the embittered ensign bent on revenge, but typical of the ruling elite of Venice as well. It's shared not only by Brabantio and Roderigo, but by the Duke of Venice himself. 'I think this tale would win my daughter too' (1.3.172), says the Duke, when Othello finishes delivering the 'round unvarnished tale' (1.3.91) of his courtship. But his attempts to appease Brabantio cut no ice, because Desdemona's father knows, as does the audience since the opening of this scene, that the Duke's mollifying platitudes are motivated by the Senate's overriding need for Othello to defend Cyprus against the Turks. As he bids the company goodnight, the couplet the Duke directs at Brabantio betrays his true attitude to the colour of Othello's skin, masquerading as a punning compliment: 'If virtue no delighted beauty lack / Your son-in-law is far more fair than black' (1.3.290–1); the Moor's sterling qualities as a man and a soldier, in other words, more than make up for the unfortunate fact of his blackness.

So endemic to Venetian culture are such attitudes that even Othello and Desdemona can't help being infected by them. That the survival of their marriage must contend not just with overt prejudice of the kind Brabantio and Iago voice, but with their own unconscious absorption of racist assumptions, is one of Shakespeare's most profound psychological insights in *Othello*. When Desdemona declares, before her father and the Senate, 'I saw Othello's visage in his mind', the context makes it clear that she's defending him, and her love for him, against the sole reason for her father's objection to her marriage. But in stating that Othello's mind, not his face, was what attracted her, that she looked through his colour to his character, Desdemona can't help validating the reason for her father's objection, just as the Duke does when he says, 'Your son-in-law is far more fair than black'. What makes her brave declaration so poignant is her blindness to the unintended insult it implies.

The first hint that Othello has internalized the Venetian view of his colour surfaces much later, as fear of Desdemona's infidelity begins to grip him: 'Nor from mine own weak merits will I draw / The smallest fear or doubt of her revolt', he tells Iago, 'For she had eyes and chose me' (3.3.190–2). She chose him, he implies, in spite of his colour, which he regards now as a defect from Desdemona's point of view. Shortly afterwards, subliminally prompted by Iago's reminder that Desdemona 'did deceive her father, marrying you' (3.3.209), Othello volunteers Brabantio's belief that her doing so was unnatural as a reason for doubting her fidelity: 'And yet how nature, erring from itself – ', he begins, giving Iago the perfect opening to cut in with 'Ay, there's the point' and hammer that line of reasoning home (3.3.231–42). Left to reflect on his dilemma after Iago's exit, Othello reviews the possible causes of his wife's betraying him, and puts the first one that springs to mind bluntly:

> Haply for I am black
> And have not those soft parts of conversation
> That chamberers have, or for I am declined
> Into the vale of years – yet that's not much –
> She's gone, I am abused, and my relief
> Must be to loathe her.

> (3.3.267–72)

The striking thing is the speed with which, under pressure from Iago's insinuations, Othello resorts to seeing and judging himself and his relationship with Desdemona through white Venetian eyes and in white Venetian terms, because those terms make sense to him. Just how deeply he has absorbed the entrenched prejudice that surrounds him becomes clear when he employs his complexion as a derogatory simile for his wife's alleged depravity: 'Her name, that was as fresh / As Dian's visage, is now begrimed and black / As mine own face' (3.3.389–91). The contrast with Aaron's truculent embrace of the same simile in *Titus* is instructive: 'Let fools do good and fair men call for grace, / Aaron will have his soul black like his face' (3.1.205–6).

The Green-Eyed Monster

The grounds of the tragedy can't be fully explained, however, by pointing to the racism that pollutes the Venetian view of Othello and even Othello's view of himself. The colour of Othello's skin is obviously a crucial factor in his downfall. His visibly alien racial identity makes him and his bride far more vulnerable to the machinations of Iago than they would have been, if Othello had been an equally noble, accomplished and indispensable white Venetian. If Desdemona had married any man 'Of her own clime, complexion and degree' (3.3.234), Iago could have planted no seeds of doubt about her fidelity in her spouse by calling her deceitful and her love unnatural, since there would have been no need to deceive her father by eloping and no talk of nature having erred from itself. Breaking Venice's unwritten law against mixed-race marriage locks Desdemona and Othello from the outset into a defensive posture, which predisposes Othello to the insecurity and suspicion that grip him so quickly at Iago's prompting. But Othello's susceptibility to misprision as a black outsider, who unconsciously endorses the white perception of his colour, is inseparable from his susceptibility as a man to misogynistic attitudes to women, sex and marriage that are as normal in Venice as racism, and that play an equally decisive part in sealing Desdemona's fate and his own.

Far from being an exceptional emotional disorder to which Othello is prone to succumb, sexual jealousy is shown to be ubiquitous in Venice. Roderigo's infatuation with Desdemona makes him jealous not only of Othello but also of Cassio. Well before Iago sets about making Othello suspect his wife with Cassio and ultimately murder her, he has no trouble persuading his 'sick fool, Roderigo, / Whom love hath turned almost the wrong side out' (2.3.48–9) that 'Desdemona is directly in love' (2.1.217) with her husband's lieutenant, and that Roderigo should undertake to murder him. The same emotion flares up in Bianca too, when Cassio gives her Desdemona's handkerchief to copy:

BIANCA
    O Cassio, whence came this?
    This is some token from a newer friend!
    To the felt absence now I feel a cause:
    Is't come to this? Well, well.
CASSIO   Go to woman,
    Throw your vile guesses in the devil's teeth
    From whence you have them! You are jealous now
    That this is from some mistress, some remembrance:
    No, by my faith, Bianca.

                                         (3.4.180–7)

Unconvinced by Cassio's denial, Bianca returns in the next scene to berate him again about the handkerchief. Its possession by Cassio she construes, like Othello as he watches them, as proof of his sexual intimacy with another woman:

What did you mean by that same handkerchief you gave me even now? I was a fine fool to take it – I must take out the work! A likely piece of work, that you should find it in your chamber and know not who left it there! This is some minx's token, and I must take out the work? There, give it your hobby-horse; wheresoever you had it, I'll take out no work on't!

                                         (4.1.147–54)

Above all, Iago displays the same contagious disposition, when he fastens automatically on sexual jealousy as a pretext for provoking it in Othello to get revenge on him and Cassio:

> I hate the Moor
> And it is thought abroad that 'twixt my sheets
> He's done my office. I know not if 't be true,
> But I for mere suspicion in that kind
> Will do as if for surety. He holds me well,
> The better shall my purpose work on him.
> Cassio's a proper man: let me see now,
> To get his place, and to plume up my will
> In double knavery. How? How? Let's see:
> After some time to abuse Othello's ear
> That he is too familiar with his wife.

(1.3.385–95)

By the end of the first scene of Act 2, Iago's 'mere suspicion in that kind' has grown stronger and spread to encompass Cassio, whom he says that he fears might be cuckolding him too. He confides to the audience that he desires Desdemona himself, not just to gratify his lust for her,

> But partly led to diet my revenge,
> For that I do suspect the lusty Moor
> Hath leaped into my seat, the thought whereof
> Doth like a poisonous mineral gnaw my inwards …
> And nothing can or shall content my soul
> Till I am evened with him, wife for wife …
> Or, failing so, yet that I put the Moor
> At least into a jealousy so strong
> That judgement cannot cure; which thing to do,
> If this poor trash of Venice, whom I trash
> For his quick hunting, stand the putting on,
> I'll have our Michael Cassio on the hip,
> Abuse him to the Moor in the rank garb –
> For I fear Cassio with my night-cap too –

(2.1.292–305)

One might be forgiven at this point for thinking that Iago's suspicion of 'the lusty Moor' is a motive invented to justify – to himself and us – the intensity of his hatred of Othello and his craving for revenge. But two acts later Emilia provides independent corroboration of her husband's having previously harboured such fears, because of its being 'thought abroad' to be the case. After Othello has called her mistress a whore, the outraged Emilia shrewdly concludes that 'The Moor's abused by some most villainous knave, / Some base notorious knave, some scurvy fellow' (4.2.141–2), unaware that the 'scurvy fellow' is her own spouse. Hearing this, and alarmed lest her outburst be overheard, Iago commands Emilia to be quiet, but she rounds on him instead: 'Some such squire he was / That turned your wit the seamy side without / And made you to suspect me with the Moor' (4.2.147–9). So Iago has been infected by the same vile slur with which he has infected Othello, and possibly by 'Some busy and insinuating rogue' (4.2.133) like himself. His stating as a fact, not a fear, that '*it is thought abroad* that 'twixt my sheets / He's done my office' lends credence to that possibility. It also evinces in Iago a sensitivity to how others see him, which is at odds with his mockery of reputation as 'an idle and most false imposition' (2.3.264–5) and in line with Othello's dread of being 'The fixed figure for the time of scorn / To point his slow and moving finger at' (4.2.55–6). Whether Iago's fear that he's been cuckolded by Othello is the product of his own diseased imagination or another's, what matters is the readiness with which it springs to his mind as a convincing motive for revenge and the readiness to be *made* jealous that he shares with Othello.

Neither Roderigo nor Bianca nor Iago becomes as fatally consumed by jealousy as Othello, but all of them fall prey like him to 'the green-eyed monster' (3.3.168) that stalks any society where the sexual desire of one human being is regarded as the property of another. To ensnare Othello and Desdemona and Cassio, Iago exploits a habit of mind and a mode of behaviour that are symptomatic of the patriarchal culture they inhabit. The play dramatizes the tragic impossibility of fulfilling the potential the couple's love possesses to transcend that culture and the misogynistic mentality it cultivates in men and women. It's no accident that both Othello and Desdemona are portrayed as having been averse to marrying before they fell in love. For from the moment they are married, the 'unhoused free condition' they both cherished is indeed 'Put into circumscription and confine' by the gender roles, power relations and propensities built into the institution of wedlock. In the first moments of their marriage after their elopement Desdemona pleads to be allowed to do what she desires to do for her own sake and Othello endorses her plea, as we've seen, because he wishes first and foremost 'to be free and bounteous to her mind'. Lest there be any doubt about the sincerity of that wish and Othello's capacity to prove the man a woman like Desdemona deserves, Iago himself is the first to dispel it. He is forced to admit in his first soliloquy that 'The Moor is of a free and open nature' (1.3.398), and obliged to admit in his second that:

> The Moor, howbeit that I endure him not,
> Is of a constant, loving, noble nature,
> And I dare think he'll prove to Desdemona
> A most dear husband.

(2.1.286–9)

What stops Othello proving a most dear husband, who goes on being free and bounteous to his wife's mind, and twists him instead into her deluded killer, is a syndrome to which they both succumb, and to which they could have succumbed in such a culture without Iago's intervention.

Who Hath Done This Deed?

Before Iago begins to turn Othello against his bride, Shakespeare gives us another glimpse of the Desdemona who belies her father's image of her as 'A maiden never bold, / Of spirit so still and quiet that her motion / Blushed at herself' (1.3.95–7): the Desdemona whose 'downright violence and scorn of fortunes' have trumpeted her love for the Moor to the world, and whose desire to perform the rites for which she loves him will not be denied; the feisty Desdemona fated to be displaced by the travesty of herself she shrinks into: the innocent, angelic wife maligned and murdered by a jealous husband, whom she nobly refuses to blame for killing her. Critics wedded to this idealized image of Desdemona as love's martyr find it difficult to square with the woman who engages in racy repartee with Iago on her arrival in Cyprus, and who proves herself a match for him. The exchange rarely receives the attention it deserves. But it's there for a good reason, which is to show Desdemona uninhibited by paternal constraints, civic authorities or the will of her husband, with whom she's waiting to be reunited. In this breathing space before her life as Othello's wife begins in earnest, she is still 'our great captain's captain' (2.1.74), in command of herself and the situation, free to pass the time in a ribald battle of wits. This playfully combative side of Desdemona, whose adroit parries bring the ripostes of Beatrice and Rosalind to mind, underscores the cost of her impending surrender to the role of demure, submissive wife.

Indeed, it's Desdemona who initiates the battle of wits with the man secretly intent on destroying her husband by vilifying her. After greeting her, Cassio welcomes Iago, then turns to welcome Emilia with a kiss, asking her husband to excuse 'this bold show of courtesy' (2.1.99) to his wife. Such a brazen liberty in public on Cassio's part lends colour to Iago's claim at the end of the scene that he fears Cassio with his nightcap too. The tenor and tone of his retort to Cassio certainly suggest that the thought of Emilia's sexual intimacy with the suave Florentine, whom Othello has just promoted instead of him, is itching to cross the embittered ancient's mind: 'Sir, would she give you so much of her lips / As of her tongue she oft bestows on me / You'd have enough' (2.1.100–2). Iago's coarse quip at his wife's expense accuses her of nagging, with a quibble that reduces her to the butt of a lewd joke between men. That prompts Desdemona to jump to Emilia's defence by protesting 'Alas! She has no speech' (2.1.102), which triggers the ensuing skirmish with Iago about the character of women, and married women in particular.

Throughout the exchange Desdemona does more than take Iago's salty innuendos in her stride and in good humour. Intermittently abetted by Emilia, she colludes in his gibes at her sex by reacting to them with mock outrage or cueing them with questions. When Iago charges both women with being 'Players in your housewifery, and housewives in / Your beds!', Desdemona exclaims in feigned reproof, 'O, fie upon thee, slanderer!'. 'Nay, it is true,' replies Iago, 'or else I am a Turk: / You rise to play, and go to bed to work' (2.1.112–13). Another cynical couplet from Iago about the fairer sex – 'She never yet was foolish that was fair, / For even her folly helped her to an heir' (2.1.136–7) – provokes the following:

DESDEMONA

> These are old fond paradoxes to make fools laugh i'th' alehouse. What miserable praise hast thou for her that's foul and foolish?

IAGO

> There's none so foul, and foolish thereunto,
> But does foul pranks which fair and wise ones do.

DESDEMONA

> O heavy ignorance, thou praisest the worst best. But what praise couldst thou bestow on a deserving woman indeed? One that in the authority of her merit did justly put on the vouch of very malice itself?

$$(2.1.138–47)$$

In the unlikely event of such a virtuous woman existing, Iago replies, she'd be good for nothing but 'To suckle fools, and chronicle small beer' (2.1.160). 'O, most lame and impotent conclusion!', exclaims Desdemona. 'Do not learn of him, Emilia, though he be thy husband. How say you, Cassio, is he not a most profane and liberal counsellor?' (2.1.160–4).

Throughout this bout of risqué badinage the pleasure Desdemona takes in her double-act with Iago is palpable. The pleasure lies in the licence it gives her to play the part of a woman scandalized and unswayed by Iago's misogynistic saws, his 'old fond paradoxes', while relishing her ironic detachment from the whole scenario and her performance in it. (That it's a conscious performance she makes clear by saying at one point, as if aside, 'I am not merry, but I do beguile / The thing I am by seeming otherwise' (2.1.122–4).) Our perception of Desdemona's capacity for self-detachment is essential to our tragic sense of her potential to be someone other than the woman she is fated to die as. It would be a mistake to take this passage at face value as a frivolous diversion, which fills the time until Othello appears, safe and sound, and the newly-weds are reunited. Ostensibly idle banter in Shakespearean tragedy usually transpires on closer inspection to be anything but idle; humorous digressions that seem to serve no purpose other than to lighten the mood with sprightly backchat and sportive wordplay turn out to have covertly tuned our attention to more serious matters.

Desdemona's impromptu verbal duel with Iago reveals a deeper irony at work of which she is unaware, and from which her ironic stance cannot protect her. As she genially quashes or deflects Iago's slurs on her sex, she is still poised on the threshold of marital reality, still free to speak her mind and express her personality for as long as this extemporal interval lasts. At the same time, she can't help doing so on the misogynistic and misogamous terms dictated by Iago, who sets the agenda for their dialogue. Iago's scurrilous portrayal of wives and women in general as lustful, devious shrews and the bane of men's lives is as old as patriarchy and as intrinsic to the play's Venetian world as racial prejudice. So inveterate are the views he rehashes that they've acquired proverbial force, as the couplets they are couched in suggest. In the very act of eliciting them from Iago expressly to dismiss them as twaddle, Desdemona concedes their force and protracts their sway over her sex. Such is the power of the misogynistic assumptions underpinning this exchange that even a woman of Desdemona's mettle can't keep them at bay when her husband begins to act on them and the pressure to conform to female stereotypes proves too strong.

Before that happens, the couple are allowed a moment of mutual delight as they are reunited. The moment is clouded, however, by Othello's sense of foreboding:

> If it were now to die
> 'Twere now to be most happy, for I fear
> My soul hath her content so absolute
> That not another comfort like to this
> Succeeds in unknown fate.

(2.1.187–91)

'The heavens forbid / But that our loves and comforts should increase / Even as our days do grow' (2.191–3), says Desdemona. But that prospect of the fulfilling life she should have been left to live with Othello vanishes as the virus of suspicion infects him and he mutates into the jealous older husband of a vivacious younger wife. That transmutation, triggered by Iago, is matched by a corresponding metamorphosis in Desdemona. It begins with her resolving to become, on Cassio's behalf, the archetypal nagging wife Iago had accused Emilia of being:

> My lord shall never rest,
> I'll watch him tame and talk him out of patience,
> His bed shall seem a school, his board a shrift,
> I'll intermingle everything he does
> With Cassio's suit …

(3.3.22–6)

Although the tone of this declaration is jocular, Desdemona is as good as her word. She pleads with Othello for Cassio's reinstatement, badgering him to fix a time as soon as possible to heal the breach: 'Why then, tomorrow night, or Tuesday morn; / On Tuesday, noon or night; on Wednesday morn! / I prithee name the time, but let it not / Exceed three days' (3.3.60–3). She continues to plague him in the same vein for another twenty lines, even after he has capitulated and said, 'Let him come when he will, / I will deny thee nothing' (3.3.75–6).

Nor does she let up in the following scene, despite the fierce interrogation about the missing handkerchief to which Othello subjects her. At first she prevaricates, saying 'I have it not about me' (3.4.55). Then, worn down by his cross-questioning and warned that its loss would mean 'such perdition / As nothing else could match' (3.4.69–70), she is driven to lie: 'I say it is not lost' (3.4.86). When Othello challenges her to prove it by fetching the handkerchief forthwith, she aggravates the situation by refusing and accusing him of diverting her from pleading Cassio's cause:

Why, so I can, sir; but I will not now.
This is a trick to put me from my suit.
Pray you, let Cassio be received again.

(3.4.88–90)

Deaf to Othello's thrice-repeated demand that she produce the handkerchief, Desdemona remains intransigent. She persists in pleading for Cassio in the face of Othello's mounting anger, until her charge that the fault lies with him – 'I' faith, you are to blame' (3.4.98) – proves too much for Othello and he storms off with an oath. As Bradley observes, 'these moments are fatal to Desdemona, who acts precisely as if she were guilty'. She acts, that is, precisely as an unfaithful, shrewish wife would be expected to act, when caught by her husband in a lie told to mask her affair with a lover she's obsessed with. That role has been lying in wait for Desdemona from the moment she married Othello, just as it would have been lying in wait for her whoever she had married, because it's built into the marital culture of her society.

So is the final stock role to which Desdemona resigns herself after Othello's physical and verbal abuse of her has escalated beyond control and her protestations of innocence have proved futile. As the part of chaste, unjustly traduced wife takes hold of her, she is overcome by a mood of listless fatalism. 'Faith, half asleep' (4.2.99), she replies, as if she's slipped into a trance, when Emilia asks how she is after Othello's most vicious diatribe. Yet she retains a subconscious awareness of the disjunction between herself and the persona being forced upon her, as the ensuing strange exchange makes apparent:

EMILIA
Good madam, what's the matter with my lord?
DESDEMONA
With whom?
EMILIA
Why, with my lord, madam.
DESDEMONA
Who is thy lord?
EMILIA
He that is yours, sweet lady.
DESDEMONA
I have none. Do not talk to me, Emilia;
I cannot weep, nor answers have I none
But what should go by water. Prithee, tonight
Lay on my bed my wedding sheets; remember,
And call thy husband hither.
EMILIA
Here's a change indeed!   *Exit.*

DESDEMONA

   'Tis meet I should be used so, very meet.
   How have I been behaved that he might stick
   The small'st opinion on my greatest misuse?

(4.2.100–11)

'I have none': with that extraordinary statement Desdemona moves into a space where she no longer recognizes or defines herself as Othello's or any man's wife. In her state of abjection she paradoxically regains possession of the self she surrendered in marriage. It's only for a moment, but it's long enough to charge her plight with the poignant sense of unrealized possibility that makes it tragic. The request for her wedding sheets to be laid on her bed locks her back into her identity and duties as a bride. But the meaning of what should have been a joyous nuptial rite has changed irrevocably, as Emilia's exclamation emphasizes. It was not uncommon in Shakespeare's day for wives to be buried in their wedding sheets, which here portend the winding sheets they are fated to become.

Desdemona's brief soliloquy after Emilia's exit is especially intriguing. Left to reflect in the hearing of the audience alone, she begins by voicing her sense of the injustice of being so abused by Othello. At least, one assumes that when she says, "'Tis meet I should be used so, very meet', the context demands that the line be understood as bitterly ironic, as meaning the reverse of its literal meaning. But, bearing in mind Bradley's observation that at times Desdemona 'acts precisely as if she were guilty', the literal meaning is not to be discounted, not least because the line's ironic effect requires that it be heard. The ambiguity is apt, for it captures Desdemona's obscure feeling that the fate overtaking her is both just and unjust. This confused sense of being at once innocent and culpable is articulated again in the question she asks in the next two lines. It's tempting to smooth its knotted diction out to produce a paraphrase that chimes with an unambiguous reading of the previous line: 'How can my behaviour have given him the slightest reason to accuse me of such gross misconduct?' But the temptation should be resisted, because the question's worded as it is for a purpose. Instead of 'How have I behaved', Desdemona says, 'How have I *been* behaved', fusing the active with the passive voice in an awkward locution. Normal usage is distorted to capture Desdemona's sense of being both the active cause of her behaviour and the passive victim of behaviour forced upon her. The Quarto's wording in the last line compounds this baffled apprehension of culpable innocence. The thrust of the rhetorical question the line completes seems to be that she is guiltless, because she has done nothing to deserve the charge Othello has levelled at her. But as a rhetorical question it also runs the risk of being taken literally and inviting the answer it does not expect. The Folio's amendment of 'my greatest misuse' to 'my *least* misuse' produces a more comfortably coherent reading of the last line in one respect, but it doesn't dispose of the misconduct on her part the line concedes or the ambiguity of the rhetorical question.

Desdemona is objectively innocent of what Othello has been led to accuse her of doing. But she has 'been behaved' by internalized forces beyond her conscious control into speaking and feeling *as if she were* a wife guilty of the 'greatest misuse'. A few moments after her three-line soliloquy, Iago enters with Emilia, who tells him how Othello 'hath so bewhored' her mistress 'That true hearts cannot bear it', prompting Desdemona to ask, 'Am I that name, Iago?' (4.2.117, 119–20), as if she were no longer sure whether she deserved to be called a whore or not. What Shakespeare is dramatizing here is the insidious process by which Desdemona is drawn into complicity with the parts she's been cast by Iago to play in Othello's credulous eyes. This unknowing acquiescence in the expectations of her patriarchal world Desdemona is ultimately powerless to resist. Hence the strange, hypnotic state in which she identifies with her mother's maid, Barbary, whose lover 'proved mad / And did forsake her' (4.3.25–6), and whose wistful 'song of "willow"' (4.3.26) she sings, adding this telling line of her own: 'Let nobody blame him, his scorn I approve' (4.3.51). With that veiled refusal to lay the blame on Othello and that veiled approval of the abuse to which he has subjected her, Desdemona's transformation from the woman who once scorned fortune with downright violence into the epitome of the meek, self-sacrificing, saintly wife is almost complete.

It becomes complete with the last words she utters before she dies. 'O sweet mistress, speak!', begs the distraught Emilia, after hearing Desdemona's cry 'O falsely, falsely murdered!'. 'A guiltless death I die', replies her mistress. 'O who hath done / This deed?', asks Emilia, to which Desdemona responds cryptically, 'Nobody. I myself', followed by 'Farewell. / Commend me to my kind lord. O, farewell!' (5.2.115, 120–3). She dies declaring herself the innocent victim of a murderer, whose identity she refuses to divulge. Instead, she first blames 'Nobody' and then blames herself in a final act of selfless devotion to her 'kind lord'. Neither of the candidates Desdemona names as her killer makes literal sense, but they both make figurative sense on the play's understanding of its heroine. For insofar as Desdemona's compliance with stereotypical gender roles has been instrumental in forging her fate, she could be regarded as an accomplice in her own murder, and in that sense of having 'done / This deed' herself. Yet insofar as her complicity is the product of unconscious conditioning as potent as that which overpowers Othello and makes him kill against his will, it's also true that 'Nobody' has 'done / This deed', in the sense that no one can be held *solely* responsible for a murder which an entire society has conspired with the killer to commit.

The Tragedy of the Handkerchief

The same intimation that the mainspring of Desdemona's murder, and thus of the tragedy, lies deeper than moralism can explain finds expression in Othello's equally enigmatic words as he gazes upon the sleeping figure of the wife he's about to kill:

> It is the cause, it is the cause, my soul!
> Let me not name it to you, you chaste stars,
> It is the cause. Yet I'll not shed her blood
> Nor scar that whiter skin of hers than snow

And smooth as monumental alabaster:
Yet she must die, else she'll betray more men.

(5.2.1–6)

Othello's reluctance to name the cause to the 'chaste stars' suggests that the unspeakable cause is Desdemona's supposed adultery, the antithesis of the chastity figured by 'that whiter skin of hers than snow / And smooth as monumental alabaster'. But that suggestion is preceded and followed by the thrice-repeated statement 'It is the cause', whose wording obscures both the nature of the cause and what the cause is of. The wording can be accounted for psychologically up to a point by Othello's unwillingness to state explicitly what he is about to do and why. But the emphatic repetition of this puzzling, impersonal statement right at the start of the soliloquy reflects Shakespeare's recognition that the fundamental cause of the tragic catastrophe is more complex than anything the characters embroiled in it can fathom. 'It is the cause, it is the cause' should prompt *us* to ask ourselves 'What is the cause?' and seek it beyond the simplistic assignment of blame to Othello's 'tragic flaw' or Iago's 'motiveless malignity' that turns the tragedy into a trite morality play.

Shakespeare is at pains throughout *Othello* to reveal the extent to which the emotions, thoughts and deeds of the protagonists are covertly governed to their detriment by cultural prescriptions they did not create. Iago's duping of Othello and Othello's murder of Desdemona would be inconceivable without the collusion of all three in a scenario dictated by the iniquitous nature of marriage in an oppressive patriarchal society. The obsessive early modern dread of cuckoldry that pervades the play is the inexorable outcome of the wife's sexual desire being subjugated to the will of her husband, whose standing as a man depends on his retaining exclusive possession of her body. Sexual jealousy within marriage in any age is hardly a male preserve, but the predisposition to such jealousy in men is inevitably stronger and more prevalent in patriarchies where so much is perceived to be at stake for the husband in the fidelity of his wife. Thus, when Othello first gives full vent in private to his fear that Desdemona may have betrayed him with Cassio, his marital predicament is conceived as typical and inevitable rather than a misfortune peculiar to him:

O curse of marriage
That we can call these delicate creatures ours
And not their appetites! I had rather be a toad
And live upon the vapour of a dungeon
Than keep a corner in the thing I love
For others' uses. Yet 'tis the plague of great ones,
Prerogatived are they less than the base;
'Tis destiny unshunnable, like death –
Even then this forked plague is fated to us
When we do quicken.

(3.3.272–81)

Once he's almost certain of Desdemona's infidelity, wanting only 'the ocular proof' (3.3.62), Othello feels his entire life disintegrating as the foundation of his identity, authority and status as a man is shattered: 'O now for ever / Farewell the tranquil mind, farewell content! / Farewell the plumed troops and the big wars / That makes ambition virtue! … Farewell: Othello's occupation's gone' (3.3.350–3). That's why the broader reason he adduces for killing his wife is 'Yet she must die, else she'll betray more men'. He portrays himself outrageously as executing Desdemona on behalf of his sex, as his sad duty to his gender, in order to justify a death unjustifiable on any grounds. That warped logic reveals the underlying rationale of such murders, which is to reassert by violence the dominion of men over women that female infidelity, whether real or imagined, threatens to subvert.

To recognize how much is riding for Othello on his wife's sexual fidelity is to understand the function and significance of the handkerchief in Shakespeare's dramatization of Cinthio's tale. Rymer notoriously failed to grasp why Shakespeare made Othello set such store by something so trivial.

> So much ado, so much stress, so much passion and repetition about an Handkerchief! Why was this not call'd the *Tragedy of the Handkerchief*? … Had it been *Desdemona*'s Garter, the Sagacious Moor might have smelt a Rat: but the Handkerchief is so remote a trifle, no Booby, on this side *Mauritania*, cou'd make any consequence from it.

For Othello, however, the 'handkerchief / Spotted with strawberries' (3.3.437–8) furnishes the requisite 'ocular proof' of Desdemona's adultery, when he sees Bianca thrust it back into Cassio's hand. As its pattern suggests, it symbolizes nothing less than the gift of her virginity in marriage, and her subsequent faithfulness, to her husband. Desdemona's exclusive possession of the handkerchief is Othello's guarantee of his exclusive sexual possession of her. By the same token, its manifest possession by Cassio turns it for Othello into material evidence of Desdemona's adultery. As Othello belatedly warns her, to give the handkerchief away would spell the doom of their relationship, because 'there's magic in the web of it' (3.4.71). An Egyptian sibyl, he explains, 'In her prophetic fury sewed the work' and gave it to his mother to 'subdue [his] father / Entirely to her love', provided that 'she kept it'; otherwise his father 'Should hold her loathed and his spirits should hunt / After new fancies' (3.4.60–2, 64–5, 74). Othello's mother gave him the handkerchief in turn to give to his wife, on the same understanding that his love for her depended on her keeping it.

There is indeed 'some wonder in this handkerchief' (3.4.102), as Desdemona says after Othello has assailed her with demands that she produce it. But its true wondrous quality consists in its being a perfect symbol of the sexual injustice of marriage on men's terms. As such it gives tangible form to the otherwise intangible emotions of fear and mistrust, resentment and insecurity, that marriage on such terms entails. As Kenneth Burke observes in his essay on *Othello*, the handkerchief is 'charged with fatal implications' by the assumption that wives by their nature are disposed to stray and must be bridled by threats. Its very triviality as a flimsy piece of cloth, too 'remote a trifle' for Rymer to take seriously, makes it an apt symbol, too, of the fragility of marriage blighted by male fears of female sexuality. When Othello collapses in an epileptic fit, crying 'Handkerchief! Confessions! Handkerchief!' (4.1.37), the pathos of his breakdown is inseparable from the bathos of his being felled by a square of fabric as insubstantial as the inference he draws from its absence. 'It is not words that shakes me thus' (4.1.41–2), he insists as he falls into a catatonic trance, triggered precisely by the words he is uttering at Iago's instigation, and especially by the word 'handkerchief'. As we saw in *Romeo and Juliet*, Shakespeare was acutely aware of the despotic power of words to determine one's fate because of what they connote. So powerful can certain words become that being in thrall to them is tantamount to being entranced, because both states entail a loss of consciousness and agency. Othello's seizure bears physical witness to his intolerable mental pain at this moment, but it's also a theatrically compelling metaphor for his possession by the stock persona of homicidally jealous husband.

'Thus credulous fools are caught,' observes Iago with satisfaction as Othello lies paralyzed before him, 'And many worthy and chaste dames even thus, / All guiltless, meet reproach' (4.1.45–7). By 'Thus' and 'even thus' he means in effect: by the susceptibility of husbands and wives to the power of a narrative hard-wired into their minds. Note that Iago's observation is couched impersonally in the plural. He's savouring the plight of Othello and Desdemona as one widely shared by other husbands and wives, not as an exceptional fate brought upon them by a psychological defect peculiar to Othello, which Iago was uniquely equipped to exploit. It's understood that any number of married couples have fallen foul, and will go on falling foul, of groundless male sexual jealousy, with or without the malign intervention of a third party such as Iago. The systemic matrix of the tragedy is physically enshrined in the handkerchief and subtly underscored by its passage through the play. The 'antique token' (5.2.214) of marital fidelity began its journey in the possession of Othello's mother, who gave it to Othello, who gives it to Desdemona, from whom it passes to Emilia, and then to Iago, through whom Cassio acquires it and gives it to his mistress, Bianca, who gives it back to Cassio. As it passes through the hands of the three couples, it ties them all together as bound by the same sexist spell, by the misogynistic magic in the web of it. 'I have a thing for you' says Emilia to Iago, meaning the handkerchief she's about to give him; 'You have a thing for me? It is a common thing' (3.3.305–6), replies Iago, quibbling on 'thing' in the vulgar sense of 'vagina'. But the knee-jerk gibe at his wife's expense, which turns on the feared loss of exclusive sexual possession, also confirms that what the handkerchief stands for is 'a common thing' indeed, not something applicable to the Moor and his bride alone.

By linking the three couples the play's main prop draws a parallel between the despised courtesan, Bianca, and the respectable wives Desdemona and Emilia, both of whom find themselves thought of and talked of as whores by their husbands, and both of whom end up killed by their husbands. Any wife subject to this matrimonial regime is always at risk of being 'bewhored' (4.2.117) by a spouse conditioned to suspect her sex of an innate propensity to whoredom. Shakespeare strengthens the link the handkerchief forges between the three women through verbal echoes attached to it. 'I'll have the work ta'en out / And give't Iago', says Emilia when she finds the 'napkin', her mistress's 'first remembrance from the Moor' (3.3.294–5, 300–1). Her first instinct, in other words, is to replicate the handkerchief by having its embroidered pattern copied. Cassio's first thought on finding it and giving it to Bianca is the same: 'I like the work well: ere it be demanded, / As like enough it will, I'd have it copied' (3.4.189–90). In her subsequent jealous altercation with Cassio, Bianca underlines the idea of duplication the handkerchief entails by harping on the phrase 'take out the work' (4.1.150, 153, 154).

The mimetic desire to reproduce the sexual bind the handkerchief represents is automatic and contagious. It crosses the boundaries of rank and sexual propriety that ostensibly divide the couples, and the wives from the whore. In the latter regard it's like the equivocal word 'housewife', which could also be used pejoratively at the time to mean a loose woman, as in its contracted form 'hussy'. Thus, in the passage quoted earlier, where he banters bawdily with Desdemona and Emilia, Iago accuses them both of being 'Players in your housewifery, and housewives in / Your beds', eliciting from Desdemona the mock reproof, 'O, fie upon thee, slanderer!' (2.1.112–14). In his description of Bianca to the audience, however, the term is unequivocally derogatory and synonymous with 'strumpet': 'A housewife that by selling her desires / Buys herself bread and clothes' (4.1.95–6, 97). The word's innate ambiguity tacitly equates the reality of the married woman's situation with that of a kept woman, a genteel whore. But when Emilia reviles Bianca in public, crying 'O fie upon thee, strumpet!', the equation is made explicit by Bianca's proud retort: 'I am no strumpet / But of life as honest as you, that thus / Abuse me' (5.1.120–3).

For Shakespeare, the relationship between Othello and Desdemona *as husband and wife* is extraordinary only in the fatal consequences of the jealousy it engenders, not in its essential character, which is indeed, like the handkerchief that epitomizes it, 'a common thing'. The answer to Rymer's sarcastic question, 'Why was this not call'd the *Tragedy of the Handkerchief?*', is that a good case could be made for calling it exactly that. In his essay 'Desdemona's Handkerchief', John Middleton Murry observes that the handkerchief is one of the two main ways in which 'the inward and invisible must be made outward and visible' in *Othello*; the other being Iago, about whose role in this regard more remains to be said. In giving visible theatrical form to what would otherwise remain 'an essence that's not seen' (4.1.16), the handkerchief serves a further purpose, however. Like the copy of Ovid's *Metamorphoses* in *Titus*, the tomb of the Andronici in the same play or the Capulet tomb in *Romeo and Juliet*, it makes the extrinsic source of the fatal compulsions gripping the protagonists graphically intelligible.

If Wives Do Fall

Lest there be any doubt about the *play's* critical detachment from the toxic patriarchal culture in which the *characters* are confined, the extraordinary exchange between Desdemona and Emilia in the final scene of Act 4 puts it beyond dispute. Still stunned by Othello's physical and verbal assault on Desdemona moments before, on the cliff-edge of the catastrophe mistress and maid are given the space and time to converse alone, woman to woman, out of the hearing of men. The first part of their dialogue, in which Desdemona likens herself to her mother's forsaken maid, Barbary, and sings the song that Barbary died singing, has already been touched upon. Its overriding mood is one of pathos and its tone plangent. But another note is sounded at its start, when Desdemona says they must do Othello's bidding and 'must not now displease him' and Emilia exclaims, 'Would you had never seen him!' (4.3.15–16). The exclamation recalls her outrage at the sight of her mistress in tears in the previous scene: 'Hath she forsook so many noble matches, / Her father, and her country, and her friends, / To be called whore?' (4.2.127–9). Desdemona, resigning herself to the chastened wife's posture of selfless devotion and the prospect of her death, denies sharing Emilia's wish that she had never seen Othello. But her resignation is not yet complete, as is evident when she remarks a few lines later, 'This Lodovico is a proper man'. 'A very handsome man', Emilia agrees. 'He speaks well', adds Desdemona. 'I know a lady in Venice', says Emilia, 'would have walked barefoot to Palestine for a touch of his nether lip' (F: 4.3.34–8). The Arden editor misses the point of this exchange, revealing his own thraldom to gender stereotypes by giving Desdemona's line in the Folio, 'This Lodovico is a proper man', to Emilia, on the purely subjective grounds that 'For Desdemona to praise Lodovico at this point seems out of character'. But the significance of Shakespeare's giving Desdemona that line did not escape Auden, when he lectured on the play: 'She may see her love for Othello as romantic, but in calling Lodovico a "proper man", she may also be thinking that he is the sort of man she should have married. In time she might well have been unfaithful.' Desdemona's unexpected turning of her mind from 'poor Barbary' (4.3.31) to the physical attractiveness and accomplished demeanour of her Venetian cousin, whose sexual desirability Emilia is keen to underscore, is all too understandable, given what Othello has just subjected her to. Lodovico epitomizes the 'many noble matches' Desdemona forsook to marry Othello and is thus a reminder of the different course her life might have taken with a husband of her own race and class. The thought may not detain her long, but it's long enough to dramatize with consummate theatrical tact what her courageous defiance of Venetian mores has cost her.

For critics sold on the idea of Desdemona as an angelic paragon of wifely fidelity, Auden doubtless presses conjecture too far when he suggests that 'In time she might well have been unfaithful'. But the suggestion gains credence from the fact that after her song Desdemona's thoughts do turn to women committing adultery. They do so unprompted by Emilia, but subconsciously triggered partly, perhaps, by thoughts of the handsome Lodovico, and partly by the last line of her song, in which the faithless lover's response to being called 'false love' by the forsaken maid is 'If I court moe women, you'll couch with moe men' (4.3.56). The line raises the idea, which Emilia will shortly develop, of women paying men back in kind for their mistreatment. But it's Desdemona who sets this train of thought in motion with a cry that implicitly arraigns her husband's abuse of her as typical of the abuse meted out to women by the opposite sex:

> O, these men, these men!
> Dost thou in conscience think – tell me, Emilia –
> That there be women do abuse their husbands
> In such gross kind?

(4.3.59–62)

'There be some such, no question', the more worldly wise maidservant assures her mistress, prompting Desdemona to ask her directly, 'Wouldst thou do such a deed for all the world?', to which Emilia boldly replies, 'Why, would not you?'. 'No, by this heavenly light!', declares Desdemona, recoiling from the alarming idea her questions have elicited. 'Nor I neither, by this heavenly light', retorts Emilia, 'I might do't as well i'th' dark' (4.3.61–6). That Desdemona, given time enough, might indeed have been driven to take the likes of Lodovico for a lover is a contingency the tragedy does not oblige us to envisage. But we're certainly expected to hear her dallying with the notion and the possibility of adultery as a direct result of what her husband has said and done to her.

The importance of this scene lies in the understanding of women and the empathy with wives that it displays, especially at this crucial point. Far from dropping the subject of adultery, Desdemona repeats her question to Emilia: 'Wouldst thou do such a deed for all the world?' Emilia's previous flippant reply has left her unsatisfied, still wanting to know what could justify a wife's committing so grievous a sin. The phrase 'for all the world', echoed six more times in the next fifteen lines, suggests the scale of the values riding on the marriage of Othello and Desdemona. Desdemona employs it rhetorically to mean that no reward could surely be great enough to persuade Emilia to have sex with another man. But Emilia takes the phrase literally in her playfully cynical mood, cutting adultery down to size with a couplet: 'The world's a huge thing: it is a great price / For a small vice' (4.3.68–9). She proceeds to defend her scandalous contention at length, asking 'who would not make her husband a cuckold to make him a monarch?'. 'Beshrew me, if I would do such a wrong / For the whole world!', protests Desdemona. 'Why,' Emilia flashes back, 'the wrong is but a wrong i'th' world; and having the world for your labour, 'tis a wrong in your own world, and you might quickly make it right' (4.3.74–5, 77–81). The levity of her tone disguises the serious point Shakespeare is making through Emilia. For it's undeniable that the deed she's defending – a wife having sexual intercourse with a man other than her husband – is illicit only because their world happens to define it as illicit; that its definition as illicit is arbitrary, because it's decided by whoever rules the world, which happens to be men; and that consequently, if women were to rule the world, there'd be nothing to stop them redefining the conduct in question as legitimate.

That is the startling burden of Emilia's sardonic banter; startling because it calls into question female adultery itself, which is 'but a wrong i'th' world' that men have made and control in their interests at women's expense. The very concept on which Othello's jealousy and justification for killing his wife depends is undermined on the threshold of her murder by a savvy female servant, who knows like Montaigne that 'The laws of conscience, which we say do proceed from nature, rise and proceed of custom'. The corollary of Emilia's argument is that Desdemona's death sentence could not be justified even if she *were* guilty of committing adultery. That inference should be too obvious to need drawing. But the alarming assumption that the tragedy consists in Othello's *mistakenly* believing his innocent wife guilty of infidelity – implying that it wouldn't be tragic if she *had* been guilty – remains sadly as widespread as the murdering of real women by real men for the same reason.

Nor is that the last of what Shaw praised as 'Emilia's really interesting speeches, which contain some of Shakespeare's curious anticipations of modern ideas'. The entire unbridled dialogue between the two women culminates in Emilia's most stunning speech, which puts their exchange on a par in importance with the exchange between the Gravedigger and his fellow Clown that opens the last act of *Hamlet*. Having confessed that she'd have no qualms about cuckolding her husband if she stood to gain enough by it, and having dismissed doing so as not just 'a small vice' but not a vice *in itself* at all, Emilia changes tack. She launches into a passionate defence of wives driven to adultery not by their desire for wealth and power, but by what is more commonly the case, their husbands' ill-treatment or sexual betrayal of *them*:

> But I do think it is their husbands' faults
> If wives do fall. Say that they slack their duties
> And pour our treasures into foreign laps;
> Or else break out in peevish jealousies,
> Throwing restraint upon us; or say they strike us,
> Or scant our former having in despite,
> Why, we have galls: and though we have some grace
> Yet have we some revenge. Let husbands know
> Their wives have sense like them: they see, and smell,
> And have their palates both for sweet and sour
> As husbands have. What is it that they do
> When they change us for others? Is it sport?
> I think it is. And doth affection breed it?
> I think it doth. Is't frailty that thus errs?
> It is so too. And have not we affections?
> Desires for sport? and frailty, as men have?
> Then let them use us well: else let them know,
> The ills we do, their ills instruct us so.

(4.3.85–102)

Emilia's cynical air of wry provocation gives way here to righteous anger at the abuse too many wives suffer at the hands of their husbands, whom she warns of the retribution such wives are entitled to exact in return. Her references to husbands who 'break out in peevish jealousies, / Throwing restraint upon us' and to those who 'strike us' are pointed glances at Othello; and the couplet that delivers the punchline of the speech might be read as a warrant for her mistress to admit the possibility let slip in her line 'This Lodovico is a proper man'. But, although it's sparked by the marital crisis of Othello and Desdemona and has a direct bearing on it, Emilia's speech is framed throughout in terms that apply to husbands and wives in general. The charge-sheet she draws up against abusive husbands is couched in the third-person plural, while the plight of abused wives is described almost exclusively in the first-person plural, from a collective female standpoint her mistress is presumed to share. Desdemona's maltreatment by Othello is thereby *explained* not as an exceptional misfortune that's unhappily befallen her, but as an experience with which Emilia and wives the world over can identify, because it's an iniquity that marriage in a man's world is prone by its nature to produce. The protagonists of Shakespearean tragedy can never be prised apart from the social milieu that shapes them.

Only a dramatist with Shakespeare's extraordinary capacity for imaginative empathy could feel impelled at such a moment in the tragedy to pull us back and make us see what a blighted marriage looks and feels like from the female point of view. Our perspective on what we're witnessing widens with Emilia's impassioned protest at the oppressive reality of wedlock for women in a society under men's sway. Just before Othello, convinced that 'Cassio did top her', kills his wife for being 'false as water' (5.2.132, 134), we hear Emilia warning all husbands on behalf of all wives that they had better 'use us well', otherwise 'The ills we do, their ills instruct us so'. The threat of revenge is levelled at husbands at large, but the inference Desdemona and we are asked to draw from it is plain: if she really had cuckolded him with Cassio, or if she were to betray him with Lodovico, Othello would have only himself as a violently jealous husband to blame. Emilia's argument cuts the ground from under the misogynistic view of women and wives that Othello shares with Iago, and that sanctions in his view her death for adultery. It frames the tragedy as a *patriarchal* tragedy, as the product of that kind of culture at that time rather than the timeless tragedy of the human condition it's so often been reduced to.

The imaginative empathy with women evinced by Emilia's fiery speech springs from the same egalitarian attitude as the tragedy's indictment of racial prejudice. For corroboration of that one need look no further than Shylock's riposte to the Jew-baiting Christians, which Emilia's speech directly echoes:

Hath not a Jew eyes? Hath not a Jew hands, organs, dimensions, senses, affections, passions? Fed with the same food, hurt with the same weapons, subject to the same diseases, healed by the same means, warmed and cooled by the same winter and summer as a Christian is? If you prick us do we not bleed? If you tickle us do we not laugh? If you poison us do we not die? And if you wrong us shall we not revenge? If we are like you in the rest, we will resemble you in that. If a Jew wrong a Christian, what is his humility? Revenge! If a Christian wrong a Jew, what should his sufferance be by Christian example? Why, revenge! The villainy you teach me I will execute, and it shall go hard but I will better the instruction.

(*MV* 3.1.53–66)

Shylock rebukes his tormentors on the grounds that they share the same physiology, faculties, emotions and needs, which render them equally vulnerable, equally mortal and equally entitled to avenge the wrongs done to them. His arraignment of their anti-

Semitism is founded on a simple, irrefutable fact that condemns every unjustified form of discrimination. The irony, of course, is that Shylock is determined to vindicate the compassionate principles that spring from that fact by violating them through revenge. But the physically grounded concept of human equality he invokes to buttress his revenge transcends the vindictive purpose for which he enlists it. Shakespeare puts into Shylock's mouth an argument which has wider implications than the character is aware of, as the speech's undiminished impact four centuries on attests. The vengeful wrath of an early-modern victim of racist bigotry is dramatized from a standpoint committed to the potential equality of all human beings.

How readily Shylock's argument could have been adapted by Shakespeare to serve the turn of a Moor as well as a Jew is not hard to imagine. Its redeployment in the service of the female sex in *The Tragedy of Othello, The Moor of Venice* affords compelling proof that racial injustice and sexual injustice were inextricably entwined in Shakespeare's mind. Emilia's speech adopts not only the same reasoning and rhetorical techniques as Shylock's, but some of the same key words too – 'senses, affections' in the latter resurfacing as 'sense' and 'affection' in the former. Emilia bases her protest at the cruelties to which wives are subjected on the same undeniable fact of physical and emotional affinity that Shylock adduces to upbraid his abusers. The immediate purpose and cultural context of her speech remain rooted like Shylock's in their historical moment, while its egalitarian rationale points likewise far beyond that moment, charging it with the same tragic tension between inhuman realities and humane possibilities. In Emilia's speech as in Shylock's the innate capacity of human beings to base their attitudes to each other, and their treatment of each other, on what they have in common as members of the same species is discovered through the denunciation of an intolerable reality. Venting their anger at indefensible forms of discrimination forces both characters to mount, on incontestable premises, an argument that does much more than justify their threats of retaliation. The fact that the enlightened import of that argument is the last thing on Shylock's or Emilia's mind as they speak does not detract from its validity. On the contrary, its validity is secured by seeing and hearing it voiced by a convincing character in the grip of a credible predicament. The universal human potential to create a true community of equals that Shakespearean tragedy reveals is never a discarnate abstraction; it's always rooted in the embodied reality of characters immersed in a version of life beyond the stage, and the prospect of its fulfilment becomes more feasible as a consequence.

Motiveless Malignity and the Curse of Service

Hazlitt caught the essential spirit of Shakespearean tragedy in the opening paragraph of his essay on *Othello*, which furnished for him a perfect illustration of how tragedy at its greatest 'excites our sympathy in an extraordinary degree'.

> That is, it substitutes imaginary sympathy for mere selfishness. It gives us a high and permanent interest, beyond ourselves, in humanity as such. It raises the great,

the remote and the possible to an equality with the real, the little and the near. It makes man a partaker with his kind. It subdues and softens the stubbornness of his will. It teaches him that there are and have been others like himself, by showing him as in a glass what they have felt, thought, and done. It opens the chambers of the human heart. It leaves nothing indifferent to us that can affect our common nature. ... It makes us thoughtful spectators in the lists of life. It is the refiner of the species; a discipline of humanity.

That's certainly the broad effect Shakespearean tragedy can and should have on us, provided its capacity to do so is perceived by those who study and stage it. Hazlitt doesn't explain, through a close analysis of the text, exactly how this effect is achieved in *Othello*, but, as a summary of the designs the play has on our hearts and minds, the passage remains invaluable. It distils, like Emilia's superb tirade, what Shakespeare is endeavouring to do throughout the tragedy. It's not just that *Othello* is crafted in such a way as to open the chambers of the human heart to what binds us to our fellow human beings, regardless of their race or gender; it's that, in doing so, 'It raises the great, the remote and the possible to an equality with the real, the little and the near'. Grand, utopian ideals, which would otherwise seem too far-fetched to be feasible, acquire a realistic immediacy by virtue of the believable characters who enact or express them in their make-believe world, which is as sexually and racially divisive as Shakespeare's and our own. The potential is placed on a par with the actual in *Othello*: the way things could be carries the same weight there, the same authority, as the way things are.

Moreover, by substituting 'imaginary sympathy for mere selfishness', by giving us an interest 'beyond ourselves, in humanity as such', *Othello* 'makes man a partaker with his kind', and thus 'subdues and softens the stubbornness of his will'. The fully realized effect of the tragedy also excites our antipathy to what Hazlitt calls 'mere selfishness', the stubborn assertion of the individual's will at the expense of others, regardless of everything that affects 'our common nature'. The quintessence of the callous self bent on subduing others to its stubborn will is personified in *Othello* by Iago. 'He has none of the "milk of human kindness" in his composition', Hazlitt observes later in the same essay; 'His indifference when Othello falls into a swoon, is perfectly diabolical.' (As Shaw has Anderson remark in *The Devil's Disciple*: 'The worst sin towards our fellow creatures is not to hate them, but to be indifferent to them; that's the essence of inhumanity.') The poetic justice of Iago's nemesis turning out to be his own wife, the play's ardent advocate of the human kindness that should follow from our innate equality, could scarcely be more perfect, or illustrate more plainly the standpoint of the dramatist who made her Iago's nemesis.

That standpoint is complicated by Shakespeare's decision to make the villain of the piece such a seductive intimate of the audience that he habitually steals the show from its tragic hero. We'll come to the reasons for that decision shortly. Before we do, taking our cue from Bradley's analysis of Iago's character, the essence of which he found in 'some of the best lines Hazlitt ever wrote', we need to dispel the myth of Iago's 'motiveless malignity'. It's a critical myth as tenacious as the critical myth that a pathological compulsion to prevaricate is the 'vicious mole' in Hamlet's nature that brings about the tragic catastrophe. The reasons for its tenacity are the same as in the case of *Hamlet* too. The first reason is that it allows the fundamental cause of the tragedy to be ascribed to something inexplicably pernicious at the core of a particular character, which lets the social forces that shaped their character, and that placed them in that culturally specific situation, off the hook. Grant that Iago's malignity is motiveless, and that Othello's 'tragic flaw' is an exceptional propensity for sexual jealousy, and the tragedy can be put down to the latter's unhappily falling prey to an unfathomably evil psychopath.

The second reason for the persistence of this view of Iago is that, like the equally persistent misconception of Hamlet, it looks plausible at first glance. Coleridge coined the phrase 'the motive-hunting of a motiveless malignity' to describe Iago's thought-process in his first soliloquy. Furnishing himself and us with a cogent motive for the 'monstrous birth' (1.3.403) gestating in his mind is certainly what he's up to in that speech. From hatred of the Moor for having chosen Cassio instead of Iago as his lieutenant – the motive emphatically established at the start of the play – he shifts to vengeance for the adultery that he suspects Othello has committed with Emilia. Then the desire to seize Cassio's post for himself triggers the desire to be revenged in the process on Cassio too, by making him the instrument of his revenge on the Moor. The hunt seems to be on again in the second soliloquy, where the thought of making Othello suspect Cassio of being 'too familiar with his wife' (1.3.395) briefly becomes Iago's stated belief 'That Cassio loves her' and 'That she loves him' (2.1.284–5). Far from being a fabrication, in other words, the jealousy Iago plans to provoke in Othello is grounded in fact, he maintains, and thus justified. 'Now I do love her too' (2.1.289), he suddenly claims to our surprise, having shown no sign of loving anybody but himself, let alone Desdemona, up to this point. 'Not out of absolute lust', he swiftly adds, 'But partly led to diet my revenge, / For that I do suspect the lusty Moor / Hath leaped into my seat' (2.1.290, 292–4).

The idea of his revenge against Othello and Cassio being fed by his own love for the woman whose love they enjoy is clearly culled from Cinthio. But it flickers across Iago's mind only for a second before it's eclipsed by the same motive of revenge for being cuckolded that he mooted in his first soliloquy: 'And nothing can or shall content my soul / Till I am evened with him, wife for wife' (2.1.296–7). If his plan to cuckold Othello in return should fail, he'll settle, he says, for putting 'the Moor / At least into a jealousy so strong / That judgement cannot cure' (2.1.298–300). He'll contrive, that is, to make Othello suffer precisely the same torment Iago suspects Othello of inflicting on him. In doing so, what's more, he'll also have wrought his revenge on Cassio. But the reason he gives now for ruining Cassio's career is not that he's usurped the lieutenancy that Iago feels should have been his by right; it's the same reason he's just given for revenging himself on Othello: 'For I fear Cassio with my night-cap too' (2.1.305). This is the first we've heard of that being a motive for queering Cassio's pitch, and it's the last we hear of it too. Three acts later, Iago produces yet another unexpected motive, but this time for wanting the disgraced and demoted Cassio killed, because 'If Cassio do remain / He hath a daily beauty in his life / That makes me ugly' (5.1.18–20).

It's not hard to see why the notion of Iago's malevolence being inexplicable, because he gives us no single, convincing reason for it, has proved so enduring. As Bradley remarks: 'Certainly he assigns motives enough; the difficulty is that he assigns so many. A man moved by simple passions due to simple causes does not stand fingering his feelings, industriously enumerating their sources, and groping about for new ones. But this is what Iago does. And this is not all. These motives appear and disappear in the most extraordinary manner.' So they do, but they are neither as many nor as diverse as this suggests. Iago may indeed give the impression of constantly inventing new reasons for revenge, plucking them out of the air to multiply the warrants for his villainy, regardless of their inconsistency. But his motive-hunting is confined to his first and second soliloquies, which furnish on closer inspection only two distinct motives that might seem incongruous rather than a plethora of mutually exclusive ones. One of these motives is revenge for being passed over for promotion by Othello in favour of Cassio; the other is revenge for the adultery he suspects Othello, and later Cassio, of committing with his wife. Both motives are set out and distinguished in a single key sentence at the start of Iago's motive-hunting in his first soliloquy: 'I hate the Moor / And it is thought abroad that 'twixt my sheets / He's done my office' (1.3.385–7; my emphasis). Note that Iago does not say, 'I hate the Moor / For [i.e. *because*] it is thought abroad that 'twixt my sheets / He's done my office'. The rumour that Othello has cuckolded him, which Iago suspects might be true, is a supplementary motive, the primary motive being: 'I hate the Moor'. The source of that hatred needs no explanation, having been drummed into us by Iago right at the start of the play. Just before the first soliloquy Iago has reasserted the strength of his loathing – 'I hate the Moor. My cause is hearted' (1.3.366–7) – without any suggestion that his reason for loathing him is other than his fury at being so publicly misprized by Othello. That this wound to his pride is still at the forefront of Iago's mind in this soliloquy is confirmed when his thoughts turn immediately from Othello to Cassio and how 'To get his place' (1.3.392) in such a way as to be avenged on both men at a stroke. Cassio must be made to pay too for his part in robbing Iago of the post he coveted.

From this point on, however, the supplementary motive of sexual revenge not only displaces the primary motive, but it also dictates the means by which Iago's revenge on both Othello and Cassio will be exacted. By the time Iago delivers his second soliloquy the primary motive has vanished behind the sexual motive, which is why a sexual motive has to be produced in a parenthetical afterthought – 'For I fear Cassio with my night-cap too' (2.1.305) – to justify Iago's revenge on Cassio on the same grounds as his revenge on Othello. Iago produces no other distinct, substantive motives for his malignity. What might sound like alternative or additional motives being mooted in the second soliloquy are merely rationalizations, restatements or elaborations of the sexual motive, or the result of confusing the means of revenge with the motive for revenge. Iago's fifth-act justification for wanting Cassio murdered, because the 'daily beauty in his life' makes Iago look ugly by comparison, isn't a separate, alternative motive for *revenge* either; it's a reason for bringing the vengeance he's already wreaked on Cassio to a lethal conclusion, and the physical and moral envy of Cassio it reveals helps explain the intensity of Iago's desire to destroy and replace the man Othello valued above him.

Bradley gets closer to the truth of what Iago's doing in his first two soliloquies when he describes him as 'pondering his design, and unconsciously trying to justify it to himself':

He speaks of one or two real feelings, such as resentment against Othello, and he mentions one or two real causes of these feelings. But these are not enough for him. Along with them, or alone, there come into his head, only to leave it again, ideas and suspicions, the creations of his own baseness or uneasiness, some old, some new, caressed for a moment to feed his purpose and give it a reasonable look, but never really believed in, and never the main forces which are determining his action. In fact, I would venture to describe Iago in these soliloquies as a man setting out on a project which strongly attracts his desire, but at the same time conscious of a resistance to the desire, and unconsciously trying to argue the resistance away by assigning reasons for the project. He is the counterpart of Hamlet, who tried to find reasons for his delay in pursuing a design which excites his aversion. And most of Iago's reasons for actions are no more the real ones than Hamlet's reasons for delay were the real ones. Each is moved by forces which he does not understand; …

This is Bradley at his brilliant best. Nor does he stop there. He rejects both the idea that Iago is driven by 'a disinterested love of evil, or a delight in the pain of others' for its own sake, and the notion that the impetus of his inhumanity is unintelligible. Indeed, he contends persuasively that Coleridge's oft-cited view of the matter has been misunderstood:

When he speaks of 'the motive-hunting of a motiveless malignity', he does not mean by the last two words that 'disinterested love of evil' or 'love of evil for evil's sake' of which I spoke just now, and which other critics attribute to Iago. He means really that Iago's malignity does not spring from the causes to which Iago refers it, nor from any 'motive' in the sense of an idea present to consciousness.

Of 'the causes to which Iago refers it', Bradley is at pains to stress, due weight must be given to 'his desire for advancement, and the ill-will caused by his disappointment'. But, although these are 'indispensable factors in the cause of Iago's action', they are, he maintains, 'neither the principal nor the most characteristic factors'.

Those factors can readily be inferred, argues Bradley, from the defining qualities of Iago's character as Shakespeare portrays him. Attend closely to what he says and does, and 'he appears, when we meet him, to be almost destitute of humanity, of sympathy or social feeling. He shows no trace of affection, and in presence of the most terrible suffering he shows either pleasure or an indifference which, if not complete, is nearly so.' Nor should this come as a surprise, given that we have from Iago's own lips at the outset ample evidence of the creed by which he lives and exhorts Roderigo to live. 'His creed', as Bradley sums it up, 'is that absolute egoism is the only rational and proper attitude, and that conscience or honour or any other regard for others is an absurdity.' The play is barely under way before Iago is voicing his contempt for those who dote on their 'obsequious bondage' to their masters, and his admiration for those like himself 'Who, trimmed in forms and visages of duty, / Keep yet their hearts attending on themselves'

(1.1.45, 49–50). Then he expounds his creed at length in the exchange with Roderigo that segues straight into his first soliloquy. Its gist is encapsulated in two sentences: 'I never found a man that knew how to love himself' and 'Our bodies are gardens, to the which our wills are gardeners' (1.3.314–15, 321–2). What Bradley dubs 'this lordship of the will' in the service of self-interest before all else is the code Iago stands or falls by, 'his practice as well as his doctrine'. The idea of the self's subjection to external ethical constraints he dismisses as claptrap: 'Virtue? A fig! 'tis in ourselves that we are thus, or thus' (1.3.320–1). As Bradley puts it: 'He professes to stand, and he attempts to stand, wholly outside the world of morality.'

As a devout exponent of absolute egoism, who keeps his heart attending on himself, it's self-evident to Bradley that 'Iago is keenly sensitive to anything that touches his pride or self-esteem'. It's here that Bradley cuts to the heart of what motivates Iago's malignity and thus explains both the form his revenge on Othello and Cassio takes and the terms in which he justifies it in his soliloquies:

> It would be most unjust to call him vain, but he has a high opinion of himself and a great contempt for others. He is quite aware of his superiority to them in certain respects; and he either disbelieves in or despises the qualities in which they are superior to him. Whatever disturbs or wounds his sense of superiority irritates him at once; and in *that* sense he is highly competitive. This is why the appointment of Cassio provokes him. This is why Cassio's scientific attainments provoke him. This is the reason of his jealousy of Emilia. He does not care for his wife; but the fear of another man's getting the better of him, and exposing him to pity or derision as an unfortunate husband, is wormwood to him; and as he is sure that no woman is virtuous at heart, this fear is ever with him.

Wounded self-regard is likewise, Bradley adds, the reason why Iago 'has a spite against goodness in men', which 'weakens his satisfaction with himself, and disturbs his faith that egoism is the right and proper thing'. Beneath the conscious motives Iago mobilizes in his soliloquies there lurks an ulterior motive of which Iago is unconscious. 'Only once', in Bradley's view, 'does he appear to see something of the truth'. It's when he uses the phrase 'to *plume up my will* / In double knavery' (1.3.392–3) in his first soliloquy to describe the purpose of his plot against Othello and Cassio. What the metaphor plainly suggests is that its purpose is to reassert with a vengeance his pleasure and pride in the feeling of superior intelligence and power Othello and Cassio have robbed him of. As Bradley explains:

> His thwarted sense of superiority wants satisfaction. What fuller satisfaction could it find than the consciousness that he is master of the General who has undervalued him and of the rival who has been preferred to him; that these worthy people, who are so successful and popular and stupid, are mere puppets in his hands, but living puppets, who at the motion of his finger must contort themselves in agony while

all the time they believe that he is their one true friend and comforter? It must have been an ecstasy of bliss to him.

Nobody has written more perceptively or convincingly than Bradley about the secret springs of Iago's far from motiveless malignity. The distinction he obliges us to draw between the overt and the covert forces that drive 'his Moorship's ancient' (1.1.32) to take such lethal measures against Othello, Desdemona and Cassio is indispensable for grasping the full significance of the character. That the full significance escapes Bradley is the inevitable result of his critical method of analysing Shakespeare's characters in isolation from the milieu that moulds the way they think, speak and act. For Bradley, the distinctive features of Iago's personality – 'the keen sense of superiority, the contempt of others, the sensitiveness to everything which wounds those feelings, the spite against goodness in men' – are the distinctive attributes of a singular individual, the innate flaws in his disposition that determine his conduct. The notion that such traits might be the widely shared products of the kind of culture Iago inhabits, and that the only singular thing about them is the appalling outcome of Iago's thraldom to them in this instance, doesn't enter into Bradley's consideration. As a result, the implications of the links he adumbrates between Iago's unconscious and conscious motives are left undeveloped.

In order to develop them we need to ask ourselves why Shakespeare decided to bring the first of the two conscious motives Iago musters to our attention at the start of the play. Bradley perceives that anger at Othello's thwarting of his military ambition does not suffice to explain the scale and intensity of the punishment Iago contrives for him, at the cost of the innocent Desdemona's life and almost at the cost of Cassio's. But he doesn't give that affront the weight it merits for unleashing Iago's rage at the deeper wounds to his ego already festering within him for the same fundamental reason. To appreciate its importance, Bradley need only have noted Shakespeare's radical rejigging of the motives for the Ensign's villainy that he found in his source. In Cinthio 'the impious Ensign', having failed to gratify his lust for Disdemona, becomes consumed with jealous hatred of her and successfully schemes to slay her himself with the duped Moor's connivance. It's only after Disdemona's murder, towards the end of the tale, that the Ensign is given cause to hate the Moor. Beside himself with grief at the loss of his beloved wife, and realizing now that the Ensign is to blame, the Moor resolves to make her killer pay. So, unable to slay the Ensign openly with impunity, 'he took away his rank and would not have him in his company, whereupon such a bitter hatred sprang up between them that no greater or more deadly feud could be imagined. The Ensign, that worst of all scoundrels, therefore set all his mind to injuring the Moor'. What was a consequence of the events culminating in the murder of the Moor's wife in Cinthio is turned into the trigger that sets them in motion in the first scene of *Othello*. Moreover, a hatred that was mutual and overt in Cinthio becomes one-sided and private in Shakespeare, who absolves his Moor of malicious intent in the matter, but compounds the unintended slight to his Ensign by having Cassio promoted over him. There could be no clearer proof of the importance Shakespeare attached to this traumatic affront to Iago's self-regard as the key to comprehending the mainspring of his iniquity.

Its importance is underscored by having Iago's first extended speech in the play devoted to divulging the grounds of his grievance to Roderigo (1.1.5–32); by the fact that, when he pauses in his first soliloquy to define his 'purpose' to himself for the first time, Iago *begins* with: 'Cassio's a proper man: let me see now, / To get his place … ' (1.3.390–2); but, above all, by the climactic moment in Act 3 when he achieves that objective, having sworn to kill Cassio at the enraged Othello's command: 'Now art thou my lieutenant', says Othello, revealing his awareness of Iago's desire for the post; to which Iago replies, in the secret heat of gratification, 'I am your own for ever' (3.3.481–2) as they exit. As the impassioned intensity of that reply attests, much more has been at stake for Iago in getting Cassio's place than promotion to the rank of lieutenant as such. If that had mattered most to him, he could have been more than satisfied with securing it by less devastating means than he's driven to employ. But satisfying 'His thwarted sense of superiority', in Bradley's phrase, won't do either to crack the problem Iago poses, because it risks reducing the ultimate cause of the tragedy to a personality disorder. It does, however, point us in the right direction.

'I know my price, I am worth no worse a place' (1.1.10), declares Iago, as he explains to Roderigo his embitterment at Cassio's promotion in his stead. His evaluation of himself is pegged to the position on the social ladder he believes he should occupy, which is why he feels so demeaned by Othello's refusal to recognize his worth with the lieutenancy. Behind the grudge Iago bears the Moor for this loss of caste lies the sense that a fundamental principle, to which 'his Moorship's ancient' (1.1.32) is wedded, has been violated:

Why, there's no remedy, 'tis the curse of service:
Preferment goes by letter and affection
And not by old gradation, where each second
Stood heir to th' first. Now, sir, be judge yourself
Whether I in any just term am affined
To love the Moor.

(1.1.34–9)

It's 'the curse of service' and the appeal to 'old gradation' that betray what's really eating at Iago: the pervasive, inescapable fact of hierarchy, and hence subordination, that governs his life and shapes his view of every aspect of his world, not just his military career. In reality, the ideal of 'old gradation', of an established order of precedence, is merely a euphemism for 'the curse of service' under which Iago has been chafing since before the play began. That much is evident from the cynical homily he delivers next to buttress his belief that 'We cannot all be masters, nor all masters / Cannot be truly followed' (1.1.41–2) by those who scorn like him the obsequious bondage on which dutiful servants dote. It's patently a considered belief, born of prior observation and experience, that Iago has already arrived at before the action of the play begins, and that his ensuing conduct bears out.

The really galling thing about being denied the lieutenancy is that it reinforces the intolerable feeling of inferiority Iago would still have to fight against even if he had won promotion. That feeling, fostered by involuntary servitude in a rigidly stratified society, breeds in Iago its inextricable antithesis: the compulsion to prove himself secretly superior to those who make him feel inferior by debasing them. Two otherwise perplexing statements by Iago in this speech appear less puzzling when read as symptomatic of the mentality it exposes. The first is 'Were I the Moor, I would not be Iago' (1.1.56), which reveals not just an envious desire to be the Moor, because then he would be the master and not the servant, but a desire not to be Iago at all, to relinquish that identity. Indeed, the following line transmutes the servant into the master, Iago into the Moor, by collapsing the distinction between them: 'In following him I follow but myself' (1.1.57). The other cryptic dictum, with which Iago's discourse on the theme of masters and servants concludes, might seem no more than a stage villain's staple confession of duplicity: 'I am not what I am' (1.1.64). But its self-cancelling formulation bespeaks something more complex than a simple disjunction between being and seeming: the simultaneous repudiation and assertion of his identity as the underling Iago, which he can neither endure nor disavow.

Tormented by the hierarchical mentality bred in him by the society that surrounds him, it's small wonder that Iago's first move against Othello, a split second later, is to pounce on Roderigo's racist cue – 'What a full fortune does the thicklips owe / If he can carry't thus!' (1.1.63) – to recruit Brabantio to his vindictive cause: 'Call up her father, / Rouse him, make after him, poison his delight, / Proclaim him in the streets, incense her kinsmen' (1.1.66–8). Note the pronominal confusion of that command, which initially conflates Brabantio with Othello, Iago's white social superior with the black general he regards, like Brabantio and Roderigo, as racially inferior. Iago's acute class resentment of Desdemona's father is reflected in his retort to the latter's cry 'Thou art a villain!': 'You are a senator!' Iago sneers back, his identity shrouded in darkness, capping Brabantio's insult by turning 'senator' into a synonymous term of abuse. By rousing Brabantio to poison Othello's delight in his bride, Iago denigrates them both in the same breath, socially and racially; he drags them down, through that foul image of bestial coupling, from their elevated positions above him to a subhuman level at which he can despise them. Although Iago shares with Brabantio and Roderigo the routine racism of Venice, whose stock slurs spring readily to his lips, he isn't *motivated* by racist hatred. He simply exploits its prevalence, because he can count on it to inflame Brabantio with hatred for the Moor for marrying his daughter, thereby putting the Moor and his marriage in jeopardy with the Senate. It's a means of achieving his objective at this point, not the reason for it. That's why Iago doesn't make a derogatory issue of Othello's race and colour again until Othello himself prompts him to, as his confidence in Desdemona's love begins to crumble in Act 3.

Iago's ruse of using Brabantio to kill the Moor's 'full fortune' in the cradle is foiled, as he anticipates, by the esteem in which the indispensable Othello is held by the Senate. The testimony of the Moor and his bride before the Senate serves only to enhance their regard for him and seal their acceptance of a marriage they wouldn't normally countenance, because they know as well as Brabantio that 'if such actions may have passage free / Bond-slaves and pagans shall our statesmen be'. It's not hard to guess, though we're obliged to imagine, the impact on Iago of seeing Brabantio defeated by his daughter and the black soldier she has eloped with. From his point of view, the racially inferior Moor, to whom he's already professionally subservient, has had the nerve to court and wed a white, high-born, Venetian beauty as if he were the equal of a man of her class and colour. And she has had the nerve not just to prefer 'a lascivious Moor' to a suitor of her own nation, race and rank in defiance of her father's will, but to brazenly proclaim her love for this 'erring barbarian' in public. They have done this, moreover, with the official blessing of the Venetian Senate. As if Othello's preferring an unqualified Florentine, 'That never set a squadron on the field' (1.1.21), to be his lieutenant instead of Iago – in contempt of loyal service and 'old gradation' – wasn't humiliating enough! Othello and Desdemona have made a mockery of the social, racial and sexual hierarchy on which Iago's very identity and sense of self-worth depend. So straight after the Senate hearing, as soon as he and Roderigo are left alone, he abandons the abortive resort to racial bigotry to undo Othello. He starts to hatch instead a sexual plot designed to put the Moor, the Moor's wife and the Moor's lieutenant in what he thinks is their place, which is subordinate to him and subject to his will like his upper-class dupe Roderigo.

Iago and Roderigo have just heard the newly-weds' moving declarations of their love, which plunge the lovelorn Roderigo into despair. But Iago senses that their absolute emotional commitment to each other makes Othello and Desdemona more vulnerable to his machinations than racial prejudice alone. Their brave mutual love poses a direct threat to his conviction that love is merely one of 'our carnal stings, our unbitted lusts' (1.3.331–2). That itch in the flesh, he believes, lasts only until the 'lust of the blood' (1.3.335) is sated, and it fades with familiarity and the passage of time. So it must prove, he insists, with Desdemona and Othello: she is as sure to tire of his body as he is of hers, and to seek sexual pleasure with a younger man – to wit, Iago promises, Roderigo himself: 'thou shalt enjoy her' (1.3.358). Iago's immediate aim in saying this is to keep his lucrative stooge keen and compliant. But the form his revenge against Othello and Cassio will shortly take is crystallizing as he speaks. The sacred oath of marital fidelity the couple have sworn must be unmasked as mere 'sanctimony and a frail vow betwixt an erring Barbarian and a super-subtle Venetian' (1.3.356–7) by fitting the Moor with horns. 'If thou canst cuckold him,' Iago says to Roderigo, 'thou dost thyself a pleasure, me a sport' (1.3.369–70).

Once Roderigo has exited, only two fiendish refinements of the means of revenge are required from Iago's soliloquy and the fledgling plot is hatched. The first is to replace Roderigo with Cassio, a more plausible candidate for the role of seducer, to ensnare him too. The second is to make Othello only *believe* that he's a cuckold, a much simpler and more satisfying trick to pull off than conspiring to make him one. What could be simpler, after all, in a society where sexual jealousy and the dread of cuckoldry are pervasive, because everything conduces to expecting the worst of women? Iago himself is plagued, as his wife later confirms, by the suspicion that Othello has already cuckolded him.

What could be more gratifying than the poetic justice of infecting the Moor with the same ubiquitous disease? Nothing could be better calculated to degrade Othello in his own mind and in Iago's eyes than convincing him that his wife, 'The divine Desdemona' (2.1.73), is just another 'subtle whore' (4.2.21) like the rest of her sex, who deserves to die for disgracing him as a man. That the true objective of Iago's revenge is the *degradation* of his victims is clear from his aside after Othello and Desdemona seal their blissful reunion on Cyprus with a kiss: 'O, you are well tuned now: but I'll set down / The pegs that make this music' (2.1.198–9). Iago's anger at Cassio's promotion over him, his resentment of his state of servitude to Othello, his resort to racist vitriol, and the misogyny that feeds his sexual insecurity all spring from the same obsession with hierarchy bred into him by a socially, racially and sexually divisive society.

The truth is that nothing could be less mysterious than the source of Iago's malignity. The idea of an inscrutably malevolent villain improvising an array of incompatible motives plucked from thin air doesn't square with the evidence furnished by the play. The two distinct motives Iago consciously cites spring from the same root motive that governs all his machinations. Nor is there anything random or arbitrary about them. On the contrary, they couldn't be more predictable, given their provenance in the characteristic mentality of the culture Iago inhabits. It's not surprising that his sexually motivated plot takes precedence from the moment Iago hits upon it, given the intrinsic vulnerability of the Moor's mixed-race marriage, Iago's prior suspicion that Othello has cuckolded him, and the readiness of the reality around them to cultivate and warrant that suspicion. That Iago fears Cassio with his nightcap too seems less of a baseless fabrication, when one recalls Cassio going out of his way to kiss a plainly game Emilia in public on the lips, knowing full well that it will nettle her husband: 'Let it not gall your patience, good Iago, / That I extend my manners' (2.1.97–8). Cassio's intimate dalliance with an equally complaisant Desdemona shortly afterwards can't help appearing to endorse his eligibility for the role of seductive rake Iago has lined up for him: 'He takes her by the palm; ay, well said, whisper. With as little a web as this will I ensnare as great a fly as Cassio. Ay, smile upon her, do: I will gyve thee in thine own courtesies. You say true, 'tis so indeed. If such tricks as these strip you out of your lieutenantry, it had been better you had not kissed your three fingers so oft' (2.1.167–73). The persons of Iago's world play so easily into his hands because the plot in which he casts them is the product of that world.

What You Know, You Know

The really disturbing thing about Iago is not that he's an unfathomable psychopath, but that he's so pathologically normal, so terrifyingly typical of the kind of world Shakespeare saw coming into being and millions of us still live in: a world rife with the narcissistic egotism Iago personifies in its most ruthless and destructive form. Although he initiates and engineers its catastrophe, Iago is neither the fundamental nor the sole cause of the tragedy, as the insufficiency of his avowed motives to explain him attests. The tragedy could have erupted in a similar form, with a similar end, and for the same reasons, without Iago's intervention or existence; Othello's ferocious jealousy could have sprung fully armed from his own mind, just like the jealousy of Leontes in *The Winter's Tale*, had Shakespeare so desired. Indeed, the fact that Iago settles for his own satisfaction on a motive rooted in his own real fears and imaginings suggests how easily the plot could be reconfigured with Iago as its protagonist, driven wild with unfounded jealousy of Cassio by the wicked Moor, or of the Moor by a smooth, conniving Cassio. There's even a hint of Cassio's potential to have shared Othello's fate in Iago's description of him as 'A fellow almost damned in a fair wife' (1.1.20) at the start of the play. Whether he simply forgot the line or it survived his deletion of it in manuscript, Shakespeare clearly decided to make nothing of the notion that Cassio was married too, finding the idea of an unwed Cassio with a mistress better suited to his plot. But the fact that he wrote it at all and put it in Iago's mouth shows how deeply embedded in his mind from the outset was the ubiquity of the fear of cuckoldry, which Iago projects here onto Cassio before he inflicts it on Othello.

To see the sexually jealous Othello latent in the sexually jealous Iago – 'the hornmad Iago ceaselessly willing that the Moor in him shall suffer', as Stephen Dedalus puts it in *Ulysses* – is to grasp the irony of Iago's thraldom to the attitudes he exploits to deceive Othello. 'By heaven,' exclaims Othello, after yet again repeating Iago's repetition of his words, 'thou echo'st me / As if there were some monster in thy thought / Too hideous to be shown' (3.3.109–11). Iago's strategy of echoing Othello to induce Othello to echo him proves insidiously effective. But it also illustrates Iago's parasitic relationship to his prey, his reliance on the assumptions and anxieties he can count on Othello sharing as a married man in the same society. The same obligation to batten on the like-minded to serve his ends is evident when Iago echoes Brabantio's warning to Othello to distrust his daughter: 'She did deceive her father, marrying you', he reminds him, refusing 'many proposed matches / Of her own clime, complexion and degree, / Whereto we see, in all things, nature tends' (3.3.209, 233–5). Iago's stock-in-trade as the villain of the piece is the fund of stereotypical reactions on which he knows men's minds like his habitually draw. But the very means he uses to make his victims destroy themselves by making them instruments of his will enslave and blind him too. The triumph of his plumed-up will turns out to be all too brief, because he can no more free himself of his time and place than Othello and Desdemona can. So he ends up the defiant but defeated victim of his own misogyny, murdering the heroic wife he didn't deserve, just like Othello.

Any residual mystery that might cling to the character of Iago dissolves with the realization that he is not a monstrous deviation from the civilized Venetian norm, but the unmasked incarnation of its actual barbarity. The iniquitous universe of *Othello* confronts in 'damned Iago', the 'inhuman dog' (5.1.62), not its demonic antithesis but its grotesque epitome. Iago differs from the principal male denizens of Venice only in the ferocity with which he espouses their values and the deadly extremes to which he will go to vindicate them and thus himself. His ploys work so well because they rely on reflecting his victims' beliefs and endorsing their expectations. By 'making noncommittal remarks that invite Othello to do the committing for himself', as Burke points out, Iago inveigles Othello into owning the 'ingeniously inculcated obsessions' that devour him. But he can do so only because Othello is as predisposed as Iago to be devoured by them. The misogyny that feeds Othello's fear of being cuckolded fits perfectly with the culture of a city where his colour makes him feel like an alien, but where he's completely at home as a man. The reason why Iago succeeds so quickly and spectacularly in persuading Othello to swallow his vile slander of Desdemona is that Othello is primed to believe it, and to believe it on the strength of mere insinuations rather than cast-iron proof. At the Moor's most susceptible, Iago can bank on the patriarchal male and the black foreigner within him craving confirmation of what they'd secretly suspected all along.

As Murry observes: 'were the seed of catastrophe not present in the relation of Desdemona and Othello, it could never be germinated by the heat of Iago's malign cunning'. That seed was planted in their relationship, the play makes plain, not by nature but by habits of mind and heart cultivated in them and in Iago by the malign ethos of their society. When Emilia begs her husband to deny that he duped Othello into murdering Desdemona for adultery, Iago's evasive mitigation of his calumny is revealing: 'I told him what I thought, and told no more / Than what he found himself was apt and true' (5.2.172–3). The alacrity with which Othello was ready to find Iago's blatant falsehood 'apt and true' renders a simplistic moral response inadequate by dividing the responsibility for Desdemona's murder between the villain and his victim. But the very last thing Iago says in the play renders such a response not just inadequate but impossible. When Othello asks Cassio, 'Will you, I pray, demand that demi-devil / Why he hath thus ensnared my soul and body?', Iago forestalls the question by brusquely interjecting: 'Demand me nothing. What you know, you know. / From this time forth I never will speak word' (5.2.298–301). To gauge the importance of Iago's refusal to explain the reason for his villainy, one need only imagine the effect of his ascribing it to anger at not being promoted, to racial hatred of the Moor, or to his belief that Othello had made a cuckold of him. To pin Iago's wickedness down to a single, clear-cut reason at this climactic juncture would be to explain the deeper causes of the tragedy away and reduce it to a morality play; whereas having the wounded Iago deny Othello and his captors the satisfaction of such an explanation reinforces the tragedy's insistence on our seeking its sources beyond moralism. When Iago says, 'Demand me nothing. What you know, you know', it can be read as his simply saying that they're wasting their time if they think he's going to tell them any more than they already know. But with his earlier reply to Emilia in mind – 'I told him what I thought, and told no more / Than what he found himself was apt and true' – it can also be read as Iago retorting, not only to Othello and Cassio, but to Lodovico, Montano, Gratiano and the rest: 'Don't ask *me* why. Ask *yourselves* why, because you know as well as I do.'

With Iago's parting shot the compass of incrimination expands to embrace the world of the play, but it doesn't stop there. Shakespeare has no intention of letting himself or us off the hook either. How else can one explain his decision to have Iago talk directly to us throughout, taking us alone into his confidence, assuming that we share his views and values, understand his reasoning and motives, and applaud his virtuosity as a villain? Or his decision to temper our moral aversion to Iago's plot by focusing our minds on its ingenuity? As Schlegel observed: 'The repugnance inspired by his aims becomes tolerable from the attention of the spectators being directed to his means: these furnish endless employment to the understanding.' Iago speaks many more lines than Othello in the tragedy with the smallest cast, as well as having the lion's share of the soliloquies and a monopoly of asides. Othello is kept at a distance from us by Shakespeare, who denies him the profound mental and emotional rapport that Hamlet and Macbeth forge with the audience through their soliloquies. That leaves Iago free to exploit his intimacy with the audience to involve us in his hatred and entrapment of Othello, to make us complicit with him and what he stands for, whether we like it or not. Shakespeare deliberately places the audience in the invidious position of allying itself with an egotistical, misogynistic bigot, hell-bent on proving *to us* his superiority to those he hates for making him feel inferior. By having Iago confidently solicit our endorsement of his right to revenge and our admiration of his infernal stratagem, the play asks us to consider to what extent we find reflected in him our own wounded egotism and fantasies of retribution. Harold Bloom for one has no doubt that 'Iago, forever beyond Othello's understanding, is not beyond ours, because we are more like Iago than we resemble Othello'. That being the case, when Iago retorts unfazed in his final speech, 'Demand me nothing. What you know, you know', we can be sure that every word of that barbed line is addressed, disconcertingly, to us too.

Equally disconcerting is the fact of Iago's kinship with his creator, which Hazlitt was the first to discern:

> He is an amateur of tragedy in real life; and instead of employing his invention on imaginary characters, or long-forgotten incidents, he takes the bolder and more desperate course of getting up his plot at home, casts the principal parts among his nearest friends and connections, and rehearses it in downright earnest, with steady nerves and unabated resolution.

After quoting this passage, Bradley adds that anyone unconvinced by it need only consider

> the curious analogy between the early stages of dramatic composition and those soliloquies in which Iago broods over his plot, drawing at first only an outline, puzzled how to fix more than the main idea, and gradually seeing it develop and clarify as he works upon it or lets it work. Here at any rate Shakespeare put a good deal of himself into Iago.

Bradley doesn't pursue the ramifications of that arresting last sentence. But it's important that we do, because Shakespeare is tacitly acknowledging that this thing of darkness called Iago is his own. He's in part a doppelganger of the dramatist who begat him, and who can't escape, any more than his audience can, a measure of complicity with his shamefully beguiling creation. That's not to say that Shakespeare approves, or is inviting our approval, of the havoc Iago wreaks for his own sadistic gratification. But the upstart crow in him will not disavow the vicarious guilty pleasure he takes, and expects us to share, in Iago's licence to outsmart and torment his betters without remorse. At the same time, we're forced to confront the appalling cost of that pleasure, as the curtain falls on a black man and his white wife lying dead together on their marriage bed with the corpse of the bride's courageous maid beside them: 'Look on the tragic loading of this bed: / The object poisons sight' (5.2.361–2). Shakespeare builds into *Othello* the knowledge that to write this tragedy like that, with such a villain contriving that denouement, and to pay to be entertained and enlightened by watching it, is to be implicated in what happens, not only in the play's world but also in the world the play reflects, where such things have happened, and are still happening, for real.

A Pageant to Keep Us in False Gaze

Shakespeare builds another vital kind of knowledge for the audience into *Othello* too: the knowledge of *how and why* such things happen and still happen. I quoted earlier Murry's observation that 'the inward and invisible must be made outward and visible' in *Othello*; one way of doing that being by means of the handkerchief, as we've seen, and the other by means of Iago, about which more now needs to be said.

Not the least of Iago's dramatic virtues is that he makes outward and visible the narratives that inwardly and invisibly grip people's hearts and minds, making them believe things that are not true and act to their cost as if they were. In this respect, he's a walking, talking incarnation of ideology in the sense of false consciousness: an object lesson in how susceptible people are to the travesties of reality implanted in them by their culture. Without Iago the tragedy could have taken essentially the same course with the same fatal conclusion, Othello having been seized by homicidal jealousy unprompted by anyone else. But *with* Iago we can see and hear ideology in action, as he fabricates an illusion to gain power over Othello, secure in the knowledge that Othello will find it as credible as Iago has found the equally false rumour of Othello's cuckolding him: 'I told him what I thought, and told no more / Than what he found himself was apt and true.' By objectifying through Iago the internalized means by which such a frame of mind normally takes hold, the tragedy throws its external, factitious origin into relief.

To recognize that there's nothing innate or natural about the patriarchal ideology Othello and Iago share is not to underestimate the tenacity of its grip on the minds of men and women. Shakespeare makes this plain too through Iago, the success of whose plot rests on his realization that Othello doesn't have to be actually cuckolded, he just has to be made to believe that he has been; and to make him believe that he has been, all that's required is to tell him a story to that effect which he finds convincing. The story need have no basis in fact or bear any relation to the truth. It need only sound and look as if it does to be believed. Like the scene of spurious aural and 'ocular proof' (3.3.363) Iago stages for Othello with Cassio's blind connivance, all that's required is 'imputation and strong circumstances' to satisfy Othello that he's been led 'directly to the door of truth' (3.3.409–10). Even before that charade takes place, the graphic sexual scenario Iago invents, casting himself as a surrogate Desdemona passionately embraced by a sleeping Cassio, suffices to clinch the matter for Othello. Deaf to Iago's dismissal of Cassio's fictitious behaviour as 'but his dream', Othello takes the bait without further thought: 'But this denoted a foregone conclusion' (3.3.429–30). Iago knows that 'Trifles light as air' can furnish 'confirmations strong / As proofs of holy writ' (3.3.325–7). He knows how needless it is to use physical force to destroy another human being, when it's enough to infect their mind, because 'Dangerous conceits are in their nature poisons' (3.3.329).

He knows that because Shakespeare knows it and is intent on the audience knowing it too by making them conscious of it. Failure to appreciate this aspect of *Othello* has spawned reams of futile commentary on the obvious impossibility of Desdemona's having cuckolded Othello at any point in the play's flagrantly incoherent time scheme – to say nothing of all the other improbabilities and inconsistencies with which the tragedy is riddled. After reviewing the play's most blatant temporal anomalies, Bradley confesses himself no wiser as to why 'Shakespeare did in *Othello* what he seems to do in no other play'. But, he adds, 'I find it hard to believe that he produced this impossible situation without knowing it'. The truth of the matter is that the impossibility of what Othello is primed to believe is *meant to be* obvious to the audience, but not to Othello, in order to dramatize the spellbinding power of the specious stories that induce us to ride roughshod over reason and self-interest, just like Othello. The same phenomenon can be observed in miniature in Iago's penchant for sententious statements that have the ring of received wisdom, such as: 'Men should be what they seem, / Or those that be not, would they might seem none' (3.3.129–30); or for remarks the apparent gist of which might strike the inattentive ear as apt, such as: 'I may not breathe my censure / What he might be: if what he might, he is not, / I would to heaven he were!' (4.1.270–2). Too much editorial ink has been spilled in misguided attempts to render these incoherent utterances coherent. They are not cryptic observations that deserve to be patiently deciphered. They are not supposed to make sense; they are supposed to sound as though they make sense when they plainly don't, in order to illustrate the seductiveness of superficial plausibility. Iago can rely on his interlocutors hearing even in sheer nonsense what he wants them to hear, which is what they expect to hear.

Our attention is repeatedly drawn by Shakespeare to the crucial role of what William Blake called 'mind-forged manacles' in creating the tragedy. His protagonists are shown to be unknowingly immured in a prison-house of narrative, shackled from first to last by tales they have been told or that they tell themselves. From the 'round unvarnished tale' Othello delivers in his defence before the Senate, we learn how he won Desdemona's heart by telling her his 'travailous history', which she devoured 'with a greedy ear' (1.3.91, 140, 150). So enthralling did she find the story of his life that she 'bade me', recalls Othello, 'if I had a friend that loved her, / I should but teach him how to tell my story / And that would woo her' (1.3.165–7). Othello rightly takes this as a flirtatious hint from Desdemona to declare his love for her. But it's also a testament to the autonomous power of the narrative to have the same spellbinding impact on the same listener regardless of the narrator. 'This only is the witchcraft I have used', says Othello, refuting Brabantio's absurd allegation with pointed irony. Nevertheless, there is a kind of witchcraft in a tale so captivating in itself that its capacity to disarm can be transferred not only to another speaker but to another auditor, as the Duke's comment attests: 'I think this tale would win my daughter too' (1.3.172). In this respect Othello's bewitching yarn is an exemplary instance of the hold cultural clichés in the guise of narratives can exert over the will, almost as if they had a mind of their own.

Iago's cynical debunking of Othello's prowess as a yarn-spinner is also a back-handed compliment from one master story-teller to another: 'Mark me with what violence she first loved the Moor, but for bragging and telling her fantastical lies' (2.1.220–1). Subjugating others to violent passions by telling them fantastical lies is Iago's forte, but before Othello falls prey to his falsehoods Shakespeare makes a point of showing Roderigo hopelessly ensnared in them too. Why? Because Roderigo's gulling and gullibility serve Iago and us as a rehearsal for Othello's. What Dr Johnson calls 'Roderigo's suspicious credulity, and impatient submission to the cheats which he sees practised upon him, and which by persuasion he suffers to be repeated' prefigure Othello's equally programmed response to a fiction he finds equally irresistible. The power of 'The tyrant custom' (1.3.230) to possess the will by activating ingrained narratives is nowhere more graphically illustrated than in the charade Iago stages with the guileless Cassio for Othello to witness as proof of Desdemona's adultery. 'I will make him tell the tale anew', Iago assures Othello, 'Where, how, how oft, how long ago, and when / He hath and is again to cope your wife' (4.1.85–7). Once Othello withdraws out of hearing, Iago informs us, his sole confidants, that the actual subject of his conversation with Cassio will be quite different, and expressly designed to make Othello 'construe / Poor Cassio's smiles, gestures and light behaviour / Quite in the wrong' (4.1.1102–4). Then we watch Othello do exactly that, misconstruing an exchange we can clearly hear but he cannot as 'the story' (4.1.131) he wants to hear, which exists entirely in his mind. The scene seeks to educate its audience in the mechanics of misprision by explaining theatrically how the trick is done.

Shakespeare strives throughout the tragedy to sharpen our awareness, and to awaken our distrust, of this irrational compulsion to connive in one's own deluding. An early warning against trusting the tales we're told unthinkingly is placed in the mouth of the senator whose response to the report that the Turkish fleet is heading for Rhodes is: 'This cannot be / By no assay of reason: 'tis a pageant / To keep us in false gaze' (1.3.18–20). The Duke's reaction shortly afterwards to Brabantio's lurid tale of how Othello must have subdued Desdemona 'with some mixtures powerful o'er the blood / Or with some dram conjured to this effect' is coolly sceptical: 'To vouch this is no proof, / Without more certain and more overt test / Than these thin habits and poor likelihoods / Of modern seeming' (1.3.107–10). And it's Emilia who asks the simple questions the play cries out for Othello to ask to break the spell of the pageant that keeps him in false gaze: 'Why should he call her whore? Who keeps her company? / What place, what time, what form, what likelihood?' (4.2.139–40). Shakespeare's concern with the role of narratives in the tragedy even finds subliminal expression in the quibbling of the Clown, whom Bradley dismisses as irrelevant: 'The clown is a poor one; we hardly attend to him and quickly forget him; I believe most readers of Shakespeare, if asked whether there was a clown in *Othello*, would answer No.' But, poor though the Clown in *Othello* might seem when compared with the Gravedigger in *Hamlet*, Lear's Fool or the Porter in *Macbeth*, it would be a mistake not to attend to him, especially when one considers the points in the play at which Shakespeare takes care to place his calculated doubletalk.

At the start of Act 3, at the turning point of the play, just before Iago plants the first seed of suspicion in Othello's mind, Shakespeare sends in the Clown to bait the musicians Cassio has hired to play an aubade for the Moor and his bride outside their quarters:

CLOWN
> Why, masters, have your instruments been in Naples, that they speak i'th' nose thus?

1 MUSICIAN
> How, sir? How?

CLOWN
> Are these, I pray you, wind instruments?

1 MUSICIAN
> Ay marry are they, sir.

CLOWN
> O, thereby hangs a tail.

1 MUSICIAN
> Whereby hangs a tail, sir?

CLOWN
> Marry, sir, by many a wind instrument that I know.

> (3.1.1–11)

The coarse gag and figurative whiff of flatulence at the musicians' expense serve no purpose as far as the plot is concerned, so the whole exchange is routinely excised from productions and overlooked by critics as redundant comic blather. But Shakespeare held the irreverent clowns and wise fools of his comedies and tragedies in higher esteem, time and again entrusting them to secrete in frivolous equivocation or crackpot sophistry the core concerns of the play. In his undeniably more modest way, the Clown in *Othello* is no exception. His opening shtick with the first musician is contrived to set up the homonymic pun that conflates 'tail' and 'tale', phallus and fiction, because it captures in a quip the phallocratic narrative ultimately responsible for this patriarchal tragedy: 'Yet she must die, else she'll betray more men'. The Clown encodes in a crude wisecrack the fact that what's at stake in *Othello* is nothing less than the notion of male supremacy. It's a classic Shakespearean device for tuning us subconsciously to matters of great moment at key points by seeming to be pointless. A few lines later, having shooed the musicians offstage, and seconds before 'Honest Iago' (1.3.295) enters to make a mockery of his fixed epithet, the Clown retorts to Cassio's query, 'Dost thou hear, mine honest friend?': 'No, I hear not your honest friend, I hear you' (3.1.21–2). Refusing to spare Cassio his compulsive quibbles (3.1.23), the Clown wilfully misconstrues Cassio's inquiry to pre-echo the issues raised by Othello's giving ear to the lies of a man he mistakes for his honest friend. And no sooner has the torrid exchange in Act 3 between Othello and Iago ended with Desdemona's fate sealed by the latter's lies than the quibbling Clown pops up again, this time to harp on the words 'lie' and 'lies' (3.4.1–13) in an otherwise superfluous bit of banter with Desdemona herself.

The tragedy's foregrounding of false narratives prises Othello and Desdemona apart from the fictions that transfix and doom them, but that neither define them nor deny the life they deserve to have lived together in the liberated world their love makes imaginable. Like Shakespeare's other tragedies, *Othello* is a lament for unlived possibilities, for the terrible toll taken on the way life should be by the way it does not have to be. As such, like Shakespeare's other tragedies, it harks forward in time as well as back, a testament to the need and the right of men and women, then and now, to realize their full potential in a just society.

The speech Othello delivers at the end of the play to distract his captors and buy time to kill himself is charged with this distinctively Shakespearean sense of tragically unrealized selfhood, of a destiny unfulfilled. It's pitched as one last hypnotic narrative, a montage of biographical tableaux that turns out to be an obituary:

When you shall these unlucky deeds relate,
Speak of me as I am. Nothing extenuate,
Nor set down aught in malice. Then must you speak
Of one that loved not wisely, but too well;
Of one not easily jealous, but, being wrought,
Perplexed in the extreme; of one whose hand,
Like the base Indian, threw a pearl away
Richer than all his tribe; of one whose subdued eyes,
Albeit unused to the melting mood,
Drops tears as fast as the Arabian trees
Their medicinable gum. Set you down this,
And say besides that in Aleppo once,
Where a malignant and a turbanned Turk
Beat a Venetian and traduced the state,
I took by th' throat the circumcised dog
And smote him – thus!

(5.2.339–54)

With that, Othello stabs *himself*. That he's mustering all the resources of his eloquence here to exert control over how he'll be remembered, forging images of himself that place him in a sympathetic and ultimately heroic light, is as undeniable as it's understandable. But his failure to heed his own instruction to 'Extenuate nothing' is less significant than the fact that, when he starts to relate the story of 'these unlucky deeds', he does so almost exclusively in the third person and the past tense, as that version of him recedes, turning into someone else he can now look back upon. So complete does his detachment from his tale of himself become that in the stunning final sentence of the speech and the suicidal act in which it issues Othello performs a complex allegory of his tragic fate. For he casts himself both as the loyal servant of the Venetian state and as the Turk, 'the circumcised dog' Venice feels threatened by and treats with contempt. As he stabs himself, he enacts the fact that he has been at once the alien victim of Venetian society and the complicit agent of his own destruction.

The fully grasped effect of these lines is crucial, because their estranged version of Othello's fate frames it as a socially scripted tragedy of which he has been the unwitting protagonist. Shortly before he kills himself, in answer to Lodovico's question, 'Where is this rash and most unfortunate man?', Othello replies: 'That's he that was Othello: here I am' (F: 5.2.280–1). The tragedy of Othello for Shakespeare lies in the gulf that yawns between those two pronouns and those two verbs: between the 'he' imprisoned forever in the past as Othello, the noble Moor deranged by homicidal jealousy, and the bewildered 'I', the unaccommodated, nameless human being left stranded in a present that has no place for all that he was capable of becoming.

CHAPTER 7
KING LEAR: SHAKESPEARE'S LEVIATHAN

A Play Fit for a King

In 1606 *King Lear* 'was played before the King's Majesty at Whitehall upon St Stephen's night in Christmas holidays', as the title page of the 1608 Quarto records. What the King's Majesty and his court made of the play that his own company, the King's Men, staged for the festive entertainment of their patron is not recorded. The Feast of St Stephen (better known now as Boxing Day) was traditionally associated with providing hospitality and giving alms to the poor. So *King Lear* may have been chosen as a play whose impassioned appeals for altruism were especially suited to the occasion and unlikely to leave its affluent audience unmoved. But whatever the reason for its performance that night and however it was received, the wonder is that Shakespeare's company got away with performing a play as seditious as *King Lear* before King James at all. As Shaw wrote when summing up his view of Shakespeare's political stance: 'whoever will read *Lear* and *Measure for Measure* will find stamped on his mind such an appalled sense of the danger of dressing man in a little brief authority, such a merciless stripping of the purple from the "poor, bare, forked animal" that calls itself a king and fancies itself a god, that one wonders what was the real nature of the mysterious restraint that kept "Eliza and our James" from teaching Shakespeare to be civil to crowned heads'.

It's hard to imagine how the subversive bearing of *King Lear* on any royal regime, including his own, could have escaped James and his court as they watched it. A mighty monarch, James's legendary precursor on the throne of Albion, is robbed not just of his royalty but of the roof over his head, and forced to feel the deprivation, the biting cold and the despair that the hungry, homeless outcasts of his kingdom must endure. A ruler who, like James, the author of *The True Law of Free Monarchies*, regards himself as divinely endowed with absolute power over his subjects, is disobeyed by his own daughters and driven insane by impotent rage and unbearable guilt. His derangement estranges him from everything he once took for granted, compelling him to call into question sovereignty itself and the unjust social order on which it's predicated. His recognition of the blame he must bear as a king and as a father is not enough, however, to redeem him. His relentless suffering is rewarded at the end not with deliverance, but with yet more anguish and a harrowing death, as he gazes in disbelief upon the lifeless lips of his dearest daughter, with whom he had hoped to live out his remaining years in peace.

Samuel Johnson found the ending of *King Lear* too distressing to reread until he came to edit the play, famously complaining in his editorial notes that 'Shakespeare has suffered the virtue of Cordelia to perish in a just cause, contrary to the natural ideas of justice, to the hope of the reader, and, what is yet more strange, to the faith of the chronicles'. What Johnson found so hard to fathom was Shakespeare's departure from previous versions of the story by killing Cordelia off, thereby sealing her father's fate too, despite having led us to expect her to be saved at the last minute and both of them to survive. When Bradley wrestled with the same question a century and a half later, what exercised him most was the fact that 'no clear reason is supplied for Edmund's delay in attempting to save Cordelia and Lear', as a result of which 'this catastrophe, unlike those of all the other mature tragedies, does not seem at all inevitable'. The absence of an adequate explanation for the glaring delay that permits the catastrophe to take place obliged Bradley to draw the obvious conclusion: 'The *real* cause lies outside the dramatic *nexus*. It is Shakespeare's wish to deliver a sudden and crushing blow to the hopes which he has excited.'

The briefest comparison of *King Lear* with its principal source puts the uncompromising mood in which Shakespeare wrote it beyond dispute. For the story of Lear and his family he relied chiefly on an anonymous older play, *The True Chronicle History of King Leir and his three daughters, Gonerill, Ragan, and Cordella*, which was published in 1605, but which had been performed in 1594 by a cast that may have included Shakespeare. To the plotline of this play Shakespeare made some crucial alterations and additions. He invented new characters, including Oswald and, most importantly, the Fool; he turned the king's folly into full-scale madness and created the storm scene in which it erupts; and he expunged virtually every trace of his source's Christian spirit, leaving the cast of *King Lear* marooned in a bleak, pagan universe. But his boldest decision as he reworked *The True Chronicle History* was his decision to destroy its benign denouement. The tragicomedy of *King Leir* concludes with Leir's sovereignty restored, Cordella reunited with Leir, and every one of the characters still alive. Shakespeare's *King Lear* terminates in unrelieved misery, with the shattered monarch, all three of his daughters and almost everyone else dead, and nothing from which the few characters left standing can take consolation. Shakespeare was familiar with the other Elizabethan versions of the Lear story related in Higgins's *Mirror for Magistrates*, Holinshed's *Chronicles of England* and Spenser's *Fairie Queene*. But in all these versions the story ends with the Lear figure restored to his throne and continuing for a time as king, while Cordelia's counterpart lives on and dies much later, long after her father's natural demise. The brutal, comfortless ending inflicted on the audience of *King Lear* is without precedent in the transmission of the tale, and clearly reflects Shakespeare's determination to confound the sanguine expectations he aroused by telling it again.

Not content with that, Shakespeare magnified the impact of Lear's fate in a fully developed parallel plot – the only one in all his tragedies – by recounting the fate of the Earl of Gloucester, which follows the same pattern of agony, enlightenment and oblivion. The terrible price Gloucester pays for aiding the king, and for the credulity that leaves him at the mercy of his treacherous son and outlaws his loyal son, is to have his eyes gouged out and be forced to feel his way like a common vagabond to the death he craves to end his suffering. Through his ordeal the once wealthy, feared and powerful earl learns the same lesson his tormented monarch is made to learn. Like Lear's madness, Gloucester's blinding uproots him from the culture that had defined his identity and his values. His view of the world, like Lear's, is turned upside down as he realizes the human cost of the privileged life he took for granted and is seized with compassion for the victims of poverty and oppression he helped to create.

Once again, Shakespeare's departures from his source are instructive. He found his inspiration for the Gloucester plot in Sidney's prose romance *Arcadia*, which includes the story of a king deposed and blinded by his wicked bastard son after being duped into seeking the death of his virtuous legitimate son. Like his counterpart in *Arcadia*, Gloucester's legitimate son, Edgar, leads his blind father on his way. But unlike him Edgar does so in disguise, concealing his identity from his grief-stricken father until the end of their journey together, when the shock of its disclosure precipitates Gloucester's death. In *Arcadia*, too, the father's demise occurs only after his virtuous son has been enthroned in his place, while the latter pardons his villainous brother on condition that he change his ways. That Shakespeare decides instead to have Edgar mortally wound his evil sibling, Edmund, and that he denies the dying Gloucester and the audience the certain knowledge that Edgar will reign after Lear, is further proof of his intention to darken the tragedy by draining every drop of solace from its final moments.

Nor does Shakespeare confine the chastening experience of degradation and enlightenment to Lear and Gloucester. Bereft of his aristocratic identity like his king and his father, on an impulse without parallel in *Arcadia* Edgar assumes the tortured persona of the demented beggar Tom o'Bedlam. As Tom he embodies the appalling misery of the abandoned poor that Lear, Gloucester and Edgar himself are compelled to acknowledge and empathize with. Unlike Gloucester and Lear, Edgar does survive his trials and resume his place among the nobility, but only to end up the presumptive king of a desolate kingdom, whose future is anything but clear. Lear's faithful counsellor, the Earl of Kent, refuses to share the rule of the realm with Edgar, preferring to follow his sovereign to the grave rather than remain in a world where, as he says, 'All's cheerless, dark and deadly' (5.3.288). He too, like Edgar, has relinquished the base-born alter ego that shrouded his identity as a peer of the realm for most of the play. In the guise of the plain-spoken Caius, he has endured the ignominy of the stocks, shared Lear's waking nightmare in the storm and borne witness to his moving reunion with Cordelia, only to behold his king and Cordelia 'dead as earth' (5.3.259).

To see the baleful arc of the monarch's fate mirrored in the fates of loyal noblemen like Gloucester, Edgar and Kent is to realize that the target on which Shakespeare's tragic vision is trained is wider than the play's title suggests. Given the deaths not only of Lear, Cordelia and Gloucester, but also of Edmund, Cornwall, Goneril and Regan, and given the presumed death of Lear's Fool and the impending death of Kent too, the final impression left by the tragedy is of a whole dispensation laid low and liquidated. Whether that was the impression the play left on James I on St Stephen's night must remain a matter for conjecture. The King's Men's royal patron may well have been as oblivious to the full import of *King Lear* as most subsequent audiences and critics of the play have been. But it's worth remembering that a few decades later, in 1649, 'the great image of authority' (4.6.154) in the shape of James's son, Charles I, was put to death by Parliament and his kingdom replaced by a Commonwealth. It's by no means unreasonable to suppose that

King Lear, more than most of Shakespeare's tragedies and history plays, helped to foster the climate of dissidence that made that revolution possible.

Nothing renders that supposition more credible than Nahum Tate's drastic redaction of *King Lear* to suit the post-revolutionary Restoration culture of Charles II. Tate cut around eight hundred lines, ditching the Fool and his insubordinate satire as well as his prophetic riddling in the process. He removed the King of France in order to turn Cordelia and Edgar into virtuous lovers, to whom Lear bequeaths his recovered kingdom. And he preserved the lives of Lear, Kent and Gloucester, whom Lear dissuades from committing suicide, dispatching them to tranquil retirement in a 'cool Cell' where, cheered by 'the prosperous Reign / Of this celestial Pair', they will pass their twilight years meditating on 'Fortunes past'. Tate's intention was 'to rectify what was wanting in the regularity and probability of the tale', and to do so above all by making his version 'conclude in a success to the innocent distressed persons' instead of in their extinction. His play ends with Edgar declaring to Cordelia: 'Thy bright example shall convince the world, / Whatever storms of fortune are decreed, / That Truth and Virtue shall at last succeed.' To bring Shakespeare's tragedy into line with the taste of his time, Tate turned it back into the bland tragicomedy Shakespeare set out to demolish. That Tate's sentimental travesty supplanted Shakespeare's *King Lear* on the English Stage from 1681 until 1838 is a testament to the implacable animus of the play that Shakespeare wrote.

As Charles Lamb observed over two hundred years ago in his essay 'On the Tragedies of Shakespeare' (1811), the trouble with Shakespeare's *King Lear* is that for Tate and his ilk

> it is too hard and stony; it must have love scenes and a happy ending. It is not enough that Cordelia is a daughter, she must shine as a lover too. Tate has put his hook in the nostrils of this Leviathan, for Garrick and his followers, the showmen of the scene, to draw the mighty beast about more easily.

Lamb was right. There is something 'hard and stony', even monstrous, about the vision of *King Lear* as Shakespeare framed it that most critics since Dr Johnson, and most productions from Tate's day to ours, have flinched from, even after Shakespeare's text began to be restored to the stage by Macready in 1838. Frank Kermode did not flinch from it, however, in his response to the play at the close of the twentieth century. In *Shakespeare's Language* Kermode doesn't hesitate to describe the dramatist's attitude to his characters in *King Lear* as one of 'authorial savagery'. 'There is a cruelty in the writing', he observes, 'that echoes the cruelty of the story, a terrible calculatedness that puts one in mind of Cornwall's and Regan's. Suffering has to be protracted and intensified, as it were, without end.' No wonder so many modern productions of *King Lear* still choose to play it for pathos as a domestic melodrama, as the tale of a vain, tyrannical patriarch redeemed too late by his angelic daughter's love, rather than meet its unforgiving gaze.

In the previous chapter on *Othello* I quoted Bradley's admission to sharing the shameful reluctance of white readers and audiences to confront the reality of Shakespeare's portrayal of the hero as an unequivocally black-skinned African. The admission prompts Bradley to this arresting conclusion, which is worth quoting again here because of its relevance to the critical and theatrical reception of *King Lear*: 'We do not like the real Shakespeare. We like to have his language pruned and his conceptions flattened into something that suits our mouths and minds.' Especially because of the way it ends, showing as little mercy to the hopes of the audience as it does to the hopes of the characters, *King Lear* has suffered more than most of the tragedies from the pressure to make it palatable onstage and in the classroom by keeping 'the real Shakespeare' it reveals at bay. But it's only if Shakespeare's Leviathan is unleashed, and the mighty beast Lamb beheld in *King Lear* is confronted head-on, that the more profound purpose of the tragedy's 'authorial savagery' becomes clear.

The question of the imaginative and emotional appeal of inhumanity to Shakespeare in his tragic vein is posed with unusual urgency by *King Lear*: inhumanity not only as a feature of the plays – the acts of physical and mental cruelty, the murders and atrocities their characters commit – but also as a disconcerting aspect of their dramatic vision. The inhuman is entwined with the human in Shakespeare's tragic imagination, and in ways that reveal how deeply at odds he was with his era. To grasp the rationale of Shakespeare's resort to inhumanity in *King Lear* is to grasp its utopian intolerance of the travesty that passed for human life in his time. The man who created *King Lear* would have known exactly what Adorno was driving at when he wrote: 'The inhumanity of art must triumph over the inhumanity of the world for the sake of the humane.' If one assumes that the tragedy was written by a playwright whose intellect and imagination were constrained by his allegiance to the social order mirrored in *King Lear*, then one's inevitably prone to mistake the characters' mood at the end for the vision of the play as a whole, and come away feeling like Kent that 'All's cheerless, dark and deadly'. But if one assumes the reverse to be the case, and reads *King Lear* as the work of a dramatist whose moral compass and imaginative standpoint were so divorced from the ethos of his age that he could write, to quote Coleridge, 'as if he were of another planet, with perfect abstraction from himself', then the inspiring and empowering vision of Shakespeare's most audacious tragedy stands revealed. For Mikhail Bakhtin, 'the essence of Shakespeare's world-consciousness', the source of his drama's enduring global appeal, is his 'belief in the possibility of a complete exit from the present order of this life'. In no tragedy of Shakespeare's is that belief dramatized more forcefully than in *King Lear*.

Echoes and Anticipations (i)

It's essential to bear in mind that the world view of the play Shelley hailed as 'the most perfect specimen of the dramatic art existing in the world' didn't spring up from nowhere. It can be traced back through Shakespeare's previous tragedies and had its roots like them in the first two *Henry VI* plays that launched his career as a dramatist. Think again of that seminal moment in *2 Henry VI* when the tragic gulf between Henry the man and Henry the monarch is first glimpsed. Think of his humiliating encounter in *3 Henry VI* with the keepers, those insolent underlings who capture him and regard his quondam royalty with contempt. Think of Henry's mounting indifference to his sovereignty and longing for death to terminate his woes. In Shakespeare's portrayal and treatment of Henry the seeds of his portrayal and treatment of Lear can already be discerned. There's even an echo of Henry in the captured Lear's poignant appeal to Cordelia, 'Come, let's away to prison. / We too alone will sing like birds i'the cage' (5.3.8–9); when freed from prison to resume a throne he has no more desire than Lear to resume, Henry describes his incarceration as having been 'such a pleasure as encaged birds / Conceive, when after many moody thoughts, / At last, by notes of household harmony, / They quite forget their loss of liberty' (3HVI 4.6.12–15). It's says a great deal about Shakespeare that the first serious subject to which he chose to devote his creative energy, and which gripped his imagination through two whole plays, was not a chauvinistic paean to a heroic English monarch, but a study of the hapless king of an England in the bloody throes of civil war, who was unfitted and unwilling to be a king, yet who for that very reason could be regarded as heroic in another sense. It's no less telling that Shakespeare remained fascinated by characters and plots that allowed him to play variations on this theme right through to and beyond *King Lear* over a decade later.

Just a few years after the *Henry VI* plays, Shakespeare returned in *Richard II* to probing the psyche and tracing the fate of a king cast in much the same mould as Henry. The debt the characterization of Richard in the last three acts owes to the characterization of Henry is as striking as the debt the portrayal of Lear owes to both. The affinities with Henry and the foretastes of Lear are unmistakable from the moment when, as the tide turns against him in Act 3, Richard replies to Aumerle's 'Remember who you are': 'I had forgot myself. Am I not king?' (*RII* 3.2.82–3). Within a hundred lines he is contemplating the abject vulnerability of whoever wears 'the hollow crown' (3.2.160) to the universal despotism of death. Realizing that beneath his regalia he is merely 'flesh and blood' (3.2.171), just as Lear does when confronted by Poor Tom in the storm, he beseeches his followers to

> Throw away respect,
> Tradition, form and ceremonious duty,
> For you have but mistook me all this while.
> I live with bread like you, feel want,
> Taste grief, need friends. Subjected thus,
> How can you say to me I am a king?

> (*RII* 3.2.172–7)

The tenor of the whole speech from which these closing lines come has clear antecedents in *2 Henry VI*. The last two lines in particular, with their inversion of the roles of ruler and ruled, hark back to Henry's 'Was never subject longed to be a king / As I do long and wish to be a subject' (*2HVI* 4.9.5–6) and the keepers' demeaning reminder that they ceased to be subjects the moment he ceased to be king. But they also point forward to Lear's sardonic reply when the blind Gloucester asks, 'Is't not the King?': 'Ay, every inch a king', says the self-deposed sovereign, 'When I do stare, see how the subject quakes' (4.6.106–7).

Like the uncrowned Henry before him and the uncrowned Lear after him, 'who hates him / That would upon the rack of this tough world / Stretch him out longer' (5.3.312–14), the uncrowned Richard yearns for the grave's deliverance. In the interim he finds solace like Henry in the liberation from his royal self that actual imprisonment grants him, and that the mere prospect of imprisonment with Cordelia affords Lear. The riveting long soliloquy Richard delivers in prison minutes before his murder concludes with a passage replete with anticipations of *King Lear*'s core concerns:

> Thus play I in one person many people,
> And none contented. Sometimes am I king;
> Then treasons make me wish myself a beggar,
> And so I am. Then crushing penury
> Persuades me I was better when a king;
> Then am I kinged again, and by and by
> Think that I am unkinged by Bolingbroke,
> And straight am nothing. But whate'er I be,
> Nor I nor any man that but man is
> With nothing shall be pleased till he be eased
> With being nothing.

(RII 5.5.31–41)

The intimation of abundance in the different selves divulged by the relinquishment of royalty; the arbitrary, insubstantial character of kingship, slipped off, then on, then off again, as readily as an actor slips in and out of a role; the collapsing of the distinction between king and beggar, as the once highest in the land identifies himself with the lowest of the low, both of them being 'but man'; the brutal reduction of the unkinged king to 'nothing', and the compulsive reworking of that word until it yields a paradoxical sense of plenitude in being bereft of everything: these will all be taken up again and developed in *King Lear*.

The whole soliloquy illustrates the most striking respect in which Richard's characterization expands upon Henry's and prefigures Lear's. The lower he sinks socially, the higher he rises in our esteem; the more he ceases to count as a king, the more admirable he becomes as a human being. As Alfred Polgar put it: 'He was, with God's blessing, a weak, empty king, and becomes, with God's ill-will, a full, fruitful man, out of whom necessity presses sweetness and wisdom. He falls upward into depth.' The same could scarcely be said of Titus Andronicus, but the protagonist of Shakespeare's first indisputable tragedy, written before *Richard II*, is in other respects a more obvious prototype of King Lear. Long before Shakespeare brought the latter to life upon the stage, he made his debut as a tragedian with a play about an irascible Roman patriarch, whose pig-headed political imprudence and impetuous cruelty to his own flesh and blood in the opening act has horrific and ultimately fatal consequences for himself and his beloved daughter. Crazed with grief and rage like Lear, Titus too becomes irrevocably alienated from the society at whose pinnacle he once stood, and whose callousness he once personified but has learned to revile. Even at the start of the play, the exercise of sovereign power holds no more appeal for him than it does for the abdicating Lear. As the tragedy proceeds, his contempt for those who rule becomes as unconfined as Lear's, when Lear mocks authority as nothing but a dog barking at a beggar (4.6.150–1). Having ceased to exist in such an intolerable world is the state to which, like Henry and Richard as well as Lear, Titus aspires. The only thing that matters to him while he lives is his belated devotion to his daughter Lavinia, 'The cordial of mine age to glad my heart' (*TA* 1.1.170), which finds such touching parallels in Lear's reborn love for Cordelia.

Not the least remarkable feature of *Titus Andronicus* that Shakespeare redeploys in *King Lear* is its conflation of disparate historical epochs within the temporal bounds of the tragedy. The timescape of *Titus* not only spans the entire history of Rome from republican dawn to imperial twilight, but also finds ways of embracing the Elizabethan present of the play's first audiences. The result, as we saw, is a compressed dramatization of a collapsing civilization from a retrospective standpoint in an era far beyond it. In *Lear* likewise, Shakespeare confounds temporal distinctions through what Stephen Booth has called its 'crazy quilt of frames of reference'. Ostensibly set centuries ago in ancient Britain, the play shuttles back and forth between the remote, mythical past, the Jacobean reality it reflects, and vantage points in futures that lie both within and beyond our imaginative grasp. The effect again, as we'll see, is to create like *Titus* an apocalyptic vision of a whole social order in terminal decline that bears an uncanny resemblance to our own. Shakespeare's second Roman tragedy is imbued with the same ominous atmosphere too, as the apocalyptic imagery that burns through it vividly attests. The sense of irrevocable doom that made *Julius Caesar* so relevant to the modern world for Auden is summed up in a single line near the end of the play: 'The sun of Rome is set. Our day is gone' (5.3.63). Several years on from *Titus Andronicus*, the desire to portray Roman society in its death-throes – a society the dominant culture of Elizabethan England revered and sought to emulate – remained as strong as ever in Shakespeare. When he envisioned a society closer to home on the brink of extinction in *King Lear*, he was adopting a dramatic standpoint that lay ready to hand in his own repertoire.

The sense *King Lear* creates of looking back on a heartless world from a position of Olympian detachment after 'the promised end' (5.3.261) is palpable in *Hamlet* too. It's vested in the prince himself from his first appearance in the second scene, when he confides to us in soliloquy, even before he meets his father's ghost, that his alienation from 'all the uses of this world' (F: 1.2.132) is complete and curable only by death. Hamlet is tormented by the same tragic conflict between his awakened self and his crippling royal role that first afflicted Henry VI and Richard II, and that tears Lear apart in his storm-lashed encounter with the beggar Edgar harbours within himself. Echoes of Richard and pre-echoes of *King Lear* are audible in Hamlet's contention that 'The King is a thing ... Of nothing' (4.2.26–8) and that 'Your fat king and your lean beggar is but variable service, two dishes but to one table' (4.3.23–4), because death dissolves the ephemeral distinction that once divided them. To see through the hoax of class society with such dispassionate clarity requires a viewpoint disengaged from that society, the posthumous viewpoint of 'doomsday' (F: 5.1.59) that pervades the graveyard scene.

The vitriolic outbursts of misanthropy and misogyny to which Hamlet gives vent are the inexorable upshot of the impossible fix in which he finds himself. His own kind, who ought to be 'the beauty of the world, the paragon of animals', he despises in such moments as 'this quintessence of dust' (2.2.272–4). And Ophelia is subjected to an unprovoked tirade against the duplicity of her sex that culminates in a scathing condemnation of marriage, on the grounds that it only breeds more sinners like Ophelia and himself. King Lear's outrage at his plight spends itself in even harsher fulminations against humanity as a whole and the female of the species in particular: 'Strike flat the thick rotundity o'the world, / Crack nature's moulds, all germens spill at once / That make ungrateful man!' (3.2.6–9); 'Down from the waist they are centaurs, though women all above. But to the girdle do the gods inherit, beneath is all the fiend's: there's hell, there's darkness, there is the sulphurous pit, burning, scalding, stench, consumption!' (4.6.121–5). 'O ruined piece of nature', cries Gloucester, catching the apocalyptic tone of Lear's diatribe, 'this great world / Shall so wear out to nought' (4.6.130–1). The misanthropic rants Shakespeare writes with such obvious relish for Hamlet and Lear should not be confused with the stance of the plays in which they feature. But they do show how close to his heart in his tragic mood lay the feeling of utter revulsion from life in his time, and how swiftly that feeling could turn into a horror of generation and evocations of the end of mankind.

It's certainly no coincidence that the play on which Shakespeare was working immediately before, and possibly at the same time as, *King Lear* was the bizarre, abortive tragedy *Timon of Athens*, parts of which were penned by Middleton. Plutarch's tale of a powerful, wealthy man, who is unhinged by fury at the ingratitude of those he had lavished gifts upon, and who withdraws into exile in the woods outside Athens to excoriate the society that once fawned on him, plainly held the same appeal for Shakespeare as the potential he saw in *The True Chronicle History of King Leir*. Like the outcast Lear at the mercy of the elements, Timon the self-styled 'Misanthropos' (4.3.54) made the perfect mouthpiece for the vicious invective the state of mankind drove Shakespeare to; and in Timon's superb arias of loathing for a world that sacrifices 'the general weal' (4.3.59) to rabid self-interest he gave free rein to it, voicing views indistinguishable in tone and tenor from those voiced in Lear's fits of 'reason in madness' (4.6.171). 'Nothing I'll bear from thee / But nakedness' (4.1.32–3), cries Timon as he banishes himself from Athens, seized by the same urge as Lear, when he cries 'Off, off, you lendings' (3.4.106), to strip away with his clothes everything that comprised his regal self and the entire society it presupposed. Lear's desire to disrobe is provoked by the need to expose his physical identity with the beggar he beholds in the shape of Poor Tom; what remains of Timon too, once divested of his opulent attire as well as his wealth, is the same bare human creature, epitomized by the same image of abject destitution: 'his poor self, / A dedicated beggar to the air, / With his disease of all-shunned poverty, / Walks, like contempt, alone' (4.2.12–15).

Through Timon's unbridled harangues runs the same mutinous utopian logic that runs through *King Lear*, standing hierarchy on its head: 'Raise me this beggar and deject that lord: / The senator shall bear contempt hereditary, / The beggar native honour' (*TIM* 4.3.9–11). If further justification were needed for describing Shakespeare's frame of mind while writing *Timon* and *King Lear* as posthumous, it's graphically furnished by his obsession with Timon's envisaging of his epitaph and eventual inscription of it on a gravestone. For his epitaph allows Timon to express and savour while alive the abhorrence of the living, and the freedom at last from their despicable existence, that he expects the grave to grant him after death:

> Why, I was writing of my epitaph.
> It will be seen tomorrow. My long sickness
> Of health and living now begins to mend
> And nothing brings me all things.

(5.2.70–3)

The anticipated future in which the living will read his epitaph morphs into the present of that astounding final line, in which Timon describes the sublime state of fulfilment non-existence will bring him as if it has already arrived. With its paradoxically positive notion of nothing, a word as close to this play's heart as to *King Lear*'s, the line recalls the last lines of Richard II's last soliloquy and looks forward to lines in *Lear* such as 'Nothing almost sees miracles / But misery' (2.2.163–4) and 'Edgar I nothing am' (2.2.192).

Echoes and Anticipations (ii)

Timon of Athens is an especially valuable guide to *King Lear*, because we find so clearly distilled in it the essence of the standpoint from which *King Lear* was conceived and created. There's something distinctly Nietzschean *avant la lettre* about *Timon of Athens*. Nietzsche could have been speaking for both the protagonist of that play and the author of *King Lear* when he wrote in *The Gay Science*: 'We children of the future, how *could* we be at home in this today? ... Being new, nameless, hard to understand, we premature births of an as yet unproven future.' But *King Lear* is less hard to understand as the vision of a child of the future 'dreaming on things to come' (Sonnet 107) when the depth of its debt to the plays from which that vision grew is borne in mind. There's manifestly more to that debt than disenchantment and rejection. The need to write at an extreme imaginative remove from the ethos of the early modern era was inherent in Shakespearean tragedy from the moment it can be seen emerging in *2 Henry VI*. At its most pressing, not least in *King Lear*, that need could spawn rabid outbreaks of misanthropy and nihilism. Yet even at its bleakest Shakespearean tragedy never sinks into mere despair.

As the closer consideration of *King Lear* to which we'll shortly turn seeks to show, the radical utopian principles that drive Shakespeare's ruthless exposure of his world's inhumanity are not only implicitly dramatized throughout the tragedy, but also overtly invoked in speeches of startling temerity. Again, it's vital to remain aware of the provenance of that radical utopianism in Shakespeare's first *Henry VI* play and of its subsequent permutations in his previous tragedies. We saw earlier in this book that the birth of Shakespearean tragedy in the portrait of a king who longs to be free of his crown was indivisible from the creation in the same play of Jack Cade, the anarchic rebel leader 'inspired with the spirit of putting down kings and princes', who declares 'then are we in order when we are most out of order', and whose war cry is 'All the realm shall be in common' (*2HVI* 4.2.31–2, 63, 178–9). As the harrowing of its royal protagonist and the agony inflicted on the Earl of Gloucester attest, *King Lear* is inspired with the same spirit of putting down kings and princes. A direct line of descent runs from the levelling plebeian wit and utopian prophecy of Lear's Fool, and from the assault on authority and social injustice by the enlightened Lear himself in Act 4, straight back to Cade. En route to the latter it passes through *Hamlet*, whose egalitarian echoes of Cade ring loud and clear in the riddling voice of the Gravedigger and in the musings on the skulls of the mighty that his labour draws from the disabused prince he outquips. Before *Hamlet* they resound in the scene of festive misrule on which *Julius Caesar* opens, and above all in the sly quibbling of the Cobbler, Cade's nameless counterpart amongst the commoners of Rome, whose insolence the tribunes struggle to contain. And before that there's a cameo role in *Richard II* for another plebeian descendant of the wild Morisco, the anonymous Gardener who encrypts his seditious creed in the language of his trade: 'Go thou, and, like an executioner, / Cut off the heads of too fast-growing sprays / That look too lofty in our commonwealth. / All must be even in our government' (3.4.32–6).

The more implicit ways in which the radical utopianism inherited by *King Lear* finds expression are no less compelling for being implicit. The sight of the king kneeling to pray for the plight of those whose houseless poverty he shares, then face to face with a beggar in whom he sees himself, dramatizes the convictions of the play with an immediacy beyond the reach of impassioned contention alone. So does the unprecedented sight in *Hamlet* of a prince conversing on equal terms with a labourer as he toils at his trade onstage and meeting his match in his own line of pithy equivocation. The dissident thrust of both characters' speeches in the graveyard is deepened by their visible theatrical parity and audible idiomatic congruence; the unbridgeable gulf that divides them in the society within and beyond the play is both acknowledged and abolished by the way their encounter is conceived, staged and phrased. The seed of these iconic encounters in *Hamlet* and *Lear* lies in the confrontation Shakespeare devised between the uncrowned Henry VI and the unnamed keepers, whose disbelief in their captive's royalty prompts him to redefine his rank with a rhetorical question that foregrounds what they have in common: 'Do I not breathe a man?' (*3HVI* 3.1.81). The same desire to bring the highest in the land into dialogue with one of the lowest later inspires the moving exchange between Richard II and the 'poor groom', which grants his 'sometimes royal master' (5.5.72, 75) a moment's solace before his murder.

An equally strong egalitarian instinct lay behind Shakespeare's creation around the same time of the scene in *Romeo and Juliet* where Romeo seeks the means of suicide from a destitute apothecary. The apothecary hesitates to oblige him for fear of incurring the death penalty prescribed for selling poison. Romeo's reply bespeaks a disillusionment with his society that goes far beyond a rejection of its tribal codes of honour and sexual conventions:

Art thou so bare and full of wretchedness,
And fearest to die? Famine is in thy cheeks,
Need and oppression starveth in thy eyes,
Contempt and beggary hangs upon thy back,
The world is not thy friend, nor the world's law;
The world affords no law to make thee rich …
There is thy gold, worse poison to men's souls,
Doing more murder in this loathsome world
Than these poor compounds that thou mayst not sell.
I sell thee poison; thou hast sold me none.
Farewell, buy food, and get thyself in flesh.

(5.1.68–73, 80–4)

At the climax of the tragedy, Romeo's words to the wretched apothecary remind us that the cruel fate of the lovers is dwarfed by the inhumanity of 'the world's law', which robs the poor and starving of their fair share of the world's wealth. To those whose eyes reflect not the light of love but 'Need and oppression', whose cheeks are not flushed with passion but hollowed by 'famine', and whose destiny is to endure nothing but 'contempt and beggary', the romantic agonies of the upper class are merely another luxury they cannot afford. On the threshold of the catastrophe these lines, reinforced by the visual impact of the emaciated creature to whom they are addressed, reveal that *Romeo and Juliet* conceals a darker, more devastating tragedy of economic exploitation, which is the precondition of its exquisite poetry.

Ten years before he wrote *King Lear* the template for that tragedy's lament for the plight of the poor and its philippics against the systemic injustice that underlies it was already in place in Romeo's admonishment of the apothecary. One can readily imagine the first six lines being addressed by an appalled Lear to Poor Tom or some imaginary mendicant, so striking is their consonance with Lear's speeches to the same effect at climactic junctures in the later play. Two of the lines in particular are redolent of the 'reason in madness' that possesses Lear in Act 4: 'The world is not thy friend, nor the world's law; / The world affords no law to make thee rich'. What's so extraordinary about them is the degree of critical detachment from his society that they evince on Shakespeare's part: the ability to stand outside it and see through it that reaches its apogee in *King Lear*. That ability entails an equally extraordinary capacity for empathy with all those who find that neither the world nor the world's law is their friend, because the world affords no law to do them the justice they deserve simply by virtue of being human.

It's Shakespeare's commitment as a dramatist to the principle of human equality, to the cause of what unites us as opposed to what divides us, that *explains* the tragedy of Romeo and Juliet, robbed of the boundless mutual love they fleetingly enjoy; the interlocking indictments of racial and sexual inequality in *Othello*; the transfiguration of the patriarchal monster Titus by compassion for his mutilated daughter and of the heartless Moor Aaron by love for his newborn son; the arraignment of Rome in *Julius Caesar* for its betrayal of the ideals of liberty and the common good it claims to espouse;

the creation in *Hamlet* of a royal hero who spurns royalty, finds a kindred spirit in a gravedigger, and perceives in the skulls of the moneyed and the mighty a portent of revolution; and the visionary utopian realism of *King Lear*.

A Better Where to Find

'He found in the world without as actual what was in his world within as possible', remarks Stephen Dedalus of Shakespeare in *Ulysses*. 'Only Shakespeare has been optimistic', observed Chesterton of the tragedies, 'when he felt pessimistic.' That creative tension between actual and possible, between pessimism and optimism, energizes Shakespearean tragedy from the start, but nowhere does it come closer to breaking point than in *King Lear*. The play is conscious of the conflict at its core and draws our attention to it at the end of Act 3, scene 2, the turning point of the tragedy. As Lear and Kent exit to seek shelter from the storm, the Fool remains onstage, steps out through the world and time of the play, and addresses the audience in their world and time in typically cryptic terms:

> This is a brave night to cool a courtesan. I'll speak a prophecy ere I go:
>> When priests are more in word than matter,
>> When brewers mar their malt with water,
>> When nobles are their tailors' tutors,
>> No heretics burned but wenches' suitors;
>> When every case in law is right
>> No squire in debt, nor no poor knight;
>> When slanders do not live in tongues,
>> Nor cut-purses come not to throngs,
>> When usurers tell their gold i'the field,
>> And bawds and whores do churches build,
>> Then comes the time, who lives to see't,
>> That going shall be used with feet.
> This prophecy Merlin shall make, for I live before his time.

(3.2.79–96)

'This is one of the Shakespearian shocks or blows that take the breath away', wrote Chesterton of that final line. It takes the breath away because of the sudden state of temporal vertigo it induces. Pitched between wry satire and self-mocking parody, the Fool's vatic doggerel fuses harsh historical realities with utopian ideals, tuning our minds to their struggle for control of the play's vision. It does so in a way designed to confound our standpoint in time, and to go on doing so because of that uncanny final line. Present, past and future converge in the Fool's pre-emptive prophecy of a prophecy, whose parting shot catapults us beyond the age in which the play was written and beyond the current moment of its performance into the virtual realm of futurity.

Shakespearean Tragedy

The Fool's Delphic utterance encapsulates the profoundly anachronistic attitude of *King Lear* to the characters and events with which it's concerned. Like the previous tragedies of Shakespeare from which it grew, regardless of when and where they purport to be set, it speaks of its time in the language of its time, but not from the standpoint of its time. That prospective standpoint emerges in *King Lear* partly as a result of Lear's decision to abdicate and divide his kingdom, but mainly as a result of the catastrophic events set in train unwittingly by Cordelia in the Lear plot and deliberately by Edmund in the Gloucester plot. Although their motives and moral dispositions place them poles apart as *dramatis personae*, Cordelia and Edmund collude as agents of the violent disruption Shakespeare's purpose demands. They are both instrumental in engineering crises designed to put epitomes of the ruling class on the rack and subvert the assumptions and values that buttress the oppressive regime Lear and Gloucester personify. They both serve to instigate a process that throws into question what seemed normal, natural and necessary from the perspective of the status quo, and that redefines the scope of the desirable, the conceivable and the possible.

Just as Edmund's evil ruse to dupe his father and supplant Edgar leads to the latter's metamorphosis into Poor Tom as well as the blindness, insight and eventual death of Gloucester, so Cordelia's defiance of her father's will in the love test leads inexorably, if unintentionally, to his physical and mental torment, his climactic encounter with Tom in the storm, the transformation of identity and consciousness he undergoes, and his anguished death in the wake of the deaths of all three daughters. But the grounds and terms of Cordelia's refusal to comply with the charade Lear has devised for his public self-aggrandizement make it clear that more than filial disobedience is at stake. When Goneril and Regan declare in turn at Lear's request why their love for him exceeds their sisters' and are each rewarded with a third of the realm, the studied hyperbole of their unctuous speeches attests to their having rehearsed their parts in a ritual whose outcome for them is foreknown. They tell him exactly what he expects to hear in exchange for their share of land and power. But Cordelia's interjected aside to the audience in response to Goneril's speech suggests that she's been taken unawares by this display of supine adulation, from whose fraudulence she recoils: 'What shall Cordelia speak? Love, and be silent' (1.1.62). Regan's sycophantic pandering to Lear's imperious vanity in the same bogus vein as Goneril prompts Cordelia to a second aside which echoes the first: 'Then poor Cordelia, / And yet not so, since I am sure my love's / More ponderous than my tongue' (1.1.76–8). But although they take us into her confidence, assuming we share her belief that genuine love can't be defined and quantified in words, these unstudied asides scarcely prepare us for the shock of Cordelia's reply when her father asks her: 'what can you say to draw / A third more opulent than your sisters?':

CORDELIA
  Nothing, my lord.
LEAR
  Nothing?

CORDELIA

   Nothing.

LEAR

   How, nothing will come of nothing. Speak again.

CORDELIA

   Unhappy that I am, I cannot heave
   My heart into my mouth. I love your majesty
   According to my bond, no more nor less.

(1.1.85–93)

This exchange marks the irruption into Lear's world of an ethos begotten by it but utterly alien to it. Cordelia rejects the role of dutiful, adoring daughter that her father expects her to play like her sisters and in doing so declines to obey her sovereign as his subject too. The private wound she inflicts on him as the child he loved most, and on whose 'kind nursery' (1.1.124) in his retirement he had counted, is aggravated by the public wound to his regal ego. But Lear's pain and his humiliation before his court and the kings of France and Burgundy matter less than preserving her moral integrity, which she prizes more than pleasing him, and more than the land, wealth and sway that pleasing him with fawning words would purchase. Cordelia prides herself on lacking what she later calls 'that glib and oily art / To speak and purpose not' (1.1.225–6) at which her sisters excel. She prefers to say nothing and be silent rather than speak with 'such a tongue' (1.1.233) as theirs. For to do so would be to succumb to the language of comparison, competition and calculation that treats love as a commodity and puts a price on it, unlike the King of France, who understands like Cordelia that 'Love's not love / When it is mingled with regards that stands / Aloof from th' entire point' (1.1.229). The fundamental importance of Cordelia's refusal to mouth the vacuous blandishments Lear's vanity requires is nowhere underlined more emphatically than in the couplet with which Edgar begins the closing speech of the play: 'The weight of this sad time we must obey, / Speak what we feel, not what we ought to say' (5.3.322–3).

The impossibility of extricating oneself from the linguistic constraints of one's society without ceasing to speak altogether becomes apparent, however, as soon as Cordelia endeavours to explain to Lear what she means by 'I love your majesty / According to my bond, no more nor less':

         Good my lord,
You have begot me, bred me, loved me. I
Return those duties back as are right fit,
Obey you, love you and most honour you.
Why have my sisters husbands, if they say
They love you all? Haply when I shall wed,
That lord whose hand must take my plight shall carry
Half my love with him, half my care and duty.

Sure I shall never marry like my sisters
To love my father all.

(1.1.95–104)

Despite the pains Cordelia takes to keep her speech plain, direct and measured in contrast to the ornate extravagance of Goneril and Regan, she can't help resorting to the language of quantification and comparison prescribed by Lear's love-test, and ends up asserting her moral superiority over her sisters. There's no denying the steely glint of spite in that last sentence, whose truthfulness can't disguise its barbed desire to hurt. It would be a mistake to see Cordelia simply as the seraphic antithesis of her wicked siblings, with whom she shares a bent for inflexible obstinacy patently bequeathed by their progenitor. But it would also be a mistake to reduce her brave intransigence in the face of Lear's mounting anger to a psychologically explicable act of retaliation against a possessive, domineering father. For that would be to explain away the uncanny aspect of her character.

The cumulative effect of Cordelia's speaking to us aside, her decision to be silent rather than reply as required, her insistence on saying 'Nothing', and the impassive precision of 'I love your majesty / According to my bond, no more nor less', is to set her apart as the voice and symbol of a sensibility that belongs to a new dispensation. In this respect, as Wilson Knight astutely inferred, 'She is of the future humanity, suffering in the present dispensation for her very virtue'. To those who belong like Lear at the start of the play to the present dispensation, Cordelia's unbending rectitude seems heartless and baffling. The truly humane are bound to sound austere and inhuman to those whose hearts and minds are wedded to the inhumanity of the world as it is. Bradley goes too far when he writes that the death of Cordelia evokes 'the feeling that what happens to such a being does not matter; all that matters is what she is' – by which he means what she embodies, what she stands for, in the tragedy. But he's responding like Knight to the uncanniness of her depiction, to her remote, otherworldly quality, which doesn't eclipse her credibility as the flesh-and-blood daughter of a king. On the contrary, the utopian potency of Cordelia is strengthened by the care Shakespeare takes to ground it in a personality realistic enough to prevent her dissolving into an allegorical abstraction.

Cordelia's embodiment of the play's utopian trajectory is underscored by the loyal Kent's intervention to plead on her behalf, when the enraged Lear disowns her:

… be Kent unmannerly
When Lear is mad. What wouldst thou do, old man?
Think'st thou that duty shall have dread to speak,
When power to flattery bows? To plainness honour's bound
When majesty falls to folly.

(1.1.146–50)

The madness of Lear, which mutates into sanity, the chastening exposure of the monarch as a mere old man, and the fall into folly that becomes an ascent into wisdom are already germinating and subtly foreshadowed here. Cordelia's confrontation with her father is the catalyst in the Lear plot for the transvaluation of values and transfiguring of perception on which the play is bent. 'See better, Lear, and let me still remain / The true blank of thine eye', is Kent's riposte to the king's command 'Out of my sight!' (1.1.158–60), an exchange which inaugurates the tragedy's concern with seeing things as they really are. With Kent's response to Lear's banishing of him on pain of death the play's perceptual revolution begins in earnest: 'Why, fare thee well, King, since thus thou wilt appear, / Freedom lives hence and banishment is here' (1.1.181–2). It's a radical reversal of perspective that Lear's Fool will endorse when he enters three scenes later: 'Why, this fellow has banished two on's daughters and did the third a blessing against his will' (1.4.100–2). Even before the first scene is over, France is possessed by the same heretical spirit as Kent and, when Burgundy declines the offer of Cordelia's hand in marriage on purely financial grounds, he's forced like Kent to enlist the language of paradox to give it voice:

Fairest Cordelia, that art most rich being poor,
Most choice forsaken and most loved despised,
Thee and thy virtues here I seize upon,
Be it lawful I take up what's cast away.
Gods, gods! 'Tis strange that from their cold'st neglect
My love should kindle to inflamed respect.
Thy dowerless daughter, King, thrown to my chance,
Is queen of us, of ours and our fair France.
Not all the dukes of waterish Burgundy
Can buy this unprized, precious maid of me.
Bid them farewell, Cordelia, though unkind;
Thou losest here a better where to find.

(1.1.252–63)

By the time the opening scene is over, we've arrived at a point where silence is deemed more eloquent than words; where banishment from society as it stands means freedom; where poverty has been redefined as wealth; where the forsaken are chosen, what's cast away embraced, and the despised loved; where to be unprized because priced at 'Nothing' (1.1.263) is to be precious; and where to have lost from one perspective is to have gained from another. All these connotations are carried by Cordelia, whose utopian provenance within the world of the play is signalled by that evocative phrase 'a better where', which echoes a dozen lines later in her allusion to 'a better place' (1.1.276) she has in mind for Lear, and re-echoes in the description of her Kent hears in Act 4: 'You have seen / Sunshine and rain at once, her smiles and tears / Were like a better way' (4.3.17–19). There's no suggestion as yet of the lengths to which the play will go to shatter the foundations of the society from whose ruins a better way might rise. A spectator or reader unfamiliar with *King Lear* would have no reason at this stage to expect the seismic shocks the tragedy has in store for its protagonists and their world, and might reasonably expect the conflict established in the opening scene to reach an edifying tragicomic resolution similar to that reached by *The True Chronicle History*, leaving the fabric of the status quo intact. But in retrospect it's remarkable how much of the ensuing tragedy is incubating in this scene.

The Whoreson and the Plague of Custom

The same can be said of the scene that immediately follows it to launch the Gloucester plot. The prose exchange between Gloucester, Kent and Edmund that starts the play has paved the way for it by foregrounding Edmund's illegitimacy as a result of his father's adultery and drawing a distinction between him and the son Gloucester has 'by order of law … who yet is no dearer in [his] account' than 'the whoreson' he's obliged to acknowledge (1.1.18–19, 22). The dialogue's parallels with Lear's love-test are apparent too in Gloucester's weighing of his sons in the scales of his affection. But it's the prejudicial designation of one son as recognized by law, with all the privileges that entails, and the other as a bastard bereft of those privileges, that fuels the soliloquy with which Edmund kickstarts the second scene:

> Thou, Nature, art my goddess; to thy law
> My services are bound. Wherefore should I
> Stand in the plague of custom, and permit
> The curiosity of nations to deprive me?
> For that I am some twelve or fourteen moonshines
> Lag of a brother? Why bastard? Wherefore base?
> When my dimensions are as well compact,
> My mind as generous and my shape as true
> As honest madam's issue? Why brand they us
> With base? With baseness, bastardy? Base, base?
> Who in the lusty stealth of nature take
> More composition and fierce quality
> Than doth within a dull stale tired bed
> Go to the creating of a whole tribe of fops
> Got 'tween a sleep and wake. Well, then,
> Legitimate Edgar, I must have your land.
> Our father's love is to the bastard Edmund
> As to the legitimate. Fine word, 'legitimate'!
> Well, my legitimate, if this letter speed
> And my invention thrive, Edmund the base
> Shall top the legitimate. I grow, I prosper:
> Now, gods, stand up for bastards!

(1.2.1–22)

A common cause unites the otherwise polarized characters of Edmund and Cordelia. Both reject the right of social conventions and the authorities that control them – what

Edmund derides as 'the plague of custom' – to dictate how they feel, think, speak and behave, when it contravenes their will. Both do so from a position of subordination to a patriarch with the power to determine their destiny. Cordelia, of course, rebels against the mores of Lear's court in the name of an ideal of love and a devotion to truth that derive from and point towards the 'better way' she symbolizes; whereas Edmund rebels against the system that debases and excludes him in order to thrive within it on its ruthless terms. But the impact of both rebellions is the same insofar as they serve to undermine the rationale of the established social order.

In this respect Edmund can be seen as a kind of double agent in the mould of Richard III, Aaron and Iago, because his villainy like theirs is secretly in league with the assault on the inhuman ethos it flagrantly exemplifies. Edmund's cynical mantra as an apostle of the actual is 'men / Are as the time is' (5.3.31–2). But the thrust of his thrilling soliloquies in the second scene is that there's nothing to stop him or anyone from being what they want to be rather than what the arbitrary, irrational conventions of their time decree, which makes him also a champion of the possible as the play begins. This Edmund is an enlightened sceptic, whose reasoning bears the unmistakeable stamp of the philosopher we know Shakespeare was reading as he wrote *King Lear*. Behind Edmund's contemptuous dismissal of 'the plague of custom' and the stringent 'curiosity of nations' stands Montaigne's attack on the insidious despotism of inveterate usage:

> For truly, *Custome is a violent and deceiving schoole-mistris.* She by little and little, and as it were by stealth, establisheth the foot of her authoritie in us; by which mild and gentle beginning, if once by the aid of time, it have setled and planted the same in us, it will soone discover a furious and tyrannicall countenance unto us, against which we have no more the libertie to lift so much as our eies; wee may plainly see her upon every occasion to force the rules of Nature …

From the rationalist perspective Edmund shares with Montaigne, the divinely ordained laws and immutable moral codes devised to regulate human conduct and maintain the status quo stand exposed as the provisional fictions of transient cultures. Everything that is currently the custom is open to question and subject to change; nothing need remain the way it happens to be now.

Hence the liberating gusto with which Edmund sweeps Gloucester's superstitious codswallop aside, and any idea of a governing deity along with it, in his second soliloquy:

> This is the excellent foppery of the world, that when we are sick in fortune, often the surfeits of our own behaviour, we make guilty of our disasters the sun, the moon and the stars, as if we were villains on necessity, fools by heavenly compulsion, knaves, thieves and treachers by spherical predominance; drunkards, liars and adulterers by an enforced obedience of planetary influence; and all that we are evil in by a divine thrusting on. An admirable evasion of whoremaster man, to lay his goatish disposition on the charge of a star.

(1.2.118–28)

The relish with which Shakespeare espouses the cause of the stigmatized bastard and the zest with which he expounds Edmund's scandalous creed betray his empathy with the man whose own father calls him 'the whoreson' (1.1.22). The fact that Edmund deploys that creed merely in the service of his own advancement does not detract from its potency as a summons to reclaim human agency and a warrant to rethink everything hitherto taken for granted. The importance Shakespeare attaches to Edmund's convictions is underscored by having him vent them at such a seminal moment in the play and in the form of soliloquies, whose privileged entente with the audience, like Cordelia's asides, gives them greater authority and prominence. Edmund's soliloquies are the explosive counterpart in the second scene of Cordelia's 'Nothing, my lord' in the first. The effect in both cases is to create a violent rupture in the given scheme of things that reveals its fragility and ripeness for transformation.

The closet kinship of Edmund and Cordelia finds further confirmation in verbal and thematic parallels between the scenes, the most conspicuous appearing in this exchange:

GLOUCESTER
    What paper were you reading?
EDMUND
    Nothing, my lord.
GLOUCESTER
    No? What needed then that terrible dispatch of it into your pocket? The quality
    of nothing hath not such need to hide itself. Let's see. Come, if it be nothing, I
    shall not need spectacles.

(1.2.31–6)

The verbatim echo of Cordelia's fateful response to Lear, coupled with the same subsequent harping on 'nothing', throws the tacit rapport between her and Edmund, and the latent links between the Lear and Gloucester plots, into sharper relief. One of those links is forged by Gloucester's saying, 'Let's see. Come, if it be nothing, I shall not need spectacles', which adumbrates the Gloucester plot's corresponding concern with seeing, both literally and metaphorically. But it's also one of the play's many instances of words predicting and procuring deeds, and the fact that it's Edmund who elicits it from his father is not fortuitous. The grim irony of Gloucester's rejoinder is that the letter is indeed nothing, inasmuch as it's a baseless fabrication, and before long Gloucester will never see anything again, thanks to his bastard's betrayal of him to Regan and Cornwall for aiding Lear.

It's Edmund's subplot against his father and brother that sets the former on the path to having his eyes gouged out onstage and paves the way for the latter's reincarnation as a bedevilled beggar. When Edgar enters, Edmund breaks off from his rant against astrological superstition to draw us deeper into complicity with this stage-scoundrel's *sotto voce* aside: 'Pat he comes, like the castrophe of the old comedy. My cue is villainous melancholy, with a sigh like Tom o'Bedlam' (1.2.134–6). The invocation of Tom o'Bedlam furnishes a subconscious cue for Edgar's creation of his alter ego in Act 2, scene 3. It's as if the uttering of the name by Edmund summons the beggar into being out of nowhere. The wry, self-conscious theatricality of Edmund's confidential quip also highlights his role here as a stage-manager, a surrogate for the dramatist himself, entrusted with putting Shakespeare's plans for Gloucester and Edgar into action. Those plans are profoundly ambivalent, as it transpires. The extreme misery inflicted on the earl and his legitimate son as a result of his whoreson's duping of them proves the means of their transmutation into agents of the play's utopianism too. By having both aspects of what they undergo, for worse and for better, spring from Edmund's vengeful ploy, Shakespeare gives his imprimatur to both the penalty the bastard makes them pay and their transcendence of it. Any residual doubt one might harbour that Edmund enjoys a special, authorial prescience and his creator's confidence should be dispelled by the same scene's final uncanny prefiguring. 'I have told you what I have seen and heard – but faintly', says Edmund to the credulous Edgar, 'nothing like the image and horror of it' (1.2.172–3). Four acts later that last phrase is recalled with a twist by Edgar. 'Is this the promised end?', asks Kent, aghast at the entrance of Lear with Cordelia's corpse; 'Or image of that horror?' (5.3.261–2) wonders Edgar, channelling Edmund, but reworking his words to lay their stress on representation rather than reality.

The Fool and the King

The brief third scene of the play returns to the Lear plot in the aftermath of the king's abdication and banishment of Cordelia and Kent. From it we are unsurprised to learn that Goneril regards the presence of Lear and his train of knights in her home as an intolerable imposition, which she plans to bring shortly to an end. The opening line does more, however, than set the tone of her exchange with her conniving steward, Oswald: 'Did my father strike my gentleman for chiding of his fool?' (1.3.1–2). It's the tragedy's first mention of Lear's nameless court jester. With his arrival onstage in the following scene the moral re-education of the British monarch that began with Cordelia's 'Nothing, my lord' continues with a vengeance. Goneril's question tells us that the fool is privileged to enjoy the protective esteem of his royal master. Before he enters in scene 4, it becomes apparent that he enjoys the latter's affection too, and something deeper than affection, which turns out to be an urgent need of him at this moment. 'Go you and call my fool hither' and 'Where's my fool?' (1.4.43, 47) make his exasperation at the prolonged absence of his jester evident early on. When his demands prove fruitless, he refuses to let the matter drop: 'But where's my fool?', he asks one of his knights, 'I have not seen him this two days.' 'Since my young lady's going into France, sir,' the knight replies, 'the fool hath much pined away.' 'No more of that,' says Lear, 'I have noted it well' (1.4.69–73), before calling yet again for the Fool to be summoned. The Fool's emotional bond with Cordelia confirms their symbolic kinship within the play. No sooner has Cordelia vanished from the scene than the Fool materializes to take over her task of telling the blunt truth to power. So closely identified were the two characters in Shakespeare's mind that he subconsciously conflated them in the six poignant words with which Lear's dying speech begins: 'And my poor fool is hanged' (5.3.304).

Lear's insistence on the summoning of his fool, Cordelia's licensed alter ego, suggests his having developed since her banishment a craving to be told truths he could never have borne to hear before the fateful day he resolved to dethrone himself, divide his kingdom, and stage a vainglorious show-trial of his daughters' love for him. As the tragedy unfolds, it becomes hard to resist the suspicion that at some level beyond his awareness or control Lear engineers in the opening scene a situation calculated to result in catastrophe and inflict upon him the extreme mental and physical suffering that he secretly feels he deserves as both a father and a king. To command his adult children to compete in public for pride of place in his heart and a commensurate share in his largesse is to foment rivalry and discord between them. By disowning the daughter he loves most in an impetuous blaze of portentous rhetoric for not pandering to his egotism, he wounds himself more deeply than he could ever wound her. And in surrendering his divided sovereignty – 'my power, / Preeminence and all the large effects / That troop with majesty' – while expecting to 'retain / The name, and all th' addition to a king' (1.1.131–3,136-7), he creates the precondition for the more profound tragic division that awaits him between the monarch and the man. This idea of Lear courting the calamity that befalls him, feeling obscurely compelled to collude in his own mortification, gains credence not only from the alacrity with which he solicits the Fool's chastening home truths and subjects himself to the violence of the storm, but also from finding it mirrored, as we'll see, in the conduct of Edgar in particular.

It's as if the true 'darker purpose' (1.1.35) Lear announces in the opening scene – a purpose of which Lear himself is unaware – is not his abdication and threefold division of the kingdom but the punitive ordeal they precipitate. Goneril speaks more truly than she knows when she says of her father in scene 3: 'Idle old man, / That still would manage those authorities / That he hath given away. Now by my life / Old fools are babes again' (1.3.17–20). For by giving away those authorities he has begun to free the old man from the clutches of the king he was, to become a babe again by waking the innocent human creature replete with potential within him, and to acquire the wisdom of the fool that his own wise fool is itching to impart. That Lear is already primed to take instruction in the art of motley from his 'all-licensed fool' (1.4.191) is evident from his exchange with the physically and vocally disguised Kent shortly before the Fool appears. Asked by Lear who he is, Kent answers: 'A very honest-hearted fellow, and as poor as the King'. To which Lear replies: 'If thou be'st as poor for a subject as he's for a king, thou art poor enough' (1.4.19–22). It's a riposte the Fool himself might have delivered satirically at his sovereign's expense. Coming from Lear, it shows a disarmingly sober awareness of his predicament, couched in the paradoxical idiom that is the jester's stock in trade. It also points forward to the erasure of the distinction between king and subject by poverty in the storm scenes, as well as harking back to France lauding Cordelia as 'most rich being poor'. The exchange is in prose, moreover, like the rest of Lear's dialogue with Kent and with the Fool in this scene. That audible shift in register from the heightened formal verse of the first scene carries subtly levelling connotations too, consistent with the humanizing course on which the throneless king is bound. The contrast with the imperious grandiloquence of the Lear who thundered 'Come not between the dragon and his wrath!' and who swore 'by the sacred radiance of the sun, / The mysteries of Hecate and the night' (1.1.110–11) could not be starker.

Once the double-act of fool and king commences, it's not long before the former's function as a surrogate for Cordelia is made explicit. 'This is nothing, fool', says Kent of the jester's trite jingle commending common sense. 'Then 'tis like the breath of an unfee'd lawyer', quips the Fool, 'you gave me nothing for't', which gives him the perfect cue to ask Lear: 'Can you make no use of nothing, nuncle?' 'Why no, boy', replies Lear, inveigled into repeating his response to Cordelia, 'nothing can be made out of nothing' (1.4.126–30). Lear has yet to learn the use that can be made of nothing and the value of nothing, which is why the Fool keeps hammering away at the word, heedless of the risk he runs of being whipped:

> I had rather be any kind o'thing than a fool, and yet I would not be thee, nuncle.
> Thou hast pared thy wit o'both sides and left nothing i'the middle. ... Now thou art
> an O without a figure; I am better than thou art now. I am a fool, thou art nothing.
>
> (1.4.176–9, 183–5)

Licensed the Fool may be, but only up to a point, which the staggering effrontery of saying that to a king blatantly ignores. Here the Fool's raillery verges upon contempt, reaching beyond mere remonstration with majesty from a standpoint that has no place for majesty at all. The Fool's pejorative use of 'nothing' to describe the self-deposed Lear secretes a positive meaning that the play's repeated harping on the word is designed to disclose, and that we've previously seen crystallizing in the speeches of Richard II and Timon. Like its use by Cordelia, it bears out John Middleton Murry's observation that in Shakespeare's plays 'a nothingness may be more real than a character, just as our unknown selves in life are sometimes more potent than our known'. In *King Lear*, to a degree unmatched by any other tragedy, the notion of nothing assumes the presence and the power of a character in its own right: the absent presence of the self's unrealized potential, its capacity to have been another kind of human being altogether.

This is the moment when that capacity, that unknown self, breaks the surface of Lear's consciousness for the first time and demands to be heard:

LEAR

> Does any here know me? Why, this is not Lear. Does Lear walk thus, speak thus?
> Where are his eyes? Either his notion weakens, or his discernings are lethargied
> – Ha! sleeping or waking? Sure 'tis not so. Who is it that can tell me who I am?

FOOL

> Lear's shadow.
>
> (1.4.217–21)

Lear will soon recover his regal composure sufficiently to rain monstrous maledictions down on Goneril – 'Into her womb convey sterility, / Dry up in her the organs of increase' (1.4.270–1) – and threaten her with the return of his forbidding former self: 'Thou shalt find / That I'll resume the shape which thou dost think / I have cast off for ever' (1.4.300–2). But not before this speech and the Fool's reply to the final, fundamental question it poses has given us a glimpse of the unconditioned creature hitherto hidden in Lear suddenly emerging and finding its voice. Under the pressure of extreme distress the carapace of kingship cracks open to reveal a nascent, nameless being, who does not recognize himself as 'King Lear' or his body, movement, speech and sight as belonging to the person who bears that name; which is why he speaks of Lear in the third person, as someone other than the 'I' and 'me' whose identity is unknown.

A shallow reading of the speech would be content with regarding it as Goneril does, as Lear's sarcastic howl of protest at his daughter's refusal to treat him with the deference she showed him before he surrendered his crown. That reading holds as far as it goes, but it stops short of registering the full import of the speech. The Fool's answer to his master's question, 'Who is it can tell me who I am?', can likewise be taken as meaning only that Lear has become, through his own folly in relinquishing his sovereignty, a shadow of the mighty monarch he once was, a king without substance because a king without a throne. The line obviously does mean that, chiming as it does with the jester's other gibes to the same effect. But in context, and with this wise fool's constant playing on 'nothing' in mind, it also begs to be read as meaning the reverse: that to be the shadow of a king is to be a man of substance. It's the choice of the word 'shadow' that clinches this reading, because it plays on the fact that it also means 'actor', as in Macbeth's 'Life's but a walking shadow, a poor player, / That struts and frets his hour upon the stage' (5.5.23–4). Taken in this sense, the line reminds us, in a flash of self-conscious theatricality, that the question it answers was posed by an actor playing the part of Lear; by an altogether different human being, in other words, capable of playing many other parts than this, who happens to be impersonating at the moment a king whose regality is imaginary – not a fact but a fiction, just like Lear's, as the unknown human being Lear harbours is starting to realize.

The tension between the shallow and the deeper readings of Lear's speech and the Fool's reply reflects the tension at this point in the play between two conceptions of what the tragedy consists in. On one hand, there's the view of *King Lear* as the tragedy of a sovereign whose rash decision to depose himself and divide his kingdom has appalling consequences for himself, his family and his country; a view which, if allowed to prevail, as it generally has, reduces *King Lear* to a cultural fossil of the Jacobean age. On the other hand, we have the visionary tragedy that can be seen evolving in this speech: a tragedy which, by the end of the play, has undermined the conventional idea of what's tragic about *King Lear* by calling the very existence of kings into question and showing the true cause of the catastrophe to be the constitutionally unjust society they serve and epitomize.

There's a further clue in this speech to the true tragedy of *King Lear* – to what makes it a *Shakespearean* tragedy – in Lear's exclamation and question, 'Ha! Sleeping or waking?', in which the exclamation registers the suddenness with which the question of which state he's in has struck him. Given the speaker and the immediate context, these words recall the second line of the moving couplet that closes Sonnet 87: 'Thus have I had thee as a dream doth flatter, / In sleep a king, but waking no such matter.' Some of the ways in which Shakespeare uses the sleeping or dreaming versus waking trope in previous tragedies have already been touched on. It crops up first in *King Lear* earlier in the fourth scene, when Lear's second call for his fool goes unanswered and he says, 'Ho, I think the world's asleep' (1.4.47). It recurs later in Poor Tom's description of himself as 'One that slept in the contriving of lust and waked to do it' (3.4.87–8); in the mock trial scene where, having been appointed a 'robed man of justice' by the crazed king, Tom says, 'Let us deal justly. / Sleepest or wakest thou, jolly shepherd?' (3.6.36, 40–1); and in the Gentleman's asking Cordelia, on the verge of her reunion with her father: 'So please your majesty, / That we may wake the King? He hath slept long' (4.7.18–19). He has indeed slept long, lost all his life in a dream of kingship, from which Shakespeare is bent on rousing him to face reality. Nor is he the only one who needs to be woken from the illusion under which he has hitherto laboured. For 'the world's asleep' too, insofar as it goes on living the same lie that creates the Lears of the world, and it will stay asleep until it wakes at last to 'deal justly' instead.

'We are asleep', observed Wittgenstein four centuries after Shakespeare, 'but in our better hours we wake up just enough to realise that we are dreaming.' It's to Montaigne, though, that we need to turn again to grasp the implications of Shakespeare's take on this idea in *King Lear*. In 'An Apologie of Raymond Sebond', whose influence on the dramatist's thinking in the play is undisputed, Montaigne writes: 'Our waking is more a sleep, than sleep itself. ... wherefore do we doubt, whether our thought and action is not another sort of dreaming, and our waking a kind of sleep?' In what sense our thought and action can be called another sort of dreaming, and our waking a kind of sleep, becomes plainer if we link this contention to Montaigne's critique 'Of Custom', from which I quoted earlier to explain Edmund's attitude. The trouble with custom, by which Montaigne means the intractable habit of thinking and acting in conventionally prescribed ways, is that it 'brings the sight of our judgement asleepe'. This somnambulant state, the indispensable mainstay of mental, social and political inertia, is sustained by the fact that

> every man holding in special regard, and inward veneration the opinions and the behaviour approved, and customes received about him, cannot without remorse leave them, nor without applause applie himselfe unto them ... verily, because wee sucke them with the milk of our birth, and forasmuch as the world's visage presents it selfe in that estate unto our first view, it seemeth we are borne with a condition to follow that course. And the common imaginations we finde in credit about us, and by our fathers seed infused in our soule, seeme to be the generall and natural.

From this thraldom to 'the common imaginations we finde in credit about us' – what we would now call ideology in the pejorative sense of the term – Shakespeare seeks to deliver *us* through Lear's violent awakening from the sleep of reason, in which 'Humanity must perforce prey on itself, / Like monsters of the deep' (4.2.50–1). As a result of that deliverance and that awakening, Montaigne tells us:

> Hee that will free himself from this violent prejudice of custome, shall find divers things received with an undoubted resolution, that have no other anker but the hoarie head and frowning wrimples of custome, which ever attends them: which maske being pulled off, and referring all matters to truth and reason, he shall perceive his judgement, as it were overturned, and placed in a much surer state.

The price Lear must pay for being placed in a much surer state, for having the mask of custom pulled off and his judgement of himself and his world turned upside down by truth and reason is to be regarded, and to regard himself, as insane. So tenacious is the sway of custom over us that, as Montaigne points out, 'whatsoever is beyond the compasse of custome, wee deeme likewise to bee beyond the compasse of reason'. Lear exits at the close of Act 1 crying, 'O let me not be mad, not mad, sweet heaven! I would not be mad' (1.5.49). His journey beyond the compass of custom, and thus beyond the compass of what masquerades as reason has just begun. Nor will it be complete until he has learned to speak what Edgar will endorse in an aside as 'matter and impertinency mixed, / Reason in madness' (4.6.170–1).

The Art of Known and Feeling Sorrows

Edgar, too, must endure his own violent awakening from the sleep of custom, as must his father. The title page of the 1608 Quarto edition underlines the importance of Edgar's kinship as a character with the king by giving second billing, after the life and death of Lear and his daughters, not to the life and death of Gloucester, but to 'the unfortunate life of Edgar, son and heir to the Earl of Gloucester, and his sullen and assumed humour of Tom of Bedlam'. Their affinity is highlighted early in the play. When Edgar announces his intention of assuming the identity of Tom, he does so on the same stage as, but unseen by, the Earl of Kent as he sleeps in the stocks. Kent has already shed his aristocratic identity in order to assume the identity and accent of a base-born man, as his fellow aristocrat Edgar is about to. Just before he falls asleep and Edgar enters, Kent's perusal of a letter from Cordelia gives him hope, prompting the reflection, 'Nothing almost sees miracles / But misery' (2.2.163–4). The aphoristic ring of the sentence enhances the substantive, personified quality its syntax lends 'Nothing', linking this iteration of the word both to its previous positive uses and to its use in the same vein by Edgar in the last sentence of the soliloquy he delivers moments later:

> I heard myself proclaimed,
> And by the happy hollow of a tree
> Escaped the hunt. No port is free, no place

That guard and most unusual vigilance
Does not attend my taking. While I may scape
I will preserve myself, and am bethought
To take the basest and most poorest shape
That ever penury in contempt of man
Brought near to beast. My face I'll grime with filth,
Blanket my loins, elf all my hair in knots
And with presented nakedness outface
The winds and persecutions of the sky.
The country gives me proof and precedent
Of Bedlam beggars, who, with roaring voices,
Strike in their numbed and mortified bare arms
Pins, wooden pricks, nails, sprigs of rosemary;
And with this horrible object, from low farms,
Poor pelting villages, sheepcotes and mills,
Sometime with lunatic bans, sometime with prayers,
Enforce their charity. Poor Turlygod, poor Tom,
That's something yet: Edgar I nothing am.

(2.2.172–92)

'Edgar I nothing am' is Edgar's version of Lear's 'this is not Lear', but with the signal difference that its contorted syntax renders it more richly ambiguous and resonant. The simple gist of the statement is that he's ceased to be Edgar, now that he's decided to adopt another name and identity. But the compacted, elliptical wording makes it read not only as a negation of Edgar but also as an emphatically positive declaration that he is now nothing; which is indeed 'something yet', inasmuch as it frees him to recreate himself as someone else entirely. The awoken Lear's potential to have been or to become someone else entirely remains implicit throughout the play. But that potential in Edgar is physically realized before our eyes in the flesh and blood form of the Bedlam beggar he's transformed himself into when we next see him. Shakespeare's creation of Poor Tom clearly answered a deeper imaginative need in him than the demands of the plot alone could explain.

Edgar is an extremely enigmatic figure, the chief mystery being why he was 'bethought / To take the basest and most poorest shape / That ever penury in contempt of man / Brought near to beast' to disguise himself, when he could have chosen like Kent a less outlandish and excruciating way of concealing his identity. Then there's the puzzle of why he sustains his full-blooded impersonation of an unhinged vagrant long after the pretext of disguise has become implausible. Edgar's role as a counterpart of Lear like his father goes some way towards explaining why Shakespeare has him driven 'to shift / Into a madman's rags, t'assume a semblance / That very dogs disdained' (5.3.185–7). The physical metamorphosis from wealthy nobleman to penniless pariah that Edgar resolves upon in his soliloquy prefigures the king's identification with the indigent denizens of his realm. His determination to subject his body to the hostility of the elements, 'And with presented nakedness outface / The winds and persecutions of the sky' anticipates Lear's decision to 'abjure all roofs', 'To wage against the enmity o'th' air' and feel 'Necessity's sharp pinch!' (2.2.397–8, 400). And his choice of a persona synonymous with lunacy mirrors the monarch's own fits of delirium. But the fact that Edgar's protracted self-laceration as Poor Tom serves no practical purpose suggests that he shares Lear's unvoiced urge to punish himself, and for a reason the play makes tacitly apparent. That unvoiced reason is his need to exact retribution from himself as Edgar, the privileged aristocratic heir of an earl, for his part in the creation and shameful neglect of the poverty-stricken underclass personified by Tom. Through the self-mutilating beggar plagued by imaginary demons, Edgar can own and expiate the guilt he shares with Lear and the rest of their class. As Tom, Edgar also serves Lear in Act 3 as visible proof of his royal guilt for the existence of the penury Tom represents and his need to expiate it by suffering the same torment himself.

Tom facilitates Edgar's exacerbation of Gloucester's guilt-ridden anguish too. Consider his glaring failure to reveal himself to his blind and broken father, when Gloucester gives him the perfect emotive cue:

> O dear son Edgar,
> The food of they abused father's wrath,
> Might I but live to see thee in my touch,
> I'd say I had eyes again.

(4.1.23–6)

Edgar persists in denying his remorseful father the consolation that lies in his gift right up until Gloucester's reported death in the final scene, despite having known that he was wrong to do so: 'Never – O fault! – revealed myself unto him / Until some half-hour past' (5.3.191–2). His belated revelation of his identity proves fatal to Gloucester: 'his flawed heart, / Alack, too weak the conflict to support, / 'Twixt two extremes of passion, joy and grief, / Burst smilingly' (5.3.195–8). Prior to that lethal revelation Shakespeare has Edgar stage-manage the mock-suicide of the man who sired him, exploiting his blindness to dupe him into thinking he has leapt in vain 'From the dread summit of this chalky bourn' (4.6.57) to the death he yearns for. 'Why I do trifle thus with his despair', Edgar seeks to assure us in an aside, 'Is done to cure it' (4.6.33–4). But his choice of the word 'trifle' betrays the sadistic aspect of his conduct that makes the episode so disturbing and its tone so difficult to define. From the absence of a motive for withholding his identity for so long, and from the inadequacy of his stated motive for contriving to prolong Gloucester's agony rather than allow him to end it, it seems not unreasonable to conclude that Edgar's justified anger at his father's credulous distrust of him finds furtive satisfaction in these ways. Even as he guides him, begs for him, defends him and comforts him, Edgar is making Gloucester pay, as surely as his brother Edmund makes him pay for the stigma of being a bastard.

As Poor Tom, Edgar is at once an object and an agent of the terrible reckoning to which Shakespeare is intent on bringing the royal family of King Lear and the noble family of the Earl of Gloucester. But what he endures, and what he witnesses the king and his father enduring, while possessed by the Bedlamite has a transformative effect on Edgar. When he drops the persona of Poor Tom to lead Gloucester on after the Dover Cliff scene, he introduces himself afresh to his father not as the latter's noble son Edgar, but as 'A most poor man, made tame to Fortune's blows, / Who, by the art of known and feeling sorrows, / Am pregnant to good pity' (4.6.217–19). Even after he has publicly reclaimed his original identity as Edgar after vanquishing Edmund, it's clear that he hasn't entirely forgotten what being Poor Tom taught him. In the closing couplets of the play that the Folio gives him, Edgar eschews the conventional note of formal resolution and reassurance one might expect in favour of words that befit the tragedy we have just witnessed:

> The weight of this sad time we must obey,
> Speak what we feel, not what we ought to say.
> The oldest hath borne most; we that are young
> Shall never see so much, nor live so long.
>
> (5.3.322–5)

The second line of the first couplet, as we've already noted, reasserts the wisdom enshrined in Cordelia's response to Lear's ill-conceived question at the start of the play. It's the wisdom that both Lear and Gloucester are constrained to acquire in the course of the tragedy, together with the need to see and speak the truth. The last line begins with a final reminder of how much seeing the reality of the world instead of blinding oneself to it matters in *King Lear*. Both lines gather between them all the power and pathos that accrue from the frequent coupling of feeling with seeing in the tragedy, as in Gloucester's denunciation of the wealthy man, who 'will not see / Because he does not feel' (4.1.71–2). We know from Edgar's description of himself as made 'pregnant to good pity' by 'the art of known and feeling sorrows' that his final speech is charged not only with the hard-won sagacity of Lear and Gloucester, but with knowledge born of his own bitter experience. It's all the more moving, therefore, to hear him acknowledge in the play's closing couplet that what he has been through and now knows can't begin to compare with what Lear and Gloucester have suffered and understood. He recognizes that they have seen more, and seen more deeply, than those who survive them can comprehend, and that in doing so they have transcended their time and thus lived far longer, figuratively speaking, than those who survive them could ever expect to live.

The King and the Beggar

Edgar may not have seen so much or lived so long as his king or his father by the end of the play, but the part played by Poor Tom in the unshackling of their minds is crucial. If any scene in *King Lear* can claim to encapsulate its vision, it's the scene in which its royal protagonist is confronted with the quintessence of human misery into which Edgar has transmuted himself. We are primed for their iconic encounter and its momentous impact on Lear by the seismic shifts in his consciousness that precede it. A decisive shift takes place at the end of the brutal Dutch auction in which Goneril and Regan bargain the retinue of one hundred knights Lear requires to be housed with him down to none. 'What need one?', asks Regan, to which Lear replies:

> O, reason not the need! Our basest beggars
> Are in the poorest things superfluous;
> Allow not nature more than nature needs,
> Man's life is cheap as beast's. Thou art a lady;
> If only to go warm were gorgeous,
> Why, nature needs not what thou gorgeous wear'st
> Which scarcely keeps thee warm. But for true need –
>
> (2.2.453–9)

On that fundamental question of what constitutes 'true need' for a human being he breaks off to beg the heavens for patience. But not before we've witnessed a king accustomed to being in the richest things superfluous inviting comparison of his plight with that of 'Our basest beggars' and refuting the attitude of those who talk and act as if 'Man's life is cheap as beast's'. What constitutes true need Lear is about to discover, when he plunges out into the night and feels for real the sharp pinch of necessity.

Lear briefly recovers his awesome powers of invocation and imprecation as he stands bare-headed in the storm and commands the furious elements to do his bidding, undaunted by the futility of conscripting them:

> You sulphurous and thought-executing fires,
> Vaunt-couriers of oak-cleaving thunderbolts,
> Singe my white head! And thou, all-shaking thunder,
> Strike flat the thick rotundity o'the world,
> Crack nature's moulds, all germens spill at once
> That make ungrateful man!
>
> (3.2.4–9)

But within a few lines the superhuman sovereign bestriding a cosmic stage is obliged to admit to his fool that he is nothing but 'A poor, infirm, weak and despised old man' (3.2.20). As his 'wits begin to turn' (3.2.67) and the cold begins to bite, Lear puts concern for the Fool's physical discomfort before his own: 'Come on, my boy. How dost, my boy? Art cold? / I am cold myself' (3.2.68–9). Turning to Kent, who has just urged him to take shelter in a nearby hovel, he says, 'Where is this straw, my fellow? / The art of our necessities is strange, / And can make vile things precious. Come, your hovel.' Then, turning back to the jester, he shows concern for his distress again: 'Poor fool and knave, I have one part in my heart / That's sorry yet for thee' (3.2.69–73). It's the first time that Lear has displayed not just an awareness of, but genuine sympathy with, the suffering of another human being. If that's a sign that he's losing what once passed for his wits, the plain implication is that he's saner without them and better served by studying 'The art of our necessities'. It's no coincidence that Shakespeare chooses this moment in the tragedy to have the Fool waylay the audience with his breathtaking, time-bending prophecy, in which the way things are is juxtaposed with the way they should be.

When we rejoin Lear, Kent and the Fool shortly afterwards on the threshold of the hovel, Lear's anger at the 'filial ingratitude' (3.4.14) of Goneril and Regan has not abated, but his new-found alertness to the needs of others has not diminished either. On the contrary, now he gives priority to the comfort of his companions over his own, telling first Kent, 'Prithee go in thyself, seek thine own ease' and then the Fool: 'In boy, go first. You houseless poverty – / Nay, get thee in. I'll pray, and then I'll sleep' (3.4.23, 26–7). With that, left alone onstage outside the hovel, the former king of Albion kneels down and begins afresh the heartfelt prayer he broke off after 'You houseless poverty' to usher the Fool in ahead of him:

> Poor naked wretches, wheresoe'er you are,
> That bide the pelting of this pitiless storm,
> How shall your houseless heads and unfed sides,
> Your looped and windowed raggedness, defend you
> From seasons such as these? O, I have ta'en
> Too little care of this. Take physic, pomp.
> Expose thyself to feel what wretches feel,
> That thou mayest shake the superflux to them
> And show the heavens more just.

(3.4.28–36)

The irascible, egotistical autocrat of the opening scene has been transfigured by his own rashness, the cruelty of 'two pernicious daughters' (3.2.22) and 'The tyranny of the open night' (3.4.2) into a man who identifies with, and feels compassion for, the most reviled outcasts of the society he once ruled. Not content with that, he acknowledges his responsibility for the unjust plight of the poor and his consequent obligation as the epitome of 'pomp' to 'shake the superflux to them' – to give the poor, in other words, the superfluous wealth of society hogged by the rich.

A lesser dramatist might well have thought Lear's moral rearmament complete by this point. But Shakespeare hasn't finished with King Lear, whose enforced enlightenment has just begun. It's just begun because Lear's prayer assumes that the remedy for the misery of the poor lies in the gift of the king. The existence of the poor and the existence of the king are taken for granted and remain unquestioned. What's needed to alleviate the wretched state of the former is for the latter to 'Take physic' by empathizing with their plight and being moved to redress it by an extreme act of regal munificence. The prayer can envisage no solution to the problem of 'houseless poverty' other than the philanthropic fiat of a more caring sovereign. It also blurs Lear's responsibility for the plight of the poor and its remedy, when he shifts it from himself ('O, I have ta'en / Too little care of this') to the personified abstraction 'pomp', which he addresses in the second person and commands to show 'the heavens' – rather than pomp itself – not just but 'more just' than they have previously been. Bold and presumptuous as its last sentence might have sounded to King James on St Stephen's night in 1606, nothing in the prayer would have prevented him and his court from hearing it as no more than a reminder of their Christian duty to be charitable befitting the occasion.

The prayer takes King Lear a long way, but not far enough for Shakespeare's liking, which explains why he needed to create Poor Tom and why he brings Lear face to face with him at precisely this juncture. In the prayer the 'houseless heads and unfed sides' of the 'Poor naked wretches' Lear conjures up in his and our mind's eye remain like 'pomp', for all their vividness, a bloodless abstraction remote from his immediate reality. But no sooner is Lear's prayer over than a cry is heard from within the hovel – 'Fathom and half, fathom and half: Poor Tom!' (3.4.37) – and an actual poor naked wretch materializes before his eyes, asking 'Who gives anything to Poor Tom?', wailing 'Tom's a-cold' and pleading 'Do Poor Tom some charity' (3.4.50, 57, 59). Lear's first reaction is to reduce the pitiful creature confronting him to a narcissistic reflection of himself: 'Didst thou give all to thy two daughters? And art thou come to this? … Nothing could have subdued nature / To such a lowness but his unkind daughters' (3.4.48–9, 69–70). But what subdued him to such lowness, Tom explains, was his depraved life as a corrupt, treacherous courtier, who 'served the lust of [his] mistress's heart and did the act of darkness with her' (3.4.84–6); who was 'false of heart, light of ear, bloody of hand; hog in sloth, fox in stealth, wolf in greediness, dog in madness, lion in prey' (3.4.90–2); and whose punishment has been to endure the blighted life of a beggar, terrorized by 'the foul fiend' (3.4.45, 50–1, 59, 78, 95) and his demonic minions.

Shakespeare's scathing portrayal in Tom of the turpitude for which courts were notorious and his depiction of the fate their denizens deserve are not the things that arrest Lear's attention, however. Transfixed by the physical appearance of the near-naked figure that faces him, he is suddenly struck by a shattering realization:

> Why, thou wert better in a grave than to answer with thy uncovered body this extremity of the skies. Is man no more than this? Consider him well. Thou ow'st the worm no silk, the beast no hide, the sheep no wool, the cat no perfume. Ha? Here's three on's are sophisticated; thou art the thing itself. Unaccommodated man is no more but such a poor, bare, forked animal as thou art. Off, off, you lendings: come, unbutton here.

> (3.4.99–107)

And with that the king starts to tear off his clothes.

It's a truly remarkable moment, made more remarkable by the thought of its having been witnessed by King James. For its implications cut much deeper than Lear's impassioned prayer for the homeless and starving, and much deeper than most critical accounts of it have been disposed to recognize. Shakespeare stages an encounter in which James's fabled antecedent on the nation's throne is compelled to realize that beneath his royal robes and a mad beggar's rags shivers the same 'poor, bare, forked animal'. Lear's prayer presupposed the continued existence of the same divisive society, in which 'pomp' would persist, but would treat its impoverished subjects with more kindness and generosity than before. But when Lear strives to tear off the tawdry trappings of majesty, which he now scorns as 'lendings', to expose the 'Unaccommodated man' they hide, he enacts the understanding that monarchy itself, and the unequal distribution of property, wealth and power it preserves, have no foundation in nature. The physical constitution, faculties and needs which he can *see* that we share as mortal human creatures cry out against the baseless disparities inflicted on us by class society. The fact that Edgar is actually a nobleman impersonating a demented beggar detracts not a jot from the subversive import of Lear's speech and action. On the contrary, it reinforces it. By having Edgar adopt Tom o'Bedlam as his alter ego, Shakespeare reveals the 'poor, bare, forked animal' normally concealed by the costly garments that distinguished the aristocracy at a glance in his day from their ill-clad inferiors. The shattering truth Lear discovers and voices as he addresses Poor Tom is already visibly incarnate, even before Lear opens his mouth, in the fellow human being facing him, whose body is both a lord's and a beggar's, as well as the body of the actor who unites them by playing them both.

The fraudulence of the hierarchical distinctions on which the entire tragedy is predicated stands revealed, as the normally unbridgeable gulf between beggar and king disappears. The fundamental equality of all human beings is not merely asserted, but dramatically demonstrated through speech and actions that give it an immediate reality beyond the reach of assertion alone. Compare, for example, Montaigne's discursive formulation of the same basic point in his essay 'Of the inequalitie that is between us':

> If we consider a Cottager and a King, a noble and a handy-crafts man, a magistrate and a private man, a rich man and a poore; an extreme disparitie doth immediately present it selfe unto our eies, which, as a man may say, differ in nothing, but in their clothes. ... For, as enterlude-plaiers, you shal now see them on the stage, play a King, an Emperor, or a Duke, but they are no sooner off the stage, but they are base rascals, vagabond abjects ... Even so the Emperor, whose glorious pomp doth so dazzle you in publike; ... View him behind the curtaine, and you see but an ordinarie man, and peradventure more vile, and more seely, than the least of his subjects.

The point is as vividly illustrated and vigorously argued by Montaigne as one would expect. But it pales in its effect when set beside the emotionally charged enactment of human equality by living individuals in the throes of a convincing predicament. Bereft of narrative context, theatrical embodiment and imaginative involvement, the egalitarian tenor of Montaigne's argument inevitably lacks the inflammatory political impetus of Shakespeare's dramatization too.

The crucial concept that underpins the radical egalitarianism of Lear's speech and his desperate urge to strip himself bare is that of 'Unaccommodated man'. The speech begins by deploring the state of utter vulnerability in which Tom's 'uncovered body' has left him. But as Lear reflects on the figure before him, the significance of what he beholds changes. The unclothed body that at first seemed deplorable suddenly seems desirable in contrast to the clothed bodies of Lear, Kent and the Fool. The latter strike him now as reprehensibly 'sophisticated', because they contrive to mask by artificial means the natural form of the human body; whereas in Poor Tom he perceives the unadorned reality of 'the thing itself', and wants at once to abolish the spurious distinctions between them. Given the sumptuary laws that regulated the kinds and colours of clothes people wore in Shakespeare's day in order to lock them visually into their rank in the social hierarchy, Lear's desire to divest himself of his 'lendings' would have had a far stronger impact on its Jacobean audiences than it does in modern productions, especially those whose costuming dispenses with any meaningful notion of rank altogether. So it's even more vital today to stress how much is at stake for Shakespeare in the idea of 'Unaccommodated man'. When everything to which human beings are obliged from birth by their society to accommodate themselves is stripped away along with their clothes, what's revealed is not just their physiological kinship with the rest of their kind, but the potential they share with their fellow human beings to be someone quite different from the person they became and believe themselves to be.

When Lear asks earlier in the play, 'Who is it that can tell me who I am?', we catch a glimpse of that potential self speaking. And in Edgar's fully realized recreation of himself as Poor Tom we're given palpable proof of the self's capacity for sustained transformation. Unlike Kent in the guise of Caius, Edgar doesn't just camouflage himself vocally and visually as another character; he *turns into* someone else when he speaks and acts as Tom, living and breathing the part with overwhelming conviction and intensity, as if that's who he really is. Two scenes later he morphs back into Edgar for a second in an aside: 'My tears begin to take his part so much / They mar my counterfeiting' (3.6.59–60). Far from undermining his credibility as the Bedlamite, however, that abrupt reversion strengthens it by emphasizing Tom's sheer incongruity with Edgar.

The existentialist philosopher Karl Jaspers once wrote:

> Although my social I is thus imposed upon me, I can still put up an *inner* resistance to it … Although I am in my social I at each moment, I no longer coincide with it … I am not solely a result of social configurations, for though my social existence determines all of my objective phenomenality, I retain my own original potential.

Centuries before Jaspers, Shakespeare had arrived at the same understanding, although he grasped it and expressed it not in the abstract terms of philosophical discourse, but theatrically and poetically through drama. Shakespeare's 'Unaccommodated man' is the repository of what Jaspers calls the 'original potential' every one of us retains: the unconditioned reserves of being that not only remain unabsorbed by our socialized selves, but that can and do 'put up an *inner* resistance' to their imposition, as Shakespeare's tragic protagonists so eloquently attest. The virtue of Shakespeare's dramatic revelation of this common human potential is that an otherwise discarnate proposition becomes incarnate in performance and thus not just imaginable but demonstrable. We see and hear the unaccommodated being within Edgar the aristocrat bodied forth as the Poor Tom he could have become for real and could become again, just as we see and hear the unaccommodated being dormant in Lear awakening as the man he could have become in defiance of the king he was doomed to be.

Attention has been drawn in earlier chapters to the ways Shakespeare finds to make visible the otherwise invisible forces of unconscious constraint and preclusion that conspire in the tragic destruction of his protagonists. But equally important are the ways he makes visible and audible through his protagonists the capacity of human beings to resist and overcome those forces. For in doing so he brings the possibility of freedom from the tyranny of a dehumanizing way of life – the possibility of feeling, thinking and acting not against but in accordance with the interests of our kind – within reach of reality. The feasibility of that prospect is reinforced by the readiness of so much that had seemed immutable to melt away under the pressure of traumatic events. The mental, emotional and physical ordeals to which Lear, Gloucester and Edgar are subjected reveal their socially defined identities to be fictions and the assumptions about themselves and their world in which those identities were anchored to be false. Nothing would appear to be more solid and fixed than the personalities and attitudes forged over lifetimes by the Lear and Gloucester we meet at the start. But the speed of their demolition, as the agonies of both men intensify, shows how fragile and provisional they had been all along.

So Distribution Should Undo Excess

The fate Shakespeare contrives for Gloucester makes that as plain as the fate he devises for Lear. Lest the obvious parallels we are meant to keep drawing between their plights escape us, Gloucester himself brings them to our attention during the storm, when he says to Kent:

> Thou sayest the King grows mad; I'll tell thee, friend,
> I am almost mad myself. I had a son,
> Now outlawed from my blood; he sought my life,
> But lately, very late. I loved him, friend,
> No father his son dearer. True to tell thee,
> The grief hath crazed my wits.

(3.4.161–6)

His mirroring of the monarch continues when, immediately after this, Poor Tom wails 'Tom's a-cold' and Gloucester, unaware that the beggar is the outlawed son whose loss has crazed his wits, ushers him into shelter from the storm, saying, 'In fellow, there, into the hovel; keep thee warm' (3.4.169–70), just as Lear had urged the Fool to take shelter in the hovel ahead of him. And in the last line Gloucester utters at the end of the scene, 'No words, no words; hush' (3.4.177), he shows that, like Lear, who only two scenes earlier had declared, 'I will say nothing' (3.2.38), he has begun to appreciate the virtue of silence.

The solicitude Gloucester displays for a beggar's comfort as well as a king's is not enough to spare him the excruciating torture that awaits him in the final scene of Act

3. The gouging out of Gloucester's eyes onstage is still generally regarded as too horrific for spectators to tolerate. Most productions opt to shift the blinding offstage or to screen the audience's view of it, leaving Gloucester's cries of agony to work upon the mind's eye. What makes the incident especially repellent is not just the nature of the atrocity – so tangibly evoked by Cornwall's grisly exclamation 'Out, vile jelly, / Where is thy lustre now?' (3.7.82–3) – but the gusto with which Regan and Cornwall commit it, spurred on rather than deterred by the unbearable pain they are inflicting on a helpless old man. The fact that the foremost function of Gloucester's blinding is to demonize Regan and Cornwall as irredeemably evil doesn't explain, however, why Shakespeare insists on the audience witnessing it. The hanging of Cordelia loses little of its impact by occurring in the offstage realm of the imagination, as her father enters cradling her corpse and howling like a wounded animal. The thought of Shakespeare deriving vicarious gratification from the savage act of mutilation he staged for his audience's entertainment may be unpalatable, but it's hard to repress, especially when the cruelty with which most of the aristocratic characters are treated by the dramatist is taken into account. This is, after all, the same dramatist who has Lear demand of his daughter's lifeless body, 'Why should a dog, a horse, a rat have life / And thou no breath at all?' (5.3.305–6). Shakespeare has no qualms about forcing a heartbroken king on the verge of death himself to face the brute fact of nature's indifference to the rank or desert of a dead princess, whose life from nature's standpoint is indeed of no more significance than that of a dog, a horse or a rat. The vicious blinding of an adulterous, credulous earl onstage by a pair of blue-blooded monsters is exceptional only in the extreme to which it takes its adoption of an attitude that is integral to the tragedy.

As an instance of horrendous physical violence inflicted with brazen relish on the nobility it's hardly without precedent in Shakespeare either. One need only recall the treatment Jack Cade gleefully metes out to the severed heads of Lord Saye and Sir James Crowmer, or the vicarious pleasure Shakespeare clearly takes in Aaron's delighted duping of Titus into letting him hack off his hand, to be reminded of how deeply rooted in the origins of Shakespearean tragedy is the enmity that finds release in the barbaric extrusion of Gloucester's eyes in *King Lear*. It would be simplistic to conclude from this scene that its creator was motivated to write it solely by a vindictive desire to have a peer of the realm robbed of his sight before the audience's eyes. The effect of the atrocity is emotionally and morally more complex than that, and in its immediate aftermath Shakespeare ensures that our compassion for the victim is unqualified. But although the pity we feel for Gloucester offsets the unspeakable cruelty to which he's been subjected, it can't eclipse it or erase our sense that Shakespeare has made him pay a terrible price for who he is and what he stands for. Nothing makes the politics of the scene more blatant than Shakespeare's extraordinary decision to have a brave, nameless servant fatally wound Cornwall in an attempt to stop the blinding and be killed for doing so by a Regan outraged at his audacity: 'A peasant stand up thus?' It's a couple of kind-hearted, equally anonymous servants, moreover, who close the scene by resolving to 'follow the old Earl and get the bedlam / To lead him where he would', and who 'fetch some flax and whites of eggs / To apply to his bleeding face' (3.7.102–30, 105–6).

As Alain Badiou has observed, 'emancipatory politics is essentially the politics of the anonymous masses; it is the victory of those with no names, of those who are held in a state of colossal insignificance by the State', but whose very lack of the property and power that constitute significance led Marx to define them as 'generic humanity': the force from which the emancipatory transformation of society as a whole must spring. The 'peasant' who has the audacity to 'stand up' against the Duke of Cornwall, like his fellow peasant-servants who succour the brutalized Earl of Gloucester, belong to the same nameless Shakespearean breed as the Gravedigger in *Hamlet*, the Porter in *Macbeth* and, of course, the Fool in *King Lear*. Their anonymity implicitly aligns them with what human beings have in common by virtue of belonging to the same genus, and their humane concern for the well-being of 'the old Earl' makes that alignment overt. The hopeful note of simple human kindness for its own sake that they strike here is sustained in the next scene, as the levelling spirit incarnate in Edgar/Poor Tom enters, comforting himself with the thought that 'The lowest and most dejected thing of fortune / Stands still in esperance' (4.1.3–4), and is followed onstage by his blind father, tenderly led by yet another personification of 'generic humanity' in the shape of an unnamed 'Old Man'.

Homeless, dispossessed and dependant for mere survival on the kindness of others, Gloucester is transfigured like Lear by the loss of everything that once mattered to him and the liberation of the nascent self within him. So transfigured, indeed, that he regards his blinding as a blessing for having brought about his Damascene conversion. When he urges the Old Man to leave him for his own safety and the aged retainer protests, 'Alack, sir, you cannot see your way', Gloucester replies:

I have no way, and therefore want no eyes:
I stumbled when I saw. Full oft 'tis seen
Our means secure us and our mere defects
Prove our commodities.

(4.1.20–3)

I can think of no finer way of glossing these lines than to quote a passage from Bradley's closing reflections on the play. What the tragedy shows, Bradley concludes from what befalls its protagonists, is that 'power and prosperity'

are worthless, or worse; it is not on them, but on the renunciation of them, that the gods throw incense. They breed lust, pride, hardness of heart, the insolence of office, cruelty, scorn, hypocrisy, contention, war, murder, self-destruction. The whole story beats this indictment of prosperity into the brain. Lear's great speeches in his madness proclaim it like the curses of Timon on life and man. But here, as in *Timon*, the poor and humble are, almost without exception, sound and sweet at heart, faithful and pitiful. And here adversity, to the blessed in spirit, is blessed. … It melts in aged hearts sympathies which prosperity had frozen. It purges the soul's sight by blinding that of the eyes. Throughout that stupendous Third Act the good are seen growing better through suffering, and the bad worse through success. The warm castle is a room in hell, the storm-swept heath a sanctuary. The judgement of this world is a lie; its goods, which we covet, corrupt us; its ills, which break our bodies, set our souls free: 'Our means secure us and our mere defects / Prove our commodities.'

Shorn of its religious rhetoric, for which the resolutely irreligious vision of *King Lear* offers scant warrant, the passage displays Bradley's unerring critical instinct for the issue at the heart of the play. As it stands, however, its slant is symptomatic of Bradley's resistance to drawing the radical political conclusions from *King Lear* readily drawn by Shaw, and his need to translate the tragedy into a more tractable parable of spiritual redemption. It's telling that Bradley doesn't dwell on the rest of the short scene from which that quotation from Gloucester comes, and which climaxes in one of the most compelling speeches in the tragedy. The core of the scene is a re-enactment by Gloucester and Poor Tom of Lear's encounter with the latter. The reminders of Lear's confrontation with the 'poor, bare, forked animal' he beholds in Tom are explicit. 'T'the last night's storm I such a fellow saw, / Which made me think a man a worm', Gloucester tells the Old Man; 'Is that the naked fellow?', he asks him, before requesting that he 'bring some covering for this naked soul', whom he even addresses as 'Sirrah, naked fellow' (4.1.34–5, 42, 46, 54), ensuring that Poor Tom's unaccommodated human state is kept foremost in our mind. Then, after Tom has assured him that he knows the way to Dover, 'Both stile and gate, horseway and footpath' (4.1.59), and thus may be counted on to lead him there, Gloucester says:

Here, take this purse, thou whom the heaven's plagues
Have humbled to all strokes. That I am wretched
Makes thee the happier. Heavens deal so still!
Let the superfluous and lust-dieted man
That slaves your ordinance, that will not see
Because he does not feel, feel your power quickly:
So distribution should undo excess
And each man have enough.

                                                    (4.1.67–74)

The echo of Lear's prayer addressing the 'Poor naked wretches' of whom he's taken too little care is so distinct that it's been common for critics to treat Gloucester's speech as if it were a restatement of Lear's and overlook the respects in which it moves beyond it. Bradley remarks that both characters 'learn the same lesson, and Gloster's repetition (noticed and blamed by Johnson) of the thought in a famous speech of Lear's is surely intentional'; and with that he relegates the quotation of both speeches in full to a footnote, deeming neither of them to merit further commentary. But it scarcely requires closer scrutiny to see that Gloucester's speech packs a punch that Lear's prayer pulls. In handing his purse to Poor Tom, Gloucester acknowledges the justice of his paying with his own misery and his own money for his part in the creation of the destitute: 'That I am wretched / Makes thee the happier.' There's no attempt to mitigate his culpability by transferring it to an impersonal abstraction, as Lear does in his prayer when he commands 'pomp' to take physic. Nor does Gloucester disguise his wish to see the same draconian poetic justice that's been meted out to him meted out forthwith to all the other 'superfluous and lust-dieted' men like him, whose selfish lack of fellow feeling blinds them to the suffering of others for which they are responsible. Instead of Lear's injunction to pomp to 'shake the superflux' to the houseless poor to 'show the heavens more just', we're given Gloucester's blunt statement of what needs to be done so that no one has too much and no one goes without: 'So distribution should undo excess / And each man have enough.' And whereas Lear's philanthropic injunction remains a wish, confined to the subjunctive realm of prayer, the impact of the solution Gloucester commends to us gains immeasurably from the fact that he enacts and illustrates what he's commending as he speaks.

Gloucester's speech evinces a clarifying and hardening of the attitude towards the rich and powerful displayed by Lear's prayer. It's a frankly punitive stance, which calls for the superfluous wealth they unjustly possess to be exacted from them by an avenging 'power' whose wrath they can *feel*, in order that it can be shared equally between everybody. It's a stance that's not only consistent with Shakespeare's scourging of the tragedy's aristocracy but provides the rationale for it too. The power so quickly felt in *King Lear* by the characters who will not see because they do not feel, and even by those such as Cordelia who do feel and see but are doomed by their rank along with them, is Shakespeare's power, and he wields it without remorse. If we had thought Gloucester's blinding, contrition and ethical epiphany more than sufficed to earn him respite from further torment by the playwright, we couldn't have been more wrong. His final speech to Tom in this scene leaves no doubt of his intention to commit suicide in Dover by plunging from 'the very brim' of 'a cliff whose high and bending head / Looks fearfully in the confined deep' (4.1.75–7). But Shakespeare has no intention of letting Gloucester off so lightly, as the surreal hoax Edgar employs to hoodwink him when they reach Dover makes clear.

In the corresponding episode in Sidney's *Arcadia*, the counterpart of Edgar frustrates his father's plan to end his life by simply refusing to bring him to the top of the rock from which he intends to hurl himself. Shakespeare decided to transmogrify this episode into the bizarre scene in which Edgar tricks Gloucester into believing he has miraculously survived a real fall from a real cliff at Dover, which is in fact an imaginary precipice Edgar has conjured out of words. Garbed now in the peasant's clothes the Old Man brought him and speaking now, as Gloucester is surprised to hear, 'In better phrase and matter' (4.6.8) than he was wont to as Poor Tom, Edgar persuades his blind father that, despite the evidence of his other senses, they have been labouring uphill towards a cliff-top and the sea can be clearly heard:

Come on, sir, here's the place. Stand still: how fearful
And dizzy 'tis to cast one's eyes so low.
The crows and choughs that wing the midway air
Show scarce so gross as beetles. Half-way down
Hangs one that gathers samphire, dreadful trade;

Methinks he seems no bigger than his head.
The fishermen that walk upon the beach
Appear like mice, and yon tall anchoring barque
Diminished to her cock, her cock a buoy
Almost too small for sight. The murmuring surge
That on th'unnumbered idle pebble chafes,
Cannot be heard so high. I'll look no more,
Lest my brain turn and the deficient sight
Topple down headlong.

(4.6.11–24)

At this point, notwithstanding the doubts sown in their minds by Gloucester's initial suspicions, an audience unfamiliar with the play would be justified in being as convinced as Gloucester by this speech that Edgar is describing a real place and reporting real sights and sounds. The scene Edgar purports to behold and hear is so vividly evoked and populated that it becomes as credible as it would be if it had been meant to establish an actual onstage location in the mind's eye and ear of the spectator. Even audiences fully aware that Gloucester is being fooled can find themselves seduced for a moment by the solidity of the illusion into believing that he is indeed standing 'within a foot / Of th' extreme verge' (4.6.25) and poised to topple from it.

It's not until Edgar informs the audience in an aside, as Gloucester prepares to plummet to his death, that he's trifling with his father's despair only to cure it that they know for sure the old man is being duped. And it's not until a worried Edgar admits in a second aside, right after his father falls forward and no further than the stage, 'Had he been where he thought, / By this had thought been past' (4.6.44–5), that the illusory status of the cliff imagined by the audience is beyond question. As was noted earlier, Edgar's claim to have deluded Gloucester for therapeutic reasons alone doesn't scotch the suspicion that his true purpose in risking his father's life with this tortuous ploy is as dark as Lear's was in dividing the kingdom. But in that regard Edgar serves also as the instrument of Shakespeare's darker purpose, which is to devise yet another ordeal for the sightless earl that's designed to exploit his blindness and our imaginative complicity in the protraction of his torment.

The virtuous cover story Shakespeare furnishes for Edgar concludes with the latter persuading his father that the gods have saved him from himself and from the 'fiend', posing as 'A poor unfortunate beggar', who lured him to 'the dread summit of this chalky bourn' (4.6.57, 68, 72). 'I do remember now', says Gloucester; 'Henceforth I'll bear / Affliction till it do cry out itself / "Enough, enough" and die' (4.6.75–7). But the avowed warrant for the affliction Gloucester has just been made to bear can't begin to justify the duplicitous ingenuity and gratuitous cruelty of the means employed to afflict him. Small wonder that both the Theatre of the Absurd and the Theatre of Cruelty have discerned in the Dover Cliff scene a foretaste of their own disquieting aesthetic. Desperate to be done with the world and die, Gloucester's hopes of merciful oblivion are raised only to be dashed. Instead of meeting a brave, dignified end charged with pathos by 'So many fathom down precipitating' (4.6.50), he drops flat on his face with a bathetic effect likely to elicit laughter from the audience. 'Away and let me die' (4.6.48), he pleads in vain as he comes round, for Edgar's manipulative charade is not over yet. 'Do but look up' (4.6.71), Edgar urges him, assuming yet another persona and feigning ignorance of his father's blindness. 'Alack, I have no eyes', Gloucester replies, before asking:

> Is wretchedness deprived that benefit
> To end itself by death? 'Twas yet some comfort
> When misery could beguile the tyrant's rage
> And frustrate his proud will.

> (4.6.62–4)

But the proud will of the tragedy, as far as Gloucester's fate is concerned, is not to be frustrated, and the benefit by which Romans of a Senecan disposition set such store is deliberately denied him. At the very moment when he might have had the consolation of knowing that the man now addressing him is his son, Gloucester is denied that too, and for no reason his son cares to explain in an aside. In fact, Edgar's reticence in this regard is rendered more unfathomable by his choosing this moment to ditch his Poor Tom persona for good. Despite having no cause to persist in deceiving his father, he insists on foisting another fiction upon him to account for the mad beggar's disappearance: Poor Tom mutates in Edgar's imagination into a demonic grotesque with 'two full moons' for eyes and 'a thousand noses, / Horns whelked and waved like the enraged sea' (4.6.70–1), last seen parting from Gloucester way up above them, on the brink of a non-existent cliff.

A Whole Dead World Galloping Over the Living Earth

Edgar's Dover Cliff hoax functions on another level, however, as an empowering parable for the audience. Viewed from this standpoint, it's an object lesson in the ease with which anyone can be duped into not only mistaking a flagrantly contrived illusion for reality, but also acting on it to their cost. It's a lesson, as we've seen, that *Othello* is especially intent on driving home. But it's driven home no less effectively through Edgar's creation on an empty stage of a landscape which the audience is induced to find credible too. All that's required of the delusion to secure its hold on the mind is that it be convincing and that, like Gloucester and like Othello, one is predisposed to be convinced. The ingenuity of the Dover Cliff scene lies in Shakespeare's using the same verbal wizardry that suspends our disbelief in the make-believe world of *King Lear* to foster our distrust of what we take to be true in the world beyond the theatre. By framing an illusion within a reality that is itself an illusion as insubstantial as the one Edgar inflicts on his father, Shakespeare confounds the distinction between imaginary and real, throwing the theatricality of everyday life into relief.

'When we are born we cry that we are come / To this great stage of fools' (4.6.178–9), says Lear later in the same scene, long aware by now that 'King' is just the role in which history happens to have cast him in a stage-play world that could be cast and staged quite differently. It's a masterstroke of Shakespeare to bring the undeceived mad monarch onstage to converse with the disabused blind earl immediately after we've watched Gloucester being beguiled by Edgar in order to open our eyes too. 'No, they cannot touch me for coining. I am the King himself' (4.6.83–4), Lear declares upon entering. But the mock crown of wildflowers he wears and his subsequent speeches leave the caustic tone in which that declaration must be delivered in no doubt. Lear has seen through the whole charade in which he has played the leading part and won't be fooled again:

> When the rain came to wet me once and the wind to make me chatter; when the thunder would not peace at my bidding, there I found 'em, there I smelt 'em out. Go to, they are not men o'their words: they told me I was everything; 'tis a lie, I am not ague-proof.
>
> (4.6.100–4)

When Gloucester recognizes 'The trick of that voice' (4.6.105) and seeks to pay obeisance to his sovereign, crying 'O, let me kiss that hand!', Lear is having none of it: 'Let me wipe it first, it smells of mortality' (4.6.129), he says, refusing to be treated any longer as if there were something that set him apart from, and placed him above, the rest of his kind.

Lear knows exactly who Gloucester is too. He also perceives that the earl has been robbed of his eyes and, seizing on that fact, insists with what at first seems wilful cruelty that Gloucester read the imaginary 'challenge' he thrusts before him. But there's method in Lear's madness, as Edgar subsequently remarks, and it soon becomes clear that Lear has fastened on the faculty of sight for a reason Gloucester will have no trouble seeing:

LEAR
Read.

GLOUCESTER
What, with the case of eyes?

LEAR
Oh ho, are you there with me? No eyes in your head, nor no money in your purse? Your eyes are in a heavy case, your purse in a light, yet you see how this world goes.

GLOUCESTER
I see it feelingly.

LEAR
What, art mad? A man may see how this world goes with no eyes. Look with thine ears. See how yon justice rails upon yon simple thief. Hark in thine ear: change places and handy-dandy, which is the justice, which is the thief? Thou hast seen a farmer's dog bark at a beggar?

GLOUCESTER
Ay, sir.

LEAR

> And the creature run from the cur – there thou mightst behold the great
> image of authority: a dog's obeyed in office.
> Thou, rascal beadle, hold thy bloody hand;
> Why dost thou lash that whore? Strip thine own back,
> Thou hotly lusts to use her in that kind
> For which thou whipp'st her. The usurer hangs the cozener.
> Through tattered clothes great vices do appear;
> Robes and furred gowns hide all. Plate sin with gold,
> And the strong lance of justice hurtless breaks;
> Arm it in rags, a pygmy's straw does pierce it.
> None does offend, none, I say none. I'll able 'em.
> Take that of me, my friend, who have the power
> To seal th' accuser's lips. Get thee glass eyes,
> And like a scurvy politician seem
> To see the things thou dost not.

(4.6.139–68)

Lear has left the philanthropic moralism of his prayer for the 'Poor naked wretches' far behind. For what is an injunction to be charitable worth, when it comes from the lips of a king? How can the spiritual regeneration of those who possess and rule provide the solution, when the problem springs from the fact of their existence? That Shakespeare was driven to write a speech in which 'the great image of authority', the sovereign himself, derides the exercise of power as nothing but a dog barking at a beggar is astonishing enough. Not satisfied with that, however, he makes Lear draw this conclusion from the pervasive corruption and hypocrisy he excoriates: 'None does offend, none, I say none.' 'None does offend', because everyone offends when inequality and injustice are structural, when the entire society is culpable. The sources of the appalling cruelty and suffering the tragedy depicts lie deeper, Lear's speech implies, than the malevolence of individuals. They lie in the institutionalized greed, exploitation and oppression of a society that creates the poor and subjects them to the rich and powerful in the first place.

King Lear offers no more compelling proof of Shakespeare's complete alienation from the travesty of human life that confronted him in Jacobean Britain. Nor could there be stronger evidence of the tragedy's keenness to command our imaginations from its vantage point beyond the war-torn, famine-ravaged, self-destructive world in which we read and stage, study and watch it today: a world swarming with millions more houseless heads and unfed sides than Shakespeare could ever have foreseen, and crippled by inequality on a scale that would have left him speechless. The great Russian film director Grigori Kozintsev described *King Lear* as 'a whole dead world galloping over the living earth beneath a sky full of stars'. That whole dead world is not only Shakespeare's world, it is our world too. For the play can be viewed as a prophetic fable, in which we witness the feudal age and ethos spawning the present age of rampant individualism and acquisitive egotism, and that age in turn destroying itself, leaving those who survive its demise dazed and exhausted, uncertain of what the future holds. *King Lear* foretells the end of our modern epoch in a mood torn between compassion and contempt: compassion for the human creatures doomed to live and die on the inhuman terms of such a society; contempt for the parts history has constrained them to play in its brutal tragedy of division and domination. For Lear *as a king* the play has as little mercy as it has regard for the sentimental pieties of its audience. But its faith in the 'Unaccommodated man' that Lear discovers within the king, and in the untapped potential of every human being that it embodies, is unquenchable.

CHAPTER 8
MACBETH: THE HABIT OF ANOTHER NATURE

Embracing the Butcher

The spirit that animates Shakespearean tragedy at its boldest is one that Bertolt Brecht, whose overtly revolutionary drama owes so much to Shakespeare, certainly understood, even if he failed to recognize the strength of that spirit in his mighty precursor. It finds uncompromising expression in the lines Brecht gives to the Chorus in *The Measures Taken* (*Die Massnahme*):

> With whom would the just man not sit down
> To help the cause of justice?
> What medicine would taste too bad
> To someone dying?
> What vile act would you not commit to
> Eradicate vileness?
> If you could change the world at last, why
> Would you be too good to change it?
> Who are you?
> Sink into the mire
> Embrace the butcher, but
> Change the world: it needs it!

No tragedy of Shakespeare's is more powerfully animated by this spirit than *Macbeth*, whose protagonist, reviled in the closing speech as 'this dead butcher' (5.9.35), is embraced in Brecht's sense by Shakespeare from the start of the play. He's embraced because his tragedy dramatizes both the inhumanity of the society that fosters his crimes and the human potential to live by the principles on which a humane society could be founded. By revealing that potential in the tormented soul of a killer, Shakespeare shows not just that the humane is inextricable from the inhumane, but how vital a tragic part inhumanity is fated to play in the liberation of mankind from its own barbarity. What more compelling way for Shakespeare to dramatize the realism of his utopian vision than to vest it in a bloodstained regicide, who butchers his way to oblivion despite his nature being 'too full o'th' milk of human kindness' (1.5.17)?

To espouse such a view of *Macbeth* is to fly in the face of readings content to construe it as a politically orthodox play of its day, in which a tyrannical regicide is defeated and beheaded in a climactic battle with forces led by the son of the king he murdered for his throne. Read from that standpoint, *Macbeth* charts the exemplary fall of a noble warrior, who succumbs to the evil promptings of the weird sisters and the goading of his ruthless wife; who kills his sleeping king in cold blood with her connivance in defiance of his conscience and suffers agonies of guilt as a consequence; who turns into a vicious despot, forced to procure further murders in a vain attempt to secure his stolen crown; who is duped into believing himself invincible by the same eldritch creatures that first lit the fuse of his ambition; and who meets his just end at the hands of the thane whose family were slaughtered at his behest. The fact that Macbeth's nemesis presents his grisly trophy to the victorious heir apparent at the end with the words 'Hail King, for so thou art. Behold where stands / Th'usurper's cursed head: the time is free' (5.9.20–1) certainly seems to set the seal on this account of *Macbeth*, whose closing speech is delivered with due regal aplomb by the newly acclaimed monarch.

The reason why this take on the tragedy continues to command credence isn't far to seek. It's because the text affords ample warrant for it, partly in the judgements passed on Macbeth by the righteous adversaries who rally to overthrow him and partly in Macbeth's perceptions of himself. But to see Macbeth solely through his own eyes and as his antagonists see him is to mistake the purview of the characters for the perspective of the play. Boiled down to the above synopsis, *Macbeth* can be made to serve as a dramatic fable with a political message in tune with the dominant ideology of its day. To those who baulk at the notion of Shakespeare writing about his time in the terms of his time, but from a standpoint far ahead of his time, that reading of the tragedy makes perfect historical sense. The trouble is that it makes sense only if the way the play is constructed and worded is discounted and the import of its astonishing poetry is sacrificed to the skeletal tenor of the plot. Once the full implications of its design and diction are unfurled, *Macbeth* demands to be read and performed as a truly visionary tragedy, which declines to comply with convention then or now. 'The chief use of the "meaning" of a poem, in the ordinary sense,' as T. S. Eliot memorably remarked, 'may be to satisfy one habit of the reader, to keep his mind diverted and quiet, while the poem does its work upon him: much as the imaginary burglar is always provided with a bit of nice meat for the house-dog.' In a similar way, readers and audiences of *Macbeth* are provided with a readily digestible meaning on which they can fasten, while the tragedy does its stealthy work upon them, transforming what it purports to mean into something else altogether.

That professed meaning slips down so smoothly because it fits with the received ideas and entrenched expectations that most spectators and critics bring to *Macbeth*. But to swallow it is as misguided as to settle for seeing *Hamlet* as the tragedy of a royal revenger fatally flawed by indecisiveness and procrastination; *Othello* as the tragedy of a devoted black husband doomed by an irrational predisposition to sexual jealousy to murder his white wife; or *King Lear* as the tragedy of an aged monarch whose foolish decision to abdicate and divide his kingdom between his daughters has catastrophic consequences. No accounts of these plays based on those assumptions can survive the close attention to form and phrasing they deserve if justice is to be done to them. Such accounts are bound to be plausible to the extent that the plays can be cited to back them up, because the plays invite the misconceptions of their meaning that they purport to endorse precisely in order to confound and eclipse them.

Supernatural Soliciting

Macbeth begins by leading us to believe that a metaphysical morality play is what it has in store. The storm-racked opening scene creates through the three witches an ominous sense of malign supernatural powers lying in wait for Macbeth even before he appears. That the witches have foreknowledge of 'When the battle's lost, and won' (1.1.4), and hence of when and where they will meet Macbeth, reinforces the feeling that whatever baleful fate awaits him is preordained. That feeling is intensified by the incantatory rhythm and rhyming couplets that govern the sinister trio's speech, giving it the formulaic ring of lines recited in a rite. The contrast with the blank verse in which the dialogue of the second scene is conducted underscores linguistically the stark divide between the occult female realm that we alone have been privileged to witness so far and the familiar male world of warfare to which the play next transports us. From this scene we learn that the battle the witches referred to has just been won after seeming lost, thanks chiefly to the ferocious valour of 'brave Macbeth' (1.2.16), whose reward will be the title of the traitor he defeated, the Thane of Cawdor. The time is now ripe for the rendezvous with Macbeth – foreknown by the witches and the audience but not by Macbeth – to take place. The fact that Macbeth is denied the prior knowledge of the encounter that we share with the witches makes him seem even more vulnerable to whatever harm they mean to cause him.

That harm is what the weird sisters have in mind is borne out by their exchange, to which again the audience alone is privy, as they await the arrival of Macbeth and Banquo on the heath in the play's third scene. The second witch has been busy since their last appearance 'Killing swine' (1.3.2), a malicious deed of which witches were commonly accused. The first witch, having been refused food and insulted by 'A sailor's wife' (1.3.4), is intent on making the sailor pay at sea for his wife's rebuff on shore:

Her husband's to Aleppo gone, Master o'th' Tiger:
But in a sieve I'll thither sail,
And like a rat without a tail,
I'll do, I'll do, and I'll do. ...
I'll drain him dry as hay:
Sleep shall neither night nor day
Hang upon his penthouse lid:
He shall live a man forbid.
Weary sev'nights nine times nine
Shall he dwindle, peak and pine:
Though his bark cannot be lost,
Yet it shall be tempest-tossed.

(1.3.7–10, 18–25)

The subliminal foreshadowing of Macbeth's sleepless torment as 'a man forbid' (i.e. cursed) in the wake of the murder deepens the impression that what follows is foredoomed. That said, the final couplet quoted qualifies the extent of the witches' power over their human victims, which includes inflicting suffering but precludes inflicting death. At the sound of Macbeth's approach – 'A drum, a drum: / Macbeth doth come' (1.3.30–1) – the witches chant as they dance in a circle:

> The weird sisters, hand in hand,
> Posters of the sea and land,
> Thus do go, about, about,
> Thrice to thine, and thrice to mine,
> And thrice again, to make up nine.
> Peace, the charm's wound up.

(1.3.32–7)

With that last line, as Macbeth and Banquo enter and come face to face with this unholy trinity, any doubt that a baneful spell of some kind has been cast on Macbeth by unearthly beings beyond his ken, and that it's about to take baneful effect, appears to have been banished.

The supernatural odds seem to have been stacked against the tragic protagonist from the outset, before he's had a chance to speak or act. Yet no sooner have the witches hailed Macbeth not only as the Thane of Glamis he now is and the Thane of Cawdor he's about to become, but also as destined to be 'king hereafter' (1.3.50), than we're obliged by Macbeth's reaction, as Banquo describes it, to begin revising our assumptions:

> Good sir, why do you start, and seem to fear
> Things that do sound so fair? – I'th' name of truth,
> Are ye fantastical, or that indeed
> Which outwardly ye show? My noble partner
> You greet with present grace, and great prediction
> Of noble having and of royal hope,
> That he seems rapt withal.

(1.3.51–7)

Having prophesied, sphinx-like, at Banquo's urging that he shall be 'Lesser than Macbeth, and greater', 'Not so happy, yet much happier' (1.3.65–6), and the begetter of kings without being one himself, the witches start to disappear, at which Macbeth cries: 'Stay, you imperfect speakers, tell me more' (1.3.70). He craves an explanation of how their 'prophetic greeting' of him as Thane of Cawdor and future king can be true, and he demands both the source of 'this strange intelligence' and their reason for imparting it (1.3.78). But the weird sisters vanish 'as breath into the wind' without answering, leaving Macbeth still longing to know more: 'Would they had stayed' (1.3.82–3). Moments later the first of the witches' predictions proves true, when Macbeth learns from Ross and Angus that he is indeed the Thane of Cawdor now. The alacrity with which he leaps to this response for our ears alone is telling: 'Glamis and Thane of Cawdor: / The greatest is behind [i.e. still to come]' (1.3.118–19). His retreat into this aside (unmarked as such in the Folio text but, like the many that follow it, plainly implied) is a sign of Macbeth's need to conceal his private thoughts about the prospect of being king from his companions. That we're justified in inferring that what lurks behind the aside must stay hidden is confirmed by Banquo's response to Macbeth's asking him *sotto voce*: 'Do you not hope your children shall be kings / When those that gave the Thane of Cawdor to me / Promised no less to them?': 'That, trusted home, / Might yet enkindle you unto the crown, / Besides the Thane of Cawdor' (1.3.120–4).

Banquo's warning of Macbeth to distrust 'The instruments of darkness', who are prone to 'tell us truths' in order 'to win us to our harm' (1.3.125–6), suggests that he already suspects the worst of his friend's keenness to pursue the matter. It naturally primes us with the same suspicion, which Macbeth reveals to be justified in an electrifying soliloquy that withholds nothing from us:

> Two truths are told
> As happy prologues to the swelling act
> Of the imperial theme. – I thank you gentlemen –
> This supernatural soliciting
> Cannot be ill; cannot be good. If ill,
> Why hath it given me earnest of success,
> Commencing in a truth? I am Thane of Cawdor.
> If good, why do I yield to that suggestion
> Whose horrid image doth unfix my hair,
> And make my seated heart knock at my ribs,
> Against the use of nature? Present fears
> Are less than horrible imaginings.
> My thought, whose murder yet is but fantastical,
> Shakes so my single state of man
> That function is smothered in surmise,
> And nothing is, but what is not.

(1.3.129–44)

Note the deft economy with which Shakespeare signals the depth of Macbeth's immersion in surmise by having him snap out of it for a second in the third line, when he remembers belatedly to thank Ross and Angus, before slipping back into a trance of self-absorption, transfixed by the 'horrid image' of himself murdering his monarch. 'Look how our partner's rapt' (1.3.145), observes Banquo to Ross and Angus, drawing attention again with the same word, 'rapt', to the mood of brooding introspection in which Macbeth is lost. So lost, indeed, that his musing on his 'horrible imaginings' (1.3.140) continues through two more engrossed asides, obliging Banquo to devise an explanation for the benefit of Ross and Angus: 'New honours come upon him, / Like our strange garments, cleave not to their mould, / But with the aid of use' (1.3.147–9). Only after his final aside does Macbeth come round from his reverie at Banquo's prodding – 'Worthy Macbeth, we stay upon your leisure' (1.3.151) – and become aware of the need to concoct a plausible excuse for his protracted fit of distraction: 'Give me your favour. My dull brain was wrought / With things forgotten' (1.3.152–3). Even then, as they ride on together to join the king, he can't let the thoughts obsessing him drop without securing Banquo's agreement to 'Think upon what hath chanced' (1.3.156) and speak of it again.

This scene repays close attention because of its crucial role in deepening our understanding of the causes, and thus the nature, of the tragedy of Macbeth. From the moment we're alerted to Macbeth's surprising display of fear at hearing 'Things that do sound so fair' and his immediate lapsing into pensive silence, it becomes increasingly apparent that the mainspring of the tragedy is to be found not in the inscrutable malice of Macbeth's supernatural solicitors, but in the all too explicable motives of his own human heart. Coleridge was the first to grasp the significance of Macbeth's reaction to the predictions with which the witches greet him:

> But O! how truly Shakspearian is the opening of Macbeth's character given in the *unpossessedness* of Banquo's mind, wholly present to the present object, – an unsullied, unscarified mirror! – and how strictly true to nature it is, that Banquo, and not Macbeth himself, directs our notice to the effect produced on Macbeth's mind, rendered temptible by previous dalliance of the fancy with ambitious thoughts …

The questions Banquo addresses to the weird sisters 'are those of natural curiosity', says Coleridge, about their capacity and willingness to tell his fortune too; they are 'all perfectly general, or rather planless', inasmuch as they harbour no intimation of preconceived design on Banquo's part.

> But Macbeth, lost in thought, raises himself to speech only by the Witches being about to depart: – Stay you imperfect speakers, tell me more: – and all that follows is reasoning on a problem already discussed in his mind, – on a hope which he welcomes, and the doubts concerning the attainment of which he wishes to have cleared up.

Hence, continues Coleridge, the pointed contrast between Banquo's disinterested wondering whither the witches have vanished and Macbeth's regretting only that they had not remained to tell him more. Hence, too, Banquo's subsequent 'wondering like any common spectator: "Were such things here as we do speak about?" whilst Macbeth persists in recurring to the self-concerning … So surely is the guilt in its germ anterior to the supposed cause, and immediate temptation!' Should surer confirmation of that be required, 'every word of his soliloquy', as Coleridge observes, 'shows the early birth-date of his guilt'.

Bradley's account of *Macbeth* a century later expands upon the inferences Coleridge draws from his acute psychological analysis of Macbeth's speech and demeanour in this seminal scene:

That the influence of the first prophecies upon him came as much from himself as from them, is made abundantly clear by the obviously intentional contrast between him and Banquo. Banquo, ambitious but perfectly honest, is scarcely even startled by them, and he remains throughout the scene indifferent to them. But when Macbeth heard them he was not an innocent man. Precisely how far his mind was guilty may be a question; but no innocent man would have started, as he did, with a start of *fear* at the mere prophecy of a crown, or have conceived thereupon *immediately* the thought of murder. Either this thought was not new to him, or he had cherished at least some vaguer dishonourable dream, the instantaneous recurrence of which, at the moment of his hearing the prophecy, revealed to him an inward and terrifying guilt. In either case not only was he free to accept or resist the temptation, but the temptation was already within him … Speaking strictly we must affirm that he was tempted only by himself. *He* speaks indeed of their 'supernatural soliciting'; but in fact they did not solicit. They merely announced events: they hailed him as Thane of Glamis, Thane of Cawdor, and King hereafter. No connection of these announcements with any action of his was even hinted by them. For all that appears, the natural death of an old man might have fulfilled the prophecy any day. In any case, the idea of fulfilling it by murder was entirely his own.

If the idea of his being the Thane of Cawdor comes as a surprise to Macbeth, the notion of his becoming king one day does not. Before the scene is over, we're left in no doubt that what's stunned Macbeth is the shock of hearing the witches openly foretelling his possession of the prize for which he's been secretly nursing 'black and deep desires' (1.4.51). Nor is it just the immediacy of his unprompted resort to murder as the means of possessing it that presupposes malice aforethought. It's also the intensity of the pressure he feels under to commit the murder *now* – indeed, to have *already* committed it – as the proleptic conclusion of his soliloquy attests: 'My thought, whose murder yet is but fantastical, / Shakes so my single state of man / That function is smothered in surmise, / And nothing is, but what is not.' The irresistible imminence of the actual murder is betrayed in the first of these lines by the adverb 'yet', which is all that's stopping the *as yet* imaginary death of Duncan from becoming a reality. But the 'horrid image' of the accomplished murder in his mind's eye is so vivid and compelling that it supplants the reality of the present moment, shaking Macbeth's being to the core as if it's actually happening.

Further proof of premeditation, of Macbeth's guilt being, as Coleridge puts it, 'in its germ anterior to the supposed cause, and immediate temptation', is provided by Lady Macbeth in the fifth scene. After reading her husband's letter describing his encounter with the weird sisters, her mind turns as swiftly as Macbeth's to murder as 'the nearest way' to be crowned with 'the golden round' (1.5.18, 28), which both had plainly coveted before that 'prophetic greeting' (1.3.78) on the heath. The king's death is sealed by her the moment she hears of his impending arrival: 'The raven himself is hoarse / That croaks the fatal entrance of Duncan / Under my battlements' (1.5.38–40). The spirits she commands in her second, chilling soliloquy to fill her 'from the crown to the toe, top-full / Of direst cruelty' and 'take [her] milk for gall' are explicitly 'murdering ministers' (1.5.42–3, 48). She imagines not only when and how Duncan will die, with a graphic brutality Macbeth's soliloquy eschews, but also herself rather than Macbeth as his undeterred murderer: 'Come, thick night, / And pall thee in the dunnest smoke of hell, / That my keen knife see not the wound it makes, / Nor heaven peep through the blanket of the dark / To cry, "Hold, hold"' (1.5.50–4). She speaks no more than the truth when she tells Macbeth, who enters at this point: 'Thy letters have transported me beyond / This ignorant present, and I feel now / The future in the instant' (1.5.56–7). So developed and demanding are her own black desires that she, too, is experiencing the murder in her mind as if she were committing it now, just like Macbeth in his first soliloquy. It's no surprise, therefore, that in the first exchange between them Lady Macbeth has no need to spell out what she means by 'He that's coming / Must be provided for' (1.5.66–7) and 'This night's great business' (1.5.68), or explain why Macbeth must 'look like the innocent flower, / But be the serpent under't' (1.5.65–6). There's no need because the dream of 'solely sovereign sway and masterdom' (1.5.70) has already ensnared them both and they both know already what they must do to realize it.

Bradley is likewise persuaded that Macbeth's 'guilty ambition, whatever its precise form, was known to his wife and shared by her. Otherwise, surely, she would not, on reading his letter, so instantaneously assume that the king must be murdered in their castle; nor would Macbeth, as soon as he meets her, be aware (as he evidently is) that this thought is in her mind.' Bradley proceeds from this to consider the implications of the speech delivered two scenes later by Lady Macbeth, in which she rebukes her husband for his reluctance to proceed with Duncan's assassination and accuses him of cowardice. 'I dare do all that may become a man', says Macbeth, 'Who dares do more, is none' (1.7.46–7); to which his wife retorts:

> What beast was't then
> That made you break this enterprise to me?
> When you durst do it, then you were a man;
> And to be more than what you were, you would
> Be so much more the man. Nor time and place
> Did then adhere, and yet you would make both:
> They have made themselves, and their fitness now
> Does unmake you. I have given suck, and know
> How tender 'tis to love the babe that milks me:
> I would, while it was smiling in my face,
> Have plucked the nipple from his boneless gums,
> And dashed the brains out, had I so sworn
> As you have done to this.

> (1.7.47–59)

Bradley comments: 'Here Lady Macbeth asserts (1) that Macbeth proposed the murder to her; (2) that he did so at a time when there was no opportunity to attack Duncan, no "adherence" of "time" and "place"; (3) that he declared he would *make* an opportunity, and swore to carry out the murder.' The apparent problem with this for Bradley (and for many other critics) is that it obliges one either to posit a lost or cut scene at the very beginning of the play, in which what Lady Macbeth reminds Macbeth of took place; or else to assume 'that Macbeth proposed, and swore to execute, the murder at some point prior to the action of the play'.

Discounting the former option as improbable (and the notion that Shakespeare simply made a mistake as equally unlikely), Bradley rightly adopts the latter as more credible, because 'we can find a good deal to say in favour of the idea of a plan formed at a past time':

> It would explain Macbeth's start of fear at the prophecy of the kingdom. It would explain why Lady Macbeth, on receiving his letter, immediately resolves on action; and why, on their meeting, each knows that murder is in the mind of the other. And it is in harmony with her remarks on his probable shrinking from the act, to which, *ex hypothesi*, she had already thought it necessary to make him pledge himself by oath.

Unfortunately, no sooner has Bradley advanced this cogent solution to the ostensible problem posed by the speech in question than he feels bound to withdraw it, on the grounds of its sequential inconsistencies with the evidence of the preceding scenes as he reads them. He's forced instead to fall back on our having to imagine an exchange between the Macbeths after scene 5 which would explain the supposed inconsistencies away. There is, however, no problem to solve, once one reminds oneself that the poetic drama of *Macbeth*, like all Shakespearean drama, is not required to meet the criteria of verisimilitude that a realist novel is expected to meet in order to be credible. Whatever contradictions, whether substantive or surmised, Lady Macbeth's speech may create for the fastidious reader, attempting to resolve them is as misconceived as attempting to rationalize the temporal discrepancies that imperil the plausibility of *Othello*, if they are strictly considered. Shakespeare has no compunction about flouting the laws of likelihood or creating incongruities when other objectives matter more and take priority at a given moment. Thus the retroactive effect of Lady Macbeth's harking back at this point to that conversation, which implicitly predates the play's action, but to which we have not been privy, is to emphasize the human origin of the regicidal impulse in Macbeth, before his encounter with the weird sisters. That effect is entirely consistent with Shakespeare's keenness, as the tragedy gathers momentum, to complicate our understanding of its causes, transforming the function and significance of the witches in the process.

Terrestrial Tragedy

Bradley rightly dismisses as 'inadequate' the notion that the witches 'are merely symbolic representations of the unconscious or half-conscious guilt in Macbeth himself'. But he goes too far when he insists that they 'are not goddesses, or fates, *or, in any way whatever, supernatural beings*. They are old women, poor and ragged, skinny and hideous, full of vulgar spite, occupied in killing their neighbours' swine or revenging themselves on sailors' wives who have refused them chestnuts' (my emphasis). They certainly possess neither the stature nor the omnipotence of goddesses or fates. But the play offers no obvious proof of their being merely human in nature, and every reason to impute a supernatural dimension, at the very least, to these prescient creatures 'That look not like th'inhabitants o'th' earth', that only seem 'corporal' and that melt away 'as breath into the wind' (1.3.41, 81–2) before the audience's eyes as well as Macbeth's. Such powers of prediction, deception and conjuration as they do possess they appear to owe to unequivocally supernatural entities in the shape of Hecate and their nameless 'masters', whose prophetic aid they invoke on Macbeth's behalf in Act 4. The supernatural aspect of the witches is as undeniable as the manifest existence in *Macbeth* of the ethereal realm whose sinister rulers they serve. Nor is it necessary to deny it, or to treat their function as *purely* figurative, in order to explain the tragedy of Macbeth in the sublunary, human terms in which Shakespeare conceived it.

It's not necessary because, as Bradley observes:

> There is no sign whatsoever in the play that Shakespeare meant the actions of Macbeth to be forced on him by an external power, whether that of the Witches, or of their 'masters', or of Hecate. ... Macbeth himself nowhere betrays a suspicion that his action is, or has been, thrust on him by an external power. He curses the Witches for deceiving him, but he never attempts to shift to them the burden of his guilt.

Nor would he be justified if he did, because, although they can 'look into the seeds of time' (1.3.58) and foretell Macbeth's future, the bearded handmaidens of Hecate cannot make it come to pass; they can predict, but they cannot coerce. By hailing Macbeth as 'king hereafter' and echoing aloud his secret thoughts at that momentous juncture, just after his triumphant display of martial valour, they tell him what he wants to hear and, in so doing, they undoubtedly exert an influence on his prior thoughts and his predisposition to act on them. But they stop short of prompting Macbeth to act to fulfil their prophecy. In fact, they never desire him, let alone incite him, to do anything he does not choose to do. Whether he acts or does not act in any way in response to their prophetic greeting is left entirely to Macbeth to decide. Nor does Macbeth ask the weird sisters what he should do, or what means he should employ, to realize his furtive ambition. No Faustian bargain, with the posthumous fate of his immortal soul at stake, is struck between them.

Likewise, when Macbeth confronts the 'Filthy hags' (4.1.114) once again in Act 4 – on his initiative, not theirs – what he hears the three apparitions they summon tell him is the confirmation he craves of the hopes and fears already preying on his mind, which have driven him to seek the witches out. 'He knows thy thought' says the first witch of the first apparition, the '*armed head*' which Macbeth addresses as 'thou unknown power', and to whose warning 'Beware Macduff, / Beware the Thane of Fife' he replies: 'Thou hast harped my fear aright' (4.1.68, 70–1, 73). From the second apparition, in the shape of '*a bloody child*', and the third apparition, '*a child crowned, with a tree in his hand*', Macbeth hears again what he wants to hear: that the fears he harbours are groundless, because 'none of woman born shall harm Macbeth' and 'Macbeth shall never vanquished be, until / Great Birnam Wood to high Dunsinane Hill / Shall come against him' (4.1.79–80, 91–3). His desperate need to be assured of his invulnerability blinds him to the riddling duplicity of these oracular pronouncements, which he misconstrues as 'Sweet bodements' (4.1.95). That they are expressly designed to dupe Macbeth and render him more vulnerable by lulling him into a false sense of security is proof positive of the malicious intent that lies behind them. That they succeed in their objective is a further measure of the witches' demonstrable capacity to influence his thinking and actions at critical junctures.

But such influence as the weird sisters have over Macbeth is drawn from them at those junctures by *his* actions, not wielded by them at their occult whim at times of their choosing. Their first appointment with him on the heath is consequent upon his fearsome prowess 'in his kingdom's great defence' (1.3.100), not determined by the arcane aims of the unearthly entities they serve. It's Macbeth who goes looking for them in Act 4, not they who seek him out; Macbeth who demands to hear from their masters what the future holds for him; Macbeth whose enforced silence as the apparitions speak ensures that *he* makes the sense that suits *him* of their specious assurances; Macbeth who insists, against the witches' express advice, on being shown, and dismayed by, the spectral dynasty of kings fated to descend from 'the blood-boltered Banquo' (4.1.122); and Macbeth who resolves, as a result of this final encounter with the witches, to act on the fear of Macduff the first apparition harped aright and 'give to th' edge o'th' sword / His wife, his babes and all unfortunate souls / That trace him in his line' (4.2.150–2).

The 'instruments of darkness' may be supernatural in origin and the motives for their malevolence mysterious, but as far as the tragedy is concerned it's the thoughts and deeds of Macbeth that summon them into being and dictate what they say to him. Their agenda is set by Macbeth, not his by them. Like the spirits Lady Macbeth summons to unsex her, they only '*tend on* mortal thoughts' (1.5.41; my emphasis): they serve or minister to the thoughts in human minds, they don't create them or plant them there; like the 'murdering ministers' she invokes in their 'sightless substances', they '*wait on* nature's mischief' (1.5.50; my emphasis) in a strictly ancillary capacity. In other words, the witches, their mistress Hecate and their unknown masters derive their point entirely from the role they play in the human drama of Macbeth, in whose terms alone they make sense. Their metaphysical provenance is immaterial when it comes to understanding the causes of the tragedy, which are in place long before the witches, those 'obscene pandars to iniquity' as Hazlitt dubs them, materialize in the opening scene. Neither the 'charm' that's 'wound up' by the dancing witches' incantation before they first greet Macbeth, nor the 'charm of powerful trouble' (4.1.18) they concoct from the gruesome ingredients of their cauldron before their last meeting with him can be held responsible for what befalls Macbeth, whatever the witches and Hecate might think. If that were indeed the case, and Macbeth was just the unfortunate victim of their gratuitous malice, there would be nothing tragic in the Shakespearean sense about his fate at all.

The redundancy of the charms as causes of the catastrophe doesn't detract, however, from their poetic power as testaments to the spellbound state in which Macbeth finds himself for reasons that owe nothing to witchcraft. The fact that the denizens of the play's supernatural domain shouldn't be *reduced* to symbols of the protagonist's subjective state doesn't mean that they don't function symbolically as well. By the same token, the fact that the ghost of old Hamlet has an objective, discarnate existence independent of young Hamlet's perception doesn't preclude his enshrining the tradition of the dead generations, which weighs like a nightmare on the mind of his living son. *Macbeth* would be theatrically and poetically impoverished without the witches and the apparitions their black arts conjure up. The *tragedy* is perfectly explicable in purely terrestrial terms and could have commenced, proceeded and concluded in much the same fashion without the intrusion of any otherworldly agency. No transcendental realm or paranormal phenomena are required to explain what Macbeth and his wife desire, why they desire it, and what happens to them as a result. But the 'imperfect speakers' on the heath and the equivocating apparitions they call up are indispensable as dramatic means of giving a form and a voice to the pressures that drive Macbeth to murder and self-destruction in spite of himself. They personify, and thus make visible and audible to the audience, psychological and emotional forces at work within Macbeth that would otherwise remain intangible abstractions. At the same time, their objective existence in the world outside Macbeth locates the source of those internalized forces in that exterior world. Through their riddling rhymes, their vatic doublespeak and the line of future monarchs brought forth at his bidding to torment him, they feed and mock the fantasies of supremacy and dread of emasculation bred in 'Bellona's bridegroom' (1.2.55) by the cut-throat warrior culture that created him.

The 'secret correspondence between him and the Weird Sisters' that Hazlitt observes is the result of their being privy to Macbeth's innermost thoughts and obliged to dance attendance on them in his terms. 'They come to him', Harold Bloom remarks, 'because preternaturally they *know* him: he is not so much theirs as they are his. This is not to deny their reality apart from him, but only to indicate again that he has more implicit power over them than they manifest in regard to him.' Nor is it to deny that, as 'spirits that know / All mortal consequences' (5.3.4–5), they have vital knowledge of facts and eventualities (Macduff's Caesarean birth, Malcolm's camouflage ruse at Birnam Wood) cruelly withheld from Macbeth until it's too late. In their figurative capacity they serve as theatrical projections of Macbeth's state of mind when he encounters them, which includes his ignorance of what will actually come to pass and consequent misreading of his predicament. In Olivier's aborted film version of the tragedy the Macbeths, according to the screenplay and shooting script, would have doubled as the first and second witches, and a dissolving shot would have suggested that the weird sisters existed entirely inside his head. Such visually arresting images would certainly have captured the sense in which the witches serve as manifestations of Macbeth's mental state; but they would have done so at the risk of reducing them to purely psychological phenomena without foundations in Macbeth's milieu as well. If Shakespeare had wanted them to be understood, like the ghost of Banquo or like Macbeth's 'dagger of the mind', as 'a false creation, / Proceeding from the heat-oppressed brain' (2.1.38–9) visible only to Macbeth, he could have made sure they were. But by insisting on their uncanny otherness he stresses instead the alien, inhuman nature of the mindset that takes possession of Macbeth and makes him turn himself into a monster against his will.

The Language of Complicity

The sense we get that 'these juggling fiends' (5.8.19) designate motives and constraints that dwell within Macbeth because they derive from the world in which he dwells is subtly reinforced by the contagious aspect of their distinctive idiom. When the cryptic, penultimate line of the witches' first scene, 'Fair is foul, and foul is fair' (1.1.9), is echoed in Macbeth's first line, 'So foul and fair a day I have not seen' (1.3.38), the echo binds them surreptitiously together in obscure complicity, blurring without dissolving the distinction between them. The same suggestion of unconscious collusion in a joint enterprise is created later when Macbeth doesn't just reply to the Third Apparition in the same rhymed pentameters all three spectres use, but completes its short final line with his first couplet, weaving his speech seamlessly into theirs:

3 APPARITION
    Macbeth shall never vanquished be, until
    Great Birnam Wood to High Dunsinane Hill
    Shall come against him.
MACBETH   That will never be.
    Who can impress the forest, bid the tree
    Unfix his earth-bound root? Sweet bodements, good.
    Rebellious dead, rise never till the Wood
    Of Birnam rise, and our high-placed Macbeth
    Shall live the lease of nature, pay his breath
    To time, and mortal custom.

(4.1.91–9)

Having Macbeth continue in the same vein to the same tune as the apparitions and sound exactly like them confirms the profound rapport between them, the depth at which they answer to his needs by mirroring his mentality and meeting his demands of them. Yet their sly prevarications also betray a veiled hostility to Macbeth that sets them and their summoners apart from him, underscoring the extrinsic provenance of the cast of mind within him that they personify.

It's not only Macbeth whose speech betrays this discursive contamination by what the weird sisters symbolize. His language is laced throughout with repetitive phrasing, alliterative locutions, incantatory rhythms and ambiguous diction that recall the witches' stylistic tics. But characters other than Macbeth are woven into the same web of complicity with them by the way they speak. This is most obviously true of Macbeth's 'dearest partner of greatness' (1.5.11), starting with the triple invocation in her second soliloquy ('Come you spirits / That tend on mortal thoughts ... Come to my woman's breasts, / And take my milk for gall ... Come thick night ... '), which makes her sound as if she were indeed the fourth witch she's sometimes been dubbed. It's the same note of solemn conjuration her husband will strike when he assures her that 'A deed of dreadful note' will be done

>   ... ere the bat hath flown
> His cloistered flight, ere to black Hecate's summons
> The shard-born beetle, with his drowsy hums,
> Hath rung night's yawning peal ...
>   ... Come, seeling night
> Scarf up the tender eye of pitiful day
> And with thy bloody and invisible hand
> Cancel and tear to pieces that great bond
> Which keeps me pale.

>   (3.2.41–5, 47–51)

Macbeth's evasive reference in that quotation to 'A deed of dreadful note' is symptomatic of the obsession with the words 'deed', 'do', 'done' and 'undone' that Lady Macbeth shares with him, and that links both of them to the witches. 'And like a rat without a tail, / I'll do, I'll do, and I'll do' chants the first witch in the play's third scene, her staccato drumming on the verb opening it to more connotations than the bawdy one the context suggests. Two scenes later the word surfaces again, employed twice with one of its cognates by Lady Macbeth, who likewise leaves its precise meaning undefined:

>   Thou'dst have, Great Glamis,
> That which cries, 'Thus thou must do', if thou have it;
> And that which rather thou dost fear to do,
> Than wishest should be undone.

>   (1.5.22–5)

Two scenes after that Macbeth harps compulsively on the past participle of the same verb in the same periphrastic style, as he begins to muster all the arguments against doing the deed: 'If it were done, when 'tis done, then 'twere well / It were done quickly' (1.7.1–2). That sentence has the ring of a riddle too, and one that could have been cackled by any of the witches.

'What is't you do?' Macbeth demands of the 'secret, black and midnight hags', when he beards them in their lair. 'A deed without a name' (4.1.1–2) is their inscrutable reply. It echoes the recurrent, euphemistic resort of both Macbeths to the word 'deed', which crops up more frequently in *Macbeth* than in any other play by Shakespeare, apart from the much longer *Richard III*. Its frequency is most marked in the wake of Duncan's murder, for which it supplies the bloodless term his murderers cling to. 'The attempt, and not the deed / Confounds us', says the anxious Lady Macbeth to herself, a heartbeat before Macbeth returns from the king's chamber to assure her, 'I have done the deed' (2.2.11–1, 15). 'A little water clears us of this deed', she tells him, in a vain attempt to dispel the horror of the deed that's gripped him and left him feeling torn in two: 'To know my deed, 'twere best not know myself' (2.2.68, 74). Nor is the use of the euphemism confined, as one might expect, to the Macbeths. ''Tis unnatural, / Even like the deed that's done' (2.4.10–11), remarks the nameless Old Man of the fearful prodigies witnessed on the night of Duncan's murder. Asked by Ross whether the identity of the murderer is known, Macduff informs him that 'Suspicion of the deed' (2.4.27) has fallen on 'the King's two sons' (2.4.25), Malcolm and Donalbain. And in the play's last instance of the noun repeatedly enlisted to sanitize the act it denotes, the Doctor comments: 'Unnatural deeds / Do breed unnatural troubles' (5.1.71–2). It's as if all three characters are infected by the urge to employ the same anaemic word the Macbeths employ to absolve themselves in speech of the crime they can't disclaim.

Nor are they the only other characters to be heard speaking unawares in ways that audibly ally them with the witches and Macbeth, implicating them by association in the latter's iniquity. Duncan himself is caught in the same subtextual net as his killer. At the end of the second scene he orders the execution of the treacherous Thane of Cawdor, instructing Ross to 'Go pronounce his present death, / And with his former title greet Macbeth'. 'I'll see it done', replies Ross, giving the king his cue to complete a second couplet with the line that closes the scene: 'What he hath lost, noble Macbeth hath won' (1.2.68). Both the line and the rhyme echo the couplet of the second witch at the start of the play, announcing the time of the meeting with Macbeth: 'When the hurly-burly's done, / When the battle's lost, and won' (1.1.3–4). Banquo falls prey to a strain of the same verbal virus too. The witches' 'Fair is foul, and foul is fair' (1.1.9) reverberates not only in Macbeth's 'So foul and fair a day I have not seen', but also in Banquo's question, 'Good sir, why do you start, and seem to fear / Things that do sound so fair?' The homophonic pun on 'fear' and 'fair' produced by Elizabethan pronunciation embroils Banquo inescapably in the dark art of equivocation. It places him, at this pregnant moment in the play, on the same linguistic wavelength as the weird sisters and Macbeth, in thrall – to borrow Banquo's own phrase – 'To th' self-same tune and words' (1.3.89).

The reverberations run the other way, too, in the discourse of doubling and replication that riddles the tragedy. The most memorable example is the witches' chanting of 'Double, double, toil and trouble' as they 'Round about the cauldron go' (4.1.4, 10, 20, 35). The belated discovery that 'Macduff was from his mother's womb / Untimely ripped', and thus not 'of woman born' in the usual fashion, causes Macbeth to say, as he squares up to Macduff at the end of the play: 'And be these juggling fiends no more believed / That palter with us in a double sense' (5.8.15–16, 19–20). But Lady Macbeth fastens on the doubling trope long before the witches and her husband, when she matches Duncan's tortuous complimentary speech, concluding 'And thank us for your trouble', with an equally elaborate accolade beginning 'All our service, / In every point twice done, and then done double, / Were poor and single business' (1.6.14–16). In doing so, she not only forges with the king a couplet that pre-echoes the witches' coupling of 'double' with 'trouble', but she also furnishes through her repetition of 'done' a subliminal cue for Macbeth's 'If it were done, when 'tis done, then 'twere well / It were done quickly', which follows sixteen lines later. The credit for the tragedy's very first use of the trope, however, must go to the anonymous Captain, who reports in the second scene that Macbeth and Banquo fought in the king's defence 'As cannons over-charged with double cracks, / So they doubly redoubled strokes upon the foe' (1.2.37–8). How apt, too, that the seminal appearance of a trope so inextricably tied to the witches should be spawned by a paean to the orgy of male violence in which Macbeth and Banquo revelled, as if 'they meant to bathe in reeking wounds, / Or memorize another Golgotha' (1.2.39–40).

Vaster Powers Without: Mirroring Macbeth

The ubiquity of these linguistic linkages and overlaps between major and minor *dramatis personae* hasn't pass unnoticed in critical commentaries on *Macbeth*. But their implications for our understanding of the play *as a tragedy* have not been appreciated. The cumulative effect of hearing, onstage or in the mind's ear, distinctive speech habits of the witches and Macbeth at home in the mouths of other characters is to involve them all in the attitude articulated in the idiom they share. When Macbeth speaks like the witches or the apparitions, he's not adopting an idiom exclusive to him and them, but one that's embedded in the wider ethos of the society he belongs to, as its employment by other characters attests. Macbeth's character, and consequently his fate, can no more be divorced from that ethos than his speech can be divorced from his native tongue. Habits of speech he unconsciously shares with other characters are the expression of habits of mind that they unconsciously share with him, and that betray their unconscious complicity in the tragedy that overtakes him.

His whole culture, in short, collaborates with Macbeth to bring about his destruction. It shares his culpability for what transpires, because it cultivates men who feel, think and act like him. To place the responsibility for the tragedy solely on Macbeth would be to treat him as a self-created individual possessed of absolute free will and full knowledge of the consequences of his decisions and deeds. It would be turn him into the protagonist of the kind of morality play whose medieval fetters Shakespeare had thrown off, as his burlesquing of the genre in the Porter scene confirms. As a critic prone to regard Shakespeare's tragic protagonists as essentially autonomous beings, hobbled like Hamlet by 'some vicious mole in nature', Bradley ought to be satisfied with proving, notwithstanding the witches' influence, 'how entirely the responsibility for his deeds still lies with Macbeth'. But Bradley is too astute a critic not to see that this won't suffice, and that a more complex formulation is required to do justice to the genesis of Macbeth's crimes:

The witches and their prophecies, if they are to be rationalised or taken symbolically, must represent not only the evil slumbering in the hero's soul, but all those obscurer influences of the evil around him in the world which aid his own ambition and the incitements of his wife. ... the inward powers of the soul answer in their essence to vaster powers without, which support them and assure the effect of their exertion. So it is in *Macbeth*. The words of the Witches are fatal to the hero only because there is in him something which leaps into light at the sound of them; but they are at the same time the witness of forces which never cease to work in the world around him, and, on the instant of his surrender to them, entangle him inextricably in the web of Fate.

Stripped of its nebulous, metaphysical diction ('the evil slumbering in the hero's soul', 'vaster powers without', 'something which leaps into light'), Bradley's formulation is fundamentally right, insofar as it recognizes the inextricability of Macbeth's 'ambition' and 'inward powers' from 'forces which never cease to work in the world'.

Bradley is unable to provide a clearer rationale for the tragedy than that. But he does at least put it in a way that points towards a more satisfactory explanation, as firmly grounded in the evidence of the text as Bradley would wish. 'The witches and their prophecies, if they are to be rationalized or taken symbolically' are best understood as embodying the external and internalized pressures that trap the appalled Macbeth in his harrowing ordeal. They demonstrate theatrically that Macbeth fashions his own fate, but that he does so under conditions and for motives that are not of his creation, and over whose ramifications he has no control. There's nothing nebulous for Shakespeare, however, about those conditions and motives, which he's not content to depict as obscure forces of evil at work within and around his protagonist, but is at pains to define much more precisely. Rather than absolve Macbeth of moral responsibility for his crimes, the aim of the play is to make us aware of the guilt the society that moulded Macbeth and fostered those crimes shares with him. In the process, we are also made conscious of factors determining Macbeth's fate of which he remains unconscious, but which are thereby brought to our attention and thus within the compass of volition for us.

The matrix of Macbeth's doom is thrown into relief by other textual and structural features of the tragedy too. The fixation on doubling in the diction of diverse characters finds parallels in the merging of identities and symmetrical events, which embed Macbeth's fate in the community that shaped it. Take the first account we have of Macbeth before he has come onstage. Fortune, the wounded Captain informs the King, had seemed to smile 'like a rebel's whore' on 'The merciless Macdonald' (1.2.9, 15) until Macbeth

Like Valour's minion, carved out his passage.
Till he faced the slave,
Which ne'er shook hands, nor bade farewell to him,
Till he unseamed him from the nave to th' chops,
And fixed his head upon our battlements.

(1.2.19–23)

Editors advise the reader to construe 'Which' as a relative pronoun meaning 'Who' and referring to Macbeth in order to make sense of this passage in the context of the speech. But that revision can't erase the primary meaning of the passage created by that dislocated pronoun and the three that follow it ('him … him … his'), which compound the confusion of Macbeth with a merciless traitor who winds up beheaded. The Captain's intended meaning is subverted by the anticipated fate of Macbeth that it secretes. The grammatical glitch betrays the ease with which the roles of Macbeth and Macdonald might be reversed, the thinness of the line that divides fealty from sedition in this ruthless feudal realm.

What Macbeth encounters in Macdonald is a version of his future self, and the same thing happens two dozen lines later in Ross's report of the victory of Duncan's army at Fife:

> Norway himself, with terrible numbers,
> Assisted by that most disloyal traitor,
> The Thane of Cawdor, began a dismal conflict,
> Till that Bellona's bridegroom, lapped in proof,
> Confronted him with self-comparisons,
> Point against point, rebellious arm 'gainst arm,
> Curbing his lavish spirit …

(1.2.52–8)

It's reasonable to assume, as most editors do, that 'Bellona's bridegroom' must be Macbeth, given that the point of this scene is to extol his heroism on the field of battle and explain the King's rewarding of him with the title of Thane of Cawdor, which he does in response to Ross's report. On that assumption, Macbeth is again being described as meeting his future mirror-image, this time in the shape of 'that most disloyal traitor, / The Thane of Cawdor', whose treacherous role he will likewise assume together with his title. The specular phrasing of 'Confronted him with self-comparisons, / Point against point, rebellious arm 'gainst arm' leaves little doubt about that. At the same time, the syntax of the whole sentence dictates that the 'him' Bellona's bridegroom confronted must refer to the subject of the main clause, 'Norway himself', rather than Cawdor. It thereby confuses Norway with Cawdor, to whom the pronoun may be taken to refer only by virtue of its proximity to his name. The use of the generic term 'Bellona's bridegroom' – the spouse of the goddess of war – only adds to the confusion, since it contains no intrinsic clue to the bridegroom's identity, which the reader or auditor is obliged to surmise.

To the objection that this is to read too much into ambiguities that are simply the result of grammatical or stylistic gaffes on Shakespeare's part, one can only reply with James Joyce that 'A man of genius makes no mistakes; his errors are volitional and are the portals of discovery'. The twinning and fusion of identities produced by both these passages is consistent with the fact that Macbeth's world is rife with prototypes and doubles of Macbeth. Even before he meets the witches, the precedents for his impending transmutation are in place in the guise of Macdonald, Cawdor and Norway. The propensity to turn traitor, to wrench power by brute force from the reigning king, lurks in them all, as it's bound to do in the inherently violent, hierarchical society they inhabit. The identification of Macbeth as a latent traitor denotes the pressure exerted on a man of his rank to act as Macbeth inexorably does. Not every man of Macbeth's rank, needless to say, feels that pressure to the same degree, let alone succumbs to it. But the capacity to have been or to become another Macbeth, like the capacity to collude with or countenance another Macbeth, is endemic to the bellicose nobility of Shakespeare's ancient Scotland, which is predisposed to breed Macbeths. The basic template for Macbeth's tragedy was built into his world before the action begins, and will go on producing such tragedies, the play implies, after its action ends. That implication is made vividly explicit in the closing scene of Polanski's film adaptation of *Macbeth*, where we see Donalbain, Duncan's younger son and the brother of Malcolm, going to meet the witches, just like Macbeth before him.

Polanski's invented epilogue finds support, it might be argued, in the historical fact that Donalbain murdered Malcolm's eldest son and seized the throne after Malcolm's death. What Shakespeare learned from Holinshed about Donalbain's eventual fate had no apparent influence on the creation of *Macbeth*, in which Donalbain plays but a fleeting part. (Unless one's inclined to detect a sinister insinuation in Lennox's answer to Caithness's question, 'Who knows if Donalbain be with his brother?': 'For certain, sir, he is not' (5.2.7–8).) But the same can't be said of what Shakespeare learned from Holinshed about Banquo, but chose to omit. Holinshed records that Macbeth was helped in the assassination of Duncan by a band of 'trustie friends, amongst whom Banquho [*sic*] was the chiefest'. Given that Banquo was supposed, according to legend, to be the ancestor of King James, Shakespeare prudently ignored his complicity in regicide and portrayed him instead as Macbeth's noble victim and the founder of an enduring dynasty to flatter the King's Men's patron. But something of Holinshed's Banquo plainly crept into Shakespeare's characterization of him, as a closer examination of his speech and conduct makes clear.

Notwithstanding the differences between his and Macbeth's initial response to the witches, Banquo soon reveals enough evidence of their affinity to impugn his depiction as a bastion of integrity. There's already a hint of unprompted collusion in that confidential exchange between Banquo and Macbeth, just after the truth of the witches' first prediction has been confirmed. 'Do you not hope your children shall be kings', Macbeth asks Banquo aside, 'When those that gave the Thane of Cawdor to me / Promised no less to them?' (1.3.120–3); to which Banquo replies, likewise aside:

> That, trusted home,
> Might yet enkindle you unto the crown,
> Besides the Thane of Cawdor. But 'tis strange:
> And oftentimes, to win us to our harm,
> The instruments of darkness tell us truths,
> Win us with honest trifles, to betray's
> In deepest consequence.

(1.3.122–8)

Macbeth's question invites Banquo's engagement in the line of thought he assumes they must both be following, given what they now know. Banquo resists the invitation, imputing to Macbeth alone the danger of acting to make the witches' prophecy come true and counselling him to mistrust them. But the fact that Banquo jumps automatically to the idea of taking such action as the tempting next step, and that he couches his counsel in terms applicable not to Macbeth but to both of them ('us'), suggests that they're more like-minded than he's aware or willing to admit. That such is the case Wilson Knight has no doubt: 'This knowledge of evil implicit in his meeting with the three Weird Sisters Banquo keeps to himself, and it is a bond of evil between him and Macbeth.'

The opening of Act 2 finds a deeply troubled Banquo on his way to bed in Macbeth's castle on the pitch-black night of Duncan's murder, accompanied by Fleance. 'There's husbandry in heaven,' he remarks to his son, 'Their candles are all out'; and then, but more to himself, he says:

> A heavy summons lies like lead upon me,
> And yet I would not sleep. Merciful powers,
> Restrain in me the cursed thoughts that nature
> Gives way to in repose.

These lines could have been written for Macbeth himself and spoken by him verbatim prior to the murder. Though the exact nature of the 'cursed thoughts' Banquo is struggling to restrain is unclear, they bespeak the anguish of a guilty mind as tormented as that of Macbeth, who looms at this moment out of the dark to put their unspoken bond beyond doubt. The first words to Macbeth out of Banquo's mouth, as soon as Fleance leaves them together, are: 'I dreamt last night of the three weird sisters: / To you they have shown some truth' (2.1.20–1). He readily agrees to exchange 'some words upon that business' (2.1.23) later with Macbeth, and even accede to whatever the latter deems advisable then, provided that in doing so he can, as he puts it, 'still keep / My bosom franchised and allegiance clear' (2.1.27–8). That proviso serves for a moment to bolster Banquo's resistance to the threat his secret bond with Macbeth poses, but his need to voice it also shows the strength of the thoughts he's having to resist.

Immediately after the discovery of Duncan's murder, Banquo's public response is to proclaim his commitment to finding out who is responsible for 'this most bloody piece of work':

> Fears and scruples shake us.
> In the great hand of God I stand, and thence
> Against the undivulged pretence I fight
> Of treasonous malice.

> (2.3.130–3)

But when we next hear him, after Macbeth's coronation but just a few minutes later in stage time, we learn from his soliloquy what he privately suspects and has resolved to do as a consequence, which is to keep his mouth shut in his own interest:

Thou hast it now, King, Cawdor, Glamis, all,
As the weird women promised, and I fear
Thou played'st most foully for't. Yet it was said
It should not stand in thy posterity,
But that myself should be the root and father
Of many kings. If there comes truth from them,
As upon thee, Macbeth, their speeches shine,
Why, by the verities on thee made good,
May they not be my oracles as well
And set me up in hope? But hush, no more.

(3.1.1–10)

'He is enmeshed in Macbeth's horror', comments Knight, 'and, after the coronation, keeps the guilty secret, and lays to his heart a guilty hope. Banquo is thus involved.' His silence makes him an accomplice after the fact in Duncan's assassination, and the echo of the witches and Macbeth in that homophonic pun again on 'fear/fair' coupled with 'foully' sets a seal on his complicity. Banquo gives no grounds in this speech for inferring that the idea of playing foully himself to ensure he becomes the 'father / Of many kings' has struck him. But Macbeth is manifestly worried that it might:

Our fears in Banquo stick deep,
And in his royalty of nature reigns that
Which would be feared. 'Tis much he dares,
And to that dauntless temper of his mind,
He hath a wisdom that doth guide his valour
To act in safety. There is none but he,
Whose being I do fear …

(3.1.48–54)

Whether Macbeth's fear of Banquo's expediting the witches' prophecy himself, as distinct from his fear of its coming to pass by some other means, is justified remains moot, but that's not the point here. The point is that Banquo is shown to have the makings of a Macbeth and, given time and opportunity, might have become one.

The same holds true, *mutatis mutandis*, of Macduff, who winds up at the end of the play the counterpart of Macbeth at the start, killing the treacherous Macbeth in loyal defence of the rightful king, Malcolm, just as Macbeth killed the traitor Macdonald in loyal defence of King Duncan. In fact, in slaying Macbeth, Macduff also becomes a regicide just like Macbeth, who is his legally enthroned sovereign when Macduff slays him in Malcolm's name and in revenge. A moral distinction must be drawn, of course, between the two men, but it's by no means a clear-cut distinction, as the structural symmetry between the parts they play implies. No one could accuse Macduff of harbouring the 'cursed thoughts' that afflict Banquo or of premeditated treachery like Macbeth's. But he stands accused nonetheless of being yet another traitor in the tragedy for abandoning his wife and his children. Shakespeare invents the scene in which Lady Macduff and her son are murdered expressly in order to put Macduff in the dock on this count, departing from his source to do so.

The scene opens with Macduff's wife complaining to Ross of her husband's flight from Scotland and desertion of her to join Malcolm in England. 'His flight was madness', she says. 'When our actions do not, / Our fears do make us traitors'. By fleeing so suddenly for what must be fear of remaining, he has made himself look guilty of treachery even if he isn't. 'You know not / Whether it was his wisdom or his fear' (4.2.3–5), replies Ross, attempting to defend Macduff's action. But Lady Macduff is adamant that her husband stands convicted of the heartless, cowardly betrayal of his family, to whom his primary allegiance as husband and father is due:

Wisdom? To leave his wife, to leave his babes
His mansion and his titles in a place
From whence himself does fly? He loves us not;
He wants the natural touch. For the poor wren,
The most diminutive of birds, will fight,
Her young ones in the nest, against the owl.
All is the fear and nothing is the love ...

(4.2.6–12)

Ross asks her to trust that her husband must have had a sound reason for acting as he has. However, he can't forebear adding: 'But cruel are the times when we are traitors / And do not know ourselves' (4.2.18–19). It's a striking remark, conceding as it does that the times are such as to turn everyone, including Ross himself and Macduff, into traitors of one kind or another, and thus traitors to themselves, who no longer know who they are. It tars them, in effect, with the same brush of treachery as Macbeth.

Shakespeare doesn't let Macduff off the hook after Ross exits either. 'Was my father a traitor, mother?', asks his son. 'Ay, that he was', replies Lady Macduff. 'What is a traitor?', asks her son. 'Why, one that swears and lies', answers his mother. 'And be all traitors, that do so?', asks her son. 'Every one that does so', replies his mother, 'is a traitor and must be hanged' (4.2.31, 46–52). A few moments later, Macduff's son is murdered onstage by Macbeth's henchmen, from whom his wife flees in vain. When Macduff is told of their deaths, he berates himself for being the cause:

Sinful Macduff,
They were all struck for thee. Naught that I am,
Not for their own demerits, but for mine,
Fell slaughter on their souls.

(4.3.227–30)

He is right to do so, insofar as by his actions he unknowingly made himself complicit with Macbeth in the butchering of his family. Shakespeare has gone to considerable lengths, without the slightest warrant in Holinshed, to call Macduff's character into question too and implicate him in the inhumanity that pervades the world of the play. He even enlists Malcolm to rack Macduff's conscience by demanding, albeit before they discover his family's fate: 'Why in that rawness left you wife and child – / Those precious motives, those strong knots of love – / Without leave-taking?' (4.3.33). The question is apparently posed by Malcolm, it transpires, as part of a convoluted ploy to test Macduff's integrity, to confirm that he's not the traitor he might covertly be. But the ironic upshot of Malcolm's ploy is that, in the process of proving Macduff a man he can trust, he reveals his own capacity to become as despicable a despot as the one he's seeking Macduff's help to defeat.

The protracted exchange between them, which begins the longest scene in the play, is regularly cut or abbreviated in performance for want of an appreciation of why it's there. Once it's seen in the context of the care Shakespeare's taken to show how much the tragic protagonist and his antagonists have in common, the point of having us envision the monster Malcolm pretends he'll be once enthroned becomes clearer. Until Malcolm reveals to Macduff's bewildered relief that he has only been pretending, audiences unfamiliar with the play have no more reason to disbelieve him than Macduff does. The tale he tells of his future self is all too familiar and plausible, finding a ready precedent in Macbeth's metamorphosis from national hero into tyrant. 'This tyrant, whose sole name blisters our tongues, / Was once thought honest', Malcolm reminds Macduff; 'I am young,' he says, 'but something / You may discern of him through me' (4.3.12–15). He invites Macduff to behold in him a budding Macbeth, who is a perfect example of how 'A good and virtuous nature may recoil / In an imperial charge' (4.3.19–20). In fact, he promises to surpass Macbeth in every conceivable form of abject depravity once he succeeds to the throne:

It is myself I mean, in whom I know
All the particulars of vice so grafted
That, when they shall be opened, black Macbeth
Will seem as pure as snow, and the poor state
Esteem him as a lamb, being compared
With my confineless harms.

(4.3.50–5)

Malcolm proceeds to describe in turn, and at length, just how insatiably lecherous and avaricious he is bent on being. Macduff's considered response to Malcolm's confession is worth pausing over. He is dismayed by the revelation but finds it entirely credible that Malcolm would exploit his sovereignty to indulge his 'Boundless intemperance' and 'stanchless avarice' (4.3.66, 78) like many a monarch before him. For, as he says, the former 'hath been / Th'untimely emptying of the happy throne, and fall of many kings' and the latter likewise 'hath been / The sword of our slain kings' (4.3.67–9, 86–7). It's a mark of Macduff, however, and a measure of what such a monarchy entails, that he's cynically prepared to tolerate his future king's degenerate indulgence of both these vices, provided they're offset by 'other graces' (4.3.90).

'But I have none', declares Malcolm, and he goes on to list all the 'king-becoming graces' as things of which he has 'no relish' (4.3.91, 95) before bringing his damning self-portrait to an apocalyptic close that smacks of Macbeth at his most defiant:

> Nay, had I power, I should
> Pour the sweet milk of concord into hell,
> Uproar the universal peace, confound
> All unity on earth.
>
> (4.3.97–100)

At that point even Macduff's readiness to acquiesce in despotism reaches its limit. Denouncing Malcolm as not just unfit to govern but unfit to live, he bids him farewell: 'These evils thou repeat'st upon thyself / Hath banished me from Scotland' (4.3.112–13). Whereupon Malcolm reveals that his vilification of himself has only been a ruse designed to verify the probity of Macduff, who need not fear for Scotland under Malcolm's rule:

> For even now
> I put myself to thy direction and
> Unspeak mine own detraction. Here abjure
> The taints and blames I laid upon myself,
> For strangers to my nature.
>
> (4.3.121–5)

The volte-face is so abrupt and absolute that it leaves Macduff dumbfounded: 'Such welcome and unwelcome things at once / 'Tis hard to reconcile' (4.3.138–9) is all he can muster in response. And no wonder, since Malcolm's unspeaking of his own detraction can't dispel the dark shadow cast over his character by the tyrannical Malcolm he's evoked with such ease. The latter may be displaced by the virtuous, virginal Malcolm for the purposes of the plot, but his counterfactual reality as a credible prospect has been too firmly established to be erased.

So Much More the Man

This tacit kinship with Macbeth of characters whose virtue is meant to throw his vice into starker relief is symptomatic of the fact 'that there is something rotten in Scotland – that something intrinsic to the structure of Scottish society, something deeper than the melodramatic wickedness of one or two individuals, generates these tendencies toward instability, conflict, sedition, and murder'. That is the conclusion at which Harry Berger arrives in his fine essay on 'The Early Scenes of *Macbeth*'. It's a conclusion which both resonates with and points beyond Bradley's perception of the way in this play 'Shakespeare has concentrated attention on the obscurer regions of man's being, on phenomena which make it seem that he is in the power of secret forces lurking below, and independent of his consciousness and will'. Shakespeare does focus our attention in *Macbeth*, as Bradley says, on 'hidden forces operating on minds unconscious of their influence'. But he also makes it plain that there's nothing mysterious, let alone metaphysical, about the nature of these forces, which are 'something intrinsic to the structure of Scottish society', not something lurking in 'the obscurer regions of man's being' and thus unfathomable. As we've seen in previous chapters, Shakespeare understood in his own terms the pernicious power of ideology, and in *Macbeth* he devised dramatic and poetic ways of showing how a savage, self-destructive mindset can take control of a man's consciousness and will, and lead him as if hypnotized, to his own baffled horror, down the road to perdition.

At the core of the mindset to which Macbeth is in thrall is a potent but toxic idea of masculinity, of what it means to be a man. So contagious is this idea in the world of the play that Lady Macbeth, far from being immune to it as a woman, craves to embody it herself:

> Come you spirits
> That tend on mortal thoughts, unsex me here,
> And fill me from the crown to the toe, top-full
> Of direst cruelty. Make thick my blood,
> Stop up th'access and passage to remorse,
> That no compunctious visitings of nature
> Shake my fell purpose, nor keep peace between
> The effect and it. Come to my woman's breasts,
> And take my milk for gall, you murdering ministers,
> Wherever, in your sightless substances,
> You wait on nature's mischief. Come thick night,
> And pall thee in the dunnest smoke of hell,
> That my keen knife see not the wound it makes,
> Nor heaven peep through the blanket of the dark
> To cry, 'Hold, hold'.

(1.5.40–54)

To be equal to the lethal man's work required of her, if she and Macbeth are to gain the 'sovereign sway and masterdom' (1.5.70) they covet, she must be void of the tender, nurturing qualities conventionally regarded as feminine. She must be unsexed to be capable of the 'direst cruelty' their ambition demands and to suppress the 'compunctious visitings of nature' that threaten its fulfilment. But even as she invokes this masculine ideal of ruthless determination to harden her 'fell purpose', Lady Macbeth can't help conceding that its adoption comes at a cost: the cost of everything within her that makes her feel remorse. The strength of her innate aversion to the atrocity she envisages committing is betrayed by her shifting responsibility for the wound from herself to her 'keen knife' and by her plea for darkness to shield her eyes and heaven's from her stabbing of Duncan.

The merciless violence that Macbeth displayed, when he unseamed Macdonald from the nave to the chops in battle, doesn't come naturally to his wife, who has to force herself into the frame of mind the killing of their king demands. But it doesn't come naturally to Macbeth either, when it's expected of him in his own home solely to satisfy his ambition, and when the intended victim is not the enemy of Duncan but Duncan himself. Of that his wife is acutely aware from the outset, as the worry that springs at once to her mind on reading his letter makes clear:

> Yet do I fear thy nature,
> It is too full o'th' milk of human kindness
> To catch the nearest way. Thou wouldst be great,
> Art not without ambition, but without
> The illness should attend it.
>
> (1.5.16–20)

That much one might have surmised from Macbeth's disclosure in his first soliloquy that imagining Duncan's murder is enough to make his hair stand on end and his heart pound in his chest 'Against the use of nature' (1.3.137–9). It's borne out, too, by the fervent wish he voiced aside after hearing Duncan make Malcolm the heir apparent of Scotland:

> Stars, hide your fires,
> Let not light see my black and deep desires.
> The eye wink at the hand; yet let that be
> Which the eye fears, when it is done, to see.
>
> (1.4.50–3)

It's the same fervent wish that Lady Macbeth is moved to voice in the following scene, when she summons darkness to conceal from her sight what she feels compelled both to do and to disown.

Strong though their initial resistance is to doing what their eyes fear to see when it is done, the drive to do it proves stronger. The prize is to be crowned with 'the golden round' at Scone. But the thing that's really at stake for Macbeth, the thing that clinches his commitment to go through with the murder, is made clear in the electrifying argument between him and his wife in the final scene of Act 1. 'We will proceed no further in this business' (1.7.31) Macbeth tells her, having reviewed and weighed at length in soliloquy all the reasons for not slaughtering Duncan as he sleeps. But the unsexed Lady Macbeth knows exactly what she must do to change her husband's mind, because she knows what matters to him more than all the scruples he can muster:

> LADY MACBETH   Was the hope drunk
> Wherein you dressed yourself? Hath it slept since?
> And wakes it now to look so green and pale,

At what it did so freely? From this time
Such I account thy love. Art thou afeard
To be the same in thine own act and valour,
As thou art in desire? Wouldst thou have that
Which thou esteem'st the ornament of life,
And live a coward in thine own esteem,
Letting 'I dare not' wait upon 'I would',
Like the poor cat i'th' adage?
MACBETH   Prithee, peace.
I dare do all that may become a man,
Who dares do more, is none.
LADY MACBETH   What beast was't then
That made you break this enterprise to me?
When you durst do it, then you were a man;
And to be more than what you were, you would
Be so much more the man.

(1.7.35–51)

This scathing assault on the courage at the heart of Macbeth's virility hits home and
he capitulates, applauding the exemplary masculinity of his wife's fearless stance in the
same terms as their argument: 'Bring forth men-children only; / For thy undaunted
mettle should compose / Nothing but males' (1.7.73–5).

The fact that what constitutes manliness is open to argument, and that a distinction
can be drawn between a restrained kind of manhood deemed becoming and a bolder
kind admired as far more manly, highlights the ideological nature of the masculine ideal
that shackles and dooms Macbeth. It's a cultural fiction of virility by which he becomes
fatally snared, not an innate proclivity with which he has the misfortune to be cursed.
The tenacity of its hold on Macbeth is shown again in Act 3, when he questions the
resolve of the murderers he's suborned to slay Banquo and Fleance. 'We are men, my
liege', the murderers assure him, to which Macbeth retorts:

Ay, in the catalogue ye go for men:
As hounds and greyhounds, mongrels, spaniels, curs,
Shoughs, water-rugs and demi-wolves are clept
All by the name of dogs. The valued file
Distinguishes the swift, the slow, the subtle,
The housekeeper, the hunter, every one
According to the gift which bounteous nature
Hath in him closed, whereby he does receive
Particular addition, from the bill
That writes them all alike: and so of men.
Now, if you have a station in the file

Not i'th' worst of manhood, say't,
And I will put that business in your bosoms
Whose execution takes your enemy off,
Grapples you to the heart and love of us,
Who wear our health but sickly in his life,
Which in his death were perfect.

(3.1.93–109)

Far from being a uniform, self-evident quality, manhood can be divided for Macbeth into ranks as distinct as those that comprise the social hierarchy whose summit he has murdered to reach. The kind of man who ranks highest for him, and the kind he commends to his fellow murderers here, is the kind who puts his own interest first and can kill without a qualm to advance or protect it.

So vital to Macbeth's image of himself is this virulent ideal that not even the horrifying sight of Banquo's ghost can break its iron grip on him. Shocked by her husband's public fit of terror at nothing she can see, Lady Macbeth takes the same tack as she did in Act 1 when his nerve failed him. 'Are you a man?', she asks him aside. 'Ay, and a bold one', replies Macbeth, 'that dare look on that / Which might appal the devil' (3.4.56–7). Unconvinced by that, she tears into him again, mocking him for making such an unmanly exhibition of himself:

O, proper stuff.
This is the very painting of your fear:
This is the air-drawn dagger which you said
Led you to Duncan. O, these flaws and starts,
Imposters to true fear, would well become
A woman's story at a winter's fire,
Authorised by her grandam. Shame itself.

(3.4.57–63)

Oblivious of the spectre Macbeth points to and proceeds to address, she keeps goading him in the same vein: 'What? Quite unmanned in folly? … Fie, for shame' (3.4.71–2). So when Macbeth eventually rallies and recovers enough to banish the ghost for good, he does so by reasserting his virility, beginning with a line that echoes his retort to his wife in their earlier dispute:

What man dare, I dare.
Approach thou like the rugged Russian bear,
The armed rhinoceros, or the Hyrcan tiger,
Take any shape but that, and my firm nerves
Shall never tremble. Or be alive again,
And dare me to the desert with thy sword;
If trembling I inhabit then, protest me

The baby of a girl. Hence, horrible shadow,
Unreal mockery, hence. [*Exit Ghost.*]
Why so, being gone
I am a man again.

(3.4.97–106)

Nor is the anxiety that afflicts Macbeth in this scene confined to him, as Macduff's distraught reaction to the news that his wife and children have been slaughtered attests. 'What, all my pretty chickens, and their dam / At one fell swoop?', he exclaims in disbelief. 'Dispute it like a man', Malcolm urges him, alarmed lest the grief-stricken warlord begin to weep. 'I shall do so,' replies Macduff, 'But I must also feel it as a man' (4.3.221–4). Then, like Macbeth, he steels himself against the emotional effeminacy he fears might overwhelm him:

O, I could play the woman with mine eyes,
And braggart with my tongue. But gentle heavens,
Cut short all intermission. Front to front
Bring thou this fiend of Scotland and myself;
Within my sword's length set him.

(4.3.233–7)

With that, like Macbeth too, he withdraws into the belligerent male persona that they share. 'This tune goes manly', says Malcolm, relieved at Macduff's reversion to martial type.

In case the decisive role played in the tragedy by this sexual ideology escapes us, Shakespeare enlists that scurrilous wise fool the Porter to bring it sharply into focus. In the immediate aftermath of Duncan's murder and its traumatic impact on Macbeth, as the dreadful knocking at the gate subsides, the self-styled 'porter of Hell Gate' (2.3.2) treats Macduff to an incongruous comic lecture on the fate booze has in store for the sexually aroused male:

Lechery, sir, it provokes and unprovokes: it provokes the desire, but it takes away the performance. Therefore much drink may be said to be an equivocator with lechery: it makes him, and it mars him; it sets him on, and it takes him off; it persuades him, and disheartens him; makes him stand to, and not stand too; in conclusion, equivocates him in a sleep and, giving him the lie, leaves him.

(2.3.28–35)

On closer inspection though, the Porter's lewd gag turns out to be anything but incongruous. It provides, in the guise of light relief from the tension of the preceding scenes, a vulgar comic version of Macbeth's plight at that point. In a sly plebeian parody of the play's 'imperial theme' (1.3.131) Macbeth's disabling agonies of conscience before and after killing his king are reduced to the embarrassment of impotent lust. This mordant caricature of Macbeth's 'Thriftless ambition' (2.4.28), which fails to be satisfied by regicide, as a failure to translate desire into deed by maintaining an erection, pinpoints and mocks the crux of the matter for Macbeth: male power and masculinity itself.

The Porter's ribald homily on the sexual humiliation and emasculated sleep of the drunkard glances back to the opening salvo of Lady Macbeth's first assault on her husband's vacillating resolve: 'Was the hope drunk / Wherein you dressed yourself? / Hath it slept since? / And wakes it now to look so green and pale, / At what it did so freely?' It's no coincidence, moreover, that the words 'equivocator' and 'equivocate', on which the Porter harps so knowingly, are echoed on the brink of doom by Macbeth. As he beholds Birnam Wood marching unbelievably on Dunsinane, he begins 'To doubt th' equivocation of the fiend, / That lies like truth' (5.5.42–3). The echo recalls the disparaging context in which the Porter uses those words to caricature his master's predicament. But it also links the Porter to the weird sisters, the source of that fiendish equivocation, who conspire with him to foreground the crucial role of gender in forging Macbeth's fate. When Macbeth and Banquo first encounter these 'hybrid monsters', as Heinrich Heine called them, Banquo is struck not only by the fact that they 'look not like th'inhabitants o'th' earth, / And yet are on't', but also by their androgynous appearance: 'You should be women, / And yet your beards forbid me to interpret / That you are so' (1.3.41–2, 45–7). Few productions of *Macbeth* have portrayed the witches as Shakespeare himself visualized them and meant them to be performed, because few productions have grasped the point of their androgyny. The effect of their embodying onstage a sexual identity which is neither female nor male but physically ambiguous should be to create a stark visual contrast with the virile warrior Macbeth, throwing into relief the rigidity of the gender role that binds him. The liminal sexual zone these epicene creatures occupy marks the boundary within which Macbeth's emphatically masculine fate unfolds. Through the visibly alien indeterminacy of their gender as much as through their gibing jingles and deadly nonsense-rhymes, the weird sisters 'scorn male power', as Terry Eagleton observes, 'and lay bare the hollow sound and fury at its heart'.

Dispossession and Disavowal

In this respect the witches serve, like the Porter, as conduits of their creator's scorn for the creed that destroys Macbeth, the creed whose essence is distilled in his resolution after banishing Banquo's ghost: 'for mine own good / All causes shall give way' (3.4.133–4). From that point on, Macbeth is irrevocably committed to what remains for most of the world the self-enthralled mantra of modernity. He hardens himself henceforth to being, as Hecate shrewdly perceives in the following scene, 'a wayward son, / Spiteful and wrathful, who, *as others do*, / Loves for his own ends' (3.5.11–13; my emphasis); and whose wayward devotion to his own ends above all is a vice not confined to him. For Knight, what grips Macbeth is 'a lust, like unruly love; a centring of reality in the self. A turning inward of the mind and its purposes, an obsession with the solitary self unharmonised with wider considerations.' Rapacious individualism in violent male pursuit of dominion over one's fellow human beings, whatever the cost to them or oneself, is the idol of the tribe by which Macbeth and his marital partner in crime are bewitched. But the price they pay from the moment of their possession by this frame of mind is to be dispossessed of themselves, as the closing lines of Macbeth's first soliloquy intimate:

> My thought, whose murder yet is but fantastical,
> Shakes so my single state of man
> That function is smothered in surmise,
> And nothing is, but what is not.

His thought of killing Duncan to advance his enthronement has taken such complete control of him at this moment that the responsibility for the murder is ascribed to the personified thought rather than to Macbeth, whose capacity to act has been usurped, leaving him lost in thought, 'rapt withal'.

This feeling of self-estrangement, of being taken over by something alien and independent of their will, becomes more acute and more conscious in Macbeth and his wife as the play proceeds. Indeed, they both exploit it repeatedly to disown their guilt by delegating it, as Macbeth does when he wishes that 'The eye wink at the hand', as if his own eye and hand were autonomous entities separate from him and from each other; or as Lady Macbeth does when she substitutes for herself as Duncan's imagined murderer her personified 'keen knife', whose eyes can't see the wound it makes. That image of a bloodstained knife with a will of its own resurfaces unforgettably in Macbeth's spellbound soliloquy as he steels himself to kill Duncan for real:

> Is this a dagger which I see before me,
> The handle toward my hand? Come, let me clutch thee.
> I have thee not, and yet I see thee still.
> Art thou not, fatal vision, sensible
> To feeling as to sight? Or art thou but
> A dagger of the mind, a false creation,
> Proceeding from the heat-oppressed brain?
> I see thee yet, in form as palpable
> As this which now I draw.
> Thou marshall'st me the way that I was going,
> And such an instrument I was to use.
> Mine eyes are made the fools o'th' other senses,
> Or else worth all the rest. I see thee still,
> And on thy blade, and dudgeon, gouts of blood,
> Which was not so before. There's no such thing.
> It is the bloody business which informs
> Thus to mine eyes.

> > (2.1.33–49)

Macbeth's apostrophe of the bloody weapon he beholds invests it with agency and intent by personifying it. The effect is to complicate the question of volition and thus our moral judgement of Macbeth on the threshold of murder. The eidetic intensity of the 'fatal vision' is such that it acquires for Macbeth the 'palpable' solidity of the actual murder weapon it prompts him to draw. He suspects it of being an hallucination, 'Proceeding from the heat-oppressed brain', and he finally dismisses it as that: 'There's no such thing.' But not before it's made us aware of Macbeth's feeling steered into this deliberate act of regicide by a force that's at once within him and outside him: 'Thou marshall'st me the way that I was going'. The phantom dagger appears unbidden to a startled Macbeth, seeming to him as 'sensible / To feeling as to sight', and with its handle turned towards his hand, compelling him to clutch it. Before it vanishes, it morphs into a dagger whose blade and hilt are stained with 'gouts of blood' from the murder about to be accomplished, easing Macbeth's passage to the deed by visualizing it as already done. It's presented, in other words, as exerting homicidal pressure upon him from without, in order to make Macbeth's involuntary thraldom to a thought – to a desire which is indeed 'A dagger of the mind, a false creation' – graphically clear to the audience.

After the dagger disappears, Macbeth is displaced in his mind's eye as Duncan's assassin by the personified thought itself, which mutates in turn metaphorically into the rapist of Lucrece:

> And withered Murder,
> Alarumed by his sentinel, the wolf,
> Whose howl's his watch, thus with his stealthy pace,
> With Tarquin's ravishing strides, towards his design
> Moves like a ghost.
>
> (2.1.52–6)

Macbeth watches himself stealing towards the king's bedchamber in figurative disguise and in the third person, as if he were watching a ghostly surrogate self from which he feels divorced. The Macbeth who stabs Duncan to death as he sleeps is no longer someone he recognizes and identifies with. As he says to his wife in the shattering wake of the murder: 'To know my deed, 'twere best not know myself' (2.2.74). His subsequent haunting by Banquo's 'horrible shadow' produces in him the same sensation of being taken over and unselved, of being turned, to his amazement, into someone else: 'Can such things be, / And overcome us like a summer's cloud, / Without our special wonder? / You make me strange / Even to the disposition that I owe' (3.4.108–11). Menteith encapsulates this tortured state of self-estrangement in his choric comment on Macbeth's frame of mind before the final battle:

> Who then shall blame
> His pestered senses to recoil and start,
> When all that is within him doth condemn
> Itself for being there?
>
> (5.2.22–5)

The man who wrote that 'All the world's a stage, / And all the men and women merely players' (*AYLI* 2.7.140–1) would undoubtedly have agreed with his fellow playwright Ben Jonson that

> our whole life is like a play: wherein every man, forgetful of himself, is in travail with expression of another. Nay, we so insist in imitating others, as we cannot (when it is necessary) return to ourselves: like children, that imitate the vices of stammerers so long, till at last they become such; and make the habit of another nature, as it is never forgotten.

Unlike Jonson, however, Shakespeare grasped the profound philosophical and political implications of the *theatrum mundi* conceit, which he exploited dramatically, in both comedy and tragedy, in ways that none of his rivals on the early modern stage could begin to grasp. For Shakespeare, Macbeth's tragedy, translated into Jonson's terms, is that he finds himself precisely 'in travail with expression of another' as the ruthlessly ambitious murderer Macbeth; and that he becomes at last so inured by 'habit' to this invasive usurper of his identity as to be unable to return to the self that once recoiled in horror from all that he was becoming: 'I am in blood / Stepped in so far, that should I wade no more, / Returning were as tedious as go o'er. / … My strange and self-abuse / Is the initiate fear, that wants hard use' (3.4.134–6, 140–1).

The same is true of Lady Macbeth, who ends up so possessed by 'the habit of another nature' that she loses herself in the bloody part she's played, as her compulsive repetition of it in the sleepwalking scene attests. To witness her obsessively washing her guilty hands, reliving things said, things heard and things done in the ghastly aftermath of the murder, is to witness her paying with a vengeance for her unsexing. But her reprising of her role as Macbeth's accomplice, during which she quotes snatches of earlier dialogues – 'To bed, to bed: there's knocking at the gate. … What's done cannot be undone' (5.1.66–8) – also underscores the grim theatricality of the original thoughts, words and deeds that she's repeating. It captures the sense in which Lady Macbeth and Macbeth himself, from the moment he becomes 'rapt withal' by the witches' greeting, become somnambulists, sleepwalking through a nightmare from which they are powerless to awaken, despite the unbearable anguish it inflicts on them. In this respect, they share the plight of Shakespeare's previous tragic protagonists for whom, to quote Montaigne again, 'waking is more a sleep, than sleep itself'. In this trance-like state, 'this fearful slumber' as Titus calls it (*TA* 3.1.253), their socialized selves dictate what they feel and think and want and do, overriding the resistance of the unconditioned human creature struggling into consciousness within them.

Hence the complex response produced in us by the tragedy's portrayal of the protagonists as manifestly guilty in one sense, and yet profoundly innocent in another. There's a passage in one of François Mauriac's journals that helps to explain this paradox and its wider bearing on Shakespearean tragedy in general as well as *Macbeth* in particular:

In *Illusions perdues*, Balzac admiringly cites the saying, 'Collective crimes implicate no one'. But what crime is not collective? Even if the murderer confronts his victim alone, his accomplices among the living and the dead could readily be found. Yet only he is tried, only he pays the penalty. … Like our human courts, like posterity, Shakespeare denounces the guilty person, the responsible individual. But by a miracle of genius he shows him to us encircled and engulfed by necessity; Shakespeare does not separate the man from the obscure forces that conjoined to culminate in a particular nature brimming with insolent guilt. In this fashion, Art prevails over History when it judges the creatures of History. To the end Shakespeare's vilest assassin preserves the excuse that at every moment of his life he is a human being caught up in a maelstrom of events that are not determined by him. His thirst to dominate does not spring from his own life; it comes from farther away.

Lear's momentous realization, at the climax of his fit of 'reason in madness', that 'None does offend, none' (4.6.164, 170–1), when the whole society is implicated in the offence in question, springs immediately to mind. As Berger observes of the pervasive complicity he discerns in *King Lear*: 'This does not mean that the audience is asked to condone duplicity, betrayal, or murder. It only means that the roots of such actions are not confined to the shallow plots of individual characters but spread down and out through the whole community or group of the play.' The same holds true of *Macbeth*. The guilt of Macbeth and of Lady Macbeth for the crimes they have committed doesn't absolve their society of its collective responsibility for their guilt, its disavowed but decisive share of the blame, because only in a society that fosters the 'thirst to dominate' could such a motive for such murders be conceivable, let alone understandable.

Even with 'Shakespeare's vilest assassin', as Mauriac points out, we remain aware that 'at every moment of his life he is a human being caught up in a maelstrom of events that are not determined by him'. It's our awareness of the human being who strives to survive within the vile assassin and merciless tyrant Macbeth that invests him with the essential innocence his wife reveals too, and that gives his fate its tragic grandeur and intensity. No critic has come closer to describing the nature and source of this quality than John Middleton Murry, who finds it crystallized most clearly in the exchange between Macbeth and his wife in the moments after the murder, when 'the discrepancy between the character and the act' at the core of Shakespearean tragedy 'is turned consciously to account':

Suddenly, Macbeth and Lady Macbeth *see themselves*, with an absolute and terrible naivety. This power that is in them to see themselves, manifested as they manifest it, convinces us, as nothing else could now convince us, of their essential nobility of soul. And by this turn the situation becomes bottomless in its profundity. That a man and a woman should, in the very act of heinous and diabolical murder, reveal themselves as naïve and innocent, convulses our morality and awakens in us thoughts beyond the reaches of our souls. … There is no word for that kind of contemplation, when two creatures, become themselves, look on the irremediable thing they did when they were not themselves.

In 'the sudden birth of childlike astonishment in the eyes of the murderers themselves' at what they have done Murry astutely perceives the hallmark of Shakespeare's tragic vision in *Macbeth*. For what's also born with that astonishment at 'the irremediable thing they did when they were not themselves' is the audience's perception of their unaccommodated inward selves, visibly and audibly present onstage. Before the murder the presence of those unsullied selves within them could be inferred from the conflicted soliloquies of both characters. But in 'the awful parenthesis', as De Quincey calls it, between the murder and the knocking at the gate, during which normal reality is suspended, the man and the woman they might otherwise have been materialize onstage as strangers, shocked to see themselves cast against their will as bloodstained killers, and wrestling desperately with that realization.

Pity, Like a Naked New-Born Babe

Lady Macbeth reveals at the outset the altogether different man Macbeth could have become, in another time and another kind of world, when she worries that her husband is not the stuff of which callous murderers are made: 'Yet do I fear thy nature', she muses in his absence, 'It is too full o'th' milk of human kindness / To catch the nearest way' (1.5.16–18). The phrase 'th' milk of human kindness' has passed into common usage and lost its original potency as a result. Its diction and imagery demand close analysis to restore its full effect. To begin with, the word 'human' is spelled 'humane' here as elsewhere in the First Folio. Shakespeare's eighteenth-century editor, Nicholas Rowe, introduced the emendation and successive generations of editors down to the present day have seen fit to preserve it, but at a cost. For in Shakespeare's day the term 'humane' had not yet split into two separate words with cognate but distinct meanings. In its original form in Lady Macbeth's line it conflates the descriptive term 'human', meaning characteristic of, or pertaining to, the genus *homo*, and the prescriptive term 'humane', meaning compassionate. The implication is that being human and being humane are inseparable, that the one entails the other, and that implication is reinforced by the noun that the adjective 'human[e]' qualifies. 'Kindness' is fully charged in this phrase with its early modern import: it means sympathetic, benevolent conduct consistent with belonging to the same *kind* as the person to whom kindness is shown. By his own wife's reluctant admission, the future homicide and fiendish 'hell hound' (5.8.3) Macbeth is 'too full' of the qualities condensed in these two words.

No less remarkable is the fact that Macbeth's 'human[e] kindness' is metaphorically described as 'milk'. For this links the whole phrase subliminally with the nourishing milk the infant sucks, out of simple human need and as a simple human right, from its mother's breasts. The inviolability of that primal right is confirmed thirty lines later by Lady Macbeth's willingness to violate it in order to be filled 'top-full / Of direst cruelty' by the 'murdering ministers' she summons to unsex her: 'Come to my woman's breasts, / And take my milk for gall' (1.5.42–3, 48); and again, two short scenes after that, when she seizes on the same imagery to steel her faltering husband's nerves for murder:

> I have given suck, and know
> How tender 'tis to love the babe that milks me:
> I would, while it was smiling in my face,
> Have plucked the nipple from his boneless gums
> And dashed the brains out, had I so sworn
> As you have done to this.
>
> (1.7.54–9)

Here the image of a breastfeeding baby implicit in the image of a mother's milk becomes vividly explicit. Lady Macbeth conjures up the most horrifying atrocity she can imagine in order to compel Macbeth to become as heartless as she has resolved to become. But in doing so she defines *ex negativo* the fundamental principle to which the tragedy is committed.

The reason why Shakespeare's evocation of helpless human infancy is so crucial to understanding the tragedy is made plain in the stunning soliloquy with which Macbeth opens the play's seventh scene. The speech displays the same tension that we've observed, at key moments in previous Shakespearean tragedies, between the historically bounded mind of an individual shaped by a particular culture and a universal human perspective that reaches back through history from the future it foreshadows. The fear Macbeth begins by voicing is that Duncan's assassination will incur retribution in 'the life to come' (1.7.7). But that swiftly gives way to a review of the grounds for also fearing 'judgement here' (1.7.8):

> He's here in double trust:
> First, as I am his kinsman, and his subject,
> Strong both against the deed. Then, as his host,
> Who should against his murderer shut the door,
> Not bear the knife myself. Besides, this Duncan
> Hath borne his faculties so meek, hath been
> So clear in his great office, that his virtues
> Will plead like angels, trumpet-tongued, against
> The deep damnation of his taking-off;
>
> (1.7.12–20)

To murder Duncan would be to break the established laws he should obey, and the ancient customs he should observe, as the kinsman, subject and host of a monarch, whose virtuous character provides no moral warrant for killing him. Up to this point, Macbeth's mind is confined within the known parameters of his class, culture and time. But none of the religious and secular prohibitions he enumerates are intimidating enough to deter him. The only thing that stops him in his tracks is his terror lest

> ... pity, like a naked new-born babe,
> Striding the blast, or heaven's cherubin, horsed
> Upon the sightless couriers of the air,
> Shall blow the horrid deed in every eye
> That tears shall drown the wind.
>
> (1.7.21–5)

What lends 'a naked new-born babe' such apocalyptic power is not only its capacity to personify pity and inspire compassion for the victim of murder, because its claim on the kindness of human beings is innate and incontestable. It's also the fact that it represents the poor, bare, forked, human animal in its most unaccommodated form, not yet defined by gender, race or rank, not yet 'cabined, cribbed, confined, bound in' (3.4.22) by history and consigned to the destiny such factors dictate. It symbolizes nothing less than the pure, indeterminate potential of humankind to deliver itself from its own inhumanity. In *The Inhuman*, his critique of 'The inhumanity of the system which is currently being consolidated under the name of development' – the 'cyborgization' of human beings that commenced, he contends, in the early modern era – Jean-François Lyotard locates the potential for resistance and transformation likewise in the native indeterminacy of childhood:

> Shorn of speech, incapable of standing upright, hesitating over the objects of its interest, not able to calculate its advantages, not sensitive to common reason, the child is eminently the human because its distress heralds and promises things possible. Its initial delay in humanity, which makes it the hostage of the adult community, is also what manifests to the community the lack of humanity it is suffering from, and which calls on it to become more human.

Writing four centuries earlier, Shakespeare enshrined this insight in the prophetic vision of 'a naked new-born babe', which flashes into the mind's eye of a medieval warlord on the brink of becoming the inhuman killer of one of his kind, solely to satisfy his 'Vaulting ambition' (1.7.27).

Blood Will Have Blood

Hence Macbeth's fear, immediately after murdering Duncan, is not that he now bears the guilt of regicide, of having betrayed 'The service and the loyalty' that he owed his sovereign's 'throne and state' (1.4.22, 25) as 'his kinsman, and his subject' (1.7.13). The thought that he's just assassinated *the king* doesn't cross his mind for a moment. What terrifies him is the thought that by committing murder he 'hath murdered sleep' (2.2.43):

> Methought I heard a voice cry, 'Sleep no more.
> Macbeth does murder sleep' – the innocent sleep,
> Sleep that knits up the ravelled sleave of care,
> The death of each day's life, sore labour's bath,
> Balm of hurt minds, great Nature's second course,
> Chief nourisher in life's feast –
>
> (2.2.36–41)

Why destroying his ability to sleep is the first thing that springs to Macbeth's mind is made clearer by what Lady Macbeth says to him following his fit of horror at the sight of Banquo's ghost: 'You lack the season [i.e. seasoning] of all natures, sleep' (3.4.139). It's the prospect of never again sleeping *as such* for killing another human being rather than as the penalty for regicide that appals him. For by forfeiting through murder the release from anguish that sleep, as 'the season of *all* natures', affords everyone, Macbeth has severed himself from humanity and from the 'innocent' state conferred by that common human blessing.

The levelling thrust of the speech is underlined by the domestic metaphors Macbeth employs, when he describes sleep as knitting up 'the ravelled sleave of care' (where 'sleave', a skein of silk, could also be heard simply as 'sleeve' by the audience) and as 'sore labour's bath', soothing the aching limbs of those who labour physically for their living. The effect of the latter metaphor is similar to that of Hamlet's reference, in his most famous soliloquy, to those who 'fardels bear' and who 'grunt and sweat under a weary life'. It reaches out from a collective standpoint, forging a bond between the experience of the aristocratic speaker and the lives of the class embodied in the play by the Porter. Two dozen lines earlier, as she waits nervously for Macbeth to return from murdering Duncan with the daggers she has planted, there's a glimpse of the same classless standpoint connected to sleep in Lady Macbeth, when she says: 'Had he not resembled / My father as he slept, I had done't' (2.2.13–14). Like Macbeth, she was not deterred from stabbing Duncan to death herself by the thought of his being her monarch, which never entered her head as she watched him sleeping. What stopped her was Duncan's resemblance, in the common human state of sleep, to her *father*, a familial relationship that cuts across classes and whose power to stay her hand owes nothing to rank.

The thing that torments Macbeth and Lady Macbeth above all, and for the same fundamental reason, is the fact of their having shed blood. 'What hands are here?', exclaims Macbeth in amazement at the sight of his own bloody hands, which seem, like the dagger of his mind, possessed by a malevolent will of their own:

> Ha: they pluck out mine eyes.
> Will all great Neptune's ocean wash this blood
> Clean from my hand? No, this my hand will rather
> The multitudinous seas incarnadine,
> Making the green, one red.
>
> (2.2.60–4)

Once again, it's not the regality of his victim that troubles him. The blood he's appalled at having shed is not the royal blood of the king as such, but the vital fluid that flows through the veins of kings and commoners alike, and that exerts its own moral authority, regardless of the rank of the person whose blood has been spilled: 'It will have blood they say: blood will have blood' (3.4.120). Likewise, when the sleepwalking Lady Macbeth recalls Duncan's corpse, as she frantically seeks to cleanse her hands of their complicity in his death, his royalty has been wiped from her mind as irrelevant: 'Yet who would have thought *the old man* to have had so much blood in him?' (5.1.39–40; my emphasis).

Had the regicidal nature of the murder mattered as much to Shakespeare as some critics would like to think it did, nothing would have been easier for him than to have the guilt-racked Macbeth fasten first and foremost upon Duncan's divinely sanctioned royalty, as Macduff does:

Confusion now hath made his masterpiece.
Most sacrilegious murder hath broke ope
The Lord's anointed temple, and stole thence
The life o'th' building. ...
                    ... O Banquo, Banquo,
Our royal master's murdered.

                                        (2.3.66–9, 85–9)

Macbeth's sole figurative glance at the dead man's regal status appears in his response to Macduff's demand that he explain why he killed the grooms in Duncan's chamber:

                    Here lay Duncan,
His silver skin laced with his golden blood,
And his gashed stabs looked like a breach in nature
For ruin's wasteful entrance; there, the murderers.
Steeped in the colours of their trade, their daggers
Unmannerly breeched with gore.

                                        (2.3.112–17)

But here Macbeth is intent on justifying the rashness of his action publicly to Macduff, Malcolm, Donalbain, Banquo and Lennox in terms calculated to carry weight with them. His gilding of the blood lacing Duncan's silver skin deifies their sovereign in order to explain why, on beholding his assassins with their blood-smeared daggers, his 'violent love' for their royal victim 'Outran the pauser, reason' (2.3.111–12). The idea of Duncan's sacrosanct royalty is adduced by Macbeth to make his lie credible and mask his real motive for killing the hapless grooms, not because it's preying on him. In private reflection by himself or with his wife, Duncan's royalty never features as a factor in what he calls 'the affliction of these terrible dreams / That shake us nightly' (3.2.19–20).

That it's the monarch who's been so brutally slain is seen, of course, to matter immensely in the world beyond the Macbeths. Shakespeare is careful to insert, straight after the discovery of the royal corpse, a short scene in which Ross and an Old Man report the bizarre phenomena convulsing the cosmos and the animal kingdom as a result, they have no doubt, of the king's assassination. 'Thou seest the heavens, as troubled with man's act, / Threatens his bloody stage', says Ross, observing how 'darkness does the face of the earth entomb / When living light should kiss it'; ''Tis unnatural', replies the Old Man, 'Even like the deed that's done' (2.4.9–11). But no such observations trouble Macbeth or Lady Macbeth, who remain unperturbed by fears of nature's distress or wrath at their killing of a king. In fact, after the exchange between Ross and the Old Man has dutifully underscored the gravity of regicide, no further concern with the subject is shown by any character, and Duncan himself is scarcely mentioned at all. The last significant reference to him in the play is made by Macbeth in conversation with his wife, and the tenor of it is telling:

> Better be with the dead,
> Whom we, to gain our peace, have sent to peace,
> Than on the torture of the mind to lie
> In restless ecstasy. Duncan is in his grave.
> After life's fitful fever, he sleeps well;
> Treason has done his worst: nor steel, nor poison,
> Malice domestic, foreign levy, nothing,
> Can touch him further.
>
> (3.2.20–7)

Far from being consumed with guilt for his treasonous dispatching of his sovereign to his death, and far from blaming that sacrilegious atrocity for the torture of their minds, Macbeth sees himself astonishingly here as having done Duncan a service by killing him and thus liberating him from the intolerable afflictions of monarchy. Such a service, indeed, that Macbeth envies the dead man the peace of the grave in which, unlike his murderer and his murderer's wife, 'he sleeps well'.

Ere Humane Statute Purged the Gentle Weal

'Better be with the dead': henceforth Macbeth is inexorably death-bound. The further atrocities he procures to save a crown he no longer wants serve merely to defer the annihilation that alone can still the 'restless ecstasy' of agonizing remorse. As his mind turns to the impending murder of Banquo, that 'deed of dreadful note' (3.2.45), the true source of Macbeth's remorse for killing Duncan is confirmed by the cause of his anguish at the prospect of Banquo's death:

> Come, seeling night,
> Scarf up the tender eye of pitiful day
> And with thy bloody and invisible hand

Cancel and tear to pieces that great bond
Which keeps me pale.

(3.2.47–51)

Macbeth summons night to commit the murder on his behalf under cover of darkness, seeking as before to disown the deed by transferring the responsibility for it to a personified abstraction. For in slaying Banquo and Fleance, the night and not Macbeth would be cancelling and tearing to pieces 'that great bond', whose hold on Macbeth keeps him pale with fear at the thought of breaking it. The 'great bond' is the moral contract that binds him as a human being to his kind, regardless of rank or any such arbitrary distinction, and that forbids his taking of another's life for his own good. It's the bond implicit in the milk of human kindness that Macbeth is too full of; the bond embodied in a naked newborn babe; the bond enshrined in the levelling imagery of sleep and blood that pervades the play.

The prophetic moral vision implicit in this imagery still awaits in our own blood-stained world the future it prefigures. In the meantime, it allows us to take the true measure of Macbeth, whose assassination of the king was a crime, but whose tragedy was that he killed one of his own kind against his will and destroyed himself by doing so. In a preternatural flash of insight before he ploughs on to his doom, Macbeth seems to grasp this too, as if suddenly privy to the anachronistic viewpoint of the play:

Blood hath been shed ere now, i'th' olden time,
Ere humane statute purged the gentle weal;
Ay, and since too, murders have been performed
Too terrible for the ear. The times have been,
That when the brains were out, the man would die,
And there an end. But now they rise again
With twenty mortal murders on their crowns,
And push us from their stools. This is more strange
Than such a murder is.

(3.4.73–81)

This extraordinary speech is triggered by the horrific first appearance of Banquo's ghost. Something stranger than the murder of Banquo has transpired, Macbeth realizes, with the passage of time: something world-changing that the shock of seeing the ghost has brought home to him with the force of an epiphany. Up until now, he reflects, one could not only shed the blood of another human being but commit the most horrendous murders with impunity. Once a man's brains had been dashed out, that was the end of the matter for his murderer. But the spilling of human blood and the violent ending of human life no longer mean what they used to mean, and from now on killing has dreadful consequences for the killer.

The direct bearing of the speech on Macbeth's experience is clear, but it describes a general phenomenon from a collective standpoint that gives it a choric quality and authority. A seismic shift in the valuation of human life that involves everyone has taken place ('But now they rise again / ... And push *us* from our stools'), transforming the perception of homicide from what it was 'Ere humane statute purged the gentle weal'. That remarkable line leaps out from the speech as the most arresting instance of prolepsis in a tragedy that carries the stamp of its author's proleptic imagination in every act. It holds the key to the speech's significance as a paradigm of the perspective from which the whole tragedy is conceived. As he utters the line, launched by the word 'humane' in its full Shakespearean sense, Macbeth too is 'transported', as his wife once was by a quite different thought, 'beyond / This ignorant present', and he feels now 'The future in the instant'. For he speaks in this line as if a 'humane statute', a benign, compassionate law made by man for the benefit of our kind, has already, indeed at some point in the distant past ('i'th' olden time'), purged the commonwealth of homicidal violence and turned it into a civilized society; which is manifestly not the case, as *Macbeth* itself bloodily confirms and the allusion to subsequent unspeakable murders concedes. The startling effect of the line is intensified, moreover, by the phrase 'the gentle weal', which constitutes a prolepsis within a prolepsis, since 'gentle' (civilized) describes the nature of the 'weal' (society) not before but *after* it was purged by the passing of a 'humane' law, as William Empson notes in *Seven Types of Ambiguity*. The era of barbarous bloodshed and murders 'Too terrible for the ear' is the era in which Macbeth's gory tragedy takes place and, as the daily news relentlessly reminds us, the era in which we have the misfortune to be still living. But for a sublime split second in this time-warping speech Macbeth thinks and talks as if he and we had long been dwelling in a peaceful, civilized community created by just, enlightened legislation, and the inhumane age of unredressed atrocities had been left far behind us.

At that moment, in other words, Macbeth sees his plight in his time as if he were looking back on it from the future foreseen in the line 'Ere humane statute purged the gentle weal'. He sees its historical reality from the same utopian perspective that audiences, then and now, are enjoined to adopt by the tragedy. That 'humane statute', whose enforcement is more urgent in our time than ever, became imaginable for Shakespeare as a result of the dawning realization in his time that, in Donne's celebrated formulation: 'No Man is an *Iland*, entire of it selfe; every man is a peece of the *Continent*, a part of the *maine* ... Any Man's *death* diminishes *me*, because I am involved in *Mankinde*'; or, as Montaigne puts it, 'chaque homme porte la forme entière de l'humaine condition', which Florio renders as 'Every man beareth the whole stampe of humane condition'. *Macbeth* is Shakespeare's tragic testament to the truth of this revolutionary realization. It takes a man who can butcher another man on the battlefield, ripping him open from navel to throat without forethought, fear or remorse, and who is lauded and richly rewarded for doing so. Then it traps him in a situation in which he feels compelled to kill again, but this time for his own advantage in his own home and unseen. And it slows the act of killing down, forcing him to ponder the chilling implications of premeditated murder before he commits it and to suffer its nightmarish consequences afterwards. It forces him to find out, and us to see, what it costs to kill one's own kind for one's own good.

Macbeth discovers that for his own good all causes will not give way, because he is not 'an *Iland*, entire of it selfe' but 'a peece of the *Continent*, a part of the *maine*' and thus innately 'involved in *Mankinde*'. Given that 'Any Man's *death*' for any reason would diminish Macbeth in Donne's view, it follows that the death he inflicts on Duncan and Banquo for his own cause does more than merely diminish him; it dehumanizes him and robs him of the will to go on living. It does so with astonishing speed too. No sooner has he committed the murder of Duncan – 'without the faintest desire or sense of glory', Bradley notes, but rather 'as if it were an appalling duty' – than the soul-destroying futility of the deed overwhelms him. When he returns with Lennox and Ross from the murdered man's chamber, he exclaims:

> Had I but died an hour before this chance,
> I had lived a blessed time, for from this instant
> There's nothing serious in mortality;
> All is but toys; renown and grace is dead,
> The wine of life is drawn, and the mere lees
> Is left this vault to brag of.

(2.3.92–7)

Macbeth's aim in this speech is to dupe Lennox, Ross, Macduff and Banquo into assuming him to be as devastated by Duncan's murder as they are. But the ironic effect of the speech on the audience, who have just witnessed Macbeth's traumatized state after the murder, is profound. As Bradley comments: 'This is no mere acting. The language here has none of the false rhetoric of his merely hypocritical speeches. It is meant to deceive, but it utters at the same time his profoundest feeling. And this he can henceforth never hide from himself for long.'

In his heart of hearts Macbeth knows from the start that his pursuit of 'sovereign sway and masterdom' is doomed to end in disaster, and that the prize he deemed 'the ornament of life' (1.7.42) would prove 'a fruitless crown', 'a barren sceptre' (3.1.60, 61). The conclusion he reaches at the end of the soliloquy that opens Act 1, scene 7 makes that crystal clear: 'I have no spur / To prick the sides of my intent, but only / Vaulting ambition, which o'er-leaps itself, / And falls on the other' (1.7.25–8). The self-defeating nature of unbridled self-assertion is underscored in the following act by Ross, who deplores the suicidal insanity of 'Thriftless ambition, that will raven up / Thine own life's means' (2.4.27–9). But no less telling than his knowledge of its self-destructive nature is Macbeth's awareness of the inadequacy of 'Vaulting ambition' as the 'only' motive he can muster for regicide. He has no incentive to murder the king other than one that he knows is bound to recoil on him. Compare Macbeth with his throne-hungry, hunchbacked theatrical progenitor, who stabs Henry VI to death with contemptuous glee before hauling his royal corpse offstage, and the hollowness of Macbeth's professed desire to seize the crown is at once apparent. 'Macbeth's agony is not properly understood', observes Knight, 'till we realize his utter failure to receive any positive joy from the imperial magnificence to which he aspired.'

Not once do we see Macbeth pausing to relish his success in grasping at last 'the round / And top of sovereignty' (4.1.86–8) for himself and his wife. Its possession brings them such excruciating mental torture that both would rather die than continue to endure it. For Lady Macbeth,

> Naught's had, all's spent,
> When our desire is got without content.
> 'Tis safer to be that which we destroy,
> Than by destruction dwell in doubtful joy.
>
> (3.2.5–8)

'Better be with the dead', Macbeth agrees, than 'eat our meal in fear, and sleep / In the affliction of these terrible dreams / That shake us nightly' (3.2.18–20). So much for what Shakespeare's mighty precursor Marlowe hymned in *Tamburlaine* as 'That perfect bliss and sole felicity, / The sweet fruition of an earthly crown'. After shaking off the shock of Banquo's ghost, Macbeth strives to remain as 'bloody, bold and resolute' (4.1.78) in the defence of his throne as the witches' Second Apparition urges him to be. But his truly 'lion-mettled' (4.1.89) defiance of the fate closing in on him can't in the end overcome his despair at the thought of where the siren call of sovereignty has led him:

> I have lived long enough: my way of life
> Is fallen into the sere, the yellow leaf,
> And that which should accompany old age,
> As honour, love, obedience, troops of friends,
> I must not look to have; but in their stead,
> Curses not loud but deep, mouth-honour, breath
> Which the poor heart would fain deny, and dare not.
>
> (5.3.22–8)

> I 'gin to be aweary of the sun,
> And wish th' estate o'th' world were now undone.
>
> (5.5.48–9)

It's an exhausted mood of absolute disenchantment, not just with the kingship he had to force himself to kill for, but with his whole 'way of life' and the entire order of things that constitutes the world of which he has been a part.

Like Lear, like Timon and like Hamlet before him, Macbeth has reached the point of being done with the world and with the man it compelled him to become. Having 'supped full with horrors' (5.5.13), the report of his wife's death at his lowest ebb leaves him locked inside a nihilistic vision of all human life as meaningless:

> She should have died hereafter;
> There would have been a time for such a word.
> Tomorrow, and tomorrow, and tomorrow,
> Creeps in this petty pace from day to day,

To the last syllable of recorded time;
And all our yesterdays have lighted fools
The way to dusty death. Out, out, brief candle,
Life's but a walking shadow, a poor player,
That struts and frets his hour upon the stage,
And then is heard no more. It is a tale
Told by an idiot, full of sound and fury
Signifying nothing.

(5.5.16–27)

The speech has too often been quoted out of context, as if it were Shakespeare's last word on the human condition instead of the bleak, contemptuous view of it to which Macbeth has been driven by his own experience and the news of his wife's demise.

But if we consider the way the speech is worded and keep its context in mind, its attunement to the tenor of the whole tragedy becomes clearer. The key to understanding it lies in the first two lines, as Murry perceives:

'Hereafter', I think, is purposely vague. It does not mean 'later'; but in a different mode of time from that in which Macbeth is imprisoned now. 'Hereafter' – in the not-Now: *there* would have been a time for such a word as 'the Queen is *dead*'. But the time in which he is caught is to-morrow, and to-morrow, and to-morrow – one infinite sameness, in which yesterdays have only lighted fools the way to dusty death. Life in this time is meaningless – a tale told by an idiot – and death also. For his wife's death to have meaning there needs some total change – a plunge across a new abyss into a Hereafter.

The speech reflects the tragic tension at the heart of the play between a conceivable time to come, in which the life of Macbeth would have been as it should have been, and the historical reality of the time in which he finds himself immured. As long as such a reality prevails, life is bound to go on feeling in the end like 'a tale / Told by an idiot, full of sound and fury / Signifying nothing'. But the prospect of alternative realities implicit in Macbeth's 'hereafter' and in his likening of the world to a stage undermines the contention that life must remain the same senseless charade it now seems to him. It betrays the yearning of the whole speech and the entire tragedy for 'some total change – a plunge across a new abyss' into a society of the future whose citizens are as full of the milk of human kindness as Macbeth.

PART IV

CHAPTER 9
ANTONY AND CLEOPATRA: MAKING DEFECT PERFECTION

Tragedy Travestied

With *Antony and Cleopatra* (1606–7) and *Coriolanus* (1607–8), the brace of Roman plays written in swift succession immediately after *Macbeth*, Shakespeare drew his career as a tragedian to a close. In doing so he was returning to the world and times he had previously explored not only in *Julius Caesar*, to which *Antony and Cleopatra* is a historical sequel, but also in *Titus Andronicus*, the tragedy that marked his debut in the genre. Given the readiness of early modern playwrights and their audiences to discern in dramatized tales of ancient Rome coded critiques of their own nation's strife-torn past and present, Shakespeare's decision to quarry Plutarch once more for the plots of his last two tragedies evinces a desire to place the vexed political issues at stake in them centre stage. That matters of deep-rooted and enduring political importance to him were on his mind in these plays is borne out, too, by the fact that in writing them he was also reaching back beyond *Titus* to tackle again themes that had fired his imagination in the *Henry VI* plays, where the seeds of Shakespearean tragedy were sown: a nation plunged by aristocratic rivals into protracted civil war in *Antony and Cleopatra*, though this time on a global scale, and class war between the rebellious commons and the patrician elite in *Coriolanus*.

In *Antony and Cleopatra*, however, the historical drama of political and military conflict is indivisible from the fate of the legendary lovers round whom the tragedy revolves. Their story links the play back to *Othello* and *Romeo and Juliet*, with which it forms a trio of love tragedies devoted to couples doomed by the transgressive nature of their relationships. All three plays secure our sympathy with and admiration for those relationships, compelling us to question the social and ideological constraints responsible for their destruction. Romeo and Juliet fall in love and are secretly married in defiance of the deadly feud between their families. Othello and Desdemona fall in love and elope in defiance of both the Venetian taboo against interracial marriage and her father's will. Given his penchant for romantic heroes and heroines of such audacity and tenacity, it's no surprise to find Shakespeare placing at the heart of his last tragedy of love a brazenly adulterous, scandalously mixed-race couple, who treat the conventions they breach and the opprobrium they attract with contempt, and who are lionized by their creator for doing so.

But it's not just their rebellious refusal to conform that holds their appeal for Shakespeare; it's also the kind of love they stand for and in whose name they rebel. When

Cleopatra insists that Antony tell her how much he loves her, and Antony replies, 'There's beggary in the love that can be reckoned' (1.1.14–15), his answer aligns them with Romeo and Juliet, who tells Romeo: 'They are but beggars that can count their worth, / But my true love is grown to such excess, / I cannot sum up sum of half my wealth' (RJ 2.6.32–4). Likewise, when Antony exalts the love between him and Cleopatra as that of 'such a mutual pair / And such a twain' (1.1.38–9), he casts it in the same mould as the mutual love fleetingly shared not only by Romeo and Juliet ('Her I love now / Doth grace for grace and love for love allow' (RJ 2.3.81–2)), but also by Othello and Desdemona, during whose courtship 'soul to soul' she was 'half the wooer' of a man wishing 'to be free and bounteous to her mind' (OTH 1.3.114, 176; 2.3.266) once wed.

What binds Shakespeare's three great love tragedies together above all is this visionary ideal of a boundless, bountiful, mutually enhancing love between equals, which all three couples share, voice and continue to enshrine. It's an ideal so enthralling when glimpsed and grasped in reality that Antony and Cleopatra, like Romeo and Juliet before them, prefer suicide to survival on the terms of a world hostile to such love. It's an ideal so threatening to a society steeped in sexual and racial inequality that the mere prospect of a 'free and bounteous' interracial marriage of true minds is enough to provoke its insidious destruction in Othello. That the ethnic and physical otherness of Cleopatra, routinely reviled in Rome as Antony's 'gipsy' whore, plays its distasteful part in straining their relationship and expediting its end too is undeniable. Nor is it unwarranted to trace Antony and Cleopatra's Shakespearean lineage back through Othello to the adulterous liaison flaunted by Aaron the Moor and Tamora, the exotic, barbarian Empress of Rome; or to the adulterous liaison between Suffolk and Margaret, the outrageous French queen consort of England. Shakespeare was drawn from the outset to such blatant violators of social and sexual mores, and to tiger-hearted, charismatic, foreign female queens in particular. When he turned his mind to Antony and Cleopatra, he was revamping a scenario for which he felt a long-standing affinity.

It's important to bear this in mind, because before we say anything else about Antony and Cleopatra and what sets it apart as a play, it's vital to stress the fundamental consistency of its vision with the vision of the Shakespearean tragedies that preceded it. That means pausing to underscore first and foremost Shakespeare's boldness in advancing such a sympathetic view of the legendary, illicit lovers and especially of Cleopatra. In the accounts of Roman historians the Egyptian queen was a wicked, wily seductress who lured Antony away from the virtuous path of duty, while Antony was depicted as a licentious, infatuated fool, emasculated and finally destroyed by his inability to resist her. Nearly all medieval and early modern takes on the story toed the same ancient Roman line, often reducing it to a didactic parable illustrating the fate that awaits those who let passion ride roughshod over reason. Cleopatra was consigned by Dante to the circle of Hell reserved for 'carnal sinners' in whom 'Reason by lust is sway'd'. Even the sceptical Montaigne saw fit to file Antony as a matter of course among those 'great persons, whom pleasure hath made to forget the conduct of their owne affaires'.

In North's 1579 translation of Plutarch's 'Life of Marcus Antonius' Shakespeare unquestionably found a richer, more complex appraisal of both his protagonists, which gave due weight to the appealing qualities of their personalities as well as to their flaws. But Plutarch's overall view of their love affair chimes with the classical Roman consensus that its effect on Antony's character and his career was disastrous, and that the bulk of the blame for his downfall lay with Cleopatra. For 'the love of Cleopatra' was deemed by Plutarch to be 'the last and extremest mischief of all other', because 'she did waken and stir up many vices yet hidden in him ... and if any spark of goodness or hope of rising were left in him, Cleopatra quenched it straight and made it worse than before'. So in elevating Antony and Cleopatra to the status of tragic hero and heroine, and in portraying their turbulent, vilified love as possessed of something sublime, Shakespeare was cutting against the grain not only of his source's judgement of them, but also of a centuries-old tradition of disparagement that was still entrenched in his own time.

It remained entrenched long after Shakespeare's time too, not least in the theatre, as a result of which *Antony and Cleopatra*, like the rest of his tragedies, continued to remain far ahead of his time, awaiting the audience it deserved. That much is clear from the fact that Dryden's eviscerated Restoration version of the play, *All for Love, or The World Well Lost* (1677), displaced Shakespeare's tragedy on the English stage almost entirely until the early nineteenth century. In *All for Love* the global scope of *Antony and Cleopatra* is shrunk to fit the confines of a domestic drama centring on the moral dilemma posed by the hero's divided loyalties; the political dimension so integral to Shakespeare's conception of the lovers' tragedy is divorced from their relationship, pared down and pushed to the edge of events along with Octavius Caesar, who only exists offstage; the nameless Clown who brings Cleopatra the means of deliverance – the plebeian counterpart of *Hamlet*'s Gravedigger and the Porter in *Macbeth* – is cut altogether as an indecorously vulgar intrusion on the queen's demise; Cleopatra herself is stripped of 'Her infinite variety' (2.2.246), turned into the sentimental stock figure of the abandoned mistress, and obliged to share the play's climactic suicide-scene with Antony instead of its being devoted to her; and 'the excellency of the moral' of the play for Dryden couldn't have been plainer: 'the chief persons represented were famous patterns of unlawful love; and their end, accordingly was unfortunate'.

The fact that Dryden's travesty supplanted Shakespeare's tragedy in the British theatre for 150 years attests to the power of *Antony and Cleopatra* in its unfettered form to provoke and challenge its audiences. How else can one explain such a sustained, culturally sanctioned preference for a version purged of those features of *Antony and Cleopatra* most audiences were apt to find least palatable? Shakespeare's conflation of the public, political domain and the private, erotic domain in the protagonists' relationship calls into question the still widespread tendency to regard them as separate rather than inextricable spheres. So the politics must be flattened into the backdrop for a morality play in which the lovers finally meet the fate their adultery demands instead of being reborn, as they are through Shakespeare's poetry, as portents of love and politics transfigured. In *Antony and Cleopatra* Shakespeare hands command of the whole fifth act of the tragedy to his heroine rather than his hero, subordinating the latter's poignant death to the dazzling apotheosis of his maligned, dark-skinned concubine. It's a theatrical violation of patriarchal propriety of a kind without precedent in Shakespearean tragedy, and a superb example of Shakespeare's penchant for making subversive points as statements of form rather than in the form of statements. But it was a violation too flagrant for the taste of Dryden, whose anodyne redaction of the tragedy restored sexual decorum by combining Cleopatra's death-scene with Antony's to prevent its eclipsing him – an alteration which continued to be adopted by productions of *Antony and Cleopatra* itself well into the twentieth century, long after *All for Love* had vanished from the stage.

In reworking and rewording Shakespeare's play Dryden, needless to say, ignored the unambiguous textual evidence that Shakespeare imagined Cleopatra, and expected her to be seen, as a North African queen, whose skin is explicitly described as 'tawny' by a Roman detractor (1.1.6) and as being 'with Phoebus' amorous pinches black' by Cleopatra herself (1.5.29). But even after Shakespeare's tragedy was more or less restored to the English stage, and right up until quite recently, it remained the norm to have the part played by white actresses just as in *All for Love*, in blithe contradiction of Cleopatra's self-portrayal. That racial difference and the prejudice it spawns are not issues that animate the dialogue in *Antony and Cleopatra* as conspicuously as they do in *Othello* is undoubtedly true. But to see the part played today by a black actor of formidable prowess, as those who saw Sophie Okonedo as Cleopatra in the National Theatre production in 2019 were fortunate to do, is to see the concern with race at the core of the play, as Shakespeare conceived and wrote it, restored at last and staring the audience in the face.

The tacit rationale for expunging Shakespeare's Clown from *All for Love* was essentially the same as that for robbing Cleopatra of the final act and cutting her character down to size in comparison with Antony's. Allowing this slyly knowing, anonymous rustic commoner, speaking in demotic prose, to materialize from nowhere at that crucial moment to steal the spotlight from a queen couldn't be countenanced by Dryden for the same reason that Sidney deplored 'mingling kings and clowns' on the Elizabethan stage: it made a mockery of the established hierarchy, which was supposed to be set in stone, by putting majesty on a par with *hoi polloi* and exposing it to unseemly quips and quibbles. The wholesale culling of clowns and jesters from the Restoration stage to which *All for Love* contributed was part of a concerted theatrical move to reinstate and secure the strict social distinctions between classes that licensed fools like Cleopatra's Clown, and like the Gravedigger and the Porter before him, contrive to undermine. The importance of the Clown in *Antony and Cleopatra* is not confined, moreover, to the levelling subtext of his bawdy badinage with his suicidal queen. His presence in the play at such a climactic juncture affords visible and audible proof of the democratic spirit that permeates its diction and design. To underestimate his symbolic importance as an uncanny incarnation of that spirit, and to treat him instead, as critics and productions too often do, as mere mood-lightening 'comic relief', is to misunderstand the tragedy and the revolutionary nature of its universality.

As a play, Dryden's *All for Love* may have become a museum piece, but as a means of grasping at a glance the reasons why *Antony and Cleopatra* stayed out of step for so long with later times, and is still out of step in profound ways with our times, it remains invaluable. The briefest comparison suffices to highlight the radical utopianism of the tragedy and pave the way for interpretations and productions that seek to do justice to Shakespeare's demonstrable intentions in writing it.

The Nobleness of Life

Those intentions can be inferred right from the opening scene, which tunes the audience immediately to the tenor of the whole tragedy. Shakespeare's strategy in the scene is similar to the one he employs at the beginning of *Othello*: set up the conventional, pejorative view of the lovers, which the audience is likely to hold and expect to see endorsed, but expressly in order to subvert it when the lovers appear in person and we hear them speak. The scene commences in Alexandria *in medias res*, with the conflict that generates the tragedy already in place rather than precipitated, as it is in the previous four tragedies, by an unforeseen, disruptive event or chain of events. We overhear two of Antony's followers, Philo and Demetrius, in mid-conversation about what Philo deplores as the shameful plight in which their legendary leader now finds himself:

> Nay, but this dotage of our general's
> O'erflows the measure. Those his goodly eyes,
> That o'er the files and musters of the war
> Have glowed like plated Mars, now bend, now turn
> The office and devotion of their view
> Upon a tawny front. His captain's heart,
> Which in the scuffles of great fights hath burst
> The buckles on his breast, reneges all temper
> And is become the bellows and the fan
> To cool a gypsy's lust.

> (1.1.1–10)

At which point Antony and his tawny-fronted gypsy paramour enter with her entourage, as if furnishing on cue, Philo invites us to believe, visible corroboration of his verdict:

> Look where they come!
> Take but good note, and you shall see in him
> The triple pillar of the world transformed
> Into a strumpet's fool. Behold and see.

> (1.1.10–13)

That we've been allowed to eavesdrop on this informal, adverse judgement passed on Antony in private by a sympathetic adherent also lends it a chorus-like authority it would not command in open dialogue.

But what we see and hear for ourselves, as Antony and Cleopatra continue in public the romantic banter evidently underway before their entrance, casts the couple in a quite different light, throwing Philo's judgement into question.

CLEOPATRA
If it be love indeed, tell me how much.
ANTONY
There's beggary in the love that can be reckoned.
CLEOPATRA
I'll set a bourn how far to be beloved.
ANTONY
Then must thou needs find out new heaven, new earth.

(1.1.14–17)

With its echoes not only of *Romeo and Juliet*'s but also of *King Lear*'s subscription to the limitless, incalculable nature of genuine love, the lovers' opening exchange strikes the keynote of their relationship, which will resound again triumphantly in the closing act. But not before the utopian ideal it evokes is forced to run the gauntlet of the reality it rebukes, as the news from Rome announced in the next line makes clear. The sudden, intrusive reminder of Rome's rival claims on Antony spurs Cleopatra to a sarcastic tirade impugning his loyalty to her and eliciting this superb response from him:

Let Rome in Tiber melt, and the wide arch
Of the ranged empire fall! Here is my space!
Kingdoms are clay! Our dungy earth alike
Feeds beast as man. The nobleness of life
Is to do thus, when such a mutual pair
And such a twain can do't, in which I bind,
On pain of punishment, the world to weet
We stand up peerless.

(1.1.34–41)

'Excellent falsehood!' (1.1.41) retorts Cleopatra, refusing to be appeased by Antony's reassurance, which she dismisses as mendacious rhetoric. At this stage in the play the sheer extravagance of the terms in which Antony affirms the priority of his commitment to Cleopatra might well lead one to think her justified in doubting his sincerity. Even at this stage though, the magnificence of the ideas expressed by the speech, and of the language in which they are couched, dwarfs whatever doubts about the speech's credibility Cleopatra's reaction may arouse.

Such doubts are offset, too, by the credibility the speech acquires from being read in the light of the previous tragedies, especially the earlier love tragedies it evokes through its image of a peerless 'mutual pair'. But that notion of mutuality, which entails an utterly unpatriarchal assumption of equality between man and woman, springs from an even more radical egalitarianism espoused by Antony in the first four lines. Rome and its mighty empire, of which Antony is a 'triple pillar', are pronounced worthless in comparison with the value he sets on the space in which 'such a twain' as they are embrace. Rome can melt away into the Tiber and the empire collapse for all he cares, because empires are made of lands, and lands in the end are just pieces of our dung-like earth, which makes no distinction between human beings and animals, let alone between the Antonys, Cleopatras and Caesars who rule kingdoms of clay and those whom they rule. Here we have the same levelling logic that produced the mighty kingmaker Warwick's dying realization: 'what is pomp, rule, reign but earth and dust?' (*3HVI* 5.2.27); that underpinned the Roman hero Titus's renouncing of Rome as 'a wilderness of tigers' (*TA* 3.1.54) whose denizens are indistinguishable from beasts; that lay behind Antony's addressing Julius Caesar's corpse as 'thou bleeding piece of earth' (*JC* 3.1.254); that led Hamlet to ask 'Why may not imagination trace the noble dust of Alexander till he find it stopping a bung-hole?' (5.1.201–2); that informed Lear's recognition of the same 'poor, bare, forked animal' (3.4.105–6) beneath his royal garb and a beggar's rags; and that moved Timon to apostrophize the 'damned earth' as our 'Common mother – thou / Whose womb unmeasurable and infinite breast / Teems and feeds all' (*TIM* 4.3.42, 176–8).

Within Antony's speech, however, this levelling impulse presses further in the extraordinary lines: 'The nobleness of life / Is to do thus, when such a mutual pair / And such a twain can do it'. They are extraordinary because they redefine nobility as the quality Antony and Cleopatra possess not by virtue of their aristocratic birth and social superiority, but by virtue of the whole way of life they enjoy as 'such a mutual pair' of matchless lovers. Through this redefinition of 'nobleness' the broader concept of social equality merges with the intimate ideal of personal equality between individuals in love; the implication being that each kind of equality is predicated on the other, and that the hierarchical notion of nobility harbours the possibility of its negation. Antony concludes his speech by commanding 'the world' to acknowledge that, as lovers in this special, exemplary sense, he and Cleopatra are 'peerless' – without equals, in other words, but without any connotation of social superiority. The ascription of global significance to the supreme example of love they set is worth noting. The play abounds in words and phrases that cast the protagonists as titanic figures on a global or even a cosmic stage. Their cumulative effect is not only to lend Antony and Cleopatra an aura of ineffable heroic grandeur, but also to suggest that the values at stake in their relationship and its fate are of universal human relevance. Antony's summoning of the world to witness at the end of his speech is allied in this respect with his earlier invocation of the 'dungy earth', which makes a mockery of kingdoms and rank, and of the 'new heaven, new earth' that would be needed to accommodate the new kind of love they stand for.

Forced by the Roman messenger's arrival to choose between the bugle call of public duty and the siren song of Cleopatra, whose 'whole character', as Hazlitt notes, 'is the triumph of the voluptuous, of the love of pleasure and the power of giving it, over every other consideration', Antony has no doubt where his priorities lie:

Now, for the love of Love and her soft hours,
Let's not confound the time with conference harsh.
There's not a minute of our lives should stretch
Without some pleasure now. What sport tonight?

(1.1.45–8)

'Hear the ambassadors' (1.1.49) is Cleopatra's truculent retort to keep Antony torn between public responsibilities and personal gratification, as he will be for much of the play. But here, at the end of this scene as at the end of his life in Act 4, which claim on him will prove the stronger is never in question:

Fie, wrangling queen,
Whom everything becomes – to chide, to laugh,
To weep, whose every passion fully strives
To make itself, in thee, fair and admired!
No messenger but thine, and all alone
Tonight we'll wander through the streets and note
The qualities of people. Come, my queen!
Last night you did desire it. [to the Messenger] Speak not to us.
          Exeunt Antony and Cleopatra with the train.

(1.1.49–55)

Antony's public snubbing of the messenger from Octavius Caesar does not escape the notice of Philo and Demetrius, who are left alone onstage to deliver the Roman verdict on what they've just witnessed. 'Is Caesar with Antonius prized so light?', Demetrius asks Philo. 'Sir,' replies Philo, 'when he is not Antony, / He comes too short of that great property / Which still should go with Antony'. 'I am full sorry,' says Demetrius, bringing the scene to an end, 'that he approves the common liar who / Thus speaks of him at Rome' (1.1.57–62).

Antony's final speech in this scene also alerts us to a fundamental paradox of Cleopatra's character, which he turns out to share with her, and which bears directly on the nature of their tragedy. I mean their ability to 'make defect perfection' (2.2.241), to borrow the phrase Enobarbus later uses to praise Cleopatra. Even at her most irrational, perverse and aggravating, Antony finds his 'wrangling queen' irresistibly entrancing; everything that should detract from her attractiveness serves only to enhance it and increase his admiration of her. By the same token, no matter how much Antony infuriates Cleopatra by his conduct, and no matter how low he sinks in the eyes of the world, nothing can diminish her passionate admiration of him; on the contrary, as the transcendent last act of the tragedy testifies, the lower he sinks in the eyes of the world, the higher he rises in her esteem. The same holds true for the audience's view of them both as the play develops. Circumstances and events conspire time and again with their flawed personalities to shatter the idealized images they project of themselves and each other. Yet those images not only survive these assaults on their veracity, but gain strength and credibility from the sceptical realism to which they're exposed.

The anchorage of the love of Antony and Cleopatra in mundane actualities is what makes its translation into poetry so convincing. That they are instinctively drawn for pleasure to the commonplace lives from which their eminence normally excludes them is revealing: 'all alone', says Antony, 'Tonight we'll wander through the streets and note / The qualities of people'. 'He would goe up and downe the citie disguised like a slave in the night', relates Plutarch, in a passage on which Shakespeare drew, 'and would peere into poore mens windows and their shops, and scold and brawle with them within the house: Cleopatra would be also in a chamber maides array, and amble up and downe the streets with him.' For Octavius, as we later learn, Antony's readiness 'to sit / And keep the turn of tippling with a slave, / To reel the streets at noon, and stand the buffet / With knaves that smells of sweat' (1.4.18–21) is the repugnant proof of his degradation. But for Shakespeare the urge Antony shares with Cleopatra to shed the identities that divide them from the lives of commoners – to release the plebeian soul within them – is intrinsic to their allure. From the Roman point of view, as expressed in Philo's closing speech, it's in these moods, 'when he is not Antony', that Antony betrays 'that great property' which defines him. But from the play's wider perspective it's Antony's and Cleopatra's ability to accommodate the plebeian and the patrician, the vulgar and the regal, within the same self and without incongruity, that constitutes their greatness.

Past the Size of Dreaming: Utopian Realism

That's why Bradley's belief that the ironic undercutting to which its protagonists are subjected disqualifies *Antony and Cleopatra* as a tragedy in the same sense as *Hamlet, Othello, King Lear* and *Macbeth* are tragedies couldn't be more wrong, though it's a belief that still has wide currency. It remains current amongst critics who endorse in effect the Roman attitude to Antony's and Cleopatra's uncouth delinquencies, which are seen as undermining the high seriousness tragic protagonists are conventionally expected to display. The judgement of such critics is basically wedded to the same principles of social and theatrical decorum that Dryden subscribed to, and that Shakespeare took pleasure in flouting. For a truer grasp of what he was about in *Antony and Cleopatra*, they would have been better to start from Anna Jameson's acute insight almost two centuries ago into the originality of his achievement:

> Great crimes, springing from high passions, grafted on high qualities, are the legitimate source of tragic poetry. But to make the extreme of littleness produce an effect like grandeur – to make the excess of frailty produce an effect like power – to heap up together all that is most unsubstantial, frivolous, vain, contemptible, and variable, till the worthlessness be lost in the magnitude, and a sense of the sublime spring from the very elements of littleness, – to do this, belonged only to Shakespeare, that worker of miracles.

To be blind to the miracle that Shakespeare works in *Antony and Cleopatra* is to fall into the same trap as Enobarbus. From a fleeting mention of a marginal figure in Plutarch called 'Domitius', Shakespeare created in Enobarbus the full-blown sardonic realist he needed to express the view of the protagonists that audiences would be most likely to adopt, but precisely in order to invalidate it. Enobarbus takes over and expands the Chorus-like role of Philo and Demetrius in the opening scene, and in his choric capacity he exerts a powerful influence on our response to his wayward master and his master's capricious mistress. His long-standing loyalty to the beleaguered Antony testifies to the latter's extraordinary magnetism, while the superlative tributes he can't help paying Cleopatra are made convincing by the fact that they proceed from such a congenital cynic:

> Age cannot wither her, nor custom stale
> Her infinite variety. Other women cloy
> The appetites they feed, but she makes hungry
> Where most she satisfies; for vilest things
> Become themselves in her, that the holy priests
> Bless her when she is riggish.

> (2.2.245–50)

Conversely, the caustic irony of Enobarbus's constant gibes at the expense of Antony and Cleopatra is all the more compelling for being tempered by his susceptibility to their mystique.

As their fortunes decline and capitulation to Octavius becomes inevitable, the disenchanted Roman perception of Antony as a strumpet's fool, who sacrificed 'his captainship' to 'The itch of his affection' (3.13.7–8), gets the better of Enobarbus. His resolution to 'follow / The wounded chance of Antony' (3.10.36) and stay loyal to him against all reason proves short-lived and he deserts Antony for Octavius. But no sooner has he done so than he regrets it: 'I have done ill, / Of which I do accuse myself so sorely / That I will joy no more' (4.6.18–20). The news that all his treasure has been sent after him by Antony with the latter's 'bounty overplus' (4.6.23) seals Enobarbus's death warrant, so unbearable is Antony's characteristic display of selfless magnanimity:

> I am alone the villain of the earth,
> And feel I am so most. O Antony,
> Thou mine of bounty, how wouldst thou have paid
> My better service, when my turpitude
> Thou dost so crown with gold! This blows my heart.

> (4.6.31–5)

With that, he goes off to find a ditch in which to die of shame and a broken heart.

Shakespeare could hardly have devised a more emphatic way of dramatizing the fate reserved for, and deserved by, those who forswear their allegiance to the ideals that Antony and Cleopatra enshrine, and that they know in their hearts they should stay true to; those who default on their debt to the higher aspirations of humanity the lovers articulate, allying themselves instead, however regretfully, to the kind of expedient pragmatism personified by Octavius Caesar, which settles cynically for the world as it finds it rather than striving to transform it. Shakespeare rightly gives the realistic mentality its due, making the case for the need to sacrifice personal desire to public duty, the claims of the self to the claims of the state, so forcefully through Antony's plight that productions and critics have often bought it as the punchline of the play. But to construe the tragedy as caused by the lovers' wilful refusal to bow to 'The strong necessity of time' (1.3.43), and put political imperatives before the demands of passion, is as misconceived as to read it purely as a tragic paean to a doomed romantic fantasy.

The tragedy of Antony and Cleopatra, as Shakespeare dramatizes it, is the tragedy of being doomed to live in a society that divorces the personal from the political, the desires of the individual from the needs of the community, because it assumes them to be incompatible. The play is written from a perspective that presupposes not just the desirability but the possibility of a world in which they are compatible, in which self-interest and the interests of society converge and neither need be sacrificed to the other. That's why, as Auden noticed, in *Antony and Cleopatra*, in pointed contrast to the other love tragedies, 'public and private life are entirely interwoven … Their worldly position is an essential part of their love. Cleopatra is Egypt and Antony is one of the rulers of the Roman empire, unlike Romeo and Juliet who are any boy and any girl separated by a family feud.' From that microcosmic first scene onwards, Antony and Cleopatra act out their private love-life in public, exactly as if there were no distinction between the two spheres, as if both dimensions of their identities coincided. Hence the lovers are never seen cloistered alone together, unlike Romeo and Juliet or Othello and Desdemona; nor are they given soliloquies disclosing hidden thoughts to which the audience alone are privy. In *Antony and Cleopatra* the realm of erotic intimacy is politicized and the realm of politics is eroticized from a standpoint that conceives them as inextricable.

As indifferent to the racial difference between them that affronts Rome as to Rome's rigid distinction between the sexes – Antony, complains Octavius, 'is not more manlike / Than Cleopatra, nor the Queen of Ptolemy / More womanly than he' (1.4.5–7) – the lovers embody the human potential to live fully as both an individual and a social being in a community of equals. That they do so in a world and at a time that makes it impossible for them to realize that potential is their tragedy. But by thinking, speaking and acting *as if* what is still far from the case for us were already the case for them – as if they had already become all that they ever dreamed of becoming – they make the *as yet* utopian a living reality on the stage before us. The imaginative transfiguration of Antony and Cleopatra, which begins in the first scene and culminates in the last act, is made more realistic, and thus more credible, by being rooted in the actuality it indicts. The exorbitant hyperbole on which the protagonists soar springs from the 'stern realism' in which, as Wilson Knight observes, the play is firmly grounded: '*Antony and Cleopatra* is fired by an intenser realism than any play from *Hamlet* to *Timon of Athens* … The play's visionary transcendence marks not a severance from reality but a consummation of it.' Antony and Cleopatra's poetically transmuted conception of themselves is what the harsh historical reality that shackles them has the capacity to become and is manifestly striving to become through them.

To grasp that is to know what Cleopatra means when she opens the final scene of the play with the words: 'My desolation does begin to make / A better life' (5.2.1–2). From where but the experience of desolation could the aspiration to a better life come? From what but defect does the desire for perfection derive? We should now be better placed to understand, too, those perplexing but profoundly important lines in which Cleopatra makes theoretically explicit a fundamental tenet of Shakespeare's dramatic art. They occur after Antony's death during her exchange with Octavius's envoy, Dolabella, in the closing scene. 'I dreamt there was an emperor Antony', says Cleopatra, to Dolabella's consternation. Then, ignoring his attempts to address her, she proceeds to deliver her magnificent eulogy of the man she loved, portraying him as a colossus supremely endowed with the virtue that broke Enobarbus's heart, and that Shakespeare plainly prized: 'For his bounty / There was no winter in't; an autumn it was / That grew the more by reaping' (5.2.85–7). But when Cleopatra asks Dolabella, 'Think you there was or might be such a man / As this I dreamt of?', and the down-to-earth Dolabella replies, 'Gentle madam, no' (5.2.92–3), his answer elicits this startling riposte:

> You lie up to the hearing of the Gods!
> But if there be nor ever were one such,
> It's past the size of dreaming. Nature wants stuff
> To vie strange forms with fancy; yet t'imagine
> An Antony were nature's piece 'gainst fancy,
> Condemning shadows quite.

> (5.2.94–9)

A preliminary paraphrase of lines 95–9, adapting the Arden editor's gloss, might run thus: 'Whether such a man as I've dreamed of exists or ever could exist, no dream could do justice to him. Nature lacks the material to compete with fancy in the creation of astonishing new forms; yet to imagine an Antony would be to create a masterpiece ("piece") of nature that would wholly surpass the insubstantial creations of fancy ("shadows").' The difficulties still posed by these lines, in which Cleopatra is clearly voicing the dramatist's reflections on his own aesthetic creed, begin to disappear once two crucial distinctions being drawn are sharpened. On one hand, we have 'nature', meaning the empirical realm of reality, as distinct from 'fancy', meaning the realm of fantasy, of things that have no existence or basis in the real world; on the other, the distinction between 'fancy' in this sense and the imagination, which is here conceived not as synonymous with 'fancy', but as a faculty which does have a basis in the real world, in the domain denoted by 'nature' in this context. What Shakespeare is saying in effect through Cleopatra is that his imaginative creation of this idealized Antony has a substantive reality of its own. It's not to be dismissed as a fanciful, impalpable illusion without foundation in the actual world in which it was forged, because the 'strange form' it takes is the product of an imagination shaped by the inadequacy of the actual world. The same applies by extension to Shakespeare's imaginative creation of the Cleopatra delivering these lines. Both characters are perfect illustrations of the utopian realism of Shakespearean tragedy.

The utopian vision of *Antony and Cleopatra* is so compelling because it's never detached from the disenchanted realism that determines and validates it.

A Lass Unparalleled

Antony and Cleopatra, as supreme members of their world's ruling aristocracy, are obviously living embodiments of the repressive, hierarchical regimes over which they hold sway. Yet, as Shakespeare portrays them, they talk and behave in ways which allow them to embody onstage at the same time values diametrically opposed to the values they exemplify as potentates. We've already seen how Shakespeare achieves this with amazing economy in the opening scene of the play, but it's in the fourth and above all the fifth act that everything the first scene prefigures finds its most powerful expression.

Take the moving second scene of Act 4, in which Antony bids his household servants farewell on the eve of battle because, as he tells them, it may be the last time they will serve him. 'Let's tonight / Be bounteous at our meal' (4.2.9–10), he says, placing the emphasis as always on bounty. Then he takes each of them by the hand in turn:

> Give me thy hand,
> Thou hast been rightly honest; so hast thou,
> Thou, and thou, and thou. You have served me well
> And kings have been your fellows.

> (4.2.10–13)

'There is the double touch,' comments John Middleton Murry, 'which makes Antony Antony – the simple humanity of his handshake with his servants and the reminder that kings have done him the like office. In comparison with Antony, and in his own accustomed sight, servants and kings are one. If kings were his servants, so his servants are now made kings.' Antony wishes, indeed, that their positions could be reversed, and that he could become his servants, so that he might show his gratitude by serving them as they have served him: 'I wish I could be made so many men, / And all of you clapped up together in / An Antony, that I might do you service / So good as you have done' (4.2.16–19). Then he says:

> Well, my good fellows, wait on me tonight;
> Scant not my cups, and make as much of me
> As when mine empire was your fellow too
> And suffered my command.

> (4.2.20–3)

'It is the same thought as before,' writes Murry.

> They serve him now, where kings served him before; and by the change it is not
> Antony that is declined, but they who are advanced. They are become kings: fellows

of empire. A pathetic illusion, some may call it. But it is something rather different from this. Royalty – it is the great burden of this play – is no external thing; it is a kingdom and conquest of the human spirit, an achieved greatness.

Just as 'the nobleness of life' was redefined by Antony in the opening scene as nothing to do with birth and rank, but as consisting in the mutual relationship of equals in love, so royalty is redefined here as the greatness born of what Murry calls 'a grace of communion between men'. Not for a moment are we blinded to the fact that kings remain kings and servants remain servants in the rigidly hierarchical society that prevails both on and beyond the stage; on the contrary, we're made acutely aware of the gulf that divides the powerful from the powerless, the sovereign from the subjugated, from the first act to the last, and nowhere more than in this scene. But although the divisive reality to which the characters must remain in thrall cannot be changed, the way we the audience perceive them can be. It can be changed by transforming the meaning of the key terms that lock the status quo into place. The rhetorical strategies of reversal and equation Antony employs to salute his servants entail the knowledge that the relationship of king to subject, or servant to master, is not immutable, but can readily be imagined as inverted, or as dissolved altogether in the fellowship of equals Antony evokes. This knowledge is articulated not only rhetorically but also theatrically. The egalitarian spirit of the scene is physically enacted by Antony, as he takes each nameless servant by the hand and his words move them to tears; it's not just verbally evoked in our imagination as an abstract prospect, but bodied forth in performance as a tangible possibility.

The scene provides a paradigm of what the tragedy accomplishes: it dramatizes the historical reality of division and subjection, which dictates the protagonists' fate, from a visionary perspective *engendered by* that dehumanizing reality. It's this capacity to perceive things from the standpoint of what should bind human beings together in a common cause that sets Shakespearean tragedy apart and explains its unparalleled ability to transcend the age in which its characters and their fates are entrenched. That is nowhere more plainly the standpoint we're invited to adopt than at the tragic climax of *Antony and Cleopatra*, when Shakespeare ushers in his base-born Clown to upstage the Empress of Egypt on the threshold of her apotheosis. The Clown's right to converse quite unfazed with a queen on his own terms is dramatically asserted through a dialogue which enacts theatrically the erasure of rank that's achieved rhetorically throughout the denouement, and never more movingly than in Cleopatra's response to Iras's anguished cry, 'Royal Egypt! Empress!': 'No more but e'en a woman, and commanded / By such poor passion as the maid that milks / And does the meanest chores' (4.15.75–9).

A similar transvaluation takes place when Cleopatra cries:

> Where art thou, Death?
> Come hither, come! Come, come, and take a queen
> Worth many babes and beggars!

> (5.2.45–7)

Cleopatra remains an imperious monarch, rating herself above all inferior mortals as a prize worth seizing by Death. As such, she enlists 'babes and beggars' as epitomes of inferiority to emphasize by contrast the inestimable value of her majesty. But in so doing she makes 'babes and beggars' the currency in which value is calculated; she makes the kind of human beings she cites as being worth least the measure of a queen's worth. Her apostrophe of Death is the subliminal trigger for the vision that links beggars and babies, and that governs the dying moments of the tragedy. 'O eastern star!', exclaims Charmian, as the venom of the asp takes hold of her mistress's life; but as before, when she insisted that she was 'No more but e'en a woman, and commanded / By such poor passion as the maid that milks / And does the meanest chores', Cleopatra rejects this grandiose appellation in favour of a more modest metaphor, in which a baby again plays a crucial part: 'Peace, peace! / Dost thou not see my baby at my breast / That sucks the nurse asleep?' (5.2.307–9). Death liberates Cleopatra from her royalty to enjoy, if only for a moment in her imagination, something far superior to royalty: the simple human bond of nurturing motherhood.

That Charmian understands this too is confirmed by the words she speaks over Cleopatra's corpse: 'Now boast thee, Death, in thy possession lies / A lass unparalleled' (5.2.313–15). ('Every other great poet the world has known', observes Murry, 'would have been compelled to write: "A queen unparalleled".') With that echo of her mistress's apostrophe of Death the inversion of the normal hierarchy of values is complete: to be an ordinary, untitled 'lass unparalleled' is to be worth more than 'a queen / Worth many babes and beggars'. So when Charmian then says, as she gazes on Cleopatra's eyelids, 'Downy windows, close, / And golden Phoebus never be beheld / Of eyes again so royal!' (5.2.315–17), the word 'royal' has once more suffered a sea change. It reinstates the 'lass unparalleled' as a monarch, whose crown Charmian makes a tender point of straightening on her head. But in the same breath it redefines true royalty as a quality that owes nothing to rank, and everything to Cleopatra's identification of herself with 'the maid that milks / And does the meanest chores'.

The reasoning behind this inversion of values is the same as the reasoning behind Hamlet's proof that 'a king may go a progress through the guts of a beggar' and the Gravedigger's proof that 'There is no ancient gentlemen but gardeners, ditchers and gravemakers' (4.3.29–30, 5.1.29–30). The inversion does not abolish the cold fact of social division in the world outside the theatre. But through it the iniquitous reality of class society is exposed to the judgement of an imaginable human realm in which neither queens nor beggars exist. 'How weak a thing is Poetry?' wrote Donne in one of his sermons, 'and yet Poetry is a counterfeit Creation, and makes things that are not, as though they were'. When Charmian says of her royal mistress, 'Now boast thee, Death, in thy possession lies / A lass unparalleled', the source of the thrill the lines deliver is that through them we join that conceivable community of equals, if only for a moment, and judge the way things once were, and still are, on their utopian terms.

CHAPTER 10
CORIOLANUS: A WORLD ELSEWHERE

Antecedents and Affinities

For his final tragedy Shakespeare turned once again to Plutarch and to Rome, but this time to a Rome at the dawn rather than the end of the Republic, and to the story in Plutarch's *Lives* that enabled him to dramatize with unprecedented starkness the political issue of inequality, which lies at the root of all his tragedies in one way or another. The Rome of *Coriolanus* reveals, through the fierce power struggle between plebeians and patricians, the raw reality and brutal consequences of systemic social injustice. Shakespeare's last tragedy returns to grapple with the theme of class-war that had gripped him at the start of his career in the Jack Cade scenes of *2 Henry VI*, the play where the beginnings of Shakespearean tragedy can be glimpsed.

As early as *Titus Andronicus*, his first fully fledged tragedy and the first of his Roman tragedies, Shakespeare had the protagonist of his final tragedy in mind. Titus's son, Lucius, is explicitly likened to the latter when he marches on Rome to exact revenge at the head of a hostile foreign army. Lucius 'threats in course of this revenge to do / As much as ever Coriolanus did', having been, as he laments, 'unkindly banished / The gates shut on me', and forced 'To beg relief among Rome's enemies, / Who drowned their enmity in my true tears / And oped their arms to embrace me as a friend' (*TA* 4.4.65–7, 5.3.103–7). The same scenario, in which a once loyal warrior rounds in vengeful wrath on his society, recurs a decade later in Alicibiades' march on Athens in *Timon* before resurfacing as a core motif of *Coriolanus*. Its focus on a figure so alienated from the nation he had shed his blood for that he defects to the enemy to exact violent retribution plainly held an abiding fascination for Shakespeare. Nor is that surprising, given that such figures have obvious affinities with Hamlet, Lear and Timon himself, all of whom also become, albeit for quite different motives, implacably estranged from the regimes that had hitherto defined their identities and governed their existence; and all of whom might also be said to wage war on their societies, albeit as internal rather than actual exiles, and as lone individuals with words as their main or their only weapons.

Although his forte is cutting a bloody swathe through the ranks of his foes on the battlefield, and his first instinct is for action or silence rather than speech, Coriolanus is more than capable of weaponizing language himself, as the bilious invective he unleashes at the plebeians' expense attests. And, although he musters an entire Volscian army to lay siege to Rome in quest of his revenge, Coriolanus still conceives of himself as the same self-sufficient loner he insists on having been all along, and is still insisting that he is at the end, even after events have conspired to prove this conception of himself fatally deluded. In his determination to resist all claims on his compassion and 'stand / As if a man were author of himself / And knew no other kin' (5.3.35–7), Coriolanus is plainly a direct descendant of the crookbacked villain of 3 *Henry VI*, who brags of feeling 'neither pity, love nor fear' and declares:

> I have no brother; I am like no brother.
> And this word 'love', which greybeards call divine,
> Be resident in men like one another
> And not in me: I am myself alone.
>
> (5.6.68, 80–3)

The characterization of Coriolanus also owes a debt in this regard to Shakespeare's portrait of an equally ferocious warrior in the shape of Macbeth, the national hero feted as 'Bellona's bridegroom', whose watchword becomes 'for mine own good, / All causes shall give way' (1.2.55, 1.5.17, 3.4.133–4).

But it's his fellow Roman general, Titus Andronicus, who has the strongest claim to be the chief prototype of Coriolanus. Like Coriolanus, Titus is adulated as the invincible champion of Rome and merciless scourge of its enemies. Like Coriolanus, Titus can slaughter without pity or compunction, as the inflexible code of honour he prides himself on obeying dictates. His icy inhumanity is illustrated, as we've seen, when Tamora's appeal to him as a parent of sons himself to spare her son the ritual butchering that awaits him falls on deaf ears, and when Titus underscores the futility of appealing to him in that capacity by killing one of his own sons without a qualm for disobeying him. But Titus is being set up by Shakespeare in his first tragedy, just as Coriolanus will be in his last, in order to be cut down to size and subjected to violent retribution. Both tragedies force an arrogant, stone-hearted, patrician monster to empathize for the first time with the suffering of another: to feel the tug of the universal bond that ties him to his fellow human beings. The horrifying sight of his raped and mutilated daughter Lavinia unites Titus with her in an emotionally shattering 'sympathy of woe' (3.1.149), from which only their deaths, in a climactic scene of gruesome carnage, can deliver them. 'Wife, mother, child, I know not' (5.2.81) is Coriolanus's response to his lifelong friend Menenius's plea that he forswear his revenge on Rome. But when mother, wife and child confront him in the flesh with the same plea, the rights of kinship will not be denied: 'I melt,' confesses Coriolanus, 'and am not / Of stronger earth than others. / ... Not of a woman's tenderness to be / Requires nor child nor woman's face to see' (5.3.28–9, 129–30). When he surrenders completely to his mother's overpowering entreaty, and the 'boy of tears' (5.6.103) inside the remorseless killing-machine stands revealed, he signs the warrant for his ignominious death at the hands of the Volscians he has betrayed.

An Inventory to Particularize Their Abundance

It's important to keep the fate inflicted on Titus Andronicus in mind as a template for the fate inflicted on Coriolanus, because it makes one less prone to reach the same conclusion about Shakespeare's last tragedy as Coleridge reached: 'This play illustrates the wonderful philosophic impartiality of Shakespeare's politics.' That misconception remains the staple assumption of most critical accounts of *Coriolanus* to this day. The politically conservative thrust of this take on the play and its author isn't hard to discern. Shakespeare is commended for weighing the case for both the rulers and the ruled in Rome without tipping the scales in favour of either faction, thereby leaving the status quo unquestioned and intact. The fact that *Coriolanus* has elicited readings, and given rise to productions, that have pinned its allegiance with equal conviction, if not equal credibility, to the patrician as well as to the plebeian point of view is taken as further proof of its author's neutrality. But to construe *Coriolanus* as adopting an impartial attitude to the class-conflict at its heart is to miss the entire point of the play, which is to call the fact of class-conflict itself into question. That the tragedy as a whole can be aligned neither with the cause of the patricians nor with the cause of the plebeians is undeniable. But it's not because the pros and cons of their respective positions are so evenly balanced that it's impossible to arbitrate between them and the play leaves us locked in a political impasse. It's because *Coriolanus* is written *about* a class-divided society, but from an imaginative standpoint *beyond* class society.

Any doubt that such is the case ought to be dispelled, at the very latest, by the impact of the final encounter between Coriolanus and his mother, the emotional and moral *coup de théâtre* in which the tragedy is designed to culminate. But it ought to be apparent from the stunning opening scene, in which the battle lines between the ruling-class elite of Rome and the rest of the populace are drawn and the values at stake in their confrontation made clear. From two telling changes he makes to Plutarch's treatment of the plebeian revolt in his 'Life of Caius Martius Coriolanus' it's obvious where Shakespeare intends our sympathies to lie. Firstly, he decides to begin the play by plunging us into the thick of the rebellion, which Plutarch doesn't mention until well into his account; and secondly, unlike Plutarch he makes the people's chief grievances their impending starvation, due to the dearth of corn created by the patricians' hoarding of grain to raise its price, and Martius's adamant opposition to letting them buy corn 'at their own rates' (1.1.184) to save themselves from starving. Few scholars would now dispute that Shakespeare was at least partly motivated to make these alterations by the blatant parallels between the situation in the play and the reality of famine and grain-hoarding that fuelled the Midlands Revolt of 1607, in which his own county, Warwickshire, was embroiled.

This is how the tragedy begins:

Enter a company of mutinous Citizens with staves, clubs and other weapons

1 CITIZEN

Before we proceed any further, hear me speak.

ALL

Speak, speak.

1 CITIZEN

You are all resolved rather to die than to famish?

ALL

Resolved, resolved.

1 CITIZEN

First, you know Caius Martius is chief enemy to the people.

ALL

We know't, we know't.

1 CITIZEN

Let us kill him, and we'll have corn at our own price. Is't a verdict?

ALL

No more talking on't. Let it be done. Away, away.

2 CITIZEN

One word, good citizens.

1 CITIZEN

We are accounted poor citizens, the patricians good. What authority surfeits on would relieve us. If they would yield us but the superfluity while it were wholesome, we might guess they relieved us humanely. But they think we are too dear. The leanness that afflicts us, the object of our misery, is as an inventory to particularize their abundance; our sufferance is a gain to them. Let us revenge this with our pikes ere we become rakes; for the gods know, I speak this in hunger for bread, not in thirst for revenge.

2 CITIZEN

Would you proceed especially against Caius Martius?

ALL

Against him first. He's a very dog to the commonalty.

(1.1.1–26)

Coriolanus begins, in other words, where *King Lear* left off a couple of years earlier. But this time it's a commoner who voices the view of the relationship between rulers and ruled that Lear arrives at only after being forced to feel what the commoners of his kingdom *in extremis* are forced to feel. The author of *King Lear* is clearly audible in the First Citizen's lines: 'What authority surfeits on would relieve us. If they would yield us but the superfluity while it were wholesome, we might guess they relieved us humanely.' That word 'superfluity' recalls not only Lear's demand that the rich and powerful, who have far too much, 'shake the superflux' to the destitute and 'show the heavens more just', but also Gloucester's denouncing of 'the superfluous and lust-dieted man' and his hard-won conviction that 'distribution should undo excess / And each man have enough' (*KL* 3.4.35–6, 4.1.70, 73–4). The First Citizen uses the same synonym for the ruling class that surfeits on the superfluity as Lear uses when he mocks 'the great image of authority' he once embodied as nothing but a farmer's dog barking at a beggar (*KL* 4.6.150–5). And in his choice of the adverb 'humanely' to describe how those in authority should treat the commoners but do not, the First Citizen rests his case on a variant of the term that has served time and again as a touchstone of the egalitarian ethics underpinning Shakespearean tragedy. By treating the plebeians humanely the patricians would be treating them in a manner befitting the fact that they belong to the same species – to the same *kind* – as them.

When Coriolanus is later compelled to parade himself, robed 'in the gown of humility', before 'the common people' and he asks them what price he must pay to secure their approval of his election to the consulship, the First Citizen answers, 'The price is to ask it kindly' (2.3.39, 74, 91). Coriolanus takes the word 'kindly' in the shallow sense of pleasantly and politely, returning it flanked by sarcastic quotation marks in his reply: 'Kindly, sir, I pray let me ha't' (2.3.75). But by 'kindly' the First Citizen means the same as he meant by 'humanely' in the opening scene of the play, and the same as the anonymous senator means in Act 3, when he pleads with the tribunes to deal with Coriolanus by lawful rather than violent means, because 'It is the humane way' (3.1.229). For confirmation of the kinship and the crucial role of the words 'human / humane' and 'kind' in the moral economy of Shakespearean tragedy, we need look back no further, of course, than *Macbeth* and the phrases 'th' milk of human kindness' (1.5.17) and 'humane statute' (3.4.74), whose full import was unpacked in the chapter on that play.

Coriolanus's bridling at 'kindly' is symptomatic of his revulsion from anything that might entail acknowledging his kinship with 'the commonalty', to whom he is indeed, as the citizens cry in unison, 'a very dog' (1.1.26) in his pitiless cruelty. For the rationale of that revulsion, which the rest of the patriciate share with him in a less visceral form and refrain from voicing openly, we need to return to the First Citizen's speech at the start of the play. After saying the patricians would be treating them 'humanely', if they'd let them have the excess grain ('the superfluity') they've been hoarding before it rots, the First Citizen continues: 'But they think we are too dear. The leanness that afflicts us, the object of our misery, is as an inventory to particularize their abundance; our sufferance is a gain to them.' The citizen's argument pivots on his bitter pun on 'dear'. At first, 'But they think we are too dear' means 'But they wouldn't do that, because relieving us humanely would cost them too much'. As the following sentence unfolds, however, the meaning of 'But they think we are too dear' turns into something different, to wit: 'But they won't relieve us humanely, because we're too precious to them as we are, in our famine-stricken state.' They *need* to keep us hungry, poor and miserable, the First Citizen explains, so that our deprivation can serve 'as an inventory to particularize their abundance' – as a graphic measure of the excessive affluence the patricians enjoy at our expense. In short, concludes the First Citizen, 'our sufferance is a gain to them': they profit by our suffering, because they wouldn't *feel* wealthy *unless* we were suffering and *seen to be* suffering. There's not a more scathing indictment of the deliberately enforced structural injustice of class society in the whole of Shakespeare, not even in *King Lear*.

The First Citizen provides us in advance with a position from which to judge the motives not only of the 'chief enemy to the people' (1.1.6–7), Caius Martius (as Coriolanus is still known at this point), but also of his fellow patrician, Menenius Agrippa, who is about to enter to forestall the plebeians' storming of the Capitol to kill their chief enemy and secure the grain they desperately need. The insurgents are initially well disposed towards Menenius as 'one that hath always loved the people' (1.1.46–7); even the First

Citizen thinks him 'honest enough' (1.1.48–9) unlike the rest of the Senate. At this stage, therefore, we are well disposed towards Menenius too. But his first attempts at quelling the insurrection cut no ice with them. His insistence that the patricians have 'most charitable care' of them (1.1.60); his warning that they 'may as well / Strike at the heaven with [their] staves, as lift them / Against the Roman state' (1.1.62–4), which pointedly does not include the plebeians; and his blaming of the dearth of grain on 'The gods, not the patricians' (1.1.68) meet with this mordant riposte from the Second Citizen:

> Care for us? True, indeed, they ne'er cared for us yet. Suffer us to famish, and their store-houses crammed with grain; make edicts for usury, to support usurers; repeal daily any wholesome act established against the rich, and provide more piercing statutes daily to chain up and restrain the poor. If the wars eat us not up, they will; and there's all the love they bear us.
>
> (1.1.74–81)

To keep stalling the incensed citizenry Menenius is forced to try distracting them with 'A pretty tale' (1.1.84). The Second Citizen is immediately on guard against this ploy: 'Well, I'll hear it, sir. Yet you must not think to fob off our disgrace with a tale' (1.1.88–9). That Plutarch makes no mention of the citizens suspecting that they are being duped confirms the care Shakespeare is taking here to put the audience on guard too before Menenius begins. To make doubly sure that neither the citizens nor we risk falling for the infamous fable of the belly, Shakespeare has the Second Citizen repeatedly interrupt Menenius during his relation of the fable to question or heckle him, to Menenius's obvious irritation. The point of the age-old fable is to reconcile the subjects of any regime to their subjugation, on the grounds that their subjugation, far from being flagrantly unjust, is not only necessary and for their own good, but a testament to their rulers' benevolence. The speciousness of the fable's logic was already transparent in Shakespeare's time: 'the tale is notorious, and as notorious that it was a tale', observed Sir Philip Sidney in his *Apology for Poetry*. As relayed by Menenius in this context, and under sceptical fire from the Second Citizen, it forfeits whatever credence it might otherwise have hoped to gain.

To defend 'The senators of Rome' as 'this good belly', against which 'all the body's members' in the shape of the plebeians have ungratefully rebelled for being 'idle and unactive, / Still cupboarding the viand, never bearing / Like labour with the rest' (1.1.91, 94–6, 143) is insensitive, to say the least, given the famished state of the rebels facing Menenius. In their eyes, the Senate is rather 'the cormorant belly', as the Second Citizen dubs it, 'the sink [i.e. cesspool] o'th' body' (1.1.116–17). But, undeterred by the citizen's attempts to derail his allegory, Menenius has the gall to conclude it by contending that, although the belly receives all 'the general food at first', it does so only in order to distribute it selflessly to all the members of the body in the form of nourishment, 'that natural competency / Whereby they live' (1.1.126, 134–5). The glaring contradiction between this contention and the citizens being up in arms precisely because in their case the belly is not nourishing its members is brazenly ignored, as Menenius spells out the mendacious moral of his fable. The mutinous, starving plebeians owe everything, he assures them, to the senators of Rome:

> For examine
> Their counsels and their cares, digest things rightly,
> Touching the weal o'th' common, you shall find
> No public benefit which you receive
> But it proceeds or comes from them to you,
> And no way from yourselves.

(1.1.144–9)

Unlike those critics who think Menenius's argument proves effective, his hungry, irate auditors show no sign of being won over by it. On the contrary, their unresponsiveness prompts Menenius to taunt the obstreperous Second Citizen as 'the great toe of this assembly', deriding him as 'one o'th' lowest, basest, poorest / Of this most wise rebellion' (1.1.150–3). In his last words to them, which concede his failure to overcome their belligerence, he drops the mask of benevolent paternalism he had initially worn: 'But make you ready your stiff bats and clubs: / Rome and her rats are at the point of battle' (1.1.156–7). So much for Menenius being 'one that hath always loved the people' and 'honest enough'. Now the plebeians and we know how this apologist for the ruling class of Rome actually sees them, which is not as members of the Roman state at all, but as the subhuman vermin infesting it.

At this point, '*Enter* Caius Martius' (1.1.158, s.d.), whose first words make it plain that he shares Menenius's contempt for the commoners; the only difference being that he sees no reason to disguise it: 'What's the matter, you dissentious rogues, / That, rubbing the poor itch of your opinion, / Make yourselves scabs? (1.1.159–61). No other Shakespearean protagonist is given opening lines so clearly calculated to dispose the audience to dislike him. But they are merely the prelude to a twenty-line diatribe in the same vitriolic vein. The citizens' demand for corn they can afford is dismissed by Martius as gross impertinence. If the nobility would only let him use his sword, he says, he'd know how to deal with them: 'I'd make a quarry / With thousands of these quartered slaves as high / As I could pitch my lance' (1.1.193–5). He mimics them complaining that 'they were an-hungry' and mocks their protesting 'That hunger broke stone walls, that dogs must eat, / That meat was made for mouths, that the gods sent not / Corn for the rich men only' (1.1.200–3). He's appalled that another troop of insurgent citizens have succeeded in forcing the Senate to grant them tribunes 'to defend their vulgar wisdoms', because 'It will in time / Win upon power and throw forth greater themes / For insurrection's arguing' (1.1.210, 214–16). And his response to the news that 'the Volsces are in arms' and war thus imminent is: 'I am glad on't. Then we shall ha' means to vent / Our musty superfluity' (1.1.219–20). In other words: then we'll have a way of getting rid of our superfluous population the way we rid ourselves of our mouldy, superfluous grain. The echo of that telling word 'superfluity', so soon after its use by the First Citizen in a different spirit, is unmissable. Nothing could drive home Martius's inhumanity more emphatically than his equation of the plebeians with the very superfluity the nobility should be yielding them to relieve them humanely.

To Unbuild the City and to Lay All Flat

The idea that the play's political sympathies are equally divided between the mutinous citizens and Coriolanus – that there's as much to be said for and against the patricians as there is for and against the plebeians – has no foundation in the text. The values on which the plebeian rebellion against the patricians is based form the ethical bedrock on which the entire tragedy is built, and their validity is not impugned by the inefficacy of Rome's citizens as a political force. Shakespeare has no illusions about the flaws in the character of the plebeians as a class. He doesn't hesitate to show them at their spineless, gullible, vacillating worst as well as at their brave, defiant, resolute best. But he also shows that their flaws are the products of their deliberate immiseration and political impotence. The implementation of their will lies in the hands of their tribunes, whom Shakespeare portrays as a canny pair of manipulative, self-serving opportunists. The shrewdest citizens know that such power as they have is purely nominal in practice and that their exercising of it is a charade contrived to maintain the façade of republican democracy. 'We have power in ourselves to do it,' says the Third Citizen of their notional right to deny Coriolanus the consulship, 'but it is a power that we have no power to do' (2.3.4–5). Coriolanus reviles 'The common file' (1.6.43) of conscripted plebeians for retreating from the Volscians in the battle for Corioles, instead of charging headlong after him, heedless of their lives, into a bloodbath. But why should they rush to throw their lives away for a Rome whose patricians regard them not as citizens but as rodents, and at the behest of a barefaced 'enemy to the people' (1.1.6–7), who views war as an ideal means of culling them?

The aspects of the plebeians and their tribunes the play finds reprehensible pale beside its onslaught on the patrician class, which Coriolanus personifies. Coriolanus is Shakespeare's most sustained and unforgiving study of a type of man the ruling class of ancient Rome prided itself on breeding; a type that sadly did not die with the Roman empire but still thrives in modern guises all over the world. In Coriolanus we behold a savage caricature of those who have a vested interest in preserving the illusion of innate superiority on which their right to dominate and exploit the rest of society as they see fit depends. What Shakespeare found in Plutarch was a character who captures perfectly the callous, predatory ethos of Rome's governing elite, stripped of all the rhetorical chicanery, bogus altruism and travesties of democracy devised to mask it. Unlike his fellow aristocrats, Coriolanus is incapable of concealing his abhorrence of the plebeians, which he spews out in torrents of abuse on the slightest provocation: 'His heart's his mouth. What his breast forges, that his tongue must vent' (3.1.259–60). As a result, he finds himself being pressurized at one point by his mother to beg the plebeians' pardon for venting his hatred of them in public, which has jeopardized his election to the consulship. The scene where this takes place has no counterpart in Plutarch. It's invented by Shakespeare partly to foreshadow Coriolanus's last, fateful submission to Volumnia in Act 5, but mainly to illustrate the patricians' cynical dissembling of convictions indistinguishable from those held by Coriolanus. As Volumnia enters to persuade him, on behalf of the assembled senators, to bend his will to theirs, Coriolanus wonders why she doesn't applaud his intransigence, since she shares his disdain for commoners, and 'was wont / To call them woollen vassals, things created / To buy and sell with groats' (3.2.9–11). He succumbs nevertheless to his mother's insistence that he perform this pantomime of contrition to mollify the furious plebeians: 'I'll mountebank their loves, / Cog their hearts from them and come home beloved / Of all the trades in Rome' (3.2.133–5).

But the patrician plot to con the people into ratifying Coriolanus's election as consul backfires. Instead of stealing their hearts and coming home beloved of the commons he despises, Coriolanus is banished from his homeland 'As enemy to the people and his country' (3.3.117). Far from being fooled by his deferential posture, the citizens and their tribunes see Coriolanus for exactly what he is and always has been: the pawn of the patriciate, the vicious attack dog of Rome's ruling class. The reason why they banish him is the same as the reason why the citizens sought to kill him right at the start of the play. Of Coriolanus's attitude to the plebeians, the tribune Brutus says early on:

> ... to's power he would
> Have made them mules, silenced their pleaders and
> Dispropertied their freedoms, holding them
> In human action and capacity
> Of no more soul nor fitness for the world
> Than camels in their war, who have their provand
> Only for bearing burdens and sore blows
> For sinking under them.
>
> (2.1.240–7)

Everything we subsequently see and hear in the play confirms this to be nothing but the truth. The two anonymous Officers laying cushions in the Capitol in the following scene are deployed as a kind of Chorus by Shakespeare to provide independent corroboration of Coriolanus's pathological loathing of the people: 'he seeks their hate with greater devotion than they can render it him, and leaves nothing undone that may fully discover him their opposite' (2.2.17–19). When Coriolanus locks horns with the tribunes, 'The tongues o'th' common mouth' (3.1.22) he despises, the thinking that lies behind his rabid hatred of them and the commoners soon becomes clear. 'You speak of the people', Brutus says to him, 'as if you were a god / To punish, not a man of their infirmity' (3.1.83–4). Coriolanus speaks of them in this way, however, not because he's congenitally arrogant, but because he knows that to speak of them as 'a man of their infirmity' – as their equal, in other words – would be to subvert the fundamental premise on which the political supremacy of the patrician class depends.

Hence his turning from Brutus to warn the 'most unwise patricians' and 'reckless senators' that to give the people power through the tribunes is to undermine their own sovereignty by dissolving the hitherto inviolable distinction between nobles and commoners, the people and the patricians: 'You are plebeians, / If they be senators, and they are no less / When, both your voices blended, the great'st taste / Most palates theirs' (3.1.92–3, 102–5). Coriolanus beseeches the Senate to 'at once pluck out / The multitudinous tongue', by which he means the tribunes of the people, in order to preserve 'the fundamental part of state' (3.1.152, 156–7), by which he means the absolute sovereignty of the patriciate. The tribunes' response to Coriolanus's demand that the Senate 'throw their power i'th' dust' (3.1.171) is to demand his arrest 'as a traitorous innovator, / A foe to th' public weal' (3.1.175–6). In the ensuing uproar patricians and plebeians physically clash onstage, and we are left in no doubt that the entire political dispensation as it stands is indeed at stake.

To arraign Coriolanus for threatening the rights and liberties of the people would be, the First Senator protests, 'To unbuild the city and to lay all flat'; to which the tribune Sicinius retorts, 'What is the city but the people?', prompting all the citizens to cry as one, 'True, the people are the city' (3.1.198–200). The First Senator identifies the fate of Rome with the fate of the patrician Coriolanus, because like the rest of his class his conception of Rome excludes the plebeians. Sicinius is well aware of that, as his sarcastic reference to Coriolanus as 'this viper, / That would depopulate the city, and / Be every man himself' (3.1.265–7) suggests. That's why his retort to the senator insists that what constitutes the city of Rome is its people, not just the patricians, whose interests Coriolanus represents. The senator is right to fear that the fate of Rome as he conceives it is now riding on the fate of Coriolanus. The conviction and execution of Coriolanus as a traitor would 'lay all flat' inasmuch as it would destroy the city as the exclusive preserve and fiefdom of the patrician class. The consul Cominius picks up the senator's phrase and spells its revolutionary implications out plainly:

> That is the way to lay the city flat,
> To bring the roof to the foundation,
> And bury all which yet distinctly ranges
> In heaps and piles of ruin.
>
> (3.1.205–8)

The triumph of the tribunes over Coriolanus, and thus of the commons over the nobility, would ultimately lead, as Cominius perceives, to the collapse of the whole system of hierarchical distinctions ('all which yet distinctly ranges') on which the hegemony of the patrician class depends. 'To bring the roof to the foundation' would be the first step towards abolishing the division of society into patricians and plebeians altogether.

A Kind of Nothing

Once that is understood, the full significance of Coriolanus's characterization and the point of the harrowing tragic fate to which Shakespeare subjects him become clearer.

Coriolanus's hatred of the commoners and constant need to assert his superiority to them are born of a horror of having anything *in common with* them, of being in any sense the same as them. They are not symptoms of a destructive personality disorder peculiar to him that constitutes his 'tragic flaw', but attitudes endemic to his class that he exhibits openly and obsessively to an extreme degree. No one has summed up the patrician mentality as Shakespeare portrays it in *Coriolanus* more incisively, or with more caustic eloquence, than Hazlitt did two hundred years ago in his essay on the play. Nor has any critic made the subversiveness of that portrayal more immediately and personally evident to their readers. From *Coriolanus* we learn, writes Hazlitt, that to the feelings of 'the great' who rule society 'the interests of humanity and justice must curtsy':

> Their interests are so far from being the same as those of the community, that they are in direct and necessary opposition to them; their power is at the expense of *our* weakness; their riches of *our* poverty; their pride of *our* degradation; their splendour of *our* wretchedness; their tyranny of *our* servitude. ... The people are poor; therefore they ought to be starved. They are slaves; therefore they ought to be beaten. They work hard; therefore they ought to be treated like beasts of burden. They are ignorant; therefore they ought not to be allowed to feel that they want food, or clothing, or rest, that they are enslaved, oppressed, and miserable.

The implicit reasoning that underpins the attitudes and actions of Coriolanus as the epitome of Rome's ruling class are made uncompromisingly explicit here.

To perceive like Hazlitt that the interests of Coriolanus and his class 'are so far from being the same as those of the community, that they are in direct and necessary opposition to them', is to realize that Coriolanus's fanatical determination to deny any bond with the base-born and his fantasies of absolute autonomy are entirely consistent with those interests. From his point of view they make perfect sense. Hence his cultivation of the 'singularity' (1.1.273) that sets him apart from 'The common file' (1.6.43); his cry to the massed ranks of the latter before Corioli: 'O, me alone! Make you a sword of me!' (1.6.76); and his preposterously egotistical rejoinder to his banishment:

> You common cry of curs whose breath I hate
> As reek o'th' rotten fens, whose loves I prize
> As the dead carcasses of unburied men,
> That do corrupt my air, I banish you.

> (3.3.119–22)

Hence, too, the image of himself he leaves in the mind of his mother as he takes his leave of her: 'I go alone, / Like to a lonely dragon that his fen / Makes feared and talked of more than seen' (4.1.29–31); the tribunes' justified fear of his tyrannical, 'Self-loving' disposition, of his eventually 'affecting one sole throne / Without assistance' (4.6.32–3); his craving 'Not to be other than one thing' (4.7.42), as Aufidius puts it; and his final, vain attempt, when faced with his suppliant mother, wife and son, to 'stand / As if a man were author of himself / And knew no other kin' (5.3.35–7).

The more figuratively inhuman Coriolanus becomes in his mind's eye and in the eyes of others, the more completely he feels severed from every 'bond and privilege of nature' (5.3.25) that betrays his brotherhood with the masses, 'the mutable, rank-scented meinie' (3.1.68). That's why the thought of being made into a sword, of becoming a mindless, insensate, deadly weapon, springs so readily to his mind in the heat of battle. It's a thought in keeping with the horrific image of him as a ruthless juggernaut that makes his domineering mother's heart swell with pride:

> Before him
> He carries noise, and behind him he leaves tears.
> Death, that dark Spirit, in's nervy arm doth lie,
> Which being advanced, declines, and then men die.
>
> (2.1.153–6)

In Cominius's reports of both his homicidal prowess at Corioles and his later generalship of the Volscian army, his dehumanization is complete: 'from face to foot / He was a thing of blood, whose every motion / Was timed with dying cries' (2.2.106–9); 'He leads them like a thing / Made by some other deity than nature' (4.6.91–2). The stonily impassive Coriolanus that Menenius recalls having met in the final act is so void of humanity that he looks more like a machine than a man: 'When he walks, he moves like an engine and the ground shrinks before his treading. He is able to pierce a corslet with his eye, talks like a knell and his hum is a battery. He sits in his state as a thing made for Alexander' (5.4.18–22).

The defence of Coriolanus as a fearless, heroic warrior, driven into exile by an ungrateful country for which he had repeatedly risked his life and suffered so many wounds, and on which he understandably sought to take revenge, doesn't pass muster. As Wilson Knight points out, the truth is that 'no deep love of his country is his. His wars are not for Rome: they are an end in themselves. Therefore his renegade attack on Rome is not strange. … From the start he had seeds of treachery in his pride, unsubdued as it was to love of country or kin.' The seeds of treachery Knight has in mind are there in Martius's wish to be no one but his Volscian enemy Aufidius, if he had to be anyone but himself: 'Were half to half the world by th' ears and he / Upon my party, I'd revolt to make / Only my wars with him' (1.1.228–30); they are discernible, too, in Coriolanus's threat to his retreating troops before Corioles: 'Mend and charge home, / Or by the fires of heaven I'll leave the foe / And make my wars on you' (1.4.39–41). But it's his sudden, unconvincingly justified decision to defect to the Volscians that puts his indifference to his country and his real motive beyond question. For his wars, *pace* Knight, are more than 'an end in themselves' for Coriolanus. The ulterior satisfaction his martial supremacy affords him is the demonstration of his 'singularity', his *unlikeness* to his fellow men and to 'the many-headed multitude' (2.3.15–16) in particular. To that end it doesn't matter to him whether he fights against the Volscians or against Rome; all that matters is having a pretext for slaughtering other human beings without mercy and *en masse* to leave no doubt of their inferiority to him. As 'a thing of blood, whose every motion' is 'timed with dying cries', Coriolanus is, after all, only taking to its logical, lethal conclusion the denial of fundamental human equality on which the sovereignty of the class that he embodies depends.

The same denial accounts for his refusal of praise or gratitude for his heroic feats on the battlefield. 'This, too', observes Knight, 'is a kind of pride':

> He instinctively rejects thanks. Partly, perhaps, because he knows his deeds are not done for Rome, or, if he does not yet know it, fears he may be forced to know it and would rather turn his mind from the matter; and, partly, because the giving and receiving of praises is a kind of payment, a levelling of differences, a mingling with inferior beings who cannot have anything to give him worth his attention. He would stand alone, unpaid, self-praised only: 'he pays himself by being proud' [1.1.30–1].

That in the end is what the tragedy turns on: Coriolanus's dread of 'a levelling of differences, a mingling with inferior beings', which would force him to confront, as the epitome of his class, his consanguinity with his kind, and thus the groundlessness of the patricians' claim to dominion over the rest of society.

The story of Coriolanus for Shakespeare is thus first and foremost the story of his inexorable degradation and demeaning death. The animus of the upstart crow against the patrician class remains as strong in his last tragedy as it was in his first. Yet, by virtue of a paradox at the heart of Shakespearean tragedy, the lower Coriolanus sinks socially in his own eyes, the higher he rises as a human being in the eyes of the audience. The arc of his abasement can be traced from Volumnia's boast in Act 1 that 'He'll beat Aufidius's head below his knee / And tread upon his neck' (1.3.48–9) to the shocking stage direction that follows her son's sordid murder in the final scene: *'Aufidius stands on him'* (5.6.131, s.d.) – an act of desecration so brutal that a Volscian lord feels compelled to rebuke Aufidius: 'Thou hast done a deed at which valour will weep. / Tread not upon him' (5.6.134–5). The trajectory that terminates in that pitiless image of abjection begins in earnest with an appalled Coriolanus being forced to 'Appear i'th' market-place' wearing 'The napless vesture of humility' to show, 'as the manner is, his wounds / To th' people', and 'beg their stinking breaths' (2.1.228–30). The disastrous upshot of his protracted humiliation as a supplicant to the commons is the further humiliation of pretending to apologize and court their despised approval again. The outcome of that futile ruse is the ignominy of being banished from Rome by the plebeians he detests. When we next see Coriolanus, he is '*in mean apparel, disguised and muffled*' (4.4.1, s.d.), dressed in the same poor clothes as the commoners who banished him, and being treated accordingly by Aufidius's snooty servants, one of whom assures his master 'I'd have beaten him like a dog but for disturbing the lords within' (4.5.53–4). As if that were not demeaning enough, Shakespeare has Aufidius pointedly fail to recognize the unmuffled Coriolanus, asking him no less than five times what his name is, until he's obliged to identify himself. By the time Cominius encounters him in the Volscian camp Coriolanus no longer answers to any name, having become 'a kind of nothing, titleless' (5.1.13). It's in this alienated state of anonymity in exile that the final, mortifying blow to his self-esteem is struck by his own mother, when she pleads successfully with him to spare Rome.

But even as the blow falls, inflicting on Coriolanus the public shame he knows will prove fatal, its effect on him is transformed into an epiphany for the audience by a sublime stage direction without parallel in Shakespeare:

> (*He holds her by the hand, silent.*)
>   O, mother, mother!
> What have you done? Behold, the heavens do ope,
> The gods look down and this unnatural scene
> They laugh at. O, my mother, mother! O!
> You have won a happy victory to Rome
> But for your son, believe it, O, believe it,
> Most dangerously you have with him prevailed,
> If not most mortal to him. But let it come.
>
>   (5.3.182–9)

The silence of that moment, as the chastened son holds his mother's hand, is charged with the whole play's commitment to the cause of our common humanity. It's a commitment that *Coriolanus* shares with all the tragedies of Shakespeare that preceded it, for the ultimate source of the catastrophe in all of them is the denial of what human beings have in common and the systemic social, sexual and racial injustice that depends on that denial. But in none of the tragedies are the *revolutionary* political implications of the universal human perspective from which they are written more clearly adumbrated than in *Coriolanus*. For *Coriolanus* is predicated on the knowledge that only the transformation of the Roman republic into a genuine 'commonwealth' (4.6.14), a classless community of truly equal citizens, could solve the otherwise intractable problems it dramatizes.

The sight of Coriolanus holding Volumnia's hand in silence and his cry, 'O, mother, mother!', are so powerful and moving because they make the play's universal human viewpoint, and the egalitarian ethics it entails, visible in a single, simple image and audible in a single, simple word. In this moment the tragedy of Coriolanus becomes an unmistakably Shakespearean tragedy. It's the counterpart in *Coriolanus* of the moment when Macbeth is unnerved on the verge of murder by a vision of 'Pity, like a naked new-born babe' (1.7.21); the moment when Lear realizes that his royal robes conceal the same 'Unaccommodated man', the same 'poor, bare forked animal' as a beggar's rags (3.4.105–6); the moment when seeing the skulls of the high and mighty being battered by a sexton's spade prompts Hamlet to observe: 'Here's fine revolution if we had the trick to see't' (F: 5.1.87–9). For at this moment in *Coriolanus*, as the universal bond between mother and son prevails, we see and hear the vulnerable, compassionate human being imprisoned within Coriolanus since childhood. There turns out to have been locked inside him all along, in the guise of 'a kind of nothing', the potential to become, like all Shakespeare's tragic protagonists, a completely different kind of person in the completely different kind of world that his fate makes conceivable *for us.* 'There is a world elsewhere' (3.3.134), declares Coriolanus as he turns his back on Rome, and that defiant declaration resonates in the mind long after the play has ended, because it enshrines the passionate conviction from which every Shakespearean tragedy draws its enduring power.

WORKS CITED

All quotations from the plays and poems are taken from The Arden Shakespeare (Third Series) editions. In the case of quotations from *Hamlet* and *Othello*, the bracketed line references indicate the points at which the text of the Folio edition is cited in preference, or in addition, to the text of the Arden edition. The punctuation of a few quotations has been silently emended to reinstate accepted editorial alternatives to the punctuation introduced or omitted by the Arden editor. Wherever a play's title is cited in the line reference after a quotation to avoid confusion about its source, I have used the following abbreviations: *Antony and Cleopatra*: AC; *As You Like It*: AYLI; *Coriolanus*: COR; *Hamlet*: HAM; *Henry VI, Part 2*: 2HVI; *Henry VI, Part 3*: 3HVI; *Julius Caesar*: JC; *King Lear*: KL; *Macbeth*: MAC; *The Merchant of Venice*: MV; *Othello*: OTH; *Richard II*: RII; *Romeo and Juliet*: RJ; *Timon of Athens*: TIM; *Titus Andronicus*: TA.

Of the two quotations from Donne, the one in the chapter on *Macbeth* can be found in *Devotions upon Emergent Occasions*, ed. Raspa (1975) and the one in the chapter on *Antony and Cleopatra* in *The Sermons of John Donne*, vol. 4, ed. Simpson and Potter (1953–62). Quotations from Dr Johnson are taken from *Samuel Johnson on Shakespeare*, ed. Woudhuysen (1989). The quotations from Coleridge, De Quincey, Goethe, Heine, Hugo, Anna Jameson and Schlegel can be found in *The Romantics on Shakespeare*, ed. Bate (1992). All quotations from Hazlitt come from his *Characters of Shakespear's Plays* (1817). *A Defence of Poetry* (1821) is the source of Shelley's remark about *King Lear*. Emerson's reflection on Shakespeare appears in John Gross's anthology *After Shakespeare* (2002). Taine's observation on *Hamlet* is taken from his *History of English Literature* (1863–4), Dowden's from *Shakspere: A Critical Study of his Mind and Art* (1875). For his comments on Brutus and on Hamlet, see Swinburne's *A Study of Shakespeare* (1880). The quotations from Chesterton can be found in *The Soul of Wit: G. K. Chesterton on William Shakespeare*, ed. Ahlquist (2012), and those from George Bernard Shaw, unless otherwise specified, in *Shaw on Shakespeare*, ed. Wilson (1961).

All quotations from A. C. Bradley's *Shakespearean Tragedy* (first published 1904) are taken from the third edition (1992). The Joyce quotation in the chapter on *Macbeth* comes from *Ulysses*. Quotations from John Middleton Murry are to be found in his study *Shakespeare* (1936). G. Wilson Knight's observations on *Macbeth* are quoted from his essays on the play in *The Wheel of Fire* (1930; 4th edition, 1949) and *The Imperial Theme* (1931; 3rd edition, 1951); the former book is also the source of the quotations from Knight's essays on *Hamlet* and *King Lear*, and the latter is where the quotations from his essays on *Antony and Cleopatra* and *Coriolanus* can also be found. The quotation from T. S. Eliot in Chapter 8 is taken from his essay 'The Use of Poetry and the Use of Criticism' (1933). Alfred Polgar's view of Richard II is quoted in Clive James, *Cultural*

Works Cited

Amnesia (2007). The quotation from François Mauriac comes from his *Journal,* 3rd series, trans. Foulke (1940). Bakhtin's comment on Shakespeare is taken from *Rabelais and his World,* trans. Iswolsky (1968). Auden's observations on *Julius Caesar, Othello* and *Antony and Cleopatra* can be found in his *Lectures on Shakespeare,* ed. Kirsch (2000). Adorno's aphorism about art in Chapter 7 appears in *Philosophy of Modern Music,* trans. Mitchell and Blomster (2004). The essay on *Othello* by Kenneth Burke quoted from in Chapter 6 is collected in *Kenneth Burke on Shakespeare,* ed. Newstok (2007). Harry Levin's description of *Hamlet* is cited by Harold Jenkins in his edition of the play (1982) for The Arden Shakespeare (Second Series). Jan Kott's summary of Hamlet's dilemma appears in *Shakespeare Our Contemporary* (1961), John Bayley's in *Shakespeare and Tragedy* (1981). Harry Berger's remarks on *King Lear* and *Macbeth* come from *Making Trifles of Terrors: Redistributing Complicities in Shakespeare* (1997). Stephen Booth's phrase quoted in Chapter 7 is borrowed from his book *King Lear, Macbeth, Indefinition and Tragedy* (1983). Both quotations from Harold Bloom are drawn from *Shakespeare: The Invention of the Human* (1999). Terry Eagleton's *William Shakespeare* (1986) is the source of his comment on the witches in *Macbeth*. The quotation in Chapter 7 from Wittgenstein can be found in *Ludwig Wittgenstein: Cambridge Letters,* ed. von Wright and McGuinness (3rd edition, 1997); the quotation in Chapter 5 from George Steiner in *After Babel* (1975); and the quotation in Chapter 7 from Alain Badiou in *The Idea of Communism,* ed. Douzinas and Zizek (2010). The translations of the quotations from Heiner Müller's essay 'Shakespeare: Eine Differenz' and Brecht's *Die Massnahme* are both mine.

INDEX

Adorno, Theodor 167, 288
alienation xiv, 6, 12, 35, 45, 46, 50, 51, 93, 114, 122,
    125, 155, 162, 169–70, 177, 219, 236, 237,
    271, 284
    see also estrangement
anachronism 37, 38, 57, 109, 111–12, 119, 175–6,
    247–8
    see also future; prolepsis; prophecy; utopia and
    utopianism
anti-Semitism 142–3
    see also race and racism
Antony and Cleopatra vii, xiii, 12, 31, 35, 46, 52,
    119, 255–69
    Antony 12, 46, 256–68
    Cleopatra 12, 35, 46, 256–8, 260–9
    Clown 257, 258, 268
    Enobarbus xiii, 263–4, 266
    Plutarch ('Life of Marcus Antonius') 255,
        256–7, 263, 263–4
    Rome 255, 256, 260, 261, 262, 265
apocalypse 37, 63–4, 170, 171, 230, 243
As You Like It 239
Auden, W. H. 63, 139, 170, 265, 288
audience xiii, 6, 11–12, 15, 16, 17–18, 22–3, 24,
    25–6, 27, 28, 31, 33, 36–7, 38, 42, 47, 50–1,
    57, 58, 63, 71, 73, 74, 84–5, 90, 91, 92, 94,
    104, 113, 114–15, 118, 120, 121, 124, 127,
    133, 138, 144, 156, 157, 159, 163, 164, 165,
    166–7, 170, 175, 176, 182, 193, 196, 198,
    202, 203, 206, 208, 209, 216, 218, 229, 238,
    240, 241, 244, 248, 249, 255, 257, 258, 259,
    262, 264, 265, 268, 276, 277, 283, 284

babies and children xiv, 7, 21, 32, 33, 38, 39–40,
    43–4, 81, 97, 122, 172, 177, 184, 211, 214,
    217, 225, 228, 229, 233, 235, 239, 241–2,
    243, 247, 268–9, 272, 284
Badiou, Alain 199, 288
Bakhtin, Mikhail 167, 288
Ball, John 108
Balzac, Honoré de 240
Bayley, John 102–3, 288
beggars 46, 104, 106–7, 109, 119, 165, 169, 170,
    171, 173, 174, 182–3, 189, 190, 192, 194–5,
    197, 202, 203, 204–5, 256, 260, 261, 268–9,
    274, 284
Berger, Harry 230, 240, 288

Blake, William 158
blood 5, 8, 11, 21, 24, 26, 32–3, 34, 43, 47, 55, 58,
    59, 63, 64, 72, 73, 77, 83, 91, 99, 121, 122,
    134, 205, 207, 217, 220, 226, 231, 237–8,
    239, 241, 243–5, 246, 247–8, 250, 271, 278,
    282, 283
Bloom, Harold 156, 218, 288
Booth, Stephen 170, 288
Bradley, A. C. xii–xiv, 68–9, 71, 88–9, 93, 112, 116,
    119, 120–1, 132, 133, 144, 145–6, 146–9,
    150, 156, 158, 159–60, 164, 166–7, 178,
    199–200, 212–13, 214–16, 222–3, 230–1,
    249, 263, 287
Brecht, Bertolt 207, 288
Burke, Kenneth 136–7, 154, 288

Charles I 165
Charles II 166
Chesterton, G. K. 97, 109, 175, 287
Cinthio, Giraldi (*Hecatommithi*) 113–14, 119, 136,
    145, 149
civil war 5, 6, 7–8, 26, 28, 55, 168, 255
class and class society 14, 18, 25–6, 55, 56, 57–8, 64,
    83, 89, 95, 103, 104, 107, 111, 113, 118, 120,
    123, 139, 151, 152, 170, 174, 176, 190, 195,
    242, 244, 255, 258, 269, 271, 273, 274, 275,
    277, 278–9, 280–1, 283, 284
    see also hierarchy; rank
Cockayne, Land of 16
Coleridge, Samuel Taylor 60–1, 68, 111–12, 118,
    120–1, 145, 147, 167, 212–13, 273, 287
commonwealth 13–14, 16–17, 22, 63, 108, 165–6,
    173, 248, 284
complicity 37, 47, 74, 82, 91, 96, 134, 156, 162, 182,
    202, 219–30, 240, 245
Coriolanus xv, 12, 13, 28, 31, 34, 35, 255, 271–85
    Act 1, scene 1 273–8
    Coriolanus 12, 28, 34, 35, 271–5, 278–85
    fable of the belly 276–7
    patricians 271, 273, 274–6, 278–81, 283
    plebeians 271–80, 283
    Plutarch ('Life of Coriolanus') 271, 273, 276, 278
    Rome 271–3, 277, 278–9, 280, 281, 282, 283,
        284, 285
    Volumnia 35, 279, 283, 284
custom and habit 92, 96, 119, 128, 180–1, 187–8,
    239, 264

Index

Dante 256

death 6, 11, 18, 21, 32, 37, 38, 41–2, 47, 51–3, 55,
70, 79, 82, 87, 91, 94–5, 97–8, 107–11, 134,
135–6, 140–1, 142, 164–5, 168, 170, 173,
176, 178, 179, 188, 190, 198, 213, 238, 244,
248–9, 250–1, 257, 264, 266, 268–9, 272
see also epitaphs; posthumous perspective

De Quincey, Thomas 241, 287

disguise 19, 20, 35, 37, 43, 47, 61, 140, 165, 184,
189, 238, 263, 283

Donne, John 248–9, 269, 287

doubles 6, 73–82, 181, 212, 218, 219, 221–2, 223–30

Dowden, Edward 112

Dryden, John (*All for Love*) 257–9, 263

Eagleton, Terry 236, 288

egalitarianism 16, 22, 43–4, 104, 106, 111, 119,
142–3, 173, 195–6, 260–1, 268, 274, 284
see also equality and inequality

Eliot, T. S. 31, 63, 208, 287

Emerson, Ralph Waldo 111, 121, 287

empathy 5, 17, 22–3, 27, 39–43, 95, 104, 122, 140,
142, 165, 174, 182, 193, 272

Empson, William 248

epitaphs 52, 104, 172
see also death; posthumous perspective

equality and inequality xiii, xiv, 17, 22, 45–6, 50,
107, 108, 111, 113, 118–19, 142–3, 144, 152,
173–4, 194–6, 201, 205, 256, 260–1, 265,
268–9, 271, 279, 283, 284
see also egalitarianism

estrangement 8, 33–4, 52, 97, 102, 117, 162, 163,
237, 238, 271
see also alienation

First Folio 3, 41, 241

Florio, John 248

future xiv, 11, 44, 45, 46, 109, 111–12, 113, 119, 170,
172, 178, 206, 214, 216, 217, 218, 224, 229,
241, 242, 247–8, 251
see also anachronism, prolepsis; prophecy;
utopia and utopianism

gender 11, 39, 94, 104, 111, 116, 131, 120, 128, 134,
136, 137, 139, 142, 144, 236, 243
see also manhood and masculinity; misogyny;
patriarchy

ghosts 64, 67, 70, 71, 75, 76, 82, 84, 87, 88, 89,
92, 93, 95, 97, 99–101, 104, 120, 218, 219,
234–5, 236, 238, 244, 247, 250

Goethe, Johann Wolfgang von 68, 71, 287

Greene, Robert 18–21, 35

Hall, Edward (*Chronicle*) 35

Hamlet vii, xiv, 10, 12, 13, 27, 35, 39, 52, 55, 56,
67–112, 119, 121–2, 141, 144–5, 147, 156,

160, 170–1, 173, 175, 199, 208, 218, 222,
244, 250, 257, 261, 263, 265, 269, 271, 284

Claudius 67, 69, 71, 72, 74–7, 79–82, 83, 84–5,
86–7, 88, 89–91, 93, 95–6, 98–9, 103, 105-7,
109, 110

doubles 73–82

Fortinbras 70, 74, 75, 82, 89, 93, 101

Gertrude 67, 78–9, 80, 82, 85, 87, 88, 89, 90,
91–2

Ghost 67, 70, 71, 75, 76, 82, 84, 87, 88, 89, 92,
93, 95, 97, 99–101, 99, 104, 170, 218

Gravedigger 13, 107, 111, 141, 160, 173, 175,
199, 257, 199, 257, 258, 269

Hamlet xiv, 10, 12, 13, 27, 35, 39, 52, 56, 67–
107, 109, 119, 144–5, 147, 156, 170–1, 173,
175, 218, 222, 244, 250, 261, 269, 271, 284

Laertes 67, 73, 74–5, 81–2, 83–4, 89, 90, 91, 93,
101, 105

language 83, 84, 85–6, 100–1, 111

madness 67, 73, 76, 80, 92, 93, 97

Mousetrap, The (*The Murder of Gonzago*) 71,
78–80, 83, 91, 105

Ophelia 67, 73, 83, 89, 92, 95–6, 101, 105, 107, 171

Polonius 67, 71, 72, 73, 74, 76, 82, 89–90, 92,
95–6, 104–5, 106, 111–12

revenge 67, 69–70, 71, 74, 75–6, 77–8, 80, 81–4,
92, 93, 95, 96, 97, 98–100, 103, 105

Rosencrantz and Guildenstern 67, 68, 71, 72,
76, 80, 89–90, 91, 92–3, 104, 105, 106

soliloquies 69–70, 73–4, 75, 78, 80–1, 86–8, 91,
92, 93–5, 98, 101, 103–4

Hazlitt, William 112, 143–4, 156, 217, 218, 261,
281, 287

Heine, Heinrich 236, 287

Henry IV Part 2 109

Henry VI Part 1 3

Henry VI Part 2 xv, 3–18, 21–2, 25, 28, 31, 32, 35,
36, 39, 52, 55, 57, 108, 110, 167–8, 170,
172–3, 255, 271

Gloucester, Duke Humphrey of 4–6, 32

Henry VI 3–7, 12–13, 14, 17–18, 22, 22–3,
23–4, 25, 33, 52, 167–8, 170

Jack Cade 6, 13–18, 21–3, 24, 25–6, 28, 32, 35,
38, 57, 108–9, 173, 198, 271

Henry VI Part 3 xv, 3, 6, 7, 11, 12, 18–21, 22–8, 31,
32–3, 35, 36, 39, 52, 55–6, 72, 167–9, 170,
249, 255, 272

Henry VI 7–12, 12–13, 22, 23–4, 25, 26–7, 33,
52, 72, 167–8, 170, 173, 249

Richard of Gloucester 11, 22–8, 32–3, 35, 38,
249, 272

Heywood, Thomas 36

hierarchy 5, 6, 11, 16, 22, 25, 57, 61, 95, 104, 108,
111, 150, 151, 152, 153, 171, 195–6, 225,
234, 258, 261, 267–9, 280
see also class and class society; rank

Higgins, John (*Mirror for Magistrates*) 164
historicist criticism xii, xiv, 112, 208
Holinshed, Raphael (*Chronicles*) 35, 164, 225, 229
Hugo, Victor 102, 287
human/humane and humanity xiv, 5, 10, 12, 39,
    40–1, 43, 46, 51, 64, 94, 97, 98–9, 101,
    103–4, 105, 107, 109, 111, 122, 143–4, 147,
    162, 167, 169, 171, 174, 178, 184, 185, 186,
    188, 192, 195–7, 199, 200, 206, 207, 232,
    237, 239, 240, 242, 241–4, 247–9, 250–1,
    261, 264, 265, 267–9, 272, 274–5, 278, 279,
    281, 282, 283, 284
    see also inhumanity; kind and kindness

imagination xiv, 5, 9, 13, 16, 22, 24, 27, 32, 36, 38,
    43, 50, 55, 64, 69, 76, 77, 88, 98, 102, 109–10,
    111, 114, 118–19, 121, 128, 142, 143–4, 152,
    154, 156, 160, 167, 168, 170, 172, 174, 186,
    187–8, 189, 190, 195, 196, 198, 201–3, 204,
    205, 208, 211, 213–14, 232, 237, 242, 248,
    255, 258, 261, 265, 266, 268, 269, 273
inhumanity xiii, 8, 21, 26, 33, 35, 37, 38, 40, 119, 122,
    143, 144, 147, 154, 167, 172, 174, 178, 181,
    206, 207, 219, 229, 243, 248, 272, 277–8,
    282
    see also human/humane and humanity
innocence 4, 32, 37, 41, 42, 43–4, 55, 61, 91, 96,
    122, 129, 132, 133–4, 142, 149, 213, 214,
    239, 240–1, 244

James I 37, 163, 165, 194, 225
Jameson, Anna 263, 287
Jaspers, Karl 196
Johnson, Samuel 31, 55, 64, 72, 101, 103, 159,
    163–4, 166, 200, 287
Jones, Ernest 69
Jonson, Ben 239
Joyce, James (*Ulysses*) 154, 224, 287
Julius Caesar 31, 55–64, 110, 170, 173, 174, 255, 261
    Act 1, scene 1 56–7
    Antony 56, 58, 59, 61, 62–3, 64, 110
    Brutus 55–6, 57, 58–64
    Cassius 58, 59, 61–2, 62–3, 64
    Julius Caesar 55–64
    Rome 55, 56, 57, 58, 60, 63, 64
justice and injustice xiii, xiv, 13, 14–15, 22, 26, 37,
    40, 45, 50, 69, 78, 93, 111, 113, 118, 133, 136,
    143, 144, 153, 163, 173, 174, 187, 200–1,
    204–5, 207, 208, 222, 271, 275, 281, 284

Kermode, Frank 166
kind and kindness 4, 10, 28, 34, 84, 93, 102, 104,
    134, 144, 171, 177, 179, 194, 196, 197, 198,
    199, 204, 207, 232, 241, 243, 247, 248–9,
    251, 271, 275, 283
    see also human/humane and humanity

King Lear 12, 13, 28, 31, 33–4, 37, 39, 40, 46, 160,
    163–206, 208, 240, 250, 260, 261, 263, 271,
    274, 275, 284
    blindness and sight 164–5, 168, 176, 179, 186,
        190, 191, 197–8, 199, 201, 202–3, 204
    Cordelia 34, 46, 163–4, 165–6, 168, 169, 176–9,
        180–1, 182, 183–4, 184–5, 187, 188, 191,
        198, 201
    custom 180–1, 187–8
    Edgar 165–6, 170, 172, 176, 177, 180, 182–3,
        184, 188–91, 195–6, 197, 199, 201–4
    Fool 160, 164, 165, 166, 173, 175–6, 179, 183–7,
        192–3, 196–7, 199
    Gloucester, Earl of 28, 164–5, 166, 168, 171,
        173, 176, 180, 181, 182–3, 188, 190–1, 197–
        205, 274
    Goneril 35, 165, 176, 178, 183, 184, 192, 193
    Kent, Earl of 165, 166, 167, 175, 178–9, 180,
        183, 184, 185, 188, 189, 192–3, 196, 197
    King Lear 12, 13, 28, 33–4, 40, 46, 164–73, 174,
        175, 176–9, 180, 181, 182, 183–8, 189–97,
        198, 199, 200–1, 202, 203–6
    King Leir, The True Chronicle History of 164,
        171, 180
    madness 164–5, 171, 174, 178–9, 188, 189, 194,
        197, 199, 203, 204
    nothing 169, 171, 172, 176–7, 178, 179, 182,
        183, 185, 186, 188–9, 197
    Poor Tom 13, 165, 168, 171, 174, 176, 182–3,
        187, 188–91, 194–7, 199, 200, 201, 203
    Regan 35, 176, 178, 182, 192, 193, 198
    sleeping and waking 180, 185, 186–8, 193
King's Men 107, 163, 165, 225
Knight, G. Wilson 112, 178, 226, 227, 236, 249, 265,
    282–3, 287
Kott, Jan 102, 288
Kozintsev, Grigori 205

Lamb, Charles 121, 166–7
language xiv, 17, 27, 45, 46–50, 83, 84, 85–6, 100–1,
    111, 121, 167, 173, 179, 219–22, 249, 260, 271
    see also names; narratives
Levin, Harry 101, 288
Lyotard, Jean-Francois 243

Macbeth xii, xiv, 12, 28, 39, 44, 55, 71, 156, 160, 186,
    199, 207–51, 255, 257, 263, 272, 275, 284
    babies and children 211, 214, 217, 225, 228,
        229, 233, 235, 239, 241–2, 243, 247
    Banquo 209, 210–13, 217, 219, 221, 222, 225–7,
        233, 234, 236, 238, 244, 245, 246–7, 249, 250
    blood 217, 220, 226, 231, 237–8, 239, 241,
        243–5, 246, 247–8, 250
    complicity 219–30, 240, 245
    doubles 212, 218, 219, 221–2, 223–30
    Duncan 235, 237, 238, 242, 243–6, 249

Index

human/humane 207, 232, 237, 239, 240, 242, 241–4, 247–9, 250–1 (*see also* inhumanity)
innocence 213, 214, 239, 240–1, 244
kind and kindness 207, 232, 241, 243, 247, 248–9, 251
Lady Macbeth 213–15, 217, 220, 221–2, 231–3, 234, 236, 237, 239, 240–2, 244–5, 246, 250
language 219–22, 249
Macbeth xiv, 12, 28, 39, 71, 156, 186, 207–51, 272, 284
Macduff 217, 218, 221, 227–30, 235, 245, 249
Malcolm 218, 221, 225, 227–8, 229–30, 232, 235, 245
manhood and masculinity 209, 214, 222, 231–6
milk 144, 207, 214, 220, 230, 231, 232, 241–2, 247, 250
Porter 159, 199, 222, 235–6, 244, 257, 258
sleep and sleepwalking 209, 226, 232, 235–6, 238, 239, 243–4, 245, 246, 247, 250
soliloquies 211–14, 220, 226–7, 232, 237, 241, 242–3, 249, 250–1
witches 209–13, 215–23, 224, 225–6, 227, 236, 239, 250
Macready, William 166
madness 32, 35, 37, 43, 67, 73, 76, 80, 92, 93, 97, 134, 154, 164–5, 171, 174, 178–9, 188, 189, 194, 197, 199, 203, 204, 228, 240
manhood and masculinity 45, 64, 104, 135, 137, 154, 155, 160, 209, 214, 222, 231–6
see also gender; misogyny; patriarchy
Marlowe, Christopher 19, 250
Marx, Karl 49, 199
Mauriac, François 239–40
Measure for Measure 163
Middleton, Thomas 171
Midsummer Night's Dream, A 39
misanthropy 39, 92–3, 95, 171, 172
misogamy 95, 130
misogyny 95–7, 126, 128, 130–1, 137, 142, 153, 154–5, 156, 171
Montaigne, Michel de 101–2, 140, 181, 187–8, 195, 239, 248, 256
moralism and morality 26, 38, 134, 148, 155, 205, 240
morality plays 98, 135, 155, 209, 222, 257
Müller, Heiner 112, 288
Murry, John Middleton 101, 102, 103, 138, 155, 157, 185, 240–1, 251, 267–8, 269, 287

names 10, 14, 19, 32, 38, 47–9, 50, 62, 70, 73, 75, 79, 90, 106, 107, 113, 114–15, 119, 122, 125, 134–5, 162, 172, 173, 183, 184, 186, 189, 198–9, 216, 220, 221, 257, 268, 283–4
see also language; narratives
narratives 47, 50, 55, 69, 113, 132, 157–62, 195
see *also* language; names

Nashe, Thomas 19
Nietzsche, Friedrich xiv, 44, 172
nihilism 39, 172, 250–1
nothing 51, 52, 69–70, 98, 106, 155, 169, 171, 172, 176–7, 178, 179, 182, 183, 185, 186, 188–9, 197, 211, 213, 237, 251, 280, 284, 285

Okonedo, Sophie 258
Olivier, Laurence 68, 218
Othello xii, 12, 35, 51, 71, 113–62, 166, 174, 203, 208, 215, 255–6, 258, 259, 263, 265
   Brabantio 114–15, 117–18, 119, 120–1, 123–5, 151–2, 154, 158–9
   Cassio 126–7, 128, 129, 130, 131, 131–2, 135, 136, 137–8, 142, 145–6, 148–50, 152–3, 154, 155, 157–8, 159, 160
   Clown 159–61
   cuckoldry 127, 128, 135, 140–1, 142, 145, 146, 152–3, 154, 155, 156, 158
   Desdemona 51, 113–18, 119–21, 123–5, 126, 127, 128–42, 145, 149, 151, 152, 153, 154, 155, 158, 159, 161
   handkerchief 126, 131–2, 136–8, 157
   Iago 28, 35, 113–15, 117, 120, 121, 122–3, 124, 125–30, 131, 134, 135, 137–8, 142, 144–51, 160–1
   jealousy, sexual 126–8, 135, 137–8, 140–1, 145–6, 152, 154, 157, 162
   Lodovico 51, 139–40, 141–2, 155, 162
   misogyny 95, 126, 128, 130–1, 137, 142
   'motiveless malignity' 135, 143–55
   narratives 157–62
   Othello 12, 35, 51, 71, 113–28, 129, 130, 131–7, 138–9, 140–1, 141–2, 145–6, 148–50, 151–3, 154–6, 157–62, 203, 255, 256, 265
   patriarchy 118, 128, 130, 134, 135, 138, 142, 155, 157, 160
   racism 113–25, 126, 142–3, 151–2, 153, 166
   revenge 122, 124, 127–8, 141–3, 145–6, 148, 152–3, 156
Ovid (*Metamorphoses*) 36, 46–7, 50, 138

patriarchy 39, 40, 48, 51, 118, 128, 130, 134, 135, 138, 142, 155, 157, 160, 166, 169, 174, 181
Peasants' Revolt 108
Peele, George 19
Plutarch 55, 171, 255, 256–7, 263–4, 271, 273, 276, 278
Polanski, Roman 225
Polgar, Alfred 169, 288
posthumous perspective 9, 53, 79, 95, 107, 170, 172
   see also death; epitaphs
potential, human xiv, 12, 25, 37, 41, 45, 49, 50, 93, 104, 111, 128, 130, 143, 144, 161, 184, 185, 189, 196, 206, 207, 243, 265, 285

prolepsis 28, 52, 213, 248
  see also anachronism; future; prophecy; utopia
    and utopianism
prophecy xiv, 59, 75, 107, 112, 136, 166, 173, 175–6,
    193, 205–6, 210–11, 213–14, 215, 216, 223,
    226, 227, 243, 247
  see also future; prolepsis; utopia and
    utopianism

race and racism 11, 39, 94, 113–25, 126, 139, 142–3,
    144, 151–2, 153, 166, 243, 255, 258
rank 6, 10, 11, 15, 19, 20, 39, 48, 56, 61, 64, 74, 94,
    98–103, 104, 107, 108, 111, 120, 138, 149,
    150, 152, 173, 196, 198, 201, 225, 234, 243,
    244–5, 247, 261, 268–9
  see also class and class society; hierarchy
realism 22, 37, 87, 144, 175, 178, 207, 215, 262, 264,
    265, 266
regicide 27, 28, 55, 67, 80, 207, 215, 225, 227, 236,
    238, 243, 244, 245, 246, 249
religion 42, 71, 74, 88, 90, 94, 95, 107, 142, 164,
    194, 200
revenge 8, 32, 33, 34–5, 37, 38–9, 42, 47, 67, 69–70,
    71, 74, 75–6, 77–8, 80, 81–4, 92, 93, 95,
    96, 97, 98–100, 103, 105, 122, 124, 127–8,
    141–3, 145–6, 148, 152–3, 156, 208, 227,
    271
revolution 14, 28, 109, 112, 166, 175, 284
revolutionary vision xiii, 98, 109, 111–12, 179, 207,
    248, 258, 280, 284
  see also utopia and utopianism
Richard II xv, 8, 9, 12, 52, 55, 108, 168–9, 170, 172,
    173, 185
Richard III 11, 22, 25, 27–8, 38, 55, 57, 122, 181, 221
Richard III, The True Tragedy of 83
Rome 33, 34, 35–6, 37–8, 40, 41, 44, 55, 56, 57, 58,
    60, 63, 64, 89, 122, 170, 173, 174, 255, 256,
    260, 261, 262, 265, 271–3, 277, 278–9, 280,
    281, 282, 283, 284, 285
Romeo and Juliet vii, xiv, 12, 45–53, 57, 86, 102,
    118–19, 137, 138, 173–4, 255–6, 260, 265
  apothecary 173–4
  audience 50–1
  books 46–7, 49–50
  death (Liebestod) 47, 51–3
  language 45, 46–50
  love 45–6
  names 47–9, 50
Rowe, Nicholas 241
Rymer, Thomas (A Short View of Tragedy) 119–20,
    121, 136, 137, 138

Schlegel, A. W. von 68, 155–6, 287
Shaw, George Bernard xiii, 98–9, 101, 102, 141, 144,
    163, 200, 287

Shelley, Percy Bysshe 167, 287
Shylock (The Merchant of Venice) 43, 142–3
Sidney, Sir Philip 9, 36, 165, 201, 258, 276
  An Apology for Poetry 9, 36, 276
  Arcadia 165, 201
sleep viii, 33, 44, 50–1, 70, 71, 77, 79, 80, 81, 94,
    112, 114, 123, 132, 134, 158, 180, 185,
    186–8, 193, 209, 226, 232, 235–6, 238, 239,
    243, 245, 246, 247, 250, 269
Sonnet 66 53
Sonnet 87 187
Sonnet 107 xiv, 112, 172
Sonnet 116 117
Sonnet 124 xiv
sovereignty 5, 7, 9–11, 12, 13, 16–17, 25, 28, 33, 36,
    99, 105–7, 110, 163, 164, 168, 170, 184, 186,
    214, 229, 231, 243, 249–50, 268, 279–80,
    283
Spenser, Edmund (The Faerie Queene) 164
Steiner, George 109, 288
Swinburne, Algernon 59, 98, 102, 287

Taine, Hippolyte 73, 287
Tate, Nahum 166
Tempest, The 16–17
theatrum mundi 239
Timon of Athens xv, 12, 31, 34, 39, 52, 171–2, 185,
    199, 250, 261, 265, 271
Titus Andronicus xv, 28, 31–44, 45, 46–7, 49, 50,
    51, 55, 122, 125, 169–70, 174, 198, 239, 255,
    271, 272
  Aaron 28, 33, 35, 38–9, 40, 41–4, 47, 122, 125,
    174, 181, 198, 256
  books 46–7
  Clown 37, 57
  revenge 33, 34–5, 37, 38–9, 42, 47
  Rome 33, 34, 35–6, 37–8, 40, 41, 44
  Tamora 32, 33, 35, 36, 39–40, 41, 43, 47, 122,
    256, 272
  Titus 32, 33–5, 36, 38–44, 46–7, 51, 52, 169–70,
    174, 198, 239, 261, 272
tyrants and tyranny 14, 16, 36, 41, 42, 57, 60–1, 63,
    76, 77, 159, 166, 181, 193, 197, 203, 207,
    229, 230, 240, 281

universality 104, 107, 143, 168, 230, 242, 258, 261,
    272, 284
utopia and utopianism xiv, 13, 16, 22, 51, 53, 56,
    111, 122, 144, 167, 171, 172–3, 175, 178,
    179, 183, 207, 248, 258–9, 260
  see also revolutionary vision

Winter's Tale, The 154
Wittgenstein, Ludwig 187, 288